T0333903

TOWARDS A
KNOWLEDGE SOCIETY
New Identities in Emerging India

Debal K. SinghaRoy

CAMBRIDGE
UNIVERSITY PRESS

CAMBRIDGE
UNIVERSITY PRESS

Cambridge House, 4381/4 Ansari Road, Daryaganj, Delhi 110002, India

Cambridge University Press is part of the University of Cambridge.

It furthers the University's mission by disseminating knowledge in the pursuit of education, learning and research at the highest international levels of excellence.

www.cambridge.org
Information on this title: www.cambridge.org/9781107065451

© Debal K. SinghaRoy 2014

First published 2014

Printed in India by Replika Press Pvt. Ltd.

A catalogue record for this publication is available from the British Library

Library of Congress Cataloging-in-Publication Data
SinghaRoy, Debal K., 1957-
Knowledge society : new identities in emerging India / Debal K. SinghaRoy.
    pages cm
Includes bibliographical references and index.
Summary: "Examines the commodification of knowledge and its mass production, the proliferation of knowledge workers, and the importance of information and communication technologies"– Provided by publisher.
ISBN 978-1-107-06545-1 (hardback)
1. Information society–India. 2. Knowledge economy–India.
3. Information technology–Social aspects–India. I. Title.
HN690.Z9I5667 2014
303.48'330954–dc23
2013048003

ISBN 978-1-107-06545-1 Hardback

With love
For Purbali and Anirudha..........

Contents

List of Tables and Figures

List of Tables

List of Figures

Preface

The progression of human society has remained intrinsically linked to the production and application of knowledge that has paved the way for its civilisational journey bringing in the spirit of rationality and scientific thinking, political liberation and social justice, material progress and economic development in society. The higher the quantum of production and application of knowledge, higher has been the degree of spread, sustenance and rejuvenation of such societal progression. Significantly the site of production of knowledge has invariably remained the human mind that possesses the potential to be developed infinitum unlike those of the other productive resources which are circumscribed by inherent limitation (UN, 2005). Human beings stand for cultivation and exploration of this potential that could be harnessed at a large scale for mass use for varieties of social, economic and political purposes. However, for long the processes of exploitation of this potential for the production, accumulation and dissemination of knowledge have remained strictly confined to limited few as these were considered to be the task of designated specialists and the philosophers (Machup, 1962; Drucker, 1968). The knowledgeable were thus a limited selected section of society and to be knowledgeable was a privilege that in many parts of the world was decided by birth and lineage. Moreover within these arrangements knowledge was viewed as the finest moral manifestation of humanity having a non-commoditised precious essence of human ontology. The relation between knowledge and market has conventionally viewed as disembedded and contradictory.

Since the second half of the last century, humanity has been experiencing phenomenal proliferation of knowledge, knowledgeable and of the application of knowledge in all domains of lives rejuvenating the course of societal progression. Against the pre-existing popular perception, knowledge has gradually emerged to be the key crucial economic resource for employment and its production, dissemination and use have acquired added significance in the backdrop of declining importance of agriculture and industry in the national economy. It has simultaneously emerged to become the major source of power and authority, social network and cultural capital, and agency of change and human capacity building at a large scale. These have made knowledge to acquire conceptual refinement and redefinition behaviourally (Machlup, 1962; Lane, 1966; Drucker, 1968; Bell, 1974), and substantially to obtain the place to be major contributors to the gross domestic product of the developed nations and most of the developing ones paving the way for the emergence of a new order and society widely designated as the knowledge, information or networked society. This society has evolved on the declining foundation of agrarian and industrial society by recognising knowledge, the brain power, as its main economic resource.

The foundation of this society has got strengthened and has been bourgeoning very fast in most parts of the globe in the wake of the revolution in the Information and Communication Technologies (ICTs), triumph of the state philosophy of neo-liberalism and unprecedented expansion of the forces of economic globalisation in every nook and corner of the globe. This society has engineered the emergence of new forms of industry, work participation, social relations, socio-cultural milieu, produced new identities and interests, domination and hegemony, marginalisation and protests affecting a vast part of pre-existing social realities, and a sense of collective existence. It has brought new flow of life, new opportunities for integration with the globalised world, produced new varieties of wealth by harnessing the creative potential of human being. Though widely described to be a new society that is presumed to promote equality, justice and dignity for all by privileging human brain power over the brawl, knowledge society however has emerged far from being an egalitarian one. Rather, it has produced new conditions for breeding marginality and format on of multiple identities by redefining the major resources of production, by imposing western values and cultural ethos over the rest, commercialising education, promoting consumer culture as to suffice the design and interests of the multinational corporations, and bringing de-contextualisation in many of the pre-existing arrangements and practices. Notwithstanding these contradictory images, knowledge society with its new technological and economic arrangements have produced significant space for intense use of knowledge, which travels not only from above, but also moves above from below, for employment, mobility, migration and formation of alternative social collectives. Thus, within the emerging socio-cultural flow of the economic interests of the neo-liberal market forces are being consolidated on one hand, and new varieties, fragmentations, disorientations and fluidity are being transported on the other in the emerging societal arrangement. It has definitely ushered a bold new world (Castells, 2006; Webster, 2006) from which the humanity can't shy away, but must face it. It also invites serious engagements of social scientists to explore, analyse and compare the emerging dynamic of this bold and smart society with new perspective.

Though India has got a knowledge-based past, traditionally the process of production, dissemination and use of knowledge has neither been made mass based nor was it commercially harnessed to be a core economic product or reserve. The traditional process of acquiring knowledge and education has remained restricted among the upper castes. The colonial administration though brought in western education, and printing press, telegraph and telephone and radio, their access was limited only to the upper strata of society. Independent India inherited from the British a predominantly agrarian society widely characterised by economic stagnation and backwardness, illiteracy and poverty, unemployment and ignorance and a slow pace of education and skill development. Immediately after independence, the Indian state initiated a host of measures for rapid industrialisation, agricultural modernisation, expansion of education and mass media to put the nation in the path of fast economic development and social transformation. Though India experienced Green Revolution in selected areas of the country, it missed the industrial revolution (Knowledge Commission of India, 2006). In areas of education and mass media, the transformation widely remained far from expectation. India started reeling under the wheel of low rate of economic growth, high rate of concentration of workforce in agriculture, low rate of capacity building and under-utilisation of its human resources. The Five Year Planning process was to be suspended by initiating annual planning in late 1980 due to increased social upheaval and resource crunch. However, in the wake of the end of Cold War, collapse of the Berlin Wall and the Union of Soviet Socialist Republic (USSR) and the emergence of economic neo-liberalism as the dominant economic force across the globe, India has introduced itself to the path of economic globalisation by accepting the Structural Adjustment Programme of the International Monetary Fund (IMF) and the World Bank and a fundamental shift in the developmental perspective of the state from socialism to economic neo-liberalism, market protection to market liberalisation can be noticed. This paradigm shift has been accompanied by increasing flow of foreign direct investment and investment by Indian private business houses in telecommunication, mass media and education. Since the mid-1990s, India has been experiencing phenomenal penetration and usage of ICTs, new and mass media, fast expansion of education and quantum increase in the pool of educated and trained man power, increasing rate of migration and mobility of vast section of people, emergence of alternative avenues of employment even in rural areas and increasing shift of the labour force towards the service sector and the emergence of the service sector to be the prime contributors the GDP of the nation. Along with these changes India stands today in the threshold of an emerging of knowledge society wherein knowledge has emerged to be the central resource for wealth and employment, power and status, mobility and interconnectivity and the key means to organise social, economic and political order of vast section of Indian population. The Indian state has now framed elaborate strategy to usher a smart knowledge society to overcome economic stagnation, to reconcile with the failure of industrialisation, to shift vast section of its work force from agriculture and industry to knowledge economy by imparting appropriate education, skill and training and to convert the twenty-first Century to be the century of India. With the vast pool of young population in its command, India is posited to emerge as the knowledge hub of the world to yield its 'demographic dividend'. However, the emergence of knowledge society in India has not been uniform, rather eclectic across the space and nor has it been a discreet process autonomous of its traditional past. Herein the new economic arrangement and socio-cultural milieu as set in motion by the emerging knowledge society has thrown open lot of new challenges and opportunities in the society by shaping its own dynamics that need a through study both methodologically and conceptually. Despite having emerged as a distinct phenomenon the emergence of knowledge society has received little attention from sociologists in particular and social scientists in general in India.

As against this backdrop, the central focus of this book is on the broad socio-historical contexts and the processes of emergence of knowledge society in India; patterns of proliferation of new economic momentum and socio-cultural milieu as set in motion by the emergence of knowledge society; their impacts on the pre-existing facets of social identity and marginality; and construction of new social identities in this emerging society. Based on empirical data collected from four metro cities, Delhi, Mumbai, Kolkata and Chennai, four district towns and seven villages located in four different directions – north, south, east and west of the country and a vast body of secondary sources of information, this study examines the interrelated processes leading to the emergence of knowledge society in India and its critical dimensions. Positing itself within the contemporary socio-economic realities, that have emerged to be part agricultural, part industrial and part service based, this study delineates the influence of pre-existing spatial (village, district towns and metro cities), caste, ethnic and gender divides in conditioning the shaping up of knowledge society in India. Conceptually grounding itself on the works of Machlap (1962), Drucker (1968), Bell (1976) Castells (2006, 2007), Toffler (1970, 1980, 1990), Evans (2004), Black (2003), Melucci (2006), Giddens 1984, 1999), Friedmen (2005), Hornby and Clarke (1996), Webster (2006), Dijk, (1999) Porat (1977), Touraine (1981) and many others, this study analyses the dynamics of knowledge society in India that have produced an era of both hope and despair in the interconnected world. It shows that despite being circumscribed by the pre-existing caste, ethnic, gender and spatial divides and marginality, knowledge society has brought into being new occupational momentum, mobility and choice, new scope of breaking the barriers of marginality, developing criticality against domination, and curving out space for construction of praxis of knowledge for liberty. Though the milieu of the redefined state along with its emerging thrust for commodification of knowledge and consumerism relentlessly try to condition knowledge as a means for expansion of economic interest of the neo-liberal market forces in contemporary society in India, the praxis of knowledge creates its own space for liberation for a vast section of marginalised people who develop multi prong strategies and articulate an alternate identities to curb out a space for livelihood security, dignity and justice in this emerging society using knowledge as their key resource. A large part of India's population is connected through a network of knowledge and information technology. The cover page of this book depicts this momentum, hope and integration of people in the emerging knowledge society in India.

My craze to research on the dynamics of knowledge society in India emerged out of my intellectual engagement both with the conceptual and with empirical issues of social development and social movements in India. The inadequacy of rural/agrarian and urban studies in addressing the transitional phase of contemporary society in India, the increasing tensions between tradition and modernity, globalism and locality, secularism and primordiality, identity and fluidity and fuzziness of emending identities, sustained poverty of the majority and flash prosperity of limited few and host of other issues and their interconnectedness with the wider world, increasing significance of service and knowledge sector in the economy, the shifting perspective of the state on economy and social welfare and the increasing flow of ICTs and globalisation have significantly provoked me to look into the issue of transition of Indian society concretely from the viewpoint of the proliferation of knowledge society in India.

My fluid thinking got consolidated out of a series of interaction with my professional colleagues in Indira Gandhi National Open University, Jawaharlal Nehru University, New Delhi, University of Edmonton and Athabasca University Canada, University of Technology, Sydney, Australia, The Open University and London City University, United Kingdom, the Open Universiteit, the Netherlands and in many other places. I am thankful to Peter (Jay) Smith, Professor of Political Science, Michael Gismondi, Professor of Sociology and Global Studies in the Athabasca University, Canada, for helping me to consolidate my early research on ICTs, distance education and globalisation. My ideas and thinking got a good degree of precision as I received the Commonwealth Fellowship in United Kingdom in 2006-07 to work on social movements in knowledge society. In fact, this fellowship has given me ample opportunities to get access to up-to-date bodies of literature on knowledge society and also to interact extensively with a large number of scholars working in this area of research. Here I am highly grateful to Ellie Chambers, Emeritus Professor of Humanities Higher Education, Institute of Educational Technology, the UK Open University, Professor Andy Northedge, Chair of Foundation Course Team Institute of Educational Technology, Open University, Dr Tim Jordan, The Open University United Kingdom, Professor Frank Webster, Professor of Sociology London City University, United Kingdom for reflecting on my thought and giving valuable suggestions to my research on knowledge society.

I got an added opportunity as I received the Australian Government Endeavour Fellowship in 2010 to look into the issues of knowledge society very closely even though I was engaged on a research on the

Environmental Issues in the Indigenous People's Movements in Australia. The emerging nature of knowledge society in Australia has helped me a lot to comprehend the Indian scenario from an additional point of view. I am thankful to Professor James Goodman, University of Technology Sydney and Professor Stuart Rosewane, University of Sydney, for providing me the platform to discuss my ideas with a lot of scholars. Their comments have been of great help in developing an insight in my research.

I am thankful to Professor Maitryee Choudhary, Professor of Sociology, Centre for the Study of Social System, Jawaharlal Nehru University, New Delhi, and Professor Uma Kanjilal, Professor Library and Information Science, Indira Gandhi National Open University, New Delhi for encouraging me and finding sense in my talking about a research in knowledge society in India. Professor Uma Kanjilal was liberal enough to share with me a lot of literature on ICT revolution and expansion and usage in India. This early encouragement has helped me a lot to get a sense of purpose in this research. I am deeply thankful to them for their liberal gesture. I am also thankful to Professor Anand Kumar for inviting me to present parts of finding of this piece of research in symposia held in Jawaharlal University under the auspice of the 60th Sociological Conference of Indian Sociological Society, held in Jawaharlal Nehru University in December 2011.

I owe my gratitude to my colleagues in the Indian Gandhi National Open University, New Delhi. I am thankful to Professor M. Aslam, the Vice Chancellor of IGNOU for his continuous interest in my research and his encouragement. I am also thankful to Professor Darvesh Gopal, Professor Pandav Nayak, Professor E. Vayunandan, and Dr Ajay Mahurkar and Dr Subha Gokhle, for their encouragement. I am sincerely thankful to the Indira Gandhi National Open University Teachers Association (Teachers) for providing me the opportunity to examine the dynamics of higher education and its politics from a close quarter.

I am thankful to the Indian Council for Social Science Research (ICSSR), New Delhi for accepting this research project and giving me the required grant to undertake this research. In fact without financial support from ICSSR it would have been highly difficult for me to undertake this piece of research that involved a large-scale survey and data collection from different parts of the country. This research needed the collection and analysis of a vast body of these data coherently and consistently from across the country. Such endeavour has been possible only with help, cooperation and encouragement of a series of experts, friends, colleagues and the respondents of this study. My sincere thanks are due to all the respondents of this study for their cooperation and willingness to spare their valuable time and information for this study. Thanks are also due to all the field investigators who have helped me to collect this vast body of data from the field. Here I am thankful to Dr T. Jitha, New Delhi, and Mr Manoj Kumar, New Delhi, Swapan Kumar Day Sarkar, Dangarhat, West Bengal, Mr Nitin More, Mumbai, Mr Sudhir Kumar, Meerut, Hemlta Kheria, Delhi, Mr Subrata Bhattacharjee, Kolkata, Mr Arun Gucchai, West Bengal, Mr Anupam Pal, West Bengal, Mr Manas Nanda, Odisha, Mr Mano, Nagerkoil, Tamil Nadu for rendering their support in collecting information for this study. I am thankful to Mr Karunakar Singh and Valarmati, PhD scholar in the department of sociology for their support.

I was to undertake additional field work and to consult new sources of information to convert the research report into a full-fledged book. The book would not have been possible without selfless dedication from my support staff in the faculty of Sociology especially from Mr Shailendra Kumar, Mr Yashwant Raj and Sonia. Mr Shailendra has played an important role not only in the additional data analysis and tabulation, but also in introducing series of corrections in all drafts of this book that went on for more than two years. Mr Yashwant Raj has played a big role in developing the charts, introducing corrections in the final draft very committedly. I am extremely thankful to them for their commitment to this piece of work.

I am thankful to my daughter Purbali SinghaRoy and to my son Aniruddha SinghaRoy for their sustained encouragement and for sacrificing their several personal demands for this research. They have been of great help not only to generate an intellectual appetite in me of contemporary social reality but also to correct my technological deficits in using ICTs. My wife Dr Prava Debal has always been the best companion and critic of my work. Her suggestions have always been fruitful to get an intellectual direction in my wisely casual life. I am ever grateful to her.

I am thankful to Cambridge University Press for bringing out this book. I am especially thankful to Debjani Mazumder, Qudsiya Ahmed and Suvadip Bhattacharjee for their relentless encouragement and support.

1

Introduction

Conceptualising Knowledge Society: Critical Dimensions and Ideal Image

I. Knowledge Society and Its Emergence

Human societies have borne witness to the continuous process of progression from an early stage of hunting–gathering to agrarian, agrarian to industrial and industrial to postindustrial and to contemporary knowledge society. These progressions have been shaped by a variety of factors including those of perceived inability and weakness of given arrangements to cope with the need of existing societies, on the one hand, and new technological discoveries, advancements of thoughts, ideals and values, on the other. These are again accompanied by the resurgence of new actions of the state, market, civil society and people; and articulation of diverse interests and identities and formation of new collectivities in society. Significantly, in the core of such discoveries and advancements, resurgence and articulation and day-to-day functioning of society lies the flame of new knowledge as the key livewire to shape social progression locating itself in the centre of all social dynamics, becoming the pivotal foundation for all transformative thoughts and social actions. This new body of knowledge integrates innovative meaning and world view to these progressions mediating itself with the interplay of conceptual abstraction and empirical realities in society; and fosters new technological, economic and social arrangements therein.

In every stage of its progression, human society has used and developed knowledge and attached emphasis on specific type(s) of knowledge in view of its own need and context. However, the intensity of such use and development of knowledge has been historically eclectic, and remained socially and technologically circumscribed. Even though at the most basic level of survival, knowledge has remained the integral component of society to observe and process information about changes in the environment, to produce new meaning and articulate its response to the challenge of change, neither all human societies historically have treated knowledge as main societal assets, nor mass-produced knowledge to make optimal use of its resources. Moreover, the capacity of mass production of knowledge has never been recognised or identified as the most important feature of human societies as these have been possible since the end of the last century through the application of Information and Communication Technologies (ICTs) and use of shared spaces for knowledge creation through globalisation. Thus, despite knowledge being the integral part of human progression, it has been seldom used to characterise a society (United Nations, 2005).

As all over the world mind is replacing the muscle, knowledge has become the highest form of power: the 'ultimate substitute' to characterise a new system in human progression. To (Toffler, 1990), 'this new system takes us to a giant step beyond mass production towards increasing customisation, beyond mass marketing and distribution towards niches and micro-marketing, to new forms of organisation, beyond nation state to operation that are both local and global, and beyond proletariat to a new *cognitariat*' (Toffler, 1990). In fact, this is possible only through the engagement of all sections of people in the production and use of knowledge. Thus, the contemporary knowledge society distinguishes itself from the previous societies as the institutions and organisations of this society 'enable people and knowledge/ information to be developed without limits, and open opportunities for all kinds of knowledge to be mass-produced and mass-utilised throughout the whole society'. At its best, it involves all members of the community in knowledge creation and utilisation to improve quality and safety of life, promote business, generate wealth, increase productivity and profit in business through the use of ICTs. Through these processes the present society, unlike the other societies, lays its foundation on two important resources: the people and knowledge that can be developed infinitium. While the former can be developed by cultivating their creativity and enriching their hidden potential, the latter can also be developed limitlessly by increasing the density of knowledge-rich environments (United Nations, 2005).

In the contemporary world knowledge in its latest avatar, as the key economic resource, has acquired distinctive connotation, usage and significance in an interrelated socioeconomic context that has been experiencing the fast expansion of the philosophy of neoliberalism, economic globalisation and revolution in the ICTs. Most significantly, the emerging socioeconomic context of the contemporary world now is being shaped by the production, distribution and use of knowledge across the globe cutting across the predefined geographical boundaries in juxtaposition with the phenomenal expansion of mass media, and education and innovative mechanisms of mass production of knowledge and its fast dissemination and intensive use in all areas of activities.

Though the knowledge society in its contemporary connotation is of recent origin, it has got a historical trajectory. It emerged from within the institutional and the technological arrangements of industrial societies to bring forth a new social, economic and technological framework of society by harnessing the creative potential stored in the human mind. Historically, the industrial revolution in the seventeenth and eighteenth centuries, which brought a severe blow to the dominance of agrarian economy, and ushered an era of advanced technology, new modes of communication, economic and social organisation and new thoughts and ideals of progress and liberation, and new hope for human wellbeing, paved the way for knowledge society in the early twentieth century in North America and Europe both through its advances and inadequacies. However, the western industrial technology-driven industrialisation that had emerged as the most aspired model for development to the whole world and continued its dominance until the late 1960s as a viable answer to underdevelopment, unemployment, poverty, backwardness, authoritarianism, conservatism, imbalanced economic development and social inequality, political centralism and bureaucratisation, economic corruption and mindless consumerism, social distortion and injustice, environmental pollution and moral degradation, crime and disharmony proved itself inadequate to prevent these problems. Again, the technological and institutional base of this society posited to become highly inadequate to manage its own complex, multidimensional and endemic social problems. As against these backdrops, the growing intricacies and adequacies of industrial society, the revolution in the information and the communication technology created a space for the emergence of an alternative arrangement 'to manage its complexity through improved human intelligence and advanced technology and to create a new economic sector through exploitation of knowledge whereby productive force could be moved away from hard core industry to knowledge sector' (Splichal, 1994). This arrangement has been envisaged not only to address the inadequacies of industrial society, but also to bring in a viable technological and economic alternative to suffice the need of contemporary society, to widen the socio-economic horizon of collective existence and to give a new direction to the pre-existing societal dynamics of society through the interpenetration of knowledge in all areas of the economic, cultural and political engagements.

As communication technology started experiencing revolution in quick succession, with the innovations in telecommunication in the 1940s and 1950s, launching of the communication satellite in the early 1960s, the early forms of Internet (ARPANet) in the late 1960s, and the massive potential of the information/electronic technologies, computer, Internet, mobile, telephone and the like arrived in the horizon in the early 1970s to lay the foundation of a new economy based on production, distribution and exchange of knowledge, a large part of the globe, initially spearheaded by the industrialised nations, got adopted to these technologies. The adoption to these technologies has been accompanied by the innovation in World Wide Waves in the late 1980s and subsequent upgradation and innovation in the computer, Internet, mobile phone and telecommunication, satellite phone, radio and television technologies, arrival of new communication platforms such as 2G and 3G, new social media such as Facebook, Twitter, blogs, email, Skype, etc., on the one hand, and economic globalisation, change in the nature of the state and thereupon the transformation of the pre-existing economic and social arrangements into a new one, on the other. This unprecedented new arrangement has got diversely described by the scholars as Knowledge Economy, Knowledge Society, Information Society, Information Age, Electronic Era, Global Village, Technetronic Age, Post Industrial Society, Third Wave, and Networked Society and many other such vocabularies. To Machlup (1962), historically as the economy developed and society became more complex the organisation of production, trade and government acquired an increasing degree of division of labour between knowledge production and physical production. This also marked quite a remarkable increase in the division of labour between pure brain work and largely physical performance in all sectors of the economic and social organisations. Since the mid twentieth century, the knowledge economy has emerged as a distinctive phenomenon by separating brain from physical work (Machlup, 1962) and has been privileging the power of the brain over the body for unleashing creative human potential through the use of ICTs rather than to restrict it (Evans, 2004). The emerging arrangements have pushed society to move forward in the path of new modes of development wherein the elements of labour, matter and energy are combined in work to accumulate knowledge. Many prefer to call it the informational mode of development that has emerged out of the material products from species, and because of the endless development of the symbolic, communicative and informational functions of the human brain (Castells, 1983).

II. Key Dimensions of Knowledge Society

Knowledge society has induced a host of transformative dynamics in society by redefining the usage of knowledge, emphasising on its application and interlocking it with the use of ICTs and trading and commoditising it through globalisation, maximising the significance information/knowledge workers by replacing historical categories like those of the agriculturalists and the industrial workers and increasing local global connectivity.

One of the key dimensions of this society is the shift in its emphasis on the application of knowledge. In this society, 'knowledge' has emerged to occupy the centre stage in the same way 'what coal and iron were to the industrial revolution and the plough was to the birth of agriculture 10,000 years ago' (Toffler, 1980). Knowledge society emphasises on the application of knowledge in all domains of society rather than its pure societal cognition. To Machlup (1962), though 'knowledge' has predominantly remained in the domain of philosopher's task and at times of the sociologists ... knowledge has always played a part in economic analysis.' In the context of the growth of technical knowledge and its increasing applicability, he asserts that knowledge has certainly become an important factor in the analysis of economic growth (Machlup, 1962, pp. 3–4). Similarly, to Drucker (1968),

> until nineteenth century, knowledge and action had almost no contact with each other. Knowledge served the inner man. The 'intellectual knowledge' is what is in a book. But as long as it is in the book, it is only 'information', if not mere data. Only when a man applies the information to do something it does become knowledge.

Herein, knowledge society is characterised by intensification of the connection between knowledge and action.

However, unlike Drucker (1968), Machlup (1962) makes no distinction between knowledge and information; and in his definition of knowledge he includes both the scientific and ordinary knowledge. To Machlup (1962)

> we may designate as knowledge anything that is known by somebody and as production of knowledge any activity by which some one learns of something that he has not known even if others have; (and) producing knowledge will mean, not only discovering, inventing, designing and planning, but also disseminating and communicating...

His understanding of knowledge is thus extensive and inclusive: 'knowledge need not be knowledge of certified events and tested theories; it may be knowledge of statements and pronouncements, conjectures and hypotheses, no matter what their status of verification may be; all knowledge regardless of the strength of belief in it or warranty for it' is knowledge (Machlup, 1962). This inclusive conceptualisation of knowledge, however, does not undermine the emerging dynamics of application of knowledge in the present era, rather shows an increasing scope in such application.

The United Nations (2005) distinguishes between information and knowledge by highlighting the difference between the explicit and tacit forms of knowledge. It recognises

> 'explicit knowledge' as information that 'refers to justified (true) belief that is codified in formal, systemic language.

It can be combined, stored, retrieved and transmitted with relative ease and through various means, including modern ICT'. The tacit knowledge on the other hand 'is a fluid mix of framed experience, values, contextual information…. It is highly personal and hard to formalize, making it difficult to communicate or share with others. Subjective insights, intuitions and hunches all fall into the category of tacit knowledge'

The explicit knowledge according to UN is information. It is like the tangible, visible part of an iceberg that can be observed, accessed and shared by others, while the tacit knowledge intangible, invisible, as if hidden 'under the water' and can be accessed on the first-person basis only.

The knowledge society, according to UN, is to recognise both categories of knowledge as one is available 'to do' while the other is available 'to be' (2005).

In essence, the knowledge society blurs differences between ideas, data, information and knowledge. All human societies function to satisfy their social, economic and cultural needs, and respond to the forces of social change and transformation based on their own skill and knowledge, the state of technological development and innovation. The inherited human tendency to know, explore and experiment suggests that each and every segment of population of a society has been endowed with the capacity to generate ideas, segregate data and information and develop skill and knowledge. While some bases of knowledge, skill, information, data and ideas are localised and inherent to the society concerned, there are also others having been acquired through interaction with a wider world or have got penetrated as exogenous agency.

In general, parlance relations between 'ideas', 'data', 'information' and 'knowledge' are diversely understood by many scholars. At times, these are understood interchangeably, while in another context to represent distinctive connotations. These are also understood in a relational and hierarchical order. In fact, for many, hierarchy of knowledge has become a reality in knowledge discourse. In explaining the hierarchical relations between ideas, data, information and knowledge, it is generally accepted that ideas are conjectures, imaginations, hunches and impressions; 'data are simple facts; information are processed data combined in meaningful structures; and knowledge is meaningfully refined and validated information. This relation generally moves upward that sees ideas to be prerequisite for data', 'data as a prerequisite for information and information are a prerequisite for knowledge' (Tuomi, 1999). Hence,

Table 1.1 *Features of Knowledge, Information, Data and Idea*

Knowledge	Interpreted, structured, verified, meaningful, transformed, and refined information, or higher forms of information
Information	Structured, meaningful, relevant, purposive and organised and processed facts or data with meaning, data endowed with relevance and purpose
Data	Observable and objective facts, statistics, symbols
Idea	Hypothesis, conjecture, nonqualified statement, part factual or nonfactual, imagination, etc.

there is a transition and a continuum. The essential features of idea, data, information and knowledge as shown in Table 1.1 are very often viewed in a hierarchical order.

Knowledge hierarchy however is not stagnant. The hierarchy of idea–data–information–knowledge could be turned the other way round in the interactive context as neither ideas, nor data, nor information, nor does knowledge stand in isolation. Rather, idea takes shape and data emerges only after the availability of knowledge and information; and that an idea can emerge only if a meaningful structure or semantics is first fixed and then used to represent information and thereafter knowledge. Following Tuomi (1999), it may be argued that ideas cannot be shaped independent of or devoid of data, information and knowledge. Instead of being raw material for information, data emerges as a result of adding value to information by putting it into a form that can not be automatically processed (Tuomi, 1999). Herein, just below/ beyond the data, there are ideas having two-way interactions. While it may be the foundation for data leading to the formation of a body of information and knowledge thereafter, it also results out of formation of information and knowledge.

This discourse depicts that the relations between knowledge, information, data and ideas are intrinsic though there are hierarchies and this hierarchical order can be reversed. Though knowledge is highly validated, refined and actionable and decides the course of its praxis, it is unalienable from ideas, data and information. In the context of knowledge society their relations are not discrete, rather more of a spiral cyclical that develops a higher spiral cycle continuously than to have a vicious or a linear one. They are a part of continuum and are subject to multiple uses through their commodification. In the knowledge society thus ideas, data, information and knowledge are put in a common basket called knowledge for application and commodification. This basket includes knowledge of all pursuits, such as economic, social, cultural, political, religious/spiritual, and repackaged as marketable commodity for employment, for the generation of wealth and power. Locating itself in the intersectionality with globalisation and ICTs, knowledge society generates a market-driven flow that mixes ideas, data, information and knowledge together and converts them into a tradable commodity for exchange both within and outside the national territory. It invites innovation, experimentation, recycling, reproduction, assimilation and repackaging of knowledge as an economic item for trade and business. A vast segment of this body of knowledge, skill, information, data and ideas especially those of the localised ones remain mostly unrecognised in the wider society due to the lack of proper certification and experimentation, even though they are a part of cultural traditions of society. Knowledge society however has taken shape based on those components of knowledge, skill, information, data and ideas that are available for wider commercial use and exploitation, and have their applicability.

The knowledge society lays its foundation on commodification of knowledge. Knowledge, information, data and ideas as the raw materials of knowledge society are used to generate profits 'for producers, manufacturers and distributors' that reach out, after a series of transformation and commercial transaction. This transformation is described as the transformation of knowledge into information or vice versa. To Hornby and Clarke (2003), knowledge gets transformed into information through several processes of value addition. As value is added to the original materials (metal, plastic, fabrics, etc.) at each stage of their processing, value is added at each stage of processing of knowledge (the raw material) for getting it transformed into information and making it a marketable commodity (Hornby and Clarke, 2003). In the wake of neoliberal market expansion, such transformation has been furthered at a massive scale. With mass commodification of knowledge/information, knowledge/information economy has emerged to be a reality as the

> primary sector of economy that engaged itself predominantly with the activities of production, distribution, transaction, handling of hardware and software, and supporting facilities of knowledge/information. It is now world widely viewed that advanced economies have shifted further from manufacturing to service provision, and have become increasingly dependent on the generation and the dissemination of knowledge/information for their economic well-being (Porat, 1977, pp. 6–7).

The relatively less-advanced economics of the world are now in the process of following the similar trend of being knowledge driven.

ICTs and globalisation are indispensable for sustenance and expansion of knowledge society. It is now widely recognised that the ICTs are the present-day equivalent of electricity of industrial era (Castells, 2001) and that ICTs and globalisation are crucial constituents of knowledge society and have emerged to be indispensible for its sustenance and expansion. Since the 1960s, the ICTs have been providing the crucial material basis for emergence of information society (Castells, 1996) through the extensive use of computer, Internet, mobile phone, entertainment devices and varieties of digital communication technologies in all the domains of life. These have come into play to redefine the ways of living and working in present society. In fact, the late twentieth century revolution in information technology has posited the humanity to 'face a quantum leap forward, the deepest social upheaval and creative restructuring of all time' (Toffler, 1980; Toffler and Toffler, 1995). Such revolution facilitated people to be part of a large-scale diffused social network through ICTs paving the way to replace the preexisting 'mass society' characterised by large-scale concentration of people with copresence and face-to-face communication (Dijk, 1999).

The ICTs that have driven progress in every field of activities, such as farming, manufacture, education, policing, medicine, entertainment, banking or whatever, now have brought into being a new society without a precedence and have intensified contemporary social processes with global connectivity (Lyon, 1988). The ICTs are no longer about simple computing, word processing or tale-talking but 'about living' and the very essence of experience wherein life itself becomes all about 'being digital' (Paschal, 2001, cf. Evans, 2004).

In all reality 'being digital' has acquired iconic globalising status through computer, World Wide Web networking, Skype, emails, blogs, Twitter, Facebook, SMS, MMS and the like. These have made humanity globally interdependent whereby 'the planet is no longer designated by just a physical location but also as a unified social space which can be culturally and symbolically perceived' (Melucci, 1996(a)). These have helped extend the horizon not only of social networking and ICT-enabled cultural reawakening but also the new frontier of economic activities across the globe. In essence, ICTs have emerged to be prime vehicles to effectively push forward local–global integration, borderless economic transaction, social interaction and political exercise of power across the globe. These have furthered the exchange, mobility, adaption, transference, transformation and transcendence of objects, image, resources, ideas and institutions that facilitate the expansion of knowledge society as the essential function of globalisation.

Thus, while the ICTs have helped demolish the barriers of geographical divides for making a virtual world a reality, *globalisation* and its neoliberal ideological framework have reinforced these processes. The combination of ICTs and globalisation in effect has helped to expand the scope of cross-border trade and services and an interconnected world with new culture and social organisation, and new conditions for social existence with diffusion and dispersal and formation of new identities. These have redefined the concepts of time and space, stability, mobility and connectivity in a variety of ways to provide a broad platform for the expansion of knowledge/information society. This society is characterised by globalisation, networking form of organisation, flexibility and instability of work, and individuation of labour, a culture of real virtually constructed by a pervasive, interconnected and diversified media system, transformation of material foundations of life, space and time through the constitution of a space of flows and timeless time

(Castells, 1996). It is now 'ordered across time and space', and is free from the hold of specific locales, recombining them across wide time, space and distances with the proliferation of the media, printed and electronic. It is in many ways a single world, having a unitary framework of experience, yet at the same time one that creates new forms of fragmentation and dispersal (Giddens, 1990).

These processes have helped the proliferation of vital political and economic forces to make the world a flat playground for several new players for new forms of economic transaction with new varieties of work and worker. To Friedman (2005) the fall of the Berlin Wall, the extensive expansion of the personal computers, Netscape, work flow, outsourcing, offshoring, uploading, insourcing supply-chaining, in-forming and the steroids as the flattening forces have merged together to convert the world into a new playground for doing business in new ways. These have brought new groups of people from China, India and the former Soviet Empire, who was earlier away, walked into the playing field. In this platform, individuals, groups, companies and universities and several other bodies from across the world concurrently collaborate for the purposes of innovation, production, education, research, entertainment, etc., that no creative platform has ever done before. This platform now operates without regard to geography, distance, time and, in the near future, even language and is going to be the centre of everything: wealth and power. The prosperity of all players now is dependent on their infrastructural capacity to connect with this flat-world platform through education, innovation, work and governance. The process of flattening has been strengthened in recent years with the emergence of a large cadre of managers, innovators, business consultants, business schools, designers, IT specialists, CEOs and workers entering into the field to develop horizontal collaboration, create new value and habits and to take advantage of this new flatter playing field (Friedman, 2005). This flattened world is now marked by the emergence of knowledge work and the knowledge worker.

Knowledge society increases the scope of knowledge works and knowledge workers. Human as a thinking animal always applies mental capability in work. However, knowledge work distinguishes from the nonknowledge work by the facts that while all works involve a mix of physical and mental work, a knowledge work is fundamentally mental work that involves analysing, problem solving, coordinating, decision-making, creatively engaging to produce and use knowledge. It covers not only the production but also of transmission of knowledge encompassing a host of intermediate processes. It integrates a host of work as knowledge work based on the intricacies of knowledge itself. For Machlup (1962), knowledge includes both 'what are known to us' and 'the process of knowing it', and also the process of letting others know. What is being communicated becomes identical with knowledge in the sense of that what is known; and 'knowledge in the sense of what is known is not really complete until it has been transmitted to some others'. The first is knowledge as a state of knowing or result, while the second meaning is knowledge as a process of transmission/distribution, or activity. From an economic point of view, the second (transmission of knowledge) is as important as the first, the state of knowing. To him, there are six varieties of communicators, transmitters or knowledge-producers: transporter, transformer, processor, interpreter, analyser and original creator. Though four basic activities related to education, research and developed communication and information are identified to be the core of knowledge work, the whole spectrum of workers from original creators to transporters of these works are designated in the knowledge society as the knowledge workers (Machlup, 1962).

It is exemplified that in every business a considerable percentage of work force, whose work consists of conferring, negotiating, planning directing, blue printing, calculating, telephoning, card punching, typing, multigraphing, recording, checking and many others, is engaged in the production of knowledge. This engagement is explicit not only in the research, development, planning and designing personnel but also in the activities of executives, administrative, supervisory, technical and clerical personnel and even of the switch board operators. Machlup (1962) observed that the increase of the factor of productivity in the American society over the years has been associated with an increase in the ratio of knowledge producing labour to the physical labour and that the knowledge economy that was contributing 29 per cent of GNP in 1958, had grown at a rate of 8.8 per cent per year over the period 1947–1958, and this occupied people represented 56.9 per cent of the national income (Machlup, 1962).

The knowledge economy experiences a continuous increase in the 'knowledge-producing workers'; a relative decline in the industrial labour, what used to be called 'productive labour'; structural change in employment leading to 'replacement of men by machines'; a succession of occupations leading to a movement from 'manual to mental', and from 'less to more highly trained labour'. Significantly, the contemporary technological revolution has also favoured the employment of knowledge-producing workers whose work participation is characterised by a high level of acquired skill and education, flexibility to change, capacity to create demand for own product, strategic thinking on production, consumption, resolution of conflict and increasing choice and liberty. Here, some of the *key features of knowledge workers* have been described below.

Skilled, Educated and Flexible to Adaptation

As the knowledge society has laid its foundation on a varied kind of intellectual and economic resource and technological arrangement, it is dependent on the productive contributions of this special category of workers who are highly trained, skilled and knowledgeable. They are not only formally educated but are also available for acquiring education throughout their lives. Hence, the knowledge workers are to be very flexible and adaptable to new technological environment, multiskilled and dynamic and should have the willingness and capacity to upgrade the educational background in view of the changing technological and economic need of society. As the knowledge society needs regular upgradation of skill and productivity, it invites the upgrading of the educational level of the entrant into the labour force, which is again upgraded continuously through life-long learning (Drucker, 1968). It has been envisioned that due to their highly skilled and educated background, the knowledge workers despite retaining the principle of division of labour, rehumanise work relations in society (Bell, 1974).

Strategic Planning, Promoting Innovation and Networking

The knowledge workers think strategically to plan for the future and to value intellectual rather than physical power, so as to maximise their output both inside and outside their work environment (Evans, 2004). They articulate strategy for technological innovation and adaptation, promote social and economic change by ushering local and global networking and stimulate new orientation to social values and global acceptability of their lifestyle.

Representing the Leading Class

The knowledge workers experience fast mobility and are integrated in the culture of conspicuous consumption. They are the ambassadors of new lifestyle in society, which is characterised by high degree of comforts both at home and in the workplace and competitive work schedule. Knowledge workers are the leading class and necessarily the ruling class in knowledge society who fundamentally distinguish themselves from other groups in history who occupied a dominant position in society in terms of their access to and control over productive resources. They collectively own the means of production as the capitalists of knowledge society (Drucker, 1968).

Experiencing Variety of Choices

Knowledge society provides ample choices for the knowledge workers enabling them to move from one predetermined occupation into another very frequently. As the worth of a worker in knowledge society is decided by his or her achieved qualities of education, skill and expertise than by ascribed qualities, he or she develops a high sense of dignity and self-esteem for him/herself. Because of these high qualities they get the opportunity for optimum gratification of their worth by engaging themselves in varieties of creative endeavours. Importantly, their increasing presence in contemporary society helps to have a forward march from a society in which careers and occupations were determined largely by the accident of birth into one in which one's position is recognised by one's achieved mental worth that provides ample freedom of choice and career options. 'The problem today is not the lack of choice for the knowledge workers but the abundance thereof. There are so many choices, so many opportunities, and so many directions in knowledge society for them' (Drucker, 1968).

Creation of Demand for Own Product

As the knowledge workers are innovative and have unlimited potential to produce socially and intellectually relevant product, they simultaneously generate demand for their contribution in society through ever-expanding knowledge networks and markets. The typical knowledge worker increasingly works longer hours as there is an ever-increasing demand for knowledge and their knowledge-producing contribution. They create the demands for their own product by introducing innovation and creativity in each and every stage of production, distribution and dissemination of their product. Indeed, they introduce creativity and innovation in work and generate demand of their produce not by compulsion, but by choice (Drucker, 1968).

Sustenance of Knowledge Workers

The arrival and sustenance of knowledge workers are more governed by the supply than by their demand dynamics. Drucker (1968) pointed out that historically the knowledge workers came first and knowledge work followed them. Because modern society has to employ people who expect and demand knowledge work, knowledge jobs have to be created and as a result the character of work has got transformed leading to a transformation of society and economy. With this transformation, one can expect increasing emphasis on work based on knowledge, and especially on skills based on knowledge. Herein old jobs will either be changed to knowledge jobs or be replaced by knowledge jobs (Drucker, 1968).

Knowledge Workers Replacing Agricultural and Industrial Workers

Knowledge society in essence has marked the declining significance of agriculture, through industrial revolution and the increasing importance of knowledge- and information-induced service sectors in the national economy and the extensive use of ICTs in all domains of lives. This society is also fast replacing history's traditional groups, namely the agricultural and the industrial workers, by the knowledge workers.

> Before the First World War, farmers composed the largest single group in every country. Farmers today are at most five percent of the population and work force – that is, one tenth of the proportion of eighty years ago … in the 1950s, industrial workers had become the largest single group in every developed country, and unionised industrial workers in mass-production industry (which was then dominant everywhere) had attained upper-middle-class income levels…. Thirty-five

years later, in 1990, industrial workers and their unions were in retreat. They had become marginal in numbers… The newly emerging dominant group is 'knowledge workers'. (Drucker, 1994, pp. 53–54)

Contradiction Encountered by Knowledge Workers

Knowledge workers are to encounter ranges of contradictions as both employee and owner of the true capital of this society: knowledge. Though they are not labourers but are still employees, they are not subordinate for they apply their knowledge, yet they have a boss. They are simultaneously capitalists, owners and also employees. They are expected to be intellectuals; however, they are governed by the code of conduct of employees. The hidden conflicts between the knowledge worker's view of himself or herself as a professional and of the social reality in which he or she is upgraded underlines the disenchantment of so many educated young people with the job available to them. Ideally, a knowledge worker is supposed to be the master of his/her mind that generates wealth through knowledge. However, he/she very often realises that his/her mind is conditioned by the forces of market and political power (Drucker, 1968).

In essence, knowledge workers use their brain and intellect to convert their knowledge resources into action. They use their mental power more than the physical to produce goods and services for society. By developing the capacity to plan, organise, research, analyse, distribute, generate, market, transform, coordinate and execute they generate a space for their autonomy and distinctive identity in society. Because of their distinctive identity, knowledge workers have emerged to be a reference group in the contemporary world.

A sustainable knowledge society emerges only by putting increasing significance of formal education, skill and training. Development of knowledge and skill especially of those varieties that creates new meaning and value addition by processing the available information by people that can be measured by greater new applicability and usefulness is the essence of knowledge society. This society endeavours to involve all members of a community in the process of development and utilisation of knowledge. These processes use people essentially as creative beings and 'to be the carriers of explicit knowledge that triggers people's creative reflection, leading to the creation of new meaning and mass production of knowledge'. As human beings are the complex embodiment of 'tacit knowledge' that is trapped in them and waits to be flushed out and formalised through proper education and training to be converted into the embodiments of 'explicit knowledge' formal education and training play a crucial role in knowledge society. In essence, knowledge society recognises people to be the key societal resource that is leveraged to produce and use knowledge by acquiring education, skills, experience and creativity (United Nations, 2005).

For strategic advantage, knowledge society puts in place optimum importance on the creation of infrastructure and effective and quality institutional mechanisms for education and research and development facilities for the enrichment of own human resources, cultivation of human creativity and mass production and utilisation of knowledge. Besides quality learning through the conventional system, it integrates continuing and lifelong learning through various flexible and innovative modes for upgradation of knowledge and skill for its members in society. It is realised that illiteracy and lack of appropriate knowledge are the major barriers to knowledge society, which are overcome not only by functional literacy but by developing capacity to use information and knowledge as tools for social and economic empowerment in society. In fact in knowledge society, as Machlup (1962) points out, education is an investment rather than a cost, and is an investment not only to the individual (earnings) but to society (culture), in line with studies on social rates of return (Machlup, 1962). It is now proven across the globe that higher extent of education and training is linked to a high degree of work participation and resource generation through the service sector of the economy leading to high degree of proliferation of knowledge economy.

Across the continent, it is depicted that higher degree expected schooling, higher rate of adult literacy, Gross Enrolment Ratio in higher education, higher rate of public expenditure on education and very high rate of penetration of ICTs are positively linked to high rate of work participation in the service sector and high contribution to GDP from this sector of economy. As shown in Table 1.2, developed countries such as Australia, UK, USA and Japan having higher degree expected schooling, higher rate of adult literacy, Gross Enrolment Ratio in higher education, higher rate of public expenditure on education and very high rate of penetration of ICTs have high rate of work participation in the service sector and get predominant contribution to GDP from this sector of economy. The developing countries such as Brazil, Pakistan, China, India and South Africa, on the other hand, with relatively lower degree of expected schooling, low rate of adult literacy

Table 1.2 *Contemporary Global Trend of Association with Service Economy*

Country	Expected Year of Schooling Years (2011)	Education			ICT	Economic Growth (2009–10)		GDP from Service Sector (%)	Employment in Service Sector (2006–09) (%)
		Literacy Rate (15 yr+) (%)	Higher Education (GER) (2009) (%)	Public Expenditure on Education % of GDP (2006–09)	Internet (%)	GNI per Capita (US$)	GDP per Capita (%)		
Australia	18.0	99.0	82.5	9.7	88.8	38,510	3.9	68.0	76.0
Brazil	13.8	88.6	34.5	9.3	45.6		6.8	69.0	62.5
United Kingdom	16.1	99.0	59.5	9.3	83.6	36,580	0.6	78.0	79.5
United States	16.0	99.0	86.5	16.2	78.1	47,020	2.0	77.0	79.0
Pakistan	6.9	54.9	5.5	2.6	10.4	2780	2.1	54.0	27.0
China	11.6	92.2	24.5	4.6	40.1	7570	9.7	43.0	36.0
Japan	15.1	99.0	58.5	8.3	79.5	34,790	5.3	59	69.0
India	10.3	83.0	13.5	4.2	11.1	3560	8.3	59.0	27.0
South Africa	13.1	89.0	6.25	8.5	17.4	10,280	1.5	66.0	71.0

Source: Compiled from World Development Report, World Bank 2012 and http://www. internetworldstats.com, www.cnbc.com/. NSSO, Employment–Unemployment in 2007-08, 64th, Round.

and Gross Enrolment Ratio in higher education, low rate of public expenditure on education and low rate of penetration of ICTs have low rate of work participation in the service sector and consequently get low contribution to GDP from this sector of the economy. Even though within the developing countries there are variations with these correlations, aspiration to be knowledge driven has been the global phenomenon; and this aspiration invites increasing investment in the educational sector of society.

It is important that as education, training and skill development have occupied the centre stage in knowledge society, the investment in this sector has no more remained a purely social, moral and noneconomic venture; rather it has been a profit-driven economic endeavour in most parts of the world. Now, new policies are put in place to make education, training and skill development to be market oriented and profit driven for the suppliers of these services. Across the globe state and private players in education have emerged to be equally active in providing market-driven self-financed academic packages and in attracting learners for cross-border trade. Even within the national territory, education has emerged to be a viable means of trade and business attracting corporate houses not only to invest in these ventures, but also to influence the state policy on the same.

III. Knowledge Society: The Popular Vision

Though the emergence of knowledge society is relatively new, it has not only sustained itself, but has also made strong impact on the social, cultural, economic and political dynamics of society and has constructed an ideal image of its own. Significantly, this image, more often than not, highlights progressive, meritocratic, democratic and a host of its other new features. In its ongoing march in the contemporary world, this society by injection of varieties of newness has brought into being a series of discontinuities and disorientations from those of the past ones, and a sign of hope at the time of despair. Against the backdrop of the inadequacies of industrial society, knowledge society has been envisioned to bring in a host of new arrangements and actions.

Society of Progress, Rationality and Positive Action and Thought

It has been widely envisioned that the arrival of knowledge society would bring about a restructuring of social structure across the globe, which would be inherently progressive and set humanity on a continuous trajectory of advancement in both economic and social terms; produce a more planned and rational society than previous political systems, replace high-risk by low-risk society; make social actors more knowledgeable and well informed in decision-making; privilege personal relationships over the purely commercial ones resulting in a more caring and participatory society; reconstruct the state to be unnecessary in future as individuals would gain time and inclination in participating in civic affairs; value the self-esteem in the management system and would decentralise all affairs of lives and action to unleash creativity; alter work relation through extensive use of knowledge, encourage diversity, progressive awakening of power structure with flexibility, equality and empowerment of so far powerless; enable the formerly powerless to build their influence together, challenging traditional structures of control, strengthening each other through an exchange of information, ideas and experiences and acting together both globally and locally to interrogate and confront the system together through ICTs; be 'less hierarchical and more democratic' than the previous societies; draw a new era impacting the economic, social and cultural aspects wherein ICTs are perceived as great social levellers; create a 'meritocratic' environment whereby all would be valued according to their intelligence; empower people in work and domestic life by their ability to use knowledge and have more control of their present condition and of their destiny (Evans, 2004); enable everyone to 'own' knowledge and to have access to the 'human capital', which is embodied within one's self (Cohen, 2003); be free of previously existing human toil and social division mainly based on inheritance and access to private property and ownership of the means of production, class ideologies and antagonisms (Gorz, 1982; Evans, 2004); alter traditional employment practises to accommodate the emerging work environments and the newly found wealth and economic progress bring stability by ushering an egalitarian social framework (Gorz, 1982).

Society with Waves of Shocks, Disorientation and Discontinuity

The emergence of knowledge society has brought into being varieties of restructuring and alteration in the pre-existing societal arrangements initiating in real lives waves of shocks, disorientation and discontinuity in society.

According to Toffler (1970) the arrival of new society has brought shock with 'the dizzying disorientation' and has set in motion an accelerated rate of change in society with the superimposition of a new culture on old one and has released a total new social force that has revolutionised the tempo of life, and has affected the very way we 'feel' the world around us. New discoveries, technologies, social arrangements erupt into social lives, 'in the form of increased turnover rates — shorter and shorter relational durations. They force a faster and faster pace of daily life. They demand a new level of adaptability. And they set the stage for the potentially devastating social illness-future shock' (Toffler, 1970).

The increasing magnitude of the production and distribution of knowledge has not only transformed the modern industrial society into a knowledge-based one but also marked a historical discontinuity with the past (Machlup, 1962), sweeping away the previous economic and social systems. To Drucker (1968) these discontinuities are marked by the emergence of information technologies to create new major industries and brand new major business and to release the creative potential embodied in people; ushering of a world economy with common process of production and distribution, to generate the 'common economic appetites, aspirations and demands cutting across the national boundaries, languages and political ideologies' building the foundation of a pluralistic society to pose political, philosophical and spiritual challenges to the pre-existing societal arrangement; 'conversion of knowledge the primary industry that supplies to the industry the essential and the central resources of production; transformation of knowledge as main cost, the main investment, the main product of the advanced economy and the livelihood of the largest group of the population' (Drucker, 1968).

The discontinuity in knowledge society is also simultaneously marked by the acquiring of several new features that altogether provide a distinctive image to this society.

The Newness in Knowledge Society

The knowledge society has been described as a new phenomenon on earth. The newness of this society has been underlined in terms of its enhanced capacity to promote new social arrangement, creation of new social divisions, providing space for new forms of social mobility, generating new forms of social conflict and identity, changing the nature of the state, emergence of new dynamics of power and the like. Let us have a glimpse on new features of this society.

Knowledge society has ushered a new societal arrangement with a genuinely new way of life that is characterised by a new code of behaviour to move society 'beyond standardisation, synchronisation, and centralisation, beyond the concentration of energy, money, and power'. To Toffler (1980) this new societal arrangement could – with some intelligent help from us – turn out to be the first truly humane civilisation in recorded history (Toffler, 1980). It has also brought a new social arrangement for power. The site of power in this society is people's mind making it both identified and diffused. Herein whoever, or whatever, wins the battle of people's minds will rule (Castells, 1996).

New Social Divisions and Mobility

While knowledge society has produced a new variety of workers, work culture, mobility and leisure activities, it has also created a new political category of new underclass those excluded from the information revolution. To Castells (1996) the counter balance to 'information wealth' is 'information poverty', and in general terms, it is the financially deprived who are also deprived of information, whether the deprivation is individual or general (Castells, 1996). Though information technology, especially the Internet, is considered to be livewire of knowledge society, it has created a vertical division in culture and society by producing several layers in terms of varied extent of access to this technology. It has produced the following four layers of culture:

- The *techno-meritocratic* culture at the top (who are enlisted on a mission of world domination or counter-domination) by the power of knowledge, followed by the hacker meritocracy strengthening the inner boundaries of the community of the technologically initiated, and making it independent of the powers;

- *The networks of all sorts* who form online communes to reinvent society and, in the process, dramatically expand computer networking and its reach;

- *Internet entrepreneurs* who discover a new planet, populated by extraordinary technological innovation, new forms of social life;

- *Self-determined individuals*, whose technological capacity gave them substantial bargaining power vis-à-vis dominant social rules and institutions'.

Knowledge society, in fact, has generated its own dynamics bringing new architecture of power, new form of the exclusion, polarisation, inequality, social asymmetries and inculcating new areas of interest, new identities and social movements and new landscape of conflicts (Castells, 2001).

Knowledge society has furthered in an unprecedented scale not only mobility of people within and beyond the territory of each society, for work, housing, leisure, religion, family relationships, criminal gains, asylum seeking and so on, but has also promoted the ever fastest exchange of images, information and wastes across the globe through use of email, blog, Facebook, Skype, SMS, MMS, etc. With the emergence of virtual world, the empirical social space has emerged to be contested identity. 'Mobility is thus to be understood in a horizontal rather than a vertical sense, and it applies to a variety of actors and not just to humans' (Urry, 2000). By increasing the movements of people, their images, ideas and actions across the globe, on the one hand, and enhancing interconnectivity among the people through ICTs and globalisation, on the other, knowledge society creates two contradictory processes and enhances social fluidity, on the one hand, and solidarity, on the other. By enhancing local global connectivity and infusing new tech-economic arrangements, it has brought new forms of mobility cutting across the caste, class, gender, ethnic and spatial divides in society.

New Focus of Social Conflicts and Identity

To Melucci (1996(a)) against the backdrops of impressive development of ICT, creation of a global media system, the disappearance of historical political cleavages, and growing collusion of cultural differences within national societies and beyond, social conflicts in knowledge society have shifted their focus from class, race and other more traditional issues to the cultural issues. To him now:

> actors in conflicts recast the question of societal ends: they probe into the nature and the limits of human intervention; they concern themselves with health and illness, birth and death. The action of movements deliberately differentiates itself from the model of political organisation and assumes increasing autonomy from political systems; it becomes intimately interweaved with everyday life and individual experience. (Melucci, 1996a, p. 9)

Touraine (1981) also highlighted the transition of society from industrial to the 'programmed one' wherein central investments have been made at the level of production management. To him in this society class domination is less reflected in organising work than in 'managing the production and data processing apparatus'. Herein the struggle is no longer between the labour and capital in the factory but between the consumers or the public and the different kinds of apparatus. 'The struggle against the apparatus is no longer carried out in the name of the worker's right, political rights, etc., but in support of population's right to choose.... Here population opposes the apparatus by which they are dominated'. In knowledge society, conflicts gradually get institutionalised wherein the trade unions gradually become the political actors. To him the present moment of the society is 'marked by the appearance of new problems which must be understood and which can no longer be explained by invoking another order of the phenomena: the laws of the capitalist development or the consequences of modernisation'. The post industrial world is characterised by new modes of development, and it invites new modes of analysis and interpretation (Touraine, 1981). This society by shaping up new networks of power and wealth produces not only new social movements, movements of movements and contestation with new social boundaries, but also construct new varieties of social identity.

Knowledge society has produced diverse varieties of identities, which are different from those of the industrial and the agrarian societies. Castells (1997) has provided an elaborate description of the formation of this identity and the sociotechnological context of emergence of this identity. To him, in the wake of technological revolution, resurgence of capitalism and the demise of the statism, knowledge society has been witnessing unprecedented proliferation of collective identity in the form of:

- *Legitimising Identity:* 'Introduced by the dominant institutions of the society to extend and rationalise their domination vis-à-vis social actors;'

- *Resistance Identity:* 'Generated by those actors that are in positions/ conditions devaluated and/or stigmatised by the logic of domination, thus building trenches of resistance and survival on the basis of principles different from or opposed to those permeating the institutions of society and;'

- *Project Identity:* 'When social actors on the basis of whatever cultural materials available to them build a new identity that redefines their position society, by so doing; seek the transformation of the whole structure.'

These identities are dynamic in nature and that 'identities that start as resistance may reduce to project and may also along with the course of history, becomes dominant in the institution of the society, thus becoming a legitimising identity to rationalise their domination.' To him in the information age as the institutions and organisations of civil society have become by and large empty shells, and are unable to relate to peoples' lives and values in most societies legitimising identities have lost their hold. There has been simultaneous emergence of resistance identities to establish their autonomy in their communal resistance. In the network society, large section of people who experience economic, cultural and political disfranchisement tend to be attracted to communal identity. They develop 'the commune of resistance' to defend their space, and their places against the placeless logic of the space of flows characterising social dominations in the information age (Castells, 1997).

New Network of Power

The information society is founded on a network of power based on the cultivation of human mind, on the one hand, and yielding of wealth out of this cultivation, on the other. However, in the process of commodification, this wealth is controlled and manipulated by the market forces to maximise their economic interests by extensive use of ICTs and mass and new media. It captures and converts people's imagination, conditions them to be global through increased interactivity and inculcation of unsatiated desire for consumption of products and services that are made available on the chain of shopping malls, or on the click of mouse or push button of the mobile phone. It reorders the contemporary world with the reappearance of the dominance of free market over people's mind that is essentially diffused in nature. With this reordering of present, Fukuyama (1992) has located the 'end of history' and the arrival of a new age of global harmony.

This global network is evolved with a social and environmental cost. To Mann (1993), the global society in which we live today is not a unitary one. Though it is not an ideological community or a state, it is a single power network wherein shock waves reverberate around it, casting down empires, transporting massive quantities of people, materials and messages, and finally threatening the ecosystem and atmosphere of the planet (Mann, 1993, cf. Urry, 2000).

The 'discontinuities' in key areas of knowledge society from those of the previous ones and its newness are compared in Table 1.3.

IV. Knowledge Society: State, Market and Knowledge

The knowledge society functions in conjunction with the neoliberal state, shifting societal perspective from modernism to postmodernism, on the one hand, and a process of insurrection of subjugated knowledge that critiques and questions pre-existing domination of established power and hierarchy, on the other. These processes widely condition the production, use and distribution of knowledge, societal orientation to cultural consumption and production and patterns of recognition to one's state of knowledge.

In the wake of globalisation and the triumph of market forces, the classical liberal state that emerged in the eighteenth and nineteenth centuries has reappeared in its new avatar as a neoliberal state

Table 1.3 *Comparative Features of Agricultural, Industrial and Knowledge Society*

Key Areas	Agricultural society	Industrial society	Knowledge society
Key Resources	Natural resources	Physical labour	Mental, intellectual capability
Source of Power	Land, animal and physical	Steam engine	Internet
Key Tools	Plough, hoe	Machine tools	Information and communication technologies
Major Products	Foods, other basic services	Industrial goods and services	Data, information, knowledge, ideas
Organisation of Production	Family, agricultural firm, small-scale production	Factory, separation of family from factory, large scale production.	Specialised organisation, work place can be anywhere and everywhere.
Major Working Categories	Agricultural workers	Industrial workers	Knowledge workers
Market	Localised markets	National and world market, colonies	Global market
Knowledge Base	Emphasis on indigenous knowledge; monopolised by a limited section. Noncommercial	Emphasis on liberal western knowledge monopolised by limited few though a process of democratisation is in the making. Commercialisation in the making	Formal education, mass based and democratisation of education. Commercialisation
Major Source of GDP and Employment	Primary sector	Secondary sector	Tertiary sector

contd...

Table 1.3 *contd...*

Production and Consumption Dynamics	Production is to meet the immediate localised consumption need	Large scale production for the national and colonial markets	Need constructed by media and supply decides the demand
Types of Industries	Family farm, household Industry	Manufacturing industries	Knowledge industries, educational institutions, business processing centre
Types of Communities	Local, informal, face to face	Formal, large and weak social relations	Mix of formal and informal, distance and virtual
Major Social Movements for Social Change	Peasant, tribal movement, localised unity	Labour movements factory or organised, class based	Global movements focused on multiple groups: environment, women, ethnic, gay, lesbian, etc.
Social Identities	Communitarian	Secular	Multiple-global
Forms of Social Mobility	Slow pace of mobility widely conditioned by primordial arrangements	Fast pace of mobility, widely vertical	Fast pace of mobility both vertical and horizontal
Forms of Spatial Mobility	Very limited, predominantly rural to rural and mostly for non-economic purpose. Insignificant incidence of immigration	Fast mobility for a limited section of people from rural to rural and rural to urban areas for both economic and non-economic purposes. Increase in immigration for a limited section of population	Extensive mobility from rural to urban areas and from urban to urban areas, predominantly for the economic purpose. Unprecedented incidences of immigration
Pace of Change	Very slow	Fast for a limited section	Very fast and all encompassing
Source of Power	Command over land, people and natural resources	Command over technology	Command over knowledge, human mind

surpassing the predominion of welfare states of the mid-nineteenth and twentieth centuries and the communist state of this period. The neoliberal state philosophy has now expanded its hold across the globe, under the condition of the late twentieth century capitalist and market expansion paving the way for further augmentation of free market or laissez-faireism. The emergence of neoliberal state one way or the other has paved the way for the curbing of state intervention in social welfare, curbing of trade unionism, ensuring market stability and investment friendly environment, encouraging private investment and international capital, breaking the political and geographical barriers for trade and investment and extensive use of ICTs in all domains of lives. Under the influence of neoliberalism, now the twenty-first century state has also undergone significant transformation widely caused by increasing exercise of authority and intervention by international institutions in its functioning. Many nation states now have become increasingly dependent on the national and multinational corporations to further the quantum of social and economic development for society.

In this system, as Sorenson (2004) points out 'political authority is disaggregated into distinct parts each of which interacts with a diverse compilation of private companies, groups and organisations as well as with their counterparts in other countries; various parts of "the state", together with different players in the market' and also with NGOs and international organisations, are involved in setting up the organisations of global economic network. In this way, a large number of different public institutions are getting involved in the marketplace in new ways, unlike the standard picture of a centralised state governing market (Sorenson, 2004). Hence, the state has become less welfarist and more Schumpeterian to encourage competitiveness and extend its activities beyond the defined geographical borders. To Jessop (2002) the state now endeavours strongly to secure economic growth and its competitive advantages for capitals both within and its borders, by promoting the economic and extra-economic conditions to project power beyond their political frontiers to shape cross-border or external economic spaces relevant to capital accumulation and its social reproduction. These are mediated through the operation of the world market as a whole (Jessop, 2002).

Again through intensified interdependence with the multinational corporations, the international agencies and the member institutions of Washington consensus, the state is posited to initiate changes to liberalise domestic market for foreign investment. The state is also driven to accept international framework of cooperation, to allow an increased role for international institutions and to make the domestic market attractive and attentive to the demands of market players. 'By setting up a new international order, they took a first step towards their own transformation. Actors from societies and markets stepped in and created a world of interdependent societies and global markets. That whole process pushed states in a new direction, towards multilevel governance. The result is postmodern state' (Sorenson, 2004).

The arrival of information age has posited the state of industrial era with serious crisis of legitimacy in its functioning. It is observed that bypassed by global networks of wealth, power and information, the modern nation-state has lost much of its sovereignty. By trying to intervene strategically in this global scene the state loses capacity to represent its territorially rooted constituencies (Castells, 1997). In the new global order, the states have emerged to be 'gamekeepers' in nature that are not involved in giving society an overall shape and are uninterested in the details, as against the 'gardening' state that presumes exceptional concerns with the patterns, regularity and ordering as to 'what is growing and what is to be weeded out'. The state that possesses a monopoly of jurisdiction or governmentality over members living within the territory or region of the society has emerged to be a contested terrain, in the wake of globalisation and ICT penetration (Bauman, 1987; cf. Urry, 2000).

Moreover, the emerging conjunction of the knowledge society, wherein the state is gradually drifting away from its welfare nature, and embarrassing of neoliberalism through economic globalisation and adaptation to the revolution in the ICTs, new principles are put in place for organising the neoliberal state, its values, norms and morals. Now, globalisation and ICTs have facilitated the process of economic liberalisation and prompted the state to get integrated with open market philosophy through fast process of exchange of goods and services, mobility of economic and intellectual resources and transnational relationships of power (Bourdien and Wacquant, 1999). In essence, the state has been part of the processes that deterritorialise 'transference' of things across existing unit boundaries, 'transform' the identity of the unit, and 'transcend' divides between inside and outside and enhance cultural exchanges and expansions and technological connectivity to further economic globalisation through ICTs (Therborn, 2000).

In the emerging world, Castells (1997) asserts that 'political ideologies that emanate from industrial institutions and organisations, from nation-state-based democratic liberalism to labour-based socialism, find themselves deprived of actual meaning in the new social context'. These states have now lost their appeal and try to survive though a series of endless adaptations and run behind the new society 'as dusty flags of forgotten wars'. Significantly, power is no longer concentrated in institutions (the state), organisations (capitalist firms), symbolic controllers (corporate media, churches). It is diffused in global networks of wealth, power, information and images. Yet, it does not disappear. 'Power still rules society; it still shapes, and dominates, us' (Castells, 1997).

Such a change in the nature of the state is also accompanied by society's orientation towards production and consumption, and its shift from modernism to postmodernism. Modernism, as an era, is circumscribed by social philosophy of enlightenment, progresses absolute moral values, universal truths, rationality, modern science, democracy and social solidarity with fixed identity and the predominance of economic philosophy of capitalism and industrialism. This economic philosophy, widely described as 'Fordism', is again characterised by mass production of goods more or less proportionate to the need of consumption. In the wake of globalisation and phenomenal proliferation of mass media and ICTs and social media while the world has been widely interconnected, these have also intensified the shaping up of postmodern era with well-articulated critiquing of social and economic philosophies of modernism and invigorating new orientation to social, cultural and economic lives. The postmodern era is characterised by 'Post-Fordism', whereby even though production techniques are specialised to meet the emerging global market requirements and high consumption and production are intensively linked, the societal value privileges consumption over production. In this postmodern and in the Fordist production process, social needs and consumption patterns are articulated through regular and intensive interplay of media in everyday lives. As the needs are not socially grounded; rather constructed on a regular basis social identities have emerged to be consumption driven and fragmented.

Questioning Hierarchy of Knowledge

The knowledge society in many ways represents a postmodern society where the relationship between power and knowledge has become intrinsic. Under neoliberal economic order, knowledge is made subject to market forces for intensive commercial use and has been fragmented in new order. Michel Foucault (1980) in his power/knowledge discourse emphasises the inseparability of the two. While for a modernist 'knowledge is power', for a postmodernist 'power is knowledge' as power creates knowledge to suffice to its own need. The shape of existing knowledge embodies the power that created it. Herein to reveal the truth and in order to hidden meanings of power–knowledge relationship one ought to take recourse to deconstruction. In this context, Foucault's argument on hierarchy of knowledge and resurrection of subjugated knowledge is crucial.

Knowledge and power are interlinked and regularly reproduced through discourses. According to Foucault, human identity is created through discourse that joins power and knowledge together to have control over life experiences and to create identity. Discourse also creates knowledge. It is again that discourse is created by those who hold power and these powerful also control the course and sustainability of discourse and thereby reproduce and exercise power. The essence of truth, morality, meaning and self-image are created through discourse in context and exercise of power. In the process of such reproduction of discourses a large part of knowledge becomes subjugated while other occupies place of privilege and becomes dominant in the knowledge hierarchy. In this hierarchy varieties of localised skills and knowledge, indigenous experiences and practises have emerged to be under privileged and occupy the lower rung of knowledge hierarchy. These are relegated to the margin, undervalued and further devaluated.

Michel Foucault (1980) has seen the emergence of local character in criticism against the dominant discourses that represents in reality an autonomous, non-centralised and independent body of knowledge.

This criticism is heralded by means of 'a return of knowledge', which he has described as an 'insurrection of subjugated knowledge'. 'The subjugated knowledge represent historical contents that have remained buried and disguised in a functionalist coherence of formal systemisation; remained disqualified as inadequate or insufficient; and remained located low down on the hierarchy beneath the required level of cognition or scientifically. The subjugated knowledge was concerned with historical knowledge of struggles, confining to the margins of knowledge. The insurrection of knowledge is opposed primarily to the effects of the centralising powers that are linked to the institution and functioning of an organised scientific discourse; are paradoxically posited vis-à-vis the meticulous, erudite, exact historical knowledge.'

To Foucault the strategy of genealogical research would have to emerge out of these oppositions and struggles to combine erudite and popular knowledge, to eliminate the hierarchy and privileges of a theoretical knowledge, to provide appropriate attention to local, discontinuous, disqualified, illegitimate knowledge against unitary body and hierarchical knowledge, to emancipate historical knowledge from that of subjection, reactivation of local and minor knowledge in opposition to the scientific hierarchisation of knowledge. This strategy would affect the intricacies of power whereby the subjugated knowledge would be released and brought into play (Foucault, 1980).

Knowledge is not only expression of domination and subjugation, but also of collective identity. In knowledge society, the ICT-driven discourse has made the knowledge both fragmented at one end and interconnected on the other. This emerging discourse has produced the space for manifestation of multiple identities both of contestation and cooperation vis-à-vis the actors and processes of domination and hegemony.

Like land in agrarian society and tools and machinery in industrial society, knowledge has emerged to be the key resource in knowledge society. As society is being structured based on the mass production and use of knowledge, in this society knowledge has become the organising principle to organise social relations surrounding it. Human history is replete with the facts that key resources of all societies are unevenly distributed among its members. Since the site of the key resource in knowledge society is individual human brain, it is posited that the knowledge society will bring a paradigm shift in the distribution process of this resource and thereby in the social relations therein.

The new technological, economic and social frameworks that emerged out of interpenetration of knowledge society has widely altered predefined social relations and cultural practices, reinforced the nexus between globalisation and ICTs, privileged the application over the cognitional dynamics of knowledge, ushered new patterns of work and work participation, reemphasised the significance of education and training, brought new orientations to lives and livelihood, exclusion and marginalisation, power and social identity and host of hopes and aspirations of a new world. The crescendos of knowledge society are posited also within a neoliberal state order, postmodern frame of social and cultural orientations. These are also accompanied by the resurgence of subjugated knowledge at the grassroots.

Knowledge society, by cultivating knowledge in the human mind to be the ultimate site for power and development, and transforming this knowledge to be the praxis for freedom, autonomy, justice, dignity and collective empowerment of humanity, has developed contestations to many of the pre-existing forms of domination and hegemony, and brought in resurgence of new hope of human existence on earth. By converting knowledge as a key resource, it has brought new forms of economic enterprise, work relations, mobility, said networks and power relation. Emerging India has acquired a new identity of its own in the changing world by its engagement with the mass production and use of knowledge in all areas of activities, initiation of economic liberalisation and bringing shift in the perspectives on development and expansion of education and ICTs, phenomenal production of educated and skilled manpower, bringing in new varieties of work, workers and work relations, fostering new sociocultural milieu in society. India's emergence in the knowledge era, however, has got added advantage because of its traditional knowledge based past and availability of huge pool of young population, and has also acquired phenomenal complexity because of pre-existing social and spatial divides that have provided the basis for people's unequal access to education, technology, economic resources and in the established power structure in society. Within these pre-existing arrangements, the emerging knowledge society is in the process of liberating one segment of society while marginalising another; and consolidating one part while fragmenting another; and has produced varieties of identities across the space being restorative at one end and transformative on the other. These dichotomies invite a critiquing of the ideal image of knowledge society and delineation of processes of marginalisation and identity formation therein in order to contextualise the emergence of knowledge society in India within the wider social processes.

2

Critiquing and Contextualising Knowledge Society

The knowledge society recognises human mind as the site of progress, power and transformation by igniting it through appropriate knowledge, which uses knowledge as the key resource to produce wealth and employment, develops mechanisms for mass production and use of knowledge and places knowledge in the inner core of its all dynamics of this society. Through its engagement with the processes of production, use and dissemination of knowledge, founded in human intellectual potential and achieved qualities, the knowledge society has emerged to be the epitome of liberty, justice, equality and dignity; and has been envisioned not only to bring qualitative changes in its key agency, the people and in the pre-existing institutional arrangements, but also in the transformative dynamics of society. Though the knowledge society itself is *sui generis*, its emergence is not autonomous of the pre-existing societal arrangements. Thus, despite bringing profound changes in the social and institutional dynamics of society across the globe, it is yet to harmonise the world with prosperity, justice, equality and dignity for all. It has rather acquired paradoxical identities being the creator of wealth, innovation and hope and transformer of culture and institutions on the one hand, and the promoters of poverty, spurring greed, hardship and despair on the other. For its sustained association with the pre-existing evils of society, the knowledge society has been described with utmost caution to be the bearers of rationality, freedom and equality for the majority of humanity. Scholars have expressed both hope and despair about the new social dynamics as engineered by knowledge society.

Doubts are also raised about the positive impact of Information and Communication Technologies (ICTs)-driven social order with deep-down apprehension that it would enhance the possibility of bringing doomsdays and disasters in human civilisation through the increasing dependency of the humanity on technology (Toffler, 1980).

Along with these apprehensions, complexities are multiplied with the functioning of multiple socioeconomic arrangements simultaneously within a given order. It is widely appreciated that regardless of the arrival of new discoveries and arrangements, the knowledge society has not been able to displace the preexisting agrarian order (the first wave) and the industrial wave (the second wave) in *toto* causing varieties of anomalies and inconsistencies in the emerging social dynamics. Toffler (1980) writes:

> today the Second Wave has not entirely spent its force. But even as this process continues, another, even more important has begun. Third Wave has begun to surge across the earth, transforming everything it touched ... Many countries, therefore are feeling the simultaneous impact of two, even three quite different waves of change, all moving at different rates of speed and with different degrees of force behind them .... Today all the high technology nations are reeling from the collision between the Third Wave and the obsolete, encrusted economies and institutions of the Second. (Toffler, 1980, pp. 25–30)

Since the late twentieth century, especially with the onset of neoliberal globalisation most of the developing nations of the world have begun encountering the powerful collusion between varieties of waves simultaneously.

Moreover, the spread of globalisation has been unequal socially and spatially making the humanity to be exposed to unequal structure of opportunity, coercion, deprivation and wellbeing. In fact, imperfect globalisation now characterises a significant feature of social structure of network society wherein the coexistence of a global structure with industrial, rural, communal or survival societies becomes the reality of all countries 'albeit with a different share of population and territory having varied degree of inclusion and exclusion' (Castells, 2004). Thus, in the wake of globalisation though the world has been horizontalised, It has not been equal. More people in more places now have the power to access the flat world platform – to connect, compete, collaborate, and, unfortunately, destroy – than ever before (Friedman, 2005). The access to this flat world has not been in equal term for all sections of people as they are posited with diverse capability and multiple social realities. The coexistence of multiple social waves and economic formation has been a part of historical reality especially for most of the developing societies. These multiple realities are seldom disconnected from the past, along with the preexisting social inequalities and exclusions. As against this backdrop, knowledge society is amenable to be viewed as a part of historical continuity and to be critiqued for its perceived foundations that are based on newness, discontinuity, democratic value and egalitarianism.

I. Questioning the Notion of Newness/Discontinuity in Knowledge Society

As the progression in human societies is not discreet or mechanical, it carries many of the elements of old society into a new one and at time many of the old dimensions also get redefined in the new context. Thus, the dimensions of newness of knowledge society and its claim for discontinuity with the past have been contested with host of empirical evidences.

It is pointed out that the *knowledge society is not a new, but as a part of evolutionary process.* Toffler (1980) has found the continuity in a cyclical movement of society wherein the new societies are evolved based on the fusion of past and future, of First Wave and Third Wave. To him, the

> 'Third Wave civilisation turns out to have many features – decentralised production, appropriate scale, renewable energy, de-urbanisation, work in the home, high levels of presumption, to name just a few – that actually resemble those found in First Wave societies. We are seeing something that looks remarkably like a dialectical return.'

This continuity reflects a strategic fusion for development based on a synthesis between the First and the Third Wave that leads to the

> 'development of both low-stream, village-oriented, capital-cheap, rural industries and certain carefully selected, high-

stream technologies with an economy zoned to protect or promote both'.

After examining trends of adoption of technologies and the development strategies of the selected developing countries, and especially of India, he observed yet just another such a transformation is now under way that would carrying forward a 'new synthesis: Gandhi, in short, with satellites' (Toffler, 1980).

In fact, knowledge society is a part of an evolutionary process and the lens of modernity is very often employed to view the information society not as an historical discontinuity. The essence of knowledge society is the scientific progress for individual and social emancipation that are surely rooted in the modern societies and have flowed over the past three centuries from industrialism, capitalism and the Enlightenment project (Black, 2003). Thus, it is not entirely new though it has heralded the end of the industrial capitalist era and the arrival of a 'service' or 'leisure' society. It is, however, more than recycled post industrialism and it goes beyond it in terms of its economic, social and political complexities (Lyon, 1988).

It is widely recognised that knowledge society *is part of latest series of innovations* in the contemporary world. While knowledge society has been characterised by the extensive use of ICTs, it is usually pointed out that such technology is merely the latest series of innovations in communications systems and technologies (Hornby and Clarke, 2003), that it is not unprecedented (Preston, 2001) and that it can be studied historically (Castells, 2001). The emergence of knowledge society has been facilitated step by step with several series of development in human history; for example, the arrival of printing in fifteenth century, expansion of commercial society, growth of knowledge and storage of information such as encyclopaedia, large-scale explosion of books and printed materials appeared in the eighteenth century, large-scale mechanisation of printing, development of the postal system and mass advertising in the second half of the nineteenth century, the invention of electric telegraph, telephone, evolution of the mass media such as popular newspapers, radio, film and television in the early twentieth century and innovations of computer, Internet and other non-print informational technologies thereafter (Black, 2003). The edifice of knowledge society is thus created on the contribution made by previous societies.

As a part of history of science and technology, the information revolution of present society has maintained several continuities with the socioeconomic features of the industrial revolution. Thus, the features of industrial revolution are also widely applied even today to describe the 'information revolution'.

Table 2.1 *Common Features of Industrial and Information Revolution*

Industrial Revolution	Information Revolution
Widespread and systematic application of science and knowledge to production	The rise of a 'knowledge society' in which both digital innovation and what Bell (1980) referred to as 'theoretical knowledge' prioritises brain over brawl
Movement of population	The dispersal of population: contrary to the 'concentration' process of industrialisation, there has occurred an outward drift of city populations and the emergence of the post-modern, polycentric, informational city (Castells, 1989)
Movement of labour between the sectors	The rise of post-industrial occupations and sectors, with majority of the workforce migrating to the service sector and, moreover, becoming engaged in 'information work' or work rich in 'information skills'
The growth of new patterns of work and new units of production	The emergence of flexible modes of working; the virtual organisation, teleworking
The emergence of new social and occupational classes	The professionalisation of society; the decline of a traditional working class synonymous with manual labour, and the parallel rise of white-collar classes and numerous professional and managerial strata (Perkin, 1989)
Specialisation of economic activity for wide markets	The expansion of markets through customisation and the niche targeting of demand: the replacement of Fordist production by post-Fordist regimes and 'just-in-time' methods
Intensive and extensive use of capital resources	Extensive capital investment in modern ICTs; by governments, multi-transnational corporations and large-scale research organisations

Source: Prepared from Phyllis Deane (1980) cf. of Rowe and Thompson (1996, pp. 14–20).

Though these crucial features of society manifest themselves differently in the ages of industrial and information revolution, they depict a host of similarities through their application.

The 'continuity' argument has been extended further with the logic that information society carries the essence of industrial society in it through the presence and furtherance of capitalism, industrialism, modernity and surveillance which are also the fundamental aspects of an industrial society. 'It is essentially an evolutionary phase of industrial capitalism, rather than a revolutionary change of gear for human society; and is neither a value-free nor a purely technoeconomic concept as it carries with it the cultural and economic practices of industrial society' (Moore and Steele, 1991; Black, 2003); and has aptly been described as 'super industrial society' (Toffler, 1990). In knowledge society, ICTs are used to restore profit and improve productivity of capitalist society and 'to replace Fordist regimes of production and economic growth by Post-Fordist capitalism essentially to repackage capitalism and to restructure the economic and technological infrastructure for corporate capital' (Black, 2003). In the process of such transformation, it has fostered 'informational capitalism' (Castells, 1997) and expanded the economy both locally and globally through the accumulation of information and development of technology to provide further boost to the economic process and encourage new forms of interaction (Evans, 2004).

Within these intersectionalities in the technoeconomic process, the knowledge society posits itself as an integral part of modernity being located in the latest stage of the 'modern project' (Giddens, 1991(a)) in the contemporary world through a new incarnation. Culturally, it has inherited the tradition of enlightenment that has laid the foundation for the development of objective science and universal morality, and thereby furthered the process of accumulation of knowledge for social and individual emancipation and progress (Black, 2003).

II. Critiquing Popular Image of Knowledge Society

Historically knowledge society was proliferated in the Western world and it is in a process of expansion in other parts of the world. Both culturally and technologically, it has been a West-driven process. Herein, notwithstanding its ideal image, the knowledge society depicts a Western bias in its onward march across the world. The expansion of this society has been accompanied by the increasing plights of workers, emerging dependency relations, inequality, exclusion and conflicts and a host of contradiction from within.

Knowledge society brings one-sided flow by promoting *western modes of globalisation and introducing new patterns of dependency to maximise western economic power.* Though the knowledge society has been described as the harbinger of new order with equality and justice and it has been projected to bring an integrated world order, it is now established by several scholars that this society has promoted predominantly the Western model of development across the globe along with its cultural output and lifestyle that dominates foods, fashion, leisure and entertainment industries. The global reach of this development has been successfully achieved with the state-of-the-art ICTs that have been proved to be extremely powerful tools to 'compress' time and space (Harvey, 1989) and to increase the 'space of flows (Castells, 1996), to move forward a globalised economy and culture with a common agenda'. With its fast expansion, rather than witnessing a flourishing of new, smaller and more flexible organisations and meeting individualised consumption needs, a new cultural imperialism has emerged in recent decades, together with a universal culture in which Western ideas, images and values predominate over a loss of local culture and imperatives (Evans, 2004).

The knowledge society was envisaged to bring into being a new societal arrangement that would have its foundation on equality and justice in all domains of life both internally and externally. However, without adequate access to modern means of communication to all sections of population, the idea of a 'just political community' has remained a chimera, that the knowledge industries have remained absolutely dominated by the giant multinational corporations, and that in the global market many countries have found their national sovereignty being threatened by the activities of these borderless economic interests. Herein as Lyon (1988) points out the dream of the poor countries to catch up with the richer ones or leapfrogging the industrial era in reality remain unrealised as they find themselves in a situation which is 'overwhelmingly not just one of interdependence, but of dependence'. Over the decades, it is also realised that in the global context the communication and cultural dominance of the north over the south has got strengthened, as it has made these communications the 'conduits of economic power'…. In reality, the expansion of knowledge economy has opened up many countries to data processing and information related services displacing the domestic production 'resulting in more job loss in the traditional varieties of activities that has created an undermining of local cultural policy and ethical values' (Lyon, 1988).

The discourse of information society has become closely wedded to:

> a neoliberal ideology that was based on the idea that an increase in an economy's wealth-creating abilities would 'trickle-down' to poorer sections of society without the government intervention. However in reality the ICTs have helped the western economic power to grow disproportionately whereby production take place in the low wage countries of the south and east, whereas ideas and intellectual skills are deployed by fewer people in the higher-waged from more advanced economies of the West (Evans, 2004).

It has been widely reported from across the world that knowledge society has *brought devaluation of non-knowledge workers* and worsening their working condition. It is found that the move away from blue-collar to white-collar work has made very little difference to power relations in the employment market as the new patterns of employment have placed the workforce in a more constrained and unequal position vis-à-vis their employers than in previous times (Castells, 1996, 1997; Evans, 2004). Knowledge society has also in many ways devaluated the non-knowledge workers. In this society, certain categories of people participate more in the information loop than others because of their access to new ICTs. This 'serves to intensify existing social inequalities, or even create large groups of "misfits" – people who do not fit in with the information society'… Here human creativity is misjudged as impressions are offered out of context in schematic, (pre-) programmed and fragmented frames' (Dijk, 1999).

Information-centred jobs favour educated, skilled and literate workforce. However, there are many in knowledge society who find themselves unable to acquire formal eduction and skills and are ultimately 'excluded from the workforce or "downgraded as workers"…' and are unable to compete in the labour market. This section of the workforce finds itself out of the emerging employment loop, relegated as underclass and remain engaged in the manual and unskilled jobs. Even though their jobs are still necessary in the information age, their inability to gain employment in a 'valued' economic sector gets socially constructed as contributing less to society and thus in turn adversely affecting their own self-image (Castells, 1996, p. 264). On the contrary, the knowledge society has placed the information rich in an advantaged position globally while disadvantaging the rest of the workers. This phenomenon has been substantiated by the fact that 'over the last 30 years the real wages have fallen, people working longer hours, vacation time is at a minimum and jobs have become insecure and largely unprotected.' Thus, in knowledge society 'contrary to past prediction', stress and hurry at work have increased; legions of teleworkers and telecottages have failed to materialise; the environment has not benefited from the 'perceived' shift away from industrialism; material and information poverty persist, and labour has been neither intellectualised nor released from monotonous patterns of work, and the imminent arrival of the paperless office has remained pure myth (Black, 2003, p. 24. cf. Sellen and Harper, 2002). Rather workers find themselves incorporated into near slave-like work conditions, practically indentured to local factories producing goods for the mighty transnational companies based in the West (Klein, 2001; Evans, 2004).

It is now widely apparent that in view of contemporary development only few of the predictions related to knowledge society have come true as the problem of profitability has not been solved and work has not been the source of empowerment (Evans, 2004). Moreover, in view of increased quantum of technology induced and enabled exploitation, exclusion, eco-vandalism and authoritarianism in the earth it is not clear that the world be transformed in the direction of enlightenment, democracy and prosperity (Muddiman, 2003).

The prediction about knowledge society has over *emphasised on technological determinism.* The emergence of this has been widely viewed in terms of technological determinism in general and ICT determinism in particular by propagating that technological development is the essential driver of social change, and information technology has transformed the information society and its economy (Masuda, 1981). However, there are also counter views to recognise that the users make their technological choice based on their social convenience, and economic necessity, that the appropriateness of technology is not decided by the technology itself but by the users who determine the success or failure of a particular system and devices and that technology does not determine what happens, it only determines what can happen (Hornby and Clarke, 2003); and that the application of new innovation 'often turns out to be quite different from that envisaged by the inventor' (Winston, 1998). Within diversified views as to whether technological change drives social change, or social change demands new technological solutions to new problems, and the persisting gaps between popular versions of information society forecasting and the multifaceted transition of contemporary economic realities one can find but 'more than one image of the information society' in the present world. It is now proven that 'technological development does not have pre-set social effects which are predictable, universal or, for that matter, just or beneficial for all. Rather social determinism may take many forms. Thus, ICTs should be seen as determined by social processes' rather than the sole determinant of social processes (Lyon, 1988). Thus while, on one hand, ICTs are recognised as the driver of economic change, these are also delineated as only instrumental rather than causative (Giddens, 1999) and as simply another system of communication whose economic consequences are far from being universally beneficial, on the other (Cassidy, 2002).

Knowledge society has brought an *extension of pre-existing inequality and exclusion*. Rather than eliminating the problem of low wage, poverty, class, gender and race divides and varieties of social disability, knowledge society has furthered them and intensified digital divides through post-industrial capitalism in everyday life. It is highlighted that the domain of exclusion has emerged to be the overriding feature of advanced or informational capitalism whose global dimension magnifies many times in the everyday inequality. As the Internet-driven global networking has converted the world into a system, conflicts rising out of inequality and exclusion have also acquired global character. Through advanced capitalism, it has brought with it for a vast section of people 'the daily affiliation of a market system, inequality, powerlessness and poverty which are too real' (Muddiman, 2003). Though a networked society is a global society, it has emerged to be deeply fragmented by the double logic of inclusion and exclusion in the global networks that structure production, consumption, communication and power relation. While it integrates the world with common economic, technological and cultural processes, it excludes those who are away from the dominant networks. Thus, even with the unitary framework there have emerged different geometries and geographies of inclusion and exclusion (Castells, 2004).

Knowledge society has emerged to be digitally divided both internally within and between nations in the form of internal divide between digitally empowered rich and the disempowered poor; linguistic cultural divide between domination of the Anglo-Saxon culture and the other world culture; divide in access of technology between the rich and the poor nation; and the divide between the values of ICT-driven affluent elite and conventional authority and hierarchies (Keniston, 2000). The encounter of the digitally divided knowledge economy with the organising principles of the pre-existing society has reinforced pre-existing social divides in many ways across the globe.

The neo-Marxist finds reinforcement of private ownership, emergence of capitalism and instability in the labour market at a global scale in the emergence of knowledge society.

They find a relationship between the emerging new market and private ownership; and argue that the new market system that has emerged since over the last 40 years has intensified the private rather than the public supply of services, private ownership of property (including 'ownership' of information through copyright, etc.), work for wage labour, provision of services, goods and information according to ability to pay and the increasing validation of the idea of competition as the main way of organising economic and social life. All this represents, for Webster (2000), an expansion and penetration of capitalism in an every wider and deeper range of human affairs. Such change adds up to a restructured, rather than a transformed, social order of a 'late'; 'disorganised'; 'informational'; 'cybernetic'; or 'digital' capitalism (Webster, 2000).

In-depth arguments are forwarded by the neo-Marxists to delineate the strengthening position of transnational corporation with mobile and the flexible power to control the market through the ICTs enabled global networks. The 'flexible' working methods, small-scale batch production, outsourcing, subcontracting and 'just-in-time' delivery methods as against mass production that are parts of knowledge society have created new markets for goods and services. These in term have resulted in the proliferation of a global consumer marketplace 'fuelled by an increasing obsession with signs and style as opposed to utility' (Amin, 1994; Lash and Urry, 1994; Webster, 2000). Along the line the process of domination of transnational corporations over the developing world has been conspicuously marked in recent decades. The internal pressure generated out of global economic interdependence also pushes the developing countries in various parts of the world in pursuing the foreign direct investment on their own society despite organised resistance from within.

The emerging work culture of the network society as described to be flexible, multiskilled knowledge based (Castells, 1996) has been explained by the neo-Marxists as phenomenon of growing insecurity of employment. Much of this insecurity according to them is experienced by the low-grade workers as pliable reserve army of labourers, which responds to the economic boom and recession. To them, many of the works are 'mislabelled' as knowledge work to 'capture the tacit expertise of the employee for competitive advantage of the organisation' (Warhurst and Thompson, 1998).

In economic terms, the advent of knowledge society has been marked by *replacement of Welfare by Entrepreneurial State.* Knowledge society posits itself in the conjunction of failure of 'welfare state' economy and the triumph of market economy. The mid-twentieth century Keynesian welfare state that attempted to compensate for the dysfunctions of the market through demand management, full employment and the provision of a social welfare for all now is being systematically replaced by a Schumpeterian Social Workfare State (SWS) that focuses its energies on meeting the conditions required for global capitalism to thrive by prioritising social order of economic competitiveness (Jessop, 1994, 2000). This state according to Webster (2006) presides over shrinkage of the publicly funded Keynesian welfare state through privatisation, cuts in welfare expenditure and promotes 'partnership' arrangements with private business houses and the voluntary sector and sometimes local communities. ICTs figure prominently in the SWS for e-governance, etc., with distinct providers and consumers. Out of changes in the state order, many advanced states abandoned liberal and humanist education paving way for vacationist educational goal that prioritises the teaching of competencies and skills (especially those linked to ICTs) that are closely linked to commerce and industry. Though the SWS contribute to the ideals of education for work, neglect public service in many areas or transfer them to the private sector (Webster, 2006), and desensitise social science education through co-option.

The knowledge society by commoditising knowledge has led to large scale *co-option of civil society initiatives and social science.* The ideological apparatus of information society creates a political climate to coopt collective initiatives and criticality within the institutionalised domain of the state. The Social Development Summit 1995 and the World Bank (2000) perspectives on redefining the state that took place in the wake of the formation of WTO, GATTS and GATS widely emphasised on the civil society engagements and people's initiatives and selective co-option of civil society activism to deliver the social goods within the given and newly formed legal arrangements, laws and procedures of the state. These initiatives have been ideologically addressed to curb the criticality of the third sphere and their inherent urge to develop contestation against the state and market. Similar efforts are also made to create a category of organic intellectuals, redefining functions of the teachers to be academic managers, librarians or computer specialists as the knowledge managers.

Within the emerging gamut of professionalisation of educational service, social science education has been deprioritised and reoriented to be demand driven than to be supply driven. Utility of knowledge is privileged over its edge for criticality. The efforts to 'question social goals, to explore the possibilities of emancipatory role, appropriateness of technology, ethical and cultural dimensions of new technology are deprioritised in this age. Social analysis that engages itself with the human conditions within technological reality is not encouraged for ideological purpose' (Lyon, 1988) as these inculcates the possibility of contestations against evolving economic order.

Knowledge society has not eliminated conflict; rather it has brought *new forms of conflicts by promoting informational capitalism.* Though knowledge society is expected to resolve old conflicts of interests and class antagonism, the 'fundamental class situations and conflicts have sharpened in this society' based on a major cleavage between technocrats (the knowledge haves) and those whose livelihood and lifestyles are governed by the technocrats (the knowledge have nots). Here opposition is brought about because 'the dominant classes dispose of knowledge and control information' (Touraine cf. Lyan, 1986). Having dual roles, ICTs on the one hand have become an effective tool for freedom, and on the other hand have emerged to be a tool in the hand of powerful to oppress the uninformed on the other leading to the exclusion of the devalued by the conquerors of technology of information society (Castells, 1997). In fact the capitalist power elites have not been undermined by the emergence of an 'informational mode of capitalism', rather have maintained their domination and embedded their own cultural codes and values within cyberspace. Within this arrangement, information has been endowed with life-enhancing qualities, and to be without information is to be deemed disempowered and disengaged; the 'information-rich' have emerged to be advantaged while the 'information-poor' are deemed to be disadvantaged on a number of levels (Castells, 1996).

The information society produces obscurity and dubiousness through its utopian image and the ideological position. It not only obscures the vested interests that shape the overall direction of information technology but also the clues as to who holds the power. Though it is promised to be egalitarian, democratic and participatory in nature, it is not evidenced that 'the centralism, monopolies and inequalities of capitalism have disappeared in this society' (Lyon, 1988).

This society has created an illusion by glorifying the power of knowledge. Though people accept the phrase 'knowledge is power' as dictum to delineate the liberating, emancipatory and empowering capacity of knowledge society, to elucidate information revolution as a social revolution and to project that a knowledge society would be of unimaginable power that would dissolve disadvantage and engineer egalitarianism, in reality knowledge only serves the dominating force (Black, 2003). This society besides promoting the domination of north over south, also provides the platform to develop one-way relation between knowledge and power (Lyon, 1988). To Drucker (1968), historically men of knowledge have not held power ... That the pen is mightier than the sword can only be called the opium of the intellectuals. But now knowledge has power. It controls access to opportunity and advancement. The learned are no longer poor... They are the true capitalist in the knowledge society. However, the men of knowledge find it hard to accept that the basic decisions on knowledge are political decisions rather than knowledge decisions; and therefore these are not in their hands (Drucker, 1968, p. 337).

Though knowledge society deifies knowledge viewing it as a sacred commodity and wraps it in an intangible mystique based on the belief that an information-rich 'learning society' acts as an antidote damaging effects of materialism, in essence knowledge society converts knowledge as a 'thing' and neatly disaggregated into data (Schumacher, 1973) 'that could be related to anything' (Ritchie, 1982). In fact, the foundation of knowledge society is based on inherent contradiction that revolves around its very perception of itself. On the one hand, it describes this society in terms of reason, enlightenment, knowledge, science, expertise and harmony with the worldly instrumentalism of digital ICTs; on the other hand, it commoditises all these as tradable items (Black, 2003).

Knowledge society having been shaped as *surveillance society* carries the dark sides of modernity that characterises control, conflicts and repression through the developed technologies of surveillance. The technological advancement has enabled the state to collect information on the citizen on each step of their movement. It has widely been used to control and command. Against the backdrop of surge of international capitalism, societies are getting 'locked in mortal combat to capture markets and conquer opposition within the lucrative high technology field', and that 'governments are so active in promoting IT and purchasing its products' and making it a powerful tool for monitoring and supervising people's activities (Lyon, 1988). Such monitoring very frequently encroaches on personal liberty of citizens, coerces their existence and imposes threat in everyday life.

III. Postmodernity, Hypermodernity and Beyond

As for Foucault (1979), knowledge is not simply a factor that determines power; it is also a product of power itself since power has the capacity to generate knowledge: 'we cannot exercise power except through the production of truth'. All knowledge is to a degree socially constructed. History has the advantage of revealing areas of knowledge which, according to current 'truth', were in the past patently false, deriving their legitimacy from the fact that power holders 'made them true'. A prominent 'regime of truth' over the last quarter of the century has been the idea of the information society. Its legitimacy is drawn from the interested party (stakeholders) which stands to gain social and professional recognition from establishing the information society as a 'given' phenomenon (Black, 2003).

The postmodernists negate 'grand theory' of capitalism that emphasises the continuity of market economics, social division of labour, colonisation of human experience and of information itself, as it oversimplifies the lived experience. It is an era of speed, of surface and of complexity and of 'life fragmented into a series of meaningless spectacles' (Bauman, 1994). To them it is a 'world where states, communities and individuals are unstable, multiple and diffuse and where material reality is obscured by signs and media babble. These phenomena mark the emergence of post-modern era and the beginning of the end of the modern age'. With the shift towards the 'postmodern condition'

> human societies have realised that the grand narratives of human improvement such as scientific socialism have ended in failure. The technical and instrumental rationality of modern science has threatened the modern world, and modernity has emerged as a phenomenon of social exclusion, domination of women, non-Europeans, nature itself. Post-modernity does not appear to provide stability in society. A multiplicity of new codes and signs thus pepper our experience in the postmodern world; and the strange alien symbol of dispossessed. In spite of the best efforts of some, such 'language games' in which values and ideas have become interest based, no longer offer us a stable, coherent or consistent view of the world. (Muddiman, 2003, p. 50)

To them, everyday life in information society experiences variety of signs and discourses through the electronic media that construct simulations for artificial hyper realities. This brings convergence of computer processing power; multimedia and networking technologies in the cyberspace to provide immense potential for fantasy, self-discovery and self-construction and the 'multiplication' of reality itself (Poster, 1995). This virtual world promises a quantum change in the way many of us experience the world. To Jordan (1999), the postmodern cyberspace 'is in the process of undermining our sense of possessing a stable, individual identity located firmly in the material world. Ever increasing numbers of Internet users and computer console addicts deconstruct, reconstruct and play with their identities through chat rooms, gaming and other multi-user facilities' (Jordan, 1999. cf. Muddiman, 2003).

Though many scholars have found potential of liberation and challenge against domination in the cyberspace activism, others 'pessimistically argue that such fractured and post human social psychology reflect accelerating deathlessness and schizophrenia in human condition and ... at the end a retract from moral engagement and the problems of the world we live in' (Robins, 1995).

Postmodern society, however, does not exclusively exist in the domain of simulation, cyberspace or the virtual world, rather it is has material base and its related consequences with 'economies of signs and space' where fashion and image, speed and flexibility dictate supply and demand (Lash and Urry, 1994). Postmodernity thus provides the 'cultural logic of late capitalism', its forms and simulations are 'characteristic embodiment of the ways in which the market system shapes our way of life' (Muddiman, 2003). These processes in essence accelerate marketisation of knowledge and become organisational capital as opposed to individual intelligence or public discourse. Postmodern knowledge, and its management and manipulation, is thus, in the end, not simply a reflection of the culture of late capitalism. It is fast becoming its property and its currency (Webster, 2000). To Lyotard (1986) in postmodern societies, knowledge becomes detached from its human context and conceptualised as an 'informational commodity indispensable to productive power' (Lyotard, 1986).

IV. Contextualising the Contradiction

Knowledge society has demonstrated significant contradictions that it has produced through its appearance and functioning. While, on the one side, it has engendered the possibility bringing balance, progressive, rational, participatory, less hierarchical, democratic social order; recognising every one of the society in terms of their inner potential; providing equality, justice and peace in society; bringing down unemployment, poverty, illiteracy, moral degradation and disharmony; widening space for social mobility, construction of new identities; bringing fundamental change in the functioning of the state, on the other, it has paved the way for an extension of industrial capitalism, promotion of Western modes of globalisation, inculcation of new form of dependency relations, worsening the conditions of workers across the world, breeding new forms of social inequality, injustice, exclusion and divides, construction of informational capitalism, expansion of the interests of the transnational corporations, conversion of the welfare state into a market-oriented workfare state and fragmentation of social reality into serious meaningless spectacles. Albeit these contradictions, knowledge society has become a social, economic and political reality across the globe. It has developed world-wide networks of profound economic, political, social and cultural order, formed its own dynamics of marginalisation and exclusion, constructed and rejuvenated distinctive identities and interests to form new social collectivities that are yet to be fully understood. This society has brought into being new kinds of challenges as the social life gets modified by the pervasive uses of ICTs. This invites effective engagement of social scientists on the issues of knowledge society. 'At this time, and in this place', as Castells (2001) narrates

> 'you will have to deal with the network society'; there is no alternative to this engagement. However, such engagement would be well served, we can perhaps conclude, by firstly unmasking the information society as the myth and ideology it surely is.... The future outcome of this society is largely undetermined, and is subjected to the contradiction between hope and despair (Castells, 2001, p. 275).

Despite elaborate state initiatives for industrialisation and agricultural modernisation in the post-independent period, India has predominantly remained an agricultural country with majority of its population living in the rural areas and is engaged in agricultural occupation for centuries. Though these initiatives have broken the stagnation in the agricultural and industrial sectors, these have neither been able to provide secured and full employment, nor been able to modernise and industrialise economy as a whole. In recent decades with the phenomenal expansion of education, ICTs and adoption to economic liberalisation the economic arrangement of the country has been experiencing a significant shift with the service sector proliferating to be the first contributor to the Gross Domestic Product (GDP) and the second largest provider of employment in the country with highest growth rate among all sectors of economy. The predominantly agricultural and part industrial society of India has started experiencing fast occupational diversification, proliferation of knowledge jobs and of knowledge society in the wake of globalisation. India is now posited with a conductive environment for the emergence and sustenance of knowledge society because of availability of a huge pool of young human resources, proliferation of educated and skilled man power and the culture of receptivity of new technologies in the contemporary era, and of her traditional past that was founded on knowledge. Though the emergence of knowledge society has become a reality, such emergence has been accompanied by a host of contradiction in Indian society.

Though India is traditionally a knowledge-based society, it is also a society based on traditional caste, class, ethnicity, gender and rural and urban divides. Within its preexisting social framework, the process of accumulation and production of knowledge was largely confined only to a limited section of the population for cognitive function than to be mass produced for application. The traditional social hierarchy has restricted the process of acquiring of knowledge to a limited few, compelling the majority to remain illiterate, ignorant, poor and powerless. Similarly, while access to advanced technology remained restricted only within a limited few, indigenous technology and practices also remained devaluated and unrecognised widely from the public parlance. The economic and social developmental initiatives in general and the educational programme in particular of post-independent India has altered too little to make majority of the people living at the bottom of social hierarchy to acquire required resource, knowledge and skill to get integrated with the main stream of the society. Rather these have sustained many facets of preexisting marginalisation and subjugated identity of vast majority of population across the space.

Significantly, the potential of knowledge society has not only been recognised but also promoted by the planners, politicians, business houses, bureaucrats, international donor agencies and media persons alike as the hope of new India in the twenty-first century and to be the panacea for economic backwardness, unemployment, environment degradation, immorality, corruption, dis-empowerment, poverty and social exclusion. The state has made profound commitment to steer a vibrant knowledge society in India to make the twenty-first century to be the century of India by liberalising its economic policies, providing new framework for the infrastructural development, expansion of education and skill, and ICTs, and producing new variety of interconnectivity, which is both physical and virtual, in the country. As a viable social and economic force, it is in the process of getting proliferated across the country at an unprecedented speed across the metro-cities, district towns and the villages – with diverse intensities and manifold implications in the processes of domination, marginalisation and identity formation for different segments of populations.

V. Continuity and Change in India: Problematising Marginalisation, Identity and Fluidity

Marginalisation is a complex process of relegating specific group(s) of people to the lower or the outer edge of the society operates as function, as cause and also as a social product. In the context of globalisation, it has been widely used to describe the social categories, which have remained only partly integrated or remain excluded from the 'mainstream' of society (UNDP, 1995, 1996). Marginalisation, however, has a composite relationship with social exclusion and vice versa. To Sen (2000), social exclusion is directly a part of capacity deprivation and that 'not being able to appear in public without shame' or inabilities to act freely with others are important deprivations. 'Being excluded from social relations can lead to other deprivations as well thereby further limiting living opportunities'. Social exclusion can thus be constitutively a part of capacity deprivation as well as instrumentally a cause of diverse capacity failure (Sen, 2000). Marginalization, however is a broader concept than social exclusion as it is linked to other operational and transformative dynamics of society

To Castells (1983), marginalisation emerges and operates in different dimensions of society. It also operates as a function of an ideology; and the ideology of marginality is reflected in different dimensions of social structure: the occupational, the spatial, the stratification system, the consumption patterns, income distribution, the culture and the psychosocial system of individual behaviour and in the power structure. Thereby marginality as a phenomenon is not a political determinant but a political outcome (Castells, 1983). Operationally, marginalisation is founded on the dynamics of social denials and deprivations, inequality and uncertainty, hierarchy and domination, legitimacy and reproduction and mobility and protest and new identity formation.

Marginalisation inculcates in its functioning dimensions of denials and deprivations by *economically* denying a large section of the society to have equal access to productive resources, opportunities of their full capacity development and utilisation; pushing them to concentrate on the underclass occupational activities, to unstable low paying jobs; making them subject to labour market segregation, un/under employment, seasonal employment, migration and economic disintegration; depriving them of technological innovations and knowledge, opportunities and choices. It *socially* relegates them to get lower social status, effective social capital, space for their social mobility and constructs their negative social images. *Politically* it denies them from having equal access to the formal power structure and participation in the decision-making processes, makes them subordinate to and dependent on the economically and politically dominant groups of the society. *Culturally* this process relegates them to periphery making them to be 'a−part society with part culture' (Redfield, 1959), 'outsider from within', alienated and disintegrated, to emerge as 'marginal man' (Park, 1982).

The process of marginalisation sets in motion several varieties of *insecurities* by dislodging a large segment of the population from habitats, pushing them to work in insecure and hazardous working condition, constraining them to accept job insecurity, making them vulnerable to accidents in high-risk factories, conditioning them to suffer basic health security, exposing them to all varieties of man made and natural calamities, compelling them to bear the burden of pollution and over consumption of natural resources by the affluent sections of society.

As marginalisation is a man-made and socially constructed process, it is *legitimised and continuously reproduced* through unequal structure of hierarchy and domination through the organised and institutionalised structure class, gender, caste and race etc. Thus, marginality gets legitimised and reproduced through the strong institutional and normative arrangements of society to sustain the hegemony of the dominant group, to provide legitimacy to exploitation and inequality, social segregation, inequality and disempowerment, through the processes of stereotyping, socialisation, enculturation so as to ensure that over a period the socially constructed marginalised categories tend to appear to be the empirical realities.

However, *marginalisation produces protest and resistance* in the form of deviant, nonconformist social behaviour of the deprived, denied and excluded and the subordinated people. It converts them from passive dropouts to active critics of the society over a period. It breeds radicalism, violence and social disruption and produces resistance identity. For many, the marginalised hold the potential of revolutionaries. They behave in violent and socially disruptive ways and hold political beliefs of a radical nature (Perlman, 1976).

Marginalisation is not isolated – rather it is relational and cumulative; and socially reproduced and culturally legitimised. It is horizontally relational with reference to the economic, social, cultural and political undercurrents of society. It is vertically (historically) cumulative with add-on impacts in the related areas of denials, deprivations, insecurity, domination, segregation and reproduction of marginality (SinghaRoy, 2010(b)). Sustained marginality generates new varieties of collective identity and urge for protest. Because 'actors in subordinate positions are never wholly dependent and are often very adept at converting whatsoever resources they possess into some degree of control over the conditions of reproduction of the system' (Giddens, 1982). They may not immediately resist domination and would rather comply. 'Compliance of the subordinate within the power relations may be explained not by lack of resistance, but by the absence of the means to implement such resistance'. Thus, there have been resistance and struggle in various forms against this domination (Mann, 1985). These struggles are reflected in the articulation and recognition of new forms of identity (Stewart, 2001).

In a transitional society, *collective identity* is constructed through the processes of interaction, and daily engagement of its members with the localised social and cultural institutional arrangements of the society – the caste, religion and ethnicity, class, on the one hand, the wider social process as engineered by the intervention of education, technology, political party, the state, market and civil society, on the other. The processes of identity construction get negotiated both with the localised conditionality, historical experience and inter-connection with the wider society that shape social identity out of individual identities. As social identities are not static, the increasing interactivity between the local and wider social forces contributes to the constant processes of shaping, transformation and rejuvenation of identities – the collective selves. The dynamic and shifting dimension of identity again gets compounded by its transformative nick that creates a source of meaning to provide legitimacy to the decisions, action and unity of the group's existence. This meaning is evolved on the basis of cultural and institutional attributes that are internalised by the members and construct their meaning around their individuation (Castells, 1997). Such a construction involves the social production of solidarity and boundary reflecting the process of inclusion and exclusion (Cerutti, 2001).

Though 'society shapes self which shapes social behaviours' (Cooley, 1902; Mead, 1934; Blumer, 1969), society itself is however not a homogenous/undifferentiated identity. It is 'highly differentiated yet organised systems of interactions and relationships encompassing a wide variety of crosscutting lines based on social class, age, gender, ethnicity, religion and more' (Stryker, 1990).Thus, though it is culture-specific discursive construction it is also a 'continually shifting description of us' and that there is no automatic connection between various discourses of identity, namely, class, gender, race, age, etc. as they can be articulated in different ways (1996). In essence, foundation of a democratic society is based on multiple identities 'that is the weaving of identities from the discourses of class, race, gender, etc. through an amount of plasticity in the formation of identity' (Barker and Galasinski, 2001). Social identity occupying a central position in human life is conditioned by inherited socio-cultural processes on the one hand and by reasons and alternative choices on the other. Here to Sen (1999), the choice to be identified is not permanent in society and there are limits to what we choose to identify with. However:

> choices do exist, and any denial to this fact leads to the uncritical and unquestioning acceptance of conformist behaviour which in turn may involve a radical shift in the identity having accepted as discovery rather than reasoned choice. For example, a shift from the holistic to sectarian identities may be a product of unquestioning acceptance of coercive arrangement.

To Sen, 'to deny plurality, choice and reasoning in identity can be a source of repression; choice is possible and important in individual conduct and social decisions even if we remain oblivious of it' (Sen, 1999).

The discourse of identity widely addresses the issues of hierarchy and domination. For Foucault (1979), power and domination work through the inscription and control of identity through various disciplinary/discursive practices (cf. Buechler, 2000). The historic blocs in power defend their power and privilege by fostering identities in which subjugation is cloaked and most people accept their domination (ruling bloc interests) as 'normal', 'common sense' and 'in their best interests'. In other words, to Longman (2010) the production of identities is a part of hegemonic processes that sustain structures of domination at the level of the person. In addition, the acceptance and performances of those identities are not without certain emotional gratifications for most people most of the time. The extent, to which such identities are embraced without question, and reproduced in performance over time, sustains the continuity of the society (Longman, 2010, p. 90).

In the wake, emergence of knowledge society with the complex processes of globalisation, initiation of new economic orders, and unprecedented flow of new technology and increasing flow of human and material objects across the globe, and the increasing migration and dislocation of people the process of formation of identities encounter both a cultural and a rational challenge. To Castells (1997):

> along with the technological revolution, transformation of capitalism, and the demise of the statism, we have experienced the widespread surge of powerful expression of collective

identity that challenge globalisation and cosmopolitanism on behalf of the singularity and people's control over their lives and environment. These expressions are multiple, highly diversified following the contours of each culture, and the historical sources of formation of each identity. They include practice of movements, aiming at the transforming human relationship at their most fundamental level. (Castells, 1997)

In India, knowledge society has brought not only new technological and economic arrangements but also new variety of work and social relations within the preexisting societal arrangement that was essentially structured to be unequal, hierarchical, divisive and exclusive. The preexisting structural arrangements of Indian society have marginalised a vast section of population through various systemic forms of discrimination, oppression, exclusion and domination. These are practised socio-historically by denying and depriving these people economically, socially, culturally and politically; by maintaining traditional caste, gender and ethnic hierarchy and domination, by proving legitimacy and by reproducing them despite resistance and protest. This structural arrangement denies these sections of population equal access to productive resources, avenues for the realisation of their productive human potential and opportunities of their full capacity development makes them subject to wage discrimination, labour market segregation and casualisation in the workforce; relegates them to get lower social status through the practice of caste, gender and ethnicity, deprives them of effective social capital, space for their social mobility, new avenues for social and human development, stigmatises and de-recognises and devaluates their contribution work in society; constructs their negative social image, denies these people from having equal access to the formal power structure and participation in the decision-making processes; subordinates them to the economically and politically dominant groups of the society; pushes them ultimately to emerge to be the underdogs, un/under represented and dis-empowered in society; relegates them to be migrants and 'marginal man', deprives them from getting access to the opportunities of education, training and other capacity building facilities through cultural barriers.

Within the pre-existing arrangement, these denials and deprivations remain legitimised and got regularly reproduced through the prevailing institutional and normative arrangements of society. These help sustain the historically inherited hegemony of the dominant group, provide legitimacy to their endeavour to exploit, social segregate, dis-empower, dominate and discriminate the weak through the socialisation, education, politicisation and enculturation. In Indian society, marginalisation is historically cumulative as the caste-, gender- and ethnicity-based inherited marginalisation is reproduced through the structural, normative and interactive process in daily life. Many of the dissents and protests of the marginalised are regularly articulated at the grassroots against deprivation and domination have led to the formation of new identities and at places have got collective expressions through several organised social movements. The broad processes of social transformation have affected the existing patterns of marginalisation and identity formation in several ways. Knowledge is being shaped in India in a societal context that is infused with the prevalence of marginalisation on the one hand and construction of new identities on the other.

Experience from various parts of the world shows that while knowledge society has been the hope of liberation, democratic, empowering and heaven of hope for a section of people, it has also been oppressive, non-egalitarian, exclusive and a phenomenon of despair for many. This emerging society has reinforced the structure of pre-existing marginality in one form or the other and also produces a new variety of marginalised form amongst the people deprived of access to education and ICTs. These induced processes have been partially layered and historically cumulative and socially relational and reflective of a continuum until and unless the old social order is questioned by the arrival of the power of knowledge. In an unequal society, unequal access to education and ICTs have reproduced pre-existing marginality of vast section in a different form. The extent of social exclusion, disabilities, disparities and de-contextualisation have been very sharp for the vast sections of the populations who are relegated to the edge of the society socially, economically and politically; and have emerged to be precarious in terms of access even to basic amenities that are crucial to get integrated with the emerging dimensions of knowledge society in meaningful terms. As against this, backdrop questions are frequently raised as to what has been the form and extent of expansion of knowledge society in India whose essentials are founded on social and spatial divides? How does the ideal image of knowledge society encounter with the pre-existing social, economic and spatial realities in India? How valid are the criticisms of knowledge society in Indian context? How has the shifting orientation of the state from socialist to neoliberalism affected the emergence of knowledge society in India? What has been the nature of state intervention in promoting the knowledge society in India? Has the emerging knowledge society been able to reduce poverty, inequality, illiteracy and stagnation of a vast segment of population in low productivity? What has been the nature and form of occupational momentum and mobility generated by the knowledge society? How has the emerging socio-cultural milieu, as generated out of the penetration of knowledge society, impacted the pre-existing social divides and occupational arrangement in society? In what way are the illiterate, semiliterate under/unskilled, migrants included and excluded from the knowledge society? Has the knowledge society been able to break the barriers of marginality in society? How does knowledge society help in the formation of alternative identities and choices cutting across the pre-defined social and economic boundaries? Will the knowledge society emerge to be the ultimate choice and a tool to construct a new world of hope, liberty, dignity and social security through growing interconnectivity among people?

Here to address these questions and to focus on the critical social (caste, gender and ethnic) and the spatial (the metropolitan cities, district towns and villages) divides this study would be based on empirical data collected from four metro cities, Delhi, Mumbai, Kolkata and Chennai, four district towns of Meerut from Uttar Pradesh, Thane from Maharashtra, Balurghat from West Bengal and Nagercoil from Tamil Nadu, and seven clusters of villages located in the Meerut district of Uttar Pradesh, South Dinajpur of West Bengal and Kanyakumari District of Tamil Nadu; and two knowledge-based organisations in Delhi and seven Internet Kiosks in the villages and district towns that are collected in the period between 2010 and 2011 and a vast body of secondary sources of information. Besides examining the interrelated processes leading to the emergence of knowledge society in India, the efficacy of the state initiatives for knowledge society, shifting state perspectives on economy, process of expansion of education and ICTs, dynamics generated by penetration of the forces of knowledge economy, its interface with new patterns of work participation and work relation, socio-cultural milieu of change and continuity, reproduction of marginality, construction of new identity and fluidity, this study also presents a critique of knowledge society that has brought into being a host of anomalies, contradictions and inconsistencies in society. These would be analysed in the context of new structurisation of Indian society in juxtaposition with local and global connectivity, emerging new economic order, technological revolution and economic neoliberalism on the one hand, and persisting poverty, marginalisation and social fragmentation of vast section of population at the grassroots on the other.

3

Strategising for Knowledge Society in India

The Shifting Backdrops and Emerging Contexts

I. The Changing Landscape

The processes of generation, accumulation and use of knowledge have remained integral parts of Indian society since the very inception of its civilisational journey that started thousands of years ago. However, a vast body of this knowledge has remained in the realm of spiritualism that looks for salvation and discovery of inner truth embodied in the nature and in human beings. These have remained integrated for long, more with the cognition, morality and ethics, and less with application for economic and societal development. Moreover, this body of knowledge, especially the process of acquiring and getting access over it, remained more restricted for limited few and got less disseminated among the common mass. The civilisational journey of India that has been shaped by the inheritance of this vast body of knowledge is seldom matched by their mass application.

India has produced local varieties of men/women of wisdom in the nooks and corners of the country having significant command over knowledge of weather, land, water, forest, health, behaviour of plant, animal and human being, localised cropping patterns, indigenous medicine, strategy for protection against natural disasters and the like. They, however, have neither emerged to be scientists in the formal sense of the term nor the process of acquiring this localised expertise has become a part of scientific learning due to the lack of systematisation, transmission, experimentation and application of this knowledge. Rather within the inundated prevalence of illiteracy and ignorance, faith in magic and supernatural phenomena among the vast mass of the country, an important part of this knowledge has remained mystified. Simultaneously, the rich body of traditional knowledge and literature that addressed the issues of health, architecture, sex, environment, economy, politics and culture remained restricted among a limited few predominantly due to caste and linguistic barriers.

The traditional hierarchical arrangement of the society based on the principle of *Varna* and Caste has historically made the process of accumulation of knowledge an absolutely graded and restricted affair in Indian society. The four-fold *Varna* division of Hindu society that authorised and encouraged only the Brahmins to practise and to have command and control over learning and the knowledge resources, deprived the vast chunk of Indian society who were mostly from the lower *Varna* and the lower caste, to have access over the world of learning and knowledge. Besides caste, the process of acquiring knowledge and getting access to knowledge through the formal institutional arrangement remained historically conditioned by class, gender and ethnic consideration in Indian society for centuries. Consequently, the indigenous knowledge and the learning processes remained a tool for domination and hegemony in the hands of a limited few who belonged to the upper echelons of caste, class, gender and ethnic hierarchy all through Indian history even though attempts were made to break barriers to access education.

With the consolidation of the British power in Indian subcontinent, the indigenous system of learning those were predominantly based on teachings from religious texts and scriptures through *Guru–Shishya Parampara* (teacher-taught tradition) and the Islamic mode of learning through Madrasa encountered phenomenal upheavals for the first time. Significantly, modern education system as initiated by the British in the Indian soil was more inclined to establish the supremacy of their education over the native one and to serve a limited purpose than to have a democratic and emancipatory function. It was meant to be for a limited few.

T. B. Macaulay's Minute of 2 February 1835 on Indian Education is quite explicit about the purpose of British education in India. He was in favour of an elitist education and therefore stated:

> it is impossible for us, with our limited means, to attempt to
> educate the body of the people We must at present do our best

to form a class who may be interpreters between us and the millions whom we govern, – a class of persons Indian in blood and colour, but English in tastes, in opinions, in morals and in intellect. To that class we may leave it to refine the vernacular dialects of the country, to enrich those dialects with terms of science borrowed from the Western nomenclature, and to render them by degrees fit vehicles for conveying knowledge to the great mass of the population.

He was assertive of the superiority of English language and the redundancy of native Indian language widely used in the educational system at that point of time.

We have to educate a people who cannot at present be educated by means of their mother-tongue. We must teach them some foreign language… that we ought to employ them in teaching what is best worth knowing, that English is better worth knowing than Sanscrit or Arabic, that the natives are desirous to be taught English, and are not desirous to be taught Sanscrit or Arabic, that neither as the languages of law nor as the languages of religion have the Sanscrit and Arabic any peculiar claim to our encouragement, that it is possible to make natives of this country thoroughly good English scholars, and that to this end our efforts ought to be directed.

He was again assertive of Western civilisational superiority over the native Indian civilisation, culture, language and education. He asserts unequivocally:

I am quite ready to take the oriental learning at the valuation of the orientalists themselves. I have never found one among them who could deny that a single shelf of a good European library was worth the whole native literature of India and Arabia. The intrinsic superiority of the Western literature is indeed fully admitted by those members of the committee who support the oriental plan of education. (Macaulay's Minute of 2 February, 1835)

Education in fact became a tool for British hegemony over colonial India.

Though the British education system was able to create an upwardly mobile middle class from among the pre-existing elite section dominated by higher castes of society to suffice to its administrative and colonial need, it was unable to make the process of acquiring knowledge mass based. Moreover, whatsoever the liberal modern education that was introduced, contributed largely to devaluate indigenous knowledge system that was traditionally practised in Indian society. It is now widely acknowledged that the colonial administration was more inclined to keep India a dependent colony on the colonial master for educational well-being and technological advancement than to promote it educationally and technologically. Though the introduction of Western education in many ways paved the way for limited modernisation, it was unable to convert the vast mass of the population living across the country to be formally skilled and 'knowledgeable'. It however created a thin layer of Indian middle class to take advantage of new avenues of employment, to be knowledgeable and to lead the social, economic and political destiny of the country, and a new pace and space for mobility for this section of population. As the state of human and social development was dismally poor, devoid of training and education, access to advanced technology and communication the vast pool of human resources remained un/ underdeveloped. Consequently, they were neither unable to elevate their economic and social status enabling them to break the barriers of marginalisation in society, nor contribute to the development of the country in effective terms.

Immediately after independence, the government of India focused on an education policy to make the learning process mass based that would contribute to nation building and develop the foundation of a modern society. The national education committees and commissions of the 1950s and 1960s emphasised on mass education, development of educational infrastructure at all levels and a shift in the perspectives on education to encourage elementary and vocational education in view of the growing need of society that envisioned to be modernised and industrialised. However, as new economic environment was looming large in the horizon, on the one hand, and India was stagnating with huge burden of illiteracy, high extent of school dropouts, very low rate of gross enrolment ratio (GER) at all levels of education, educational imbalances by region, religion, caste and gender, on the other, the New Education Policy 1986 propagated democratisation, increasing access, quality and equity in higher education. This policy directives in many ways have paved the way for fast proliferation of educational institutions at all levels, establishing the alternative system of education in the form of adult and extension education in the educational system of the country and establishing new professional and technical educational institutions and increasing private investment in the primary and secondary levels of education since the late 1980s. However, the process of such proliferation has got phenomenal momentum with the flow of globalisation, economic liberalisation and introduction of Structural Adjustment Programme by the Indian State since the early 1990s and fast process of penetration of information and communication technologies (ICTs) since the mid-1990s. Importantly, along with conventional education, the strategies for lifelong learning and reaching out of education to the doorstep of the marginalised segments of population, to the school college and university dropout and to the existing work force for their skill enhancement through open and distance learning by making extensive use of electronic media and ICTs have started getting state patronage. This arrangement by introducing several innovative techniques such as developing quality self-instructional course material, integrating course curriculum with audio, video, radio and teleconferencing, providing the learners the opportunity of their own space and pace and need-based learning has revolutionised educational arrangement and significantly contributed to the mass production of educated and skilled manpower in the country.

Technological Transformation

Similarly, India also remained technologically backward all through the colonial rule. Though the British introduced railways, telecommunication system, road and airways and modern tools and machines, the extent of spread of these technologies was very limited and again only restricted segments of population had got the capacity to have access over them. Thus, notwithstanding these induced processes, India remained educationally and technologically backward all through the colonial rule immediately adversely impacting the performance of all sectors of economy– agriculture, industry and service. In fact, with the vast resources of the country regularly drained out, and little care for the development and expansion of infrastructure, major parts of India were made to reel under sustained economic stagnation and backwardness.

Independent India inherited a backward technological framework in agriculture, industry and telecommunication from the British. The state initiatives of early independent India only brought a slow shift in the technological front notwithstanding its venture for heavy industrialisation and agricultural modernisation. The state sponsored land reform and rapid industrialisation programmes of the 1950s hardly met the desired goal, even though India's search for alternative agricultural and industrial revolution remained persistent. The Green Revolution of the late 1960s and early 1970s though increased productivity in agriculture with the intensive use of advanced technology but its positive impacts remained restricted only among the upper strata of landed gentry and that too only in the limited parts of the country. In many ways, these furthered regional imbalances and class inequality in rural India. The state-controlled initiatives for industrialisation through market regulation as a panacea for low rate of economic growth, persistent unemployment, poverty, illiteracy and economic stagnation and backwardness has remained highly elusive. The telecommunication and the mass communication networks similarly were far away from getting the mass character and remained confined only among the limited segments of population across the country at times being a status symbol and at times a tool of hegemony.

However, with the increasing urgency for alternative avenues of employment (as agriculture and industry are unable to absorb all workforce) for the functionally literate, educated, highly skilled and trained manpower, and the need for a high rate of economic growth to address the issues of unemployment, poverty, illiteracy, ill health and socioeconomic backwardness and to meet the problem of population explosion India's search for alternative entered into a new threshold as waves of the ICT revolution started reaching the doorstep of India since the late 1980s. The pre-existing tele and mass communication networks those were highly insufficient to facilitate India to get integrated globally got paradigmatically rejuvenated when revolution in the information technology and forces of globalisation started swaying all realms of Indian society since the last decade of the last century. India has started experiencing confluence of fast proliferation of computers, satellite communications, landline and mobile phone, Internet, radio and television to provide the technological and information bases for the knowledge revolution in India. This dramatic acceleration in the development of information technologies, the enhanced speed of accumulation, dissemination and exchange of knowledge, unprecedented proliferation of technical and higher educational institutions across the country, emergence of highly qualified and professional manpower and the emergence of new knowledge-based industries have now become defining characteristics of socioeconomic mosaic of India today.

Along with these developments, the socioeconomic framework of society has also got initiated with an increasing quantum of urbanisation, occupational diversification, migration and mobility, quantum rise in new business processing centres, shopping malls, mass communication, transport, entertainment, recreation, tourism, fashion and varieties of other activities which were hitherto unknown in India. This scenario has also seen the fast proliferation both of providers and users of these services and activities across the country in an unprecedented speed and scale.

Shift in the State Perspectives on Economic Transformation

Concurrently, these changes have been accompanied by a shift in the perspectives on economic transition in society. The well-articulated paths of socialism and mixed economy those were the defining characteristic features of Indian political economy have undergone phenomenal changes in view of emerging technological, economic and the political scenario within the country, on the one hand, and the changing nature of commitments and obligations of the state towards the obligatory principles of several international declarations, conventions, summits, treaties and agreements of UNO, and its organs such as those of the UNDP, WTO, World Bank and the International Monetary Fund and other agencies, on the other, since last two decades. The pre-1980s political conviction for a socialist economy with centralised planning, nationalisation of banking and heavy industries, promotion of medium and small industries, economic self-sufficiency, export promotion and import restriction has been shifted for an open market policy in view of globalisation and changes taking shape across the globe, especially in the western world.

With the market emerging to be the powerful institution to engineer the process of development in contemporary world along with the failure of the controlled and centralised regime of the state, and most of the world economics in one form or the other now getting embraced with the decentralised market mechanism, open trade policy as against the centralised planning; and the ideas of economic liberalisation, state, market and the civil-society partnership becoming the integral parts of globalisation (World Bank, 1997). The Indian state has also got integrated with the world market initiating the policy of economic liberalisation. The broad framework of economic globalisation, as emanates from the directives of the international financial institutes and the bilateral agencies that work under the auspices of the United Nations (UN) (like the World Bank, International Monetary Fund and the other members of the Washington Consensus (1990) for initiation of Structural Adjustment Programme, UNDP's framework on human development since the 1990s, Resolution of the Social Development Summit, Copenhagen 1995 and formulation of Millennium Development Goal by the UNDP 2000, General Agreements of the Trades and Tariffs (GATT) and in the General Agreements of the Trades in Services (GATS) and such other agencies and conventions) have made most of the member states of UN to introduce strict state policies relating to fiscal discipline for trade liberalisation, liberalisation of inflows of foreign direct investment (FDI), privatisation, deregulation (to abolish barriers to entry and exit) and secure property rights (www.cid.harvard.edu). Significantly, India has accepted these policy directives for economic liberalisation since the early 1990s.

As a signatory of the World Summit for Social Development (1995), Copenhagen, India is committed to promote 'dynamic, open and free markets', while recognising the need:

> to intervene in markets, to the extent necessary, to prevent or counteract market failure, promote stability and long-term investments, ensure fair competition and ethical conduct, and harmonise economic and social development, ... to foster international cooperation in macroeconomic policies, liberalisation of trade and investment so as to promote sustained economic growth and the creation of employment, and exchange experiences on successful policies and programmes aimed at increasing employment and reducing unemployment (UNDP, 1995).

Hence, the World Bank also suggests the member states:

to accept a redefinition of the state's responsibilities.... This will include strategic selection of the collective actions that states will try to promote, coupled with greater efforts to take the burden off the state, by involving citizens and communities in the delivery of core collective goods.... Even with more selectivity and greater reliance on the citizenry and on private firms (World Bank, 1997, p. 3).

Similarly, GATT, GATS and Trade Related Aspects of Intellectual Property Right (TRIPS) are integral components of free-market philosophy. Under the principles of GATT of WTO, all member countries will provide equal market access for foreign exporters and importers of services and investors to do business. Ideas and knowledge emerging out of research, innovation, invention and application of advanced technology are important parts of trade. The WTO agreement on TRIPS aims to grant the creators 'the right to prevent others from using their inventions, designs or other creations and to use that right to negotiate payment in return for other using them'. Under the GATS trading is extended from banking, telecommunications, tourism, professional, etc., services to health care, education and energy, etc., social sectors through well-defined four modes of trading services: cross-border supply, consumption abroad, commercial presence and presence of natural persons. It has been stipulated that Most Favoured Nation treatment and equal opportunity be given to service providers from all WTO members. This agreement will provide market access and national treatment to all service providers from all WTO members; would ensure that government would make and modify all relevant laws and regulations governing services accordingly; and would ensure progressive liberalisation of the services sector as a goal of GATS, which is to be achieved through negotiations (WTO, 2001).

Significantly, since the early 1990s, the developmental perspectives of India started experiencing a paradigm shift in its integration with the global economy. Such integration was indeed warranted following the change in the external political, economic and technological climate, on the one hand, and a host of internal economic crisis, on the other. Specifically, in 1991, against the backdrop of deteriorating trade balances, sharp decline in foreign exchange reserves, financial profligacy and excessive borrowings the Government of India initiated structural reform programmes in the trade and the industrial policies. These measures included dismantling the licensing for domestic investment, removing many of control on foreign trade, reforming the financial sector and tax system, reducing the high rates of tariffs and taxes on imports of foreign goods and services and initiation of several measures to promote private and FDIs in several key industrial and service sectors of economy. Subsequently, since the Eighth Five Year Plan (1992–97), radical economic reforms are designed to remove hindrance to private investment in all sectors of the economy. The Planning Commission in its Eighth Five Year Plan (1992–97) recognised that 'the economy has passed through difficult circumstances during the last couple of years. The growing fiscal gap and the sudden depletion of foreign exchange resources created a situation that puts severe strains on the economic system leading to drastic import curbs, high rate of inflation and recession in industry'. In this background, the

> 'Eighth Plan is being launched at a time which marks a turning point in both international and domestic economic environment. All over the world centralised economies are disintegrating. On the other hand, economies of several regions are getting integrated under a common philosophy of growth, guided by the market forces and liberal policies. The emphasis is on autonomy and efficiency induced by competition. We cannot remain untouched by these trends … If planning has to retain its relevance, it must be willing to make appropriate mid-course corrections and adjustments. In that process, it may be necessary to shed off some of the practices and precepts of the past which have outlived their utility and to adopt new practices and precepts, in the light of the experience gained by us and by other nations' (Planning Commission, 1992).

This significant shift in the economic perspective has paved the way for economic liberalisation and thereafter with its continuity India has emerged to be an important site of market penetration and favourable destination of the FDI because of emergence of huge middle class and availability of required natural and trained human resources and the cheap labour force. As per the global survey of corporate investment plans carried out by KPMG International (a global network of professional firms providing audit, tax and advisory services), released in June 2008, India will see the largest overall growth in its share of foreign investment, and it is likely to become the world leader for investment in manufacturing (www.ibef.org/). India has been ranked at the second place in the global FDI in 2010 and remains among the top five favourable destinations for FDI for the international investors during 2010–12 according to the UN Conference on Trade and Development (UNCTAD) (http://fdiindia.in/). Significantly in July 2013 the government of India has unleashed a big reform in FDI raising the FDI limit in the telecom sector from 74 per cent to 100 per cent and in the insurance sector from 26 per cent to 49 per cent, those are expected to bring far-reaching changes in Indian economy especially in the knowledge sector.

The Demographic Transition

While the whole world is experiencing the phenomenal proliferation of the ageing population, significantly India has been witnessing the highest concentration of young population in the world with 65 per cent of its population belonging to the age group of below 35 years; and 47 per cent below 20 years; and most importantly 41 per cent of Indian population belong to the age group of 13–35 years, the official cohort of young population in India. Because of its young population India has the labour force, which according to the Planning Commission of India, is expected to decline in most developed countries and even in China. However, it is expected to increase in India over the next 20 years. To the Planning Commission (2013), this 'demographic dividend' can add to our growth potential through its impact on the supply of labour and also, via the falling dependency ratio, on the rate of domestic savings… (Planning Commission, 2013). Quoting data from global market research firm Euromonitor, the CNBC reports its story entitled 'India's Secret Weapon: Its Young Population' that:

> the median age of India's population as a whole is 28, significantly lower than that of regional peers China and Japan, at 37.6 and 44.4, respectively. India's workforce, those between 15 and 64, is expected to rise from almost 64 per cent of its population in 2009 to 67 per cent in 2020.

Meanwhile, China is expected to start declining from 2014 resulting in a labour shortfall by 2050, according to some estimates. It is suggested that 'as the population's working age expands, savings increase – and that turns into a source of funding for investment. This will be beneficial for the country's competitiveness as other countries age' (CNBC, 2012). Hence, according to the Planning Commission of India 'to reap this demographic dividend we must ensure that our younger citizens come into the labour force with higher levels of education and skills that needed to support rapid growth'. Knowledge revolution is in the offing in India to transform the human capital of the country including the youth below the age of 25 years. This transformation is posited with the possibility of a generational change, and a systemic transformation to address the concerns of the entire knowledge spectrum. 'This massive endeavour involves creating a roadmap for reform of the knowledge sector that focuses on enhancing access to knowledge, fundamentally improving education systems and their delivery, re-shaping the research, development and innovation structures, and harnessing knowledge applications for generating better services' (Bhatia, 2010).

II. Envisioning an Era of Hope and Global Integration with It

In view of the changing technoeconomic environment across the globe, and demographic transition in the country the Indian state has been posited to take its strategic advance of huge human resources and harness the benefits of knowledge revolution. Hence, in the globalised world, India seeks to innovate new strategies and new applications of the knowledge revolution adapted to local needs, conditions and culture so as to make the expansion of knowledge society sustainable and mass based (Jacobs and Asokan, 2003). The Knowledge Commission of India desires the twenty-first century to be fashioned to be a century of knowledge civilisation; and wishes India to strategise its knowledge policy to be globally competitive for

> 'enhancing access to knowledge, reinvigorating institutions where knowledge concepts are imparted, creating a world class environment for creation of knowledge, promoting applications of knowledge for sustained and inclusive growth and using knowledge applications in efficient delivery of public services' (National Knowledge Commission of India, 2008).

In India, the emergence of knowledge society has been seen by the state, market, civil society and a large section of population as an era of hope that would bring a new epoch in economy, in politics and in culture. It has been recognised as a great transformer, promoter and innovator to bring wealth, peace, prosperity and equality in society. The state has envisioned knowledge society as a societal arrangement that uses knowledge through all its constituents to empower and enrich its people, to transform knowledge as a powerful tool to drive societal transformation, to promote a learning society which is committed to innovation, to acquire the capacity to generate, absorb, disseminate and protect knowledge, to use knowledge to create economic wealth and social good for all its constituents and to enlighten its people to take an integrated view of life as a fusion of mind, body and spirit. It has also been envisioned to be egalitarian and integrative and transformative and protective for the well-being of the nation (Planning Commission of India, 2001a). Here, India also shares the UN's perspective that has visualised knowledge society to be an effective arrangement to break the barriers to knowledge to develop human capabilities in all areas throughout the globe and among the poor and the rich alike, to promote participation for collective action for both the individuals and the civil societies, and to further economic opportunities (UNDP, 2001a).

Knowledge society according to the perspective of Indian state would have three key drivers. The first would be driven by societal transformation for a just and equitable society, the second by wealth generation and the third would be driven by promotion of knowledge that are not only the one generated in its research laboratories but also its traditional knowledge, generated by communities over centuries in laboratories of life (Planning Commission, 2001).

Experts have viewed the past progression of Indian economy in agriculture and industry with a sense of lamentation to foresee the knowledge-based future with a host of possibility and hope. The Planning Commission of India states:

> we missed the industrial revolution but we should not miss the information and knowledge revolution. This can happen only if we properly synergise our competencies with innovative planning, use all our natural endowments and leverage these by the use of IT. Indeed, the nation has not secured the fullest returns possible from the industrial, electronics and computer

revolutions. Leap flogging into knowledge era looks eminently possible today for our societal transformation in the twenty-first century, which is going to be the century of hope for India. (Planning Commission of India, 2001a).

According to Planning Commission, we did not get the opportunity to participate in the transformation as an industrial society; our chances to undergo transformation to a knowledge society are extremely bright due to its several endowments, and especially because we were already a leading knowledge society in the millennia gone by. By using the native strengths of the people and enunciating appropriate national plans, this transformation can be further accelerated and used to solve the basic problems of the nation and develop it as a sustainable knowledge society (Planning Commission, 2001).

The Planning Commission (2001a) in its report 'India as Knowledge Super Power: Strategy for Transformation' also asserts that the twenty-first century will be the century of knowledge; and only those nations will survive and succeed, which will build themselves by understanding the dynamics of knowledge and create true knowledge societies. It further observes that:

> India has a number of strengths. India enjoys a broad based and diversified science and Technology (S&T) infrastructure.... It is the Indian minds today, which are making waves internationally in knowledge based industry; India having become the most sought after destination for software being just one example of this emerging scenario in this century.

It also recognises that in the emerging world scenario comparative advantage in the new world economy will be shifting to those with the ability to absorb, assimilate and adopt the spectacular developments in new knowledge and harness them for national growth (Planning Commission, 2001a).

The Ambani and Birla Report on a Policy Framework for Reforms in Education in India (2000) explicitly states that the contemporary world knowledge is rapidly replacing raw materials and labour as the most critical input for survival and success. Knowledge has become the new asset. More than half of GDP in the major OECD countries is now knowledge based. About two-thirds of the future growth of world GDP is expected to come from knowledge-led businesses. The Report suggests that:

> As the developed world moves to forging an information society founded on education, India cannot remain behind as a non-competitive labour oriented society. India has to envision to being a competitive knowledge economy. India has to create an environment that does not produce industrial workers and labourers but one that fosters knowledge resources. Such resources must be at the cutting edge of knowledge, be competitive and innovative. Education development has a major role to play in shaping knowledge resources and, in turn, placing India in the vanguard in the information age. (Ambani and Birla Report, 2000)

Education and ICTs being the key enablers in knowledge society demand ever fastest expansion in the globalising world. So as to ensure such expansion, state policies are now put in place to liberalise investment in technical and higher education and in telecommunication services both through the public and private market players. Through the policy of liberalisation, India's domestic economy has got integrated with the world market; and the IT sector of India has emerged to be a favourable destination for unprecedented FDI.

It is again that owing to cost effectiveness widely due to the availability of quality ICT personnel at a relative cheap cost, India has emerged to be a highly lucrative place for off-shore trading and outsourcing of work from the developed countries. In fact, India's emergence as a knowledge society is linked to the creation and application of computer hardware and software and the ICTs that have spurred the growth of the global IT industry over the past two decades, on the one hand, emergence of highly trained human resources and application of these resources in all sectors of economy, on the other (TRAI 2011).

Over the decades, India has acquired several positive dimensions for fast integration with the waves of knowledge economy. It has borne willingness not only to a phenomenal expansion of ICT devices across the country, but also to a phenomenal cost reduction of the ICT devices and in the cost of the services provided by those devices. This has enabled a vast segment of the population to get integrated with the flow of ICT revolution, notwithstanding the ICT divides.

According to the TRAI (2011) in contemporary India, ICTs now offer unprecedented economic opportunities to combine and leverage resources across markets, value chains, products, services and technologies. It has been a stimulus for creativity, improved productivity, continuous technological innovation, economic growth, societal benefit and greater inclusion. It has been a key enabler for reducing distance, connecting people and speeding information flows and processes for greater inclusion and enhanced societal interaction. The evolution of technology and automation has enabled functions such as knowledge-intensive man–machine and machine–machine interactions to be flexible and user friendly (TRAI, 2011, Recommendations on Telecom Equipment Manufacturing Policy: New Delhi).

III. The Challenges to and Strategies for Expansion of Knowledge Society in India

India encounters a host of challenges in its efforts for the expansion of a knowledge society especially caused by the prevailing state of illiteracy, low level of skill development and acquisition of knowledge among a vast segment of population, lack of quality assurance in knowledge and skill development, class divide and historically inherited patterns of social unequally and exclusion and rural–urban divides in the country. These are again compounded by the emerging state of technological and digital divides. India today stands between two conflicting worlds: one pushes back with the dark influence of illiteracy, incapability, exclusion and inequality and the other trying to push forward with the advancement of education, ICTs and other advanced technologies, for integration with knowledge society. In view of such dichotomies, the Government of India has suggested several strategies both to encounter these challenges and to pave the way to usher a socially meaningful knowledge society in the coming decade.

A sustainable knowledge society needs strategy for minimising knowledge skill and learning gap: In India, the existing bases of knowledge, skill and learning are widely characterised by historical gaps between men and women, rural and urban areas, high and low castes, tribes and nontribes, rich and poor. To achieve the status of a learner-based knowledge society, the state has emphasised on the need for the expansion *of education at all levels* and has explicitly recognised that 'knowledge super power can only be built upon the foundation of a civil society that is nearly fully literate and has a capacity to absorb new and relevant knowledge' (Planning Commission, 2001(a)). This policy initiative has recognised people to be the core capital of all segments of population in a knowledge-driven economy and has emphasised on the need for constant development of human capital with thrust on skill upgradation, knowledge generation, assimilation, dissemination and use of knowledge in all realms of activities. Here, the major areas of policy interventions include revamping of education system, expansion of quality educational institutions, expansion of gross enrolment ratio in all levels of education, encouraging of vocational education and training, encouraging open distance learning for mass quality education, developing linkages among knowledge institutions and host of other initiatives as placed the Eleventh and Twelfth Five Year Plans.

The Indian, states has intensively realised that *knowledge society needs a strategic revamping of the education system, expansion of quality education and gross enrollment ratio in all levels of education:* The recommendations of NKC are crucial in this regard. While comparing the state of Indian education in view of the emergence of knowledge society, the Ambani and Birla Report (2001) observes that while the larger world embraces the information age, the world of education in India encompasses different 'worlds' that live side by side. One world includes only a fortunate few with access to modern institutions, computers, Internet access and expensive overseas education. A second world wants to maintain *status quo* – teachers, administrators, textbook publishers, students – all have reasons to prefer things to remain as they are or change only gradually. The third world struggles with fundamental issues such as no books, wrong books, teachers with poor commitment, learning of irrelevant material, classrooms with hundred students, dirty floors and no toilets. India cannot hope to succeed in the information age on the back of such three disparate worlds (Birla Ambani Report). In this backdrop, the recommendations of the Planning Commission (2001(b)) and (2011) are very crucial. The commission has suggested for not only the expansion of GER at all levels through diverse means but also quality assurance in education, and use of ICT, reducing the rural and urban divides, etc.

Knowledge society is an integrated aspect of emerging global economy. Herein to be globally competitive, India would have to expand and nurture its knowledge resources by training and educating the youth and the adult alike and by upgrading their skill. According to the National Knowledge Commission, the full potential of knowledge economy is dependent on supply of quality human resources; and India ought to take advantage of knowledge revolution to inculcate the required qualities among the young workers. As against this backdrop, the Commission recognises 'education as the key enabler for the development of an individual and for altering the socio-economic landscape of a country' and has emphasised on the need to increase access to quality education, to revamp the education system in view of the changes taking shape across the globe, to broaden the scope of Right to Education for all Indian children and to reorient school, higher, professional and vocational education to meet the critical need of the knowledge economy (National Knowledge Commission, 2007).

For the school education, the NKC has proposed generational changes in the school system that would encourage decentralisation, local autonomy in management of schools and flexibility and reforms in the curriculum and examination systems by encouraging learning to be a process of critical understanding. The higher education would look forward to ensure expansion, excellence and inclusion of this sector of learning by increasing GER in higher education to 15 per cent and above by 2015, by encouraging private participation, philanthropic contributions and industry linkages with the higher education, establishing 1500 universities by 2015, partly restructuring the existing ones, creating models for community colleges that would provide credit and non-credit courses leading to two year associate degrees both in general and in employment-oriented programmes, and by creating the flexibility for students to pursue higher education later in life.

As the penetration of knowledge is to be all encompassing as strategic intervention, there should be encouragement for *Vocational Education and Training* for special segments of population so as to enable them to integrate themselves with the knowledge society: Given that 93 per cent of the country's labour force is in the unorganised sector, the NKC has recommended VET programme for the school dropouts and the existing workforce in the unorganised sector, and to increase flexibility of VET within the mainstream education system, and to expand capacity through innovative delivery models, including 'robust public private partnerships'. While recognising the fact that India has the reservoir of the world's youngest population with the median age of 24 and this demographic structure can work in favour of India only if the youths are provided with required skill to seize the opportunity of employment globally, the Eleventh Five Year Plan proposed the Skill Development Mission. This mission has aimed to provide 'within a five-to eight-year timeframe, a pool of trained and skilled workforce, sufficient to meet the domestic requirements of a rapidly growing economy, with surpluses to cater to the skill deficits in other ageing economics, thereby effectively leveraging India's competitive advantage and harnessing India's demographic dividend'. This proposed mission among various other things would assess skill deficits sector regionwise and meet the gaps by planned action within a given time frame; realign and reposition existing public sector infrastructure, polytechnics and VET in school to get into public–private partnership mode. It also aims to launch and enlarge the 50,000 Skill Development Centres (SDCs) eventually to convert them into 'Virtual Skill Development Resource Network' for Web-based learning (Planning Commission, Eleventh Five Year Plan Vol. I, 2008, p. 92). The Twelfth Five Year Approach Paper emphasised on the need of a National Vocational Education Qualification Framework (NVEQF) to ensure mobility. According to the Planning Commission (2012), the vocational curriculum needs to be integrated and closely aligned with academic curriculum containing modules on various generic and specific vocational skills and that the same need to be evolved in consultation and active involvement of industry. Finally, vocational education at the school level and vocational training through Industrial Training Institutes (ITIS) and ITCs need to be expanded and be introduced to flexible learning pathways integrated to schooling on one end and higher education on the other through NVEQF (Planning Commission, 2012).

Encouraging learning of English language: In the knowledge era, English has emerged to be the powerful medium of integration of local society with global processes and an important vehicle for sociocultural exchanges across the globe. Similarly at the national stage, understanding and command over the English language has emerged to be the most important determinant of access to higher education, employment possibilities and social opportunities. The NKC recommends that the teaching of English as a language should be introduced, along with the first language (either mother tongue or the regional language) of the child, starting from Class I. As the foundation of a knowledge society is to be based on scientific knowledge in all areas of activities, the NKC has also recommended to invigorate research and development in the country; and it has suggested a massive investment in education and research at all levels, together with renovation and reform of the university system and the fostering of a global outlook in research.

Realising the fact that a knowledge society needs both a mass and class education for the mass production and use of knowledge, the Commission has emphasised on the role of open and distance education in knowledge society. To the Commission, development of open and distance education and open educational resources is imperative to achieve the objectives of expansion, excellence and inclusion in higher education. Today, more than one-fifth of the students enrolled in higher education are in the ODE stream and the NKC recommends that the distance education should focus on creating a national ICT infrastructure, improving regulatory structures, developing web-based common open resources, establishing a credit bank and providing a national testing service. To supplement this, NKC also recommends that the production of quality content and leveraging global open educational resources needs to be focused on in a comprehensive manner. It has also emphasised on the need to encourage open access for all study material, research papers, books, periodicals, etc.

The knowledge society is also a networked society and it needs a consistent process of sharing of information for innovation and excellence: The key to successful research today demands live consultations, data and resource sharing. Towards this end, NKC has recommended the establishment of a high-end national knowledge network connecting all our knowledge institutions in various fields and at various locations throughout the country, through an electronic digital broadband network with gigabyte capacity (National Knowledge Commission, 2006).

The recommendations of NKC have also been reinforced by the Planning Commission of India. The Eleventh Five Year Plan (2007–12) has placed high priority on education as a central instrument for achieving rapid and inclusive growth with specific emphasis on expansion, excellence and equity. The Planning Commission also proposed an allocation of ₹ 3 trillion, a five-fold increase over the Tenth Plan and an increase in share of education in the total plan from 7.7 per cent to 20 per cent of plan allocation, representing a credible progress towards the target of 6 per cent of GDP. Significantly, the Planning Commission has been propagating several revolutionary measures that would aim to:

- create a common service delivery platform including State Wide Networks, Common Service Centres and Last Mile Connectivity, and making use of e-governance in the implementation of all major flagship programmes of the government for better citizen-centric delivery of services.

- expand and modernise existing public sector infrastructure for skill development to get into public–private partnership mode with functional and governance autonomy through the National Skill Development Mission.

- encourage competition among enterprises, greater diffusion of knowledge and increased support to early-stage technology development initiatives and grassroots level innovators by framing a National Innovation Policy.

- ensure minimum standards and norms for public and private schools, encouraging the role of private providers, giving special focus on disadvantaged groups and educationally backward areas by reorienting Sarva Shiksha Abhiyan.

- ensure expansion, inclusion and rapid movement in quality Higher and Technical Education through establishment of new government and private-funded institutions, establishing 30 new Central Universities and 14 World Class Universities; launching a National Mission in education through ICT coverage in all the Universities and colleges, strengthening the Open Universities and reforming statutory bodies and scaling up SAKSHAT as the education portal for 50 crore people.

- develop Public Libraries including Rural Public Libraries with special collection and technological support for visually challenged and hearing impaired. For the expansion of the bases of the knowledge society library and the information services have emerged to be the key facilitators. The changing scenario invites new initiatives for modernising management of libraries to ensure greater community participation.

- develop an appropriate legislative framework for incentivising innovators and commercialisation of public-funded research and development.

- strengthen professional education, strategic research programmes, promotion of best clinical practises, technology upgradation in industry and setting internationally acceptable pharmacopoeial standards. Undertake modernisation of Intellectual Property Rights to address the needs of human resources development, training and awareness and also infrastructure besides regular updation of the IT facilities (Planning Commission of India, 2007).

The Planning Commission (2001a) has also recommended for quality universal elementary education by enhancing reach and quality of education at all levels, ensuring quality education by attracting quality teachers, linking higher and technical education with industry, encouraging private initiatives to increase access and enhance quality, encouraging technology-based education, encouraging demand-driven nonformal institutions, making women's education free up to college level, encouraging educational institutions to set up formal networks with other institutions for resource sharing and for synergistic development of the entire educational system (Planning Commission, 2001). It states a people's movement marching towards knowledge society should be started to facilitate such transformation. This movement would focus on: Time-bound programme for universal elementary education by the year 2010, spreading awareness of pride in our nation's past heritage and skill sets, mounting a massive campaign on education in human values, and inculcating community solidarity, social harmony and environmental responsibility.

The Approach Paper to Twelfth Five Year Plan points out that higher education is essential to build a workforce capable of underpinning a modern, competitive economy. However, it emphasised on excellence and quality assurance. It has proposed:

- a strategic shift from mere expansion to improvement in quality higher education,

- increasing the GER and bringing it broadly in line with the global average,

- a holistic and balanced expansion approach to target under-represented sections of society, consolidating and improving the capacity and quality of the existing institutions,

- bridging regional imbalances and disparities across disciplines and to address special economic, social and technological needs of the country, stepping up both public and private investment in higher education,

- improving the employability of graduates by integrating critical thinking, communication, collaboration and creativity (the '4Cs') with education,

- developing a large sector offering short-cycle qualifications in the form of associate degrees catering to intermediate skills in the higher education within the National Vocational Education Qualifications Framework,

- bringing back the 'lost' research culture of Indian universities so as to create new knowledge and improving teaching standards (Planning Commission, 2012).

Minimising social, cultural and spatial gaps: Contemporary India lives in many centuries together with lots of traditional sociocultural and economic diversities juxtaposing with advanced thoughts and actions of the twenty-first century. India has inherited a host of cultural, religious, linguistic values, traditions and customs that encounter modern secular values, traditions and customs and localised practises even though pluralism and diversities have been parts of Indian social reality. Many times these diversities are physically conditioned, suffer from the problems of connectivity and function as the barriers to accommodate new values and ideas. Herein, the significance of connectivity – physical (good highways, railways, airline and waterways routes) and electronic (long-distance telephone, television and the Internet) – has got added emphasis in the developmental perspective of India for removing all barriers of space and time from social interaction.

Minimising rural–urban divides: In India, rural and urban divides are conspicuously marked in both cultural and economic terms. Though the process of urbanisation has been fastened in recent years, more than 65 per cent of the Indian population live in rural areas; a vast majority of them slog in a life situation that is conditioned by inadequate employment, education, health care, road, transport, water, sanitation, electricity, etc., facilities. Herein, to reduce rural–urban divides, the process of 'rurbanisation' has got a place of prominence in the contemporary development discourse that has been envisioned to bring in rural prosperity through physical and electronic connectivity, to bring down the rural–urban migration to the zero level by providing rural areas with all desirable amenities that are currently available in cities and by generating employment and other attractions as cities do; by mitigating gaps between rural and urban areas in knowledge and digital divides through the use of appropriate and advanced ICTs. Now, with the advent of buried optical fibre, cellular telephony, Internet, Wireless Application Protocol-enabled telephones, Internet over cable TV, Voice (and now Video), etc., India is to look for not only convergence of technologies but also convergence of governance that would minimise the rural–urban divides in effective terms (Planning Commission, 2001b).

Minimising gaps among population and between various sectors of economy: It is imperative that all segments of population be made active and productive members of society and they take part in the economic and societal transformation of India. New systems of education, training, learning, ranging from agriculture to industry are crucial towards such endeavour. It is envisioned that empowering every single Indian with knowledge in his or her respective sphere will help in improving the 'national efficiency' in every single walk of life, ranging from agriculture to industry to knowledge-based service industries. A new paradigm in the Indian social and economic transformation is proposed to be evolved by designing, developing and deploying the high-technology tools and methods in all sectors to increase productivity and release of surplus manpower from the traditional sector. It is proposed that the surplus manpower can be upgraded with proper education and training and be redeployed in agro-based industries, service sector and IT Industry (Planning Commission, 2001b).

Such endeavour needs to collaborate efforts of all stakeholders of society – the people, civil society, state and market – for the creation of an amicable environment. Indeed, the real challenge now as Pitroda narrates:

> is to create an appropriate environment to engage and empower local communities and various other stakeholders and at the same time build effective models of collaboration including public–private partnerships and partnerships between academia, industry and local communities at large to bring about generational changes in our knowledge institutions and infrastructures needed to respond to the opportunities for growth and prosperity in the 21st century for all our people (Pitroda, 2008, p. 111).

IV. Nonstate Initiatives for Knowledge Society

In India, a host of state initiatives is being supplemented in the IT and educational sector by the nonstate players. These initiatives play crucial roles in augmenting knowledge revolution in India in all sectors of the economy: agriculture, industry, service across the rural and urban spaces. For example, according to e-India with the support of the United States Agency for International Development (USAID), under its Feed the Future initiative, Sathguru Management Consultants and its long-time partner in agriculture and life sciences development projects in South Asia, the College of Agriculture and Life Sciences at Cornell University, Ithaca, NY, established the Agricultural Innovation Partnership (AIP) to increase food security and improve the quality of life in the targeted regions in the Indo-Gangetic plains. In order to integrate ICT learning into the agricultural curriculum, AIP has created e-learning centres to deliver ICT-enabled courses to students at partner Indian agricultural universities leveraging on the technological expertise of US partner universities. Similarly, the initiative of Unique Identification Authority of India under the auspices of the Planning Commission of India engaged the Sify Technologies Ltd, a private nonstate actor for training and certification of personnel to undertake such massive job. The Mexus Education Pvt Ltd offers ICTs aid to maximise engagement to bring about a balance in the expected level of knowledge with the educational degree attained, to bring effectiveness of digital aid and the pedagogy adopted in the classroom. The APEX Foundation has been working to evolve several Degree/Diploma/Certificate courses by integrating the working environment of the industry and institutions with learning environment. The Edutor Technologies India Pvt Ltd has been working for harnessing ability towards education by using Tablet PCs to make learning intuitive and engaging and transforming the students' personal learning experience (http://eindia.eletsonline.com/2012). Similarly, varieties of institutions are engaged in health, food, employment and related areas. Investments are also made in business houses and the international agencies to make the workforce of the country to be ICT enabled.

A host of initiatives has been set in motion in India by the civil society to enhance the usage of ICTs in every domain of activities. For example, the Digital Empowerment Foundation, a Delhi-based not-for-profit organisation has been engaging community to find solutions to bridge the digital divide. The American India Foundation is a leading international development organisation working as 'the Digital Equaliser' to bridge the 'digital divide' by providing computers, Internet and training to underresourced schools. The World Summit Award has created a global hub for everyone who sees the crucial importance of excellent e-Content creation within the new Information Society. The National Institute for Smart Government, Hyderabad, is promoting e-governance with a focus on Strategic Planning, developing appropriate architectures and standards, providing high-level consultancy services and capacity building at the national level. The GeSCI is providing strategic advice to developing countries on the effective use of ICTs for education and community development to improve the quality of teaching and learning through the strategic and effective use of ICTs thereby transforming education, empowering communities and promoting development. The NASSCOM Foundation is working for the application of ICT for empowering and transforming the lives of the underserved. The ITVidya.com as a community platform is promoting 'Sharing' of IT Knowledge among its members. The One World South Asia is working to bring people through IT networking for human rights and sustainable development from across the globe. One World is the world's favourite and fastest-growing civil society network online, supporting people's media to help build a more just global society. JILIT,

JIL Information Technology Ltd, is providing services and solutions in the area of software development and consultancy for construction, cement, power and education sectors. The Tata Consultancy Services through its Global Network Delivery Model is promoting innovation in networking and helping global organisations address their business challenges effectively. Dataquest is useful information for vendor and user communities. The Society for Research and Initiatives for Sustainable Technologies and Institutions is providing organisational, intellectual and logistics support to the Honey Bee Network to 'systematically documenting, disseminating and developing grassroots green innovations, providing intellectual property rights protection to grassroots innovators, working on the situ and ex situ conservation of local biodiversity, and providing venture support to grassroots innovators'. The Trivial File Transfer Protocol (TFTP) as a technical support organisation is promoting developmental issues through appropriate technology and supporting the use of ICTs in expanding the existing activities in areas of education, hygiene, child rehabilitation and economic empowerment (Digital Empowerment Foundation, 2007).

Similarly, the e-Choupal, Ujjain, Madhya Pradesh, has become a Web-based initiative of ITC's International Business Division that 'offers the farmers of India all the information, products and services they need to enhance farm productivity, improve farm-gate price realisation and cut transaction costs'. The e-Seva, Hyderabad, Andhra Pradesh, is working 'to provide real-time online transactions, to improve government-customer interface at all levels, improve service quality and innovation, improve operational efficiency and provide cost-effective services'. The Fast, Reliable, Instant and Effective Network for Disbursement of Services, Thiruvananthapuram, Kerala, promotes government–customer interface, operational efficacy and cost-effective services. The Gramdoot, Jaipur, Rajasthan, is helping to bridge the digital divide between rural India and the rest of the world by creating the infrastructure, to provide cable TV, telephony and Internet connectivity to all gram panchayats and to develop a business model in rural broadband connectivity. The N-Logue Telecentres, Madurai, Tamil Nadu, is undertaking research to increase access devices for rural Internet and telephone and has established 30 public access Internet kiosks in villages across Madurai, Tamil Nadu. The Vidyal Information Service

Provider (VISP), Tiruchirapalli, Tamil Nadu, is working to empower the weaker sections of the rural community through the use of ICT. The Warana Wired Village, Kolhapur, Maharashtra, is working to provide computerised facilitation booths in the villages, which are linked up to the central computer network at Warana (Harris and Rajora, 2006). Many more such initiatives are in the making in the nooks and corners of the country to integrate the society with a new body of connectivity education and knowledge. In fact, a strong foundation for a vibrant knowledge society is in the making with participation of both the state and non-state actors.

V. Old Challenges in the New Context

It is now widely acknowledged that the transformation of a predominantly agrarian society into a full-fledged knowledge one is largely dependent on the society's substantive capacity to create, absorb, disseminate, protect and use knowledge for the creation of economic wealth and societal good through the participation of all sections of the population. This capacity demands inculcation of human capabilities by withering away the inherited disparities and disabilities. The social realities of contemporary India are embedded with a host of contradictions. Though India has achieved 9.4 per cent economic growth in 2006–2007 (notwithstanding recent slowdown to 6 per cent in 2012), 36 per cent of its population lives below the poverty line. Though it has been described to be a food-surplus country, 27 per cent of world's undernourished people live in India. The quantum of marginal workers (who do not get more than 180 days of employment) within total workers have phenomenally increased from 9 per cent in 1991 to 22.2 per cent in 2001 and thereafter to 24.8 per cent in 2011.

Significantly, the socially and the economically weaker sections of Indian society have remained the end victims of these anomalies and deprivations. The quantum of these disparities and social dichotomies have not only multiplied over the decades, but also acquired added complexities with eclectic forms of economic development, decline in bases of the traditional sources of economy and sliding of social significance of traditional sources of livelihood security and indigenous knowledge system. The prevailing state of disparities and disabilities has emerged to be severe obstacles for the expansion of equitable and sustainable knowledge society in India.

Though India is still a predominantly rural and agrarian society, its traditional social and economic orders are profoundly shaken in recent decades with the advancement of industrialisation and modernisation, globalisation, penetration of ICTs and mass media. However, these advancements have not been able to replace the old order by a new one and completely delink them from the traditional past. The knowledge society in India is presumed to be the latest series of societal progressions positing its foundation on the secular credential of 'knowledge'. It is also expected to introduce new technological, economic and social arrangements that would lay the foundation of a society with greater inclusion, equality, justice, mobility and choice for its members. However, the historical experiences of developmental initiatives in India are replete with the evidence of reinforcement of traditional social divisions and cleavages based on caste, class, ethnicity and gender in the new context. It is posited to shape its course in Indian course within these pre-existing social cleavages, which are compounded by emerging spatial divides between urban and rural areas, economic and technological separations between agrarian and industrial, formal and informal economies, linguistic split between English-speaking upwardly mobile Indian literati and non-English-speaking Bharatiyas or Hindustani, political divides between the Indian elite and the common man who have insufficient access to higher and technical education, professional skill and the ICTs. Herein, the new emerging order as put in motion by the knowledge society is posited with the possibilities of generation of new dynamics of inclusion, exclusion and dispersal on the one hand and reinforcement of old disabilities and disparities in social arrangements in a modified form in many parts of the country on the other. It is posited to combine the both too. It is worth examining empirically.

4

Education for Knowledge Society in India

I. Education as a Critical Investment and Mainstreaming Mechanism

Education has always remained a key factor of human development and economic reconstruction of a country and its national integration. Accordingly, all nation states frame policies on education that promote, generate and circulate skilled and educated manpower and train and socialise the new generation keeping in view both the short-and long-term needs of the nation. In knowledge society, the significance of education has been multiplied to become the key means for generation of wealth and employment, formation of knowledge-based networks, ushering of knowledge and technological revolution, converting knowledge as the main source of livelihood and mobility, integration of society with the global socioeconomic and technological forces and transformation of all members as creative beings. Education in this society is not an end in itself, but a means of social welbeing and a source for collective use and reflection. It is no more a social service, but a long-term investment that aims to ensure inexhaustible development of the country through mass production and application of knowledge by cultivating human brains for a desired end. With the knowledge and ICTs revolution in the offing, most nations are now profoundly engaged in 'creating, organising, accessing and processing and recirculating knowledge in an unprecedented speed so as to ensure their place in the advantage of emerging knowledge society.

Since the second half of the twentieth century, with the growing realisation that knowledge and its application have become basis for the development of advanced economics, efforts are made to integrate the education with new types of activities. Thus, in the changing global scenario, mass education has emerged to be a universal phenomenon; national education system finds itself in an increasingly global market place, higher education institutions are under pressure from the government to use state power to secure their policy goals and balance between public and private providers of education; and financing of higher education has been shifted in favour of private players (Palfreyman, Tapper, and Thomas, 2012).

Most aspiring nations are now endeavouring to integrate each and every generation society with the appropriate educational arrangement. In order to cultivate each mind to be a site of resource, these societies apply multiprong strategy to enhance the quality and quantity of learning by making 'proper' mix of primary, secondary and tertiary education, as well as life-long learning (UN, 2005) so as to ensure that they can take competitive advantage of the emerging knowledge-based economy. Thus, the process of acquiring education becomes multidimensional in knowledge society that simultaneously engages nonformal, formal, continuous and lifelong processes of learning at all levels to ensure that no human mind remains uncultivated and unused as human mind is the main site and source of development. These initiatives are posited to open up broad avenues for the limitless development of people and information and rebuild social organisations for mass production and mass utilisation of knowledge, supposedly pairing the way for the evolvement of a 'smart knowledge society' (UN, 2005).

Education has always been recognised in India as an enabling mechanism and an emancipatory force and a means to transform physical endowment into intellectual entity that enhances opportunities and choices for individuals and groups paving the way for their human development, social inclusion and empowerment in society all of which augment a person's quality of life. Most importantly, it is now considered to be a 'critical investment for human development' (Ninth Five Year Plan, 1997), and invasive instrument for bringing about social, economic and political inclusion and a durable integration of people, particularly those excluded from the mainstream of society to the national lives (National Human Development Report, Government of India (GOI), 2001). In the emerging technoeconomic context and shifting perspective on social development, India has reinforced its position that a well-educated population, adequately equipped with knowledge and skill, is not only essential to support economic growth, but is also a precondition for growth to be inclusive (Planning Commission, 2012). In the context of globalisation and ICT revolution, the Ambani and Birla Report (2001) states

> Education is becoming even more vital in the new world of information, where knowledge is rapidly replacing raw materials and labour as the most critical input for survival and success. India has to see education not just as a component of social development, but as a means of securing her future in an information society, resplendent with knowledge, research, creativity and innovation... The imperative for India is to raise standards of the vast majority with poor education, break the education sector free from its inertia and forge a society that places knowledge as the cornerstone of its development. Therefore, a vision for education in India has to inspire creation of a knowledge-based society, induce competitiveness, and yet foster a sense of co-operation (Birla Ambani Report 2001: P.1).

The knowledge society is being shaped in India in the context of neoliberal globalisation and economic liberalisation that promised to bring forth a fast economic growth and social development in the country. In view of the above changes, a perceptive reorientation in the state perspective on education and skill development has rather been explicit since the Eighth Five Year Plan 1992–1997, coinciding with the introduction of Structural Adjustment Programmes of World Bank and IMF that pledge to undertake reexamination and reorientation of the role of government in developmental initiatives. It reads:

> Eighth Plan is being launched at a time which marks a turning point in both international and domestic economic environment. All over the world centralised economies are disintegrating. On the other hand, economies of several regions are getting integrated under a common philosophy of growth, guided by the market forces and liberal policies... If planning has to retain its relevance, it must be willing to make appropriate mid course corrections and adjustments (Planning Commission, 1992, p. 7).

These midcourse corrections and reorientations while, on the one hand, have asked for increasing state and market-driven initiatives for the creation of new institution, infrastructure and innovation in education, on the other, have opened up scope and the condition for integration of this arrangement with the global market forces. As in knowledge society, the state has emerged to be more of 'workfare' than to be 'welfare' in nature; a drive towards the market-oriented education has started becoming more obvious henceforth initiating the process of extensive commodification of education.

In the wake of globalisation and the proliferation of knowledge-based industries across the globe, and highest concentration of young population in the country, India has attracted huge investment in education from both the public and private investors. In view of changing economic policy and growing need for a massive infrastructure to suit the emerging need of society, the state has been encouraging the private sector in getting engaged in education at all levels. Within the broad policy framework, the state now explicitly accepts that 'the private sectors' legitimate role in expanding education needs to be recognised, and further strengthened through right policies, proper regulation, innovative public–private partnerships (PPPs) in achieving objectives of access, quality and equity in education' (Planning Commission, 2013).

In recent years, the government's expenditure on education, including those of the state and the central government, has phenomenally increased from ₹1,29,366 crores in 2007–2008 to ₹ 3,31,524 in 2012–2013 that comprised 9.8 per cent and 11.7 per cent, respectively, of the total government expenditure in the country (GOI, 2013). The private sector is also making a big dent in India's education sector now. According to the PricewaterhouseCoopers (PwC) report (2010), the education sector in India is estimated to be around US$ 25 billion. According to estimates by HDFC Bank, private equity investment in education was US$ 190 million in 2010. Further, these estimates suggest that investments in the kindergarten to class XII segments grew to US$ 20 billion in 2011 and are further expected to grow to US$ 33 billion in 2012 (http://www.investindia.gov.in/?q=education-sector). The Overseas Indian Facilitation Centre based on the research of a consulting firm Technopak reports that the private education sector is estimated to reach US$ 70 billion by 2013 and US$ 115 billion by 2018, and that enrolment in kindergarten to 12th standard (K–12) would be growing to 351 million, requiring an additional 34 million seats by 2018 (OIFC, 2013, http://www.oifc.in/sectors/education). According to a report 'Education in India: Securing the Demographic Dividend,' published by Grant Thornton, the primary and secondary education, or K–12 sector, is expected to reach US$ 50 billion in 2015 from US$ 24.5 billion in 2008, growing at an estimated compound annual growth rate (CAGR) of 14 per cent. Further, according to another report, '40 Million by 2020: Preparing for a New Paradigm in Indian Higher Education' released by Ernst & Young, the higher education sector in India is expected to witness a growth of 18.0 per cent CAGR till 2020. At present, the sector witnesses expenditures of more than ₹ 46,200 crore (US$ 8.38 billion), which are estimated to grow at an average rate of more than 18.0 per cent to over ₹ 2,32,500 crore (US$ 42.17 billion) in 10 years'. Significantly, the education sector has attracted FDI worth ₹ 3239.76 crore (US$ 597.68 million) during April 2000 to December 2012, according to the data released by the Department of Industrial Policy and Promotion (http://www.ibef.org/industry/education-sector-india.aspx). Along with these changes, there has been substantive increase in the state funding in education and phenomenal expansion of the educational institutions and visible change in the patterns of enrolment and retention of students in educational institutions in India.

Increasing in Public Expenditure in Education

In India, an overview on the educational expenditure of the state shows that in 1950–1951, of the total GDP of India, an amount of ₹ 64.46 crore, accounting to 0.64 per cent of the GDP, was allocated for education. In 1980–1981, the allocation shot up to ₹ 3884.20 crore accounting for 2.98 per cent of the GDP (See Table 4.1). It gradually increased to 3.84 per cent in 1990–1991, and 4.28 per cent of the GDP in 2000–2001. The Planning Commission of India proposed an increase in the share of education from 7.7 per cent in Tenth Five Year Plan to 20 per cent in Twelfth Five Year Plan representing a target of 6 per cent of GDP. However, it declined to 3.77 per cent of GDP in 2008–2009. Though during the period under consideration, there has been an increase in

Table 4.1 *Educational Expenditure as a Percentage of Public Expenditure and GDP*

Year	% of Public Expenditure		% of GDP	
		Decadal Growth		Decadal Growth
1951–52	7.92	–	0.64	–
1960–61	11.99	51.4%	1.48	131%
1970–71	10.16	–15%	2.11	43%
1980–81	10.67	5%	2.98	41%
1990–91	13.37	25%	3.84	29%
2000–01	14.42	8%	4.28	11%
2008–09	13.63	–5%	3.56	–12%
2010–11(BE)	15.63		3.36	

Source: UGC, 2012; MHRD, 2012.

overall public expenditure in education from 7.92 per cent in 1951–1952 to 11.99 in 1960-61, this expenditure declined to 10.6 per cent in 1970–1971. This declining trend was put on hold in 1990–1991 when the public expenditure in education was increased to 13.37 per cent. Though this expenditure was 14.12 per cent of the total expenditure in 2000–2001 with a growth rate of 8 per cent over the last decade, it declined to 13.63 per cent of the total public expenditure in 2008–2009. In 2012-13 budget estimets expenditure on education has increased to 15.63 per cent. An analysis on the expenditure on education shows that the total budget expenditure in 2011-12 formed 3.36 per cent of the GDP. When the provision for education for all departments including education department is taken into account this percentage works out to be 4.17 per cent. If the shares of expenditure on education of the centre and the states are described separately, it would show an increasing trend of Centre's share from 0.53 per cent in 2000-01 to 1.05 per cent in 2009-10 while a declining trend of states share from 3.76 per cent to 3.05 per cent during the same period (Govt. of India, 2013).

India is to clear the burden of illiteracy, on the one hand, and to promote secondary, higher, professional, vocational and technical education, on the other, with quality assurance to match the global standard in the emerging world scenario. In India, however, there has been unequal focus of the state on the various sectors of education.

For example, while in 1970–1971 of the total educational budget, 41.6 per cent was allocated to elementary education, it has constantly increased to 52.53 per cent during 2007–2008. However its share has declined to 50.21 per cent in 2011–12. The second-highest allocation was received by secondary education, and it has got 29.10 per cent of the total share in 1970–1971. Though its share has declined to 28.67 per cent in 2008–2009, its share has again increased to 30.6 per cent in 2011-12 (BE) and it still continues to occupy the second place. Higher education got 12.2 per cent budgetary allocation in 1970–1971 and its share increased to 14.71 per cent in 2000–2001. Though higher education has got only 11.83 per cent allocation in 2008–2009 its share has increased to 12.91 per cent in 2011-12. Technical education received 5.40 per cent budget expenditure on education in 1970–1971. Though it marginally declined in the subsequent decades, it received 5.3 per cent of the allocation in 2008–2009 and further to 4.79 per cent in 2011–12. It is important that there has been significant increase in the private investment in technical education in this period. The proportional budgetary allocation has declined for adult education from 2.20 per cent to 0.45 per cent and other educational programmes from 9.50 per cent to 1.4 per cent during the same period (see Table 4.2). The budget estimate of 2011–2012 shows a quantum jump for budget allocation in higher education and considerable decline for the elementary and secondary education in absolute term.

Table 4.2 Distribution of Total Budget (Centre + State) for Education by the Sub-sector of Education (Revenue Accounts), India

| Year | % of total budget allocated for | | | | | | |
	Elementary Education	Secondary Education	Adult Education	University Education	Technical Education	Other Educational Programme	Total
1970–71	41.6	29.10	2.20	12.20	5.40	9.50	100.00
1980–81	45.50	30.70	0.80	14.30	4.10	4.60	100.00
1990–91	46.30	32.20	1.60	13.40	4.40	2.10	100.00
2000–01	47.61	31.60	0.36	14.71	4.04	1.68	100.00
2007–08	52.32	28.67	0.45	11.83	5.33	1.40	100.00
2011–12 (BE)	50.21	30.60	0.40	12.91	4.79	1.09	100

Note: BE stands for Budget Estimate
Source: Department of Education, Ministry of Human Resource Development (2010–2011, 2011–12).

II. Expansion of the Educational Institutions in India

In recent years, there has been a phenomenal growth in the educational institutions at all levels in India. Table 4.3 shows that while in 1951 there were only 209.7 thousand primary schools and 13.6 thousand upper primary and 7.4 thousand secondary/senior secondary level schools, the absolute numbers of these schools increased to 408.4 thousand, 90.6 thousand and 37.1 thousand respectively, in the year 1970–1971, again to 560.9 thousand, 151.5 thousand and 79.8 thousand in 1990–1991, and further to 748.5 thousand, 447.6 thousand and 200.2 thousand, respectively, in 2010–2011. The colleges for general education and professional education altogether increased from 0.6 thousand in 1950–1951 to 3.3 thousand in 1970–1971, 5.8 thousand in 1990–1991 and further to 32.9 thousand in 2010–2011. The University and the university-level institutions grew from 0.03 thousand in 1950–1951 to 0.08 thousand in 1970–1971, to 0.18 thousand in 1990–1991 and further to 0.66 thousand in 2010–2011.

Table 4.3 *Expansion of Educational Institutions in India (in Thousands)*

Year	Primary	Upper Primary	Secondary/ Senior Secondary Level	College for General Education	College for Professional Education	University/ University level Institutions
1950–51	209.7	13.6	7.4	0.4	0.2	0.03
1970–71	408.4	90.6	37.1	2.3	1.0	0.08
1990–91	560.9	151.5	79.8	4.9	0.9	0.18
2010–11 (P)	748.5	447.6	200.2	32.9*		0.66

*Note: (i) P stands for Provisional, (ii) *Includes all Institutes for post matric courses.*
Source: MHRD, 2012.

Thus, despite an uneven trajectory, educational institution has started expanding phenomenally in recent years in absolute terms. The expansion in educational institution has been accompanied by increase in Gross Enrolment Ratio (GER) in all levels of education.

Increasing Gross Enrolment Ratio

Increasing GER is not only an indicator of the state of educational accomplishment of a society, but also shows a society's readiness for integration with knowledge society. In India, low GER in education system has remained a prime concern for several decades. In 1991, while the GER at primary level was 78.6 per cent, it increased to 81.6 per cent in 2001 and to 104.3 per cent in 2011 (see Table 4.4). At the secondary level, such increase was from 19.3 per cent in 1991 to 33.3 per cent in 2001 and to 52.1 per cent in 2011 and at the tertiary level from 6 per cent to 8.1 per cent in 2001 and to 18.8 per cent in 2011.

Table 4.4 *Changing Gross Enrolment Ratio (GER) at Different Levels of Education in India*

	Primary Class I–VIII (6–13 years)			Secondary Class IX–XII (14–17 years)			Tertiary (18–13 years)		
	1991	2001	2011	1991	2001	2011	1991	2001	2011
Boys	90.3	90.3	104.9	31.2	38.2	55.5	8	9.3	20.9
Girls	65.9	72.4	103.7	6.3	27.7	48.4	4	6.7	16.5
Total	78.6	81.6	104.3	19.3	33.3	52.1	6	8.1	18.8

Note:
* *GER is the total enrolment of pupils in grade or cycle or level of education, regardless of age, expressed as percentage of the corresponding eligible official age-group population in a given school/college/university year.*
* *2011 is provisional.*

Source: World Bank, 2012; MHRD, 2012.

In India, in general, boys have relatively higher GER than girls. Though the GER has increased at all levels, such increase has not been devoid of the pre-existing caste and gender divide in Indian society. Significantly, at the primary level, the gender gap between the boys and the girls shows a declining trend in recent years, while at the secondary and the higher education levels, the girl students have got relatively a low GER than the boys. It is again that starting from the secondary and above levels of education, the scheduled caste and the scheduled tribe students have lower rates of GER than against the overall trend. Again, the girl students studying at the secondary and the above levels from these groups are doubly disadvantaged first in relation to the overall trends and then in terms of gender divide within their own groups.

As shown in Table 4.5 at the elementary (I–VIII class) level of education, the overall GER in 2000–2001 was 81.6 per cent and for the boys and girls these were to the extent of 90.3 per cent and 72.4

Table 4.5 *Gross Enrolment Ratio (GER)*

Age Group	Year	All Categories			SC			ST		
		Boys	Girls	Total	Boys	Girls	Total	Boys	Girls	Total
6–14 (Classes I–VIII)	2000–01	90.3	72.4	81.6	97.3	75.5	86.8	102.2	73.5	88.0
	2010–11	104.9	103.7	104.3	117.3	116.9	117.1	120.5	118.7	119.7
16–18 (Classes XI–XII)	2000–01	38.2	27.7	33.3	37.2	26.9	32.6	31.0	19.8	25.7
	2010–11	55.5	48.4	52.1	57.3	52.2	54.9	45.4	37.3	41.5
18–24 (Higher Edn.)	2000–01	9.3	6.7	8.1	7.7	3.6	5.8	5.8	2.6	4.2
	2010–11	20.9	16.5	18.8	13.0	9.0	11.1	13.1	7.5	10.3

Note: For higher education of SC and ST the provisional data of 2009–2010 is used.
Source: Selected Educational Statistics 2005–2006, MHRD, 2012.

per cent, respectively. At this level of education, the scheduled caste and the scheduled tribe students acquired a relatively higher level of GER mostly due to encouragement provided by the state. Thus, while among the scheduled caste and scheduled tribe, total GERs are 86.8 per cent and 88 per cent, respectively, for the boys and the girls of these communities GERs are to the extent of 97.3 per cent for SC boys and 75.5 per cent for SC girls, 102.2 per cent for ST boys and 73.5 per cent for ST girls, respectively. Significantly, the improvement in the GER is positively linked to a decline in gender divides in education. In 2010–2011, while the overall GER at this level of education improved to 104.3 per cent, the GER for the boys and the girls improved to 104.9 per cent and 103.7 per cent showing a decline in gender divides in GER. For the scheduled caste, the total GER improved to 117.1 per cent and for the boys and girls these improved to 117.3 per cent and 116.9 per cent, respectively, from the previous period of 2000–2001. Similarly, for the scheduled tribes, while the overall GER improved to 119.7 per cent for boys and girls, this improved to 120.5 per cent and 118.7 per cent, respectively, in 2010–2011 showing a declining gender divide in GER.

In the secondary level of education in 2000–2001, the overall GER was 33.3 per cent and it improved to 52.1 per cent in 2010–2011. For the boys and girls, these improved from 38.2 per cent and 27.7 per cent to 55.5 per cent and 48.4 per cent during the same period.

For the scheduled caste, while the total GER improved from 32.6 per cent to 54.9 per cent, for the boys and girls, these improved from 37.2 per cent and 26.9 per cent in 2000–2001 to 57.3 per cent and 52.2 per cent in 2010–2011. Again for the scheduled tribes, the total GER at this level of education improved from 25.7 per cent in 2000–2001 to 41.5 per cent in 2010–2011 and for the boys and girls these improved from 31 per cent and 19.8 per cent to 45.4 per cent and 37.3 per cent, respectively, during this period.

At the higher level of education, the overall GER improved from 8.1 per cent in 2000–2001 to 18.8 per cent in 2010–2011 and for the boys and girls these improved from 9.3 per cent and 6.7 per cent in 2000–2001 to 20.9 per cent and 16.5 per cent in 2010–2011, respectively. For the scheduled castes, the total GER in higher education improved from 5.8 per cent in 2000–2001 to 11.1 per cent in 2010–2011 and for the boys and girls these improved from 7.7 per cent to 13 per cent, 3.6 per cent to 9 per cent during the same period. For the scheduled tribes, the total GER in higher education increased from 4.2 per cent in 2000–2001 to 10.3 per cent in 2010–2011 and for the boys and girls these improved from 5.8 per cent to 13.1 per cent and 2.6 per cent to 7.5 per cent during this period. This shows that despite the expansion of educational institutions low GER has remained linked to secondary and higher education in the country and that traditional caste, ethnic and gender divide have remained attached to GER at this level of education; and that higher GER is linked to low rate of gender divide.

III. The Foundation Stone: State of Expansion of Literacy and Elementary Education

Elementary education is the crucial foundation stone for human resource generation of the country. For long, India remained a country with high incidences of illiteracy and school dropouts. However, in recent years, with several state measures the quantum of student's enrolment and their retention in the school system has increased. As can be seen from Table 4.6, over the decades the literacy rates in India have increased and the rural and urban and gender divides in literacy rates also have started declining especially in the last two decades. In 1951, 18.33 per cent of the Indian population was literate while the rural and urban literacy rates were 12.1 per cent and 34.6 per cent and the overall male and female literacy rates were 27.16 per cent and 8.86 per cent, respectively. The rural–urban gap in literacy kept on increasing from

Table 4.6 *Rural Urban Literacy Rate 1951–2011, India*

Year	Persons				Persons			Work Participation in Agriculture
	Total	Rural	Urban	Rural-Urban Gap	Male	Female	Gender Gap	
1951	18.33	12.1	34.6	22.5	27.16	8.86	18.30	
1961	28.30	22.5	54.4	31.9	40.40	15.3	25.05	
1971	34.45	27.9	60.2	32.3	45.96	21.97	23.98	72.05
1981	43.57	36.0	67.2	31.2	56.38	29.76	26.62	66.52
1991	52.21	44.7	73.1	22.4	64.13	39.29	24.84	66.92
2001	65.38	59.4	80.3	20.9	75.85	63.20	21.59	58.40
2011	74.04	82.14	65.46	16.7	82.14	65.46	16.86	51.0

Source: Census of India, 2001

22.5 per cent in 1951 to around 32 per cent level in 1961. This trend continued till 1971 and started showing a decendency in 1981 and thereafter. As in 1991 literacy rate of the country increased to above 52 per cent, the rural–urban divide in literacy rate declined to 22.4 per cent. In 2001, overall literacy rates of the country increased to 65.38 per cent and in 2011 to 74.4 per cent; and simultaneously the rural–urban gap also declined in literacy rates to 20.9 per cent in 2001 and 16.7 per cent in 2011. Along the line, again the gender gap in literacy increased from 18.30 per cent in 1951 to 25 per cent in 1961 and to 26.62 per cent in 1981, but with an increase in literacy it declined to 23.98 per cent in 1971 and consistently declined to 24.84 per cent in 1991, 21.59 per cent in 2001 and further to 16.86 per cent in 2011.

Significantly, low level of literacy has remained positively linked to high intensity in rural–urban and gender divides in literacy and high intensity of work participation in agriculture and vice versa in India. Thus, the declining rural–urban and gender gaps in literacy impacted the occupational structure of the country as a whole and patterns of work participation in agriculture in particular, which are reflected in the decline in work participation in agriculture from 72.05 per cent in 1971 to 58.40 per cent in 2001 further to 50.2 per cent in 2011 and increasing rural-to-urban migration and withdrawal of women from extra-mural manual agricultural activities.

Gender, Caste and Regional Divides in Educational Expansion in India

In India, while the urban and the metro centres have high rates of literacy, the remote and the rural areas usually lag behind. Again, the spread of literacy has been unequal among the states/union territories. Among the selected states, West Bengal and Uttar Pradesh lag behind Maharashtra and Tamil Nadu. The literacy rate is again linked to the process of urbanisation.

In 1991, while at the national level, the literacy rate was 52.21 per cent, for the states of West Bengal, Tamil Nadu, Maharashtra, Delhi and Uttar Pradesh, these were 64.87 per cent, 62.66 per cent, 64.87 per cent and 75.29 per cent, 40.06 per cent, respectively. While at the national level, the literacy rate increased from 65.38 per cent in 2001 to 74.04 per cent in 2011 (Tables 4.6 and 4.7) for Uttar Pradesh it

Table 4.7 *Changing Literacy Rates among the Social Categories in the Selected States*

State/ district/ city/ towns	1991						2001						2011					
	Total	Male	Female	Gap	SC	ST	Total	Male	Female	Gap	SC	ST	Total	Male	Female	Gap	SC	ST
West Bengal	64.87	76.56	52.32	24.2	56.46	36.79	69.22	77.58	60.22	17.36	71.90	55.21	77.8	82.67	71.16	11.52		
Tamil Nadu	62.66	73.75	51.33	22.4	46.74	27.89	73.47	82.33	64.55	17.78	63.19	41.53	80.33	86.81	73.86	12.95		
Maha-rashtra	64.87	76.56	52.32	24.2	56.46	36.79	77.27	86.27	67.51	18.76	71.90	55.21	82.9	89.82	75.84	14.34		
Delhi	75.29	82.01	66.99	15.62	57.60	Nil	81.82	87.37	75.0	12.37	70.85	Nil	86.34	91.3	80.93	10.10		
Uttar Pradesh	41.06	55.7	25.3	30.04	26.85	35.70	57.36	70.23	42.98	27.25	46.27	35.13	69.72	79.24	59.26	20.0		

Source: Census of India, 1991, 2001, 2011.

increased from 57.36 per cent to 69.72 per cent, West Bengal from 69.2 per cent to 77.8 per cent, Tamil Nadu from 73.47 per cent to 80.33 per cent and Maharashtra from 77.27 per cent to 82.90 per cent

Significantly, along with the overall increase in literacy rate, gender gap has declined for all the states. For example, for West Bengal, it declined from 24.2 per cent in 1991 to 17.36 per cent in 2001 to 11.52 per cent in 2011, Tamil Nadu from 22.4 per cent to 17.78 per cent to 12.95 per cent, Maharashtra 24.2 per cent to 18.76 per cent to 14.34 per cent, Delhi 15.62 per cent to 12.37 per cent to 10.10 per cent, and Uttar Pradesh 30.04 per cent to 27.25 per cent to 20 per cent during the same period, respectively. In all the states, though the scheduled castes have a low rate of literacy than the overall rate of literacy, and the scheduled tribes have a low rate of literacy than the scheduled castes, in general literacy rate has increased for all social categories across the regions. In West Bengal, the literacy rates for the scheduled castes and scheduled tribes increased from 56.46 per cent and 36.79 per cent in 1991 to 71.90 and 55.21 per cent in 2001, respectively, for these groups. In Tamil Nadu, these increased from 46.74 per cent and 27.89 per cent to 63.19 per cent and 41.53 per cent, Maharashtra 56.46 per cent and 36.79 per cent to 71.90 per cent and 55.21 per cent and Uttar Pradesh it changed from 26.85 per cent and 35.7 per cent to 46.21 per cent and 35.13 per cent, respectively, for these groups in the period between 1991 and 2001. As Uttar Pradesh has been divided into two states, it shows stagnation in the literacy rate for the tribes.

IV. The Secondary and Vocational Education: Emerging New Horizon

The changing technoeconomic environment does not only need manpower with functional literacy but also demands qualified manpower grounded in necessary skill and knowledge. This situation necessitated to empower the young generation with 'above elementary level' of education and skill to take the massive challenge of carrying forward the economy in the desired path of economic growth and social development. The state of secondary and higher secondary education in India are undergoing a massive change in view of improvement in the primary sector, growing need of manpower with secondary/higher secondary level of education, and growing aspirations for higher level of education among a vast section of learners. Now, the overall GER has become above 49 per cent with 52.4 per cent for boys and 45.9 per cent for girls. In 2011–2012, ₹ 9483 crore accounting to 1.05 per cent of the GDP was spent on these levels of education. At present, there are more than 2 lakh secondary and senior secondary schools in the country. In view of the increasing flow of students, government proposes to encourage more and more private sectors' engagement in this level of education.

India since long has realised the need of vocational education at the secondary stage to provide for diversification of educational opportunities so as to enhance individual employability, reduce the mismatch between demand and supply of skilled manpower and provide an alternative for those pursuing higher education (Planning Commission, 2012). The Planning Commission of India (2008; Vol. II) observed in its Eleventh Five Year Plan that

> rapid changes in the technology and increasing demand for skill has made it necessary that young people should acquire more than eight years of elementary learning to acquire necessary skill to complete successfully in the labour market. With Universal Elementary Education becoming a reality, near universalization of secondary education has become a logical next step.

India still has a high dropout rate at the high and the higher secondary levels of education. In view of such dropouts and inability of prevailing higher education system to accommodate huge flow of students to it immediately, on the one hand, and immanent need for skill in several areas of activities, on the other, contemporary emphasis has been on skill development and vocational training for this segment of young population. State has framed policies for skill development and vocational trainers programme that specifically aims to equip young individuals with marketable skills through technical and vocational training that could be gainfully and professionally used in the industrial, manufacturing and service sector. Such trainings are provided in India by ITIs and the ITCs under the auspices of the Ministry of Labour and Employment, Government of India, through the Directorate General of Employment and Training (DGET). Several other ministries and departments also take initiatives for the vocational training and skill development. There are a total of 6906 ITIs and ITCs in India with a total seating capacity of 9.53 lakhs. In view of the emerging local needs and the changing global scenario, growing emphasis has been on skill development programmes by linking them strongly with market and industry and lifelong learning, etc., for all sections of the workforce right from operators/workers to college-qualified students to junior to mid-and-senior level executives (National Skill Development Corporation, 2012). Here, the Planning Commission of India recommends the need for establishing flexible learning pathways integrated to schooling, on the one end, and higher education, on the other, through National Vocational Education Qualification Framework. It says, PPPs in financing, service delivery and provision of workspaces and training of trainers should be promoted. 'We should aim to increase the percentage of the workforce that has received formal skills through vocational education and training from 12.0 per cent at present to 25.0 per cent by the end of the Twelfth Plan. This would mean that about 70 million more people have to be imparted formal skills in the next five years' (Planning Commission, 2012). Significantly, along with increasing emphasis on the vocational skill and education, there is an emphasis on the private intervention in this crucial sector.

V. Higher and Technical Education in India: Unfolding New Horizons and Challenges

Higher education in knowledge society is no more a luxury, but an essential tool for nation's social and economic development (UNESCO, 2001). It has been assigned the special role to train and educate new generation of manpower who would promote the cause of nation building, introduce and improve technological innovation, augment economic prosperity, accommodate new ideas and actions, create bases of critical thinking, generate and disseminate knowledge through regular research and also contest the same with all openness and democratic values.

In the emerging technoeconomic environment, higher education needs a huge investment for fast expansion and quality assurance. Planned expenditure in higher and technical education has significantly increased in India over the planned period. A glance of this increase is shown in Table 4.8. Higher education was allocated from ₹ 530 crore in the Sixth Plan ₹ 1200 crore in the Seventh Plan ₹ 1060 in the Eighth Plan to ₹ 2500 crore in the Ninth Plan, ₹ 9600 crore in the Tenth Plan ₹ 84,940 in the Eleventh Plan and further ₹ 1,10,700 in the Twelfth Plan.

Table 4.8 Planned Expenditure in Higher and Technical Education

	6th Plan ('80–'85)	7th Plan ('85–'90)	8th Plan ('92–'97)	9th Plan ('97–'02)	10th Plan ('02–'07)	11th Plan ('07–'12)	12th Plan ('12–'17)
Planned Expenditure (₹ in crore)	530	1200	1060	2500	9600	84,940	1,10,700

Source: Planning Commission: Tenth Five Year Plan and Eleventh Five Year Plan, and Twelfth Five Year Plan.

Higher education, however, receives meagre share of the total expenditure in education and of the GDP despite the crucial role it plays in nation building, its increasing demand and manifold increase in the student population at these levels of education. The changing patterns of expenditure in higher education as a share of total expenditure on education are shown in Table 4.9.

Table 4.9 Share of Public Expenditure on Higher Education in GDP and Education Expenditures

Year	Expenditure on Edn as % of GDP	Expenditure on Higher Edn as % of Expenditure on Edn	Expenditure on Higher Edn as % of GDP
1981–1982	2.49	15.25	0.38
1991–1992	3.59	10.16	0.34
2000–2001	3.91	12.14	0.60
2010–2011	3.80	23.45	0.80

Source: UGC educational statistics 2012.

Expenditure on higher education has increased in India as per cent of GDP from 2.49 per cent in 1981–1981 to 3.59 per cent in 1991–1992, 3.91 per cent in 2000–2010 and to 3.80 per cent in 2010–2011. In terms of expenditure on higher education as per cent of expenditure on all education, it was declined from 15.25 per cent 1981–1982 to 10.16 per cent in 1991–1992, but increased to 12.14 per cent in 2000–2001 and sharply to 23.45 per cent in 2010–2011. As far as the expenditure on higher education or per cent of total GDP is concerned, it was declined from 0.38 per cent in 1981–1982, to 0.34 per cent in 1991–92. However there after it increased to 0.60 per cent in 2000–2001 and 0.80 per cent in 2010–2011. Despite the increasing trend, it has been widely recognised that in view of the huge concentration of youth population and their high rate of retention and completion of secondary level of education, growing demand for higher and technical education in the country and simultaneous growing demand for highly educated and skilled manpower and the proliferation of a knowledge-based economy and huge requirement of research, on the one hand, state commitment for quality, equity and unprecendented expansion in higher education on the other, the given budgetary allocation appears to be highly inadequate.

A Paradigm Shift in Higher Education

As the higher educational scenario of the country has again been marked by increasing demand for quality higher and technical education, short supply of government institutions to suffice to this demanded increasing affordability of a small section of parents to pay children's higher education by paying higher fee, cultural/moral readiness of Indian parents to pay for higher education of their children even at the cost of their self-denial, the private penetration in higher education has merged to be unprecedented in the higher and technical education in contemporary India. These private players have made their presence felt in one form or the other in the nooks and corners of the country bringing a paradigm shift in the educational scenario. As under the aegis economic liberalisation states perspective on higher education tilts in favour of the market forces the private education institutions boom in contemporary India. In fact, a new policy framework is now put in place for a shift in educational perspective and market penetration in this sector of education.

The Birla Ambani Report (2001) elucidates this shift very clearly that specifically recommends the state to privatise education at all levels in view of changing need for the knowledge-based economy in India. The Committee recommends the government 'to leave higher and professional education to the private sector', 'support disciplines that have no market orientation', 'keep the economy free from state controls to foster new opportunities that will create a market for graduates from the education system', 'progressively reduce the funding for universities and make them adopt the route of self-sufficiency', 'promote credit market for private finance of cost of higher education', 'enact a Private University Bill to encourage establishment of new private universities in the fields of science and technology and management', 'allow FDI in education in the areas of science, technology and management and related areas', 'depoliticise of universities and educational institutions and banning of political activity on campuses of universities and educational institutions' and 'encourage for market-oriented education through private investment'.

The Planning Commission of India (2012) also suggests that 'private sector growth in higher education (including technical) should be facilitated and innovative PPPs should be explored and developed and "not-for-profit" tag in higher education sector should, perhaps, be reexamined in a more pragmatic' (Planning Commission, 2012).

Though the Private University Bill for establishing private university in the country is pending in the Parliament, many provincial governments have already enacted private university bills and started allowing the private universities to operate in their respective states. The process of recognition of private higher education institutions at the central level by the University Grants Commission of India (UGC), All India Council for Technical Education (AICTE), Distance Education Council (DEC) and National Accreditation Council (NAC), Medical Council of India (MCI), Dental Council of India (DCI) and other bodies are effectively initiated. Through these mechanisms many of the private educational entrepreneurs have made significant dents in the higher education system in the country and have acquired the status of university and deemed university for their private technical, management and professional institutions. As the Foreign University Bill is yet to be enacted to facilitate the foreign universities to open their campus in India, the UGC has set up a committee to smoothen the process.

It is important that in recent years the share of private higher education institution and student enrolment therein has significantly increased. The Planning Commission reports that private higher education accounts for about four-fifths of enrolment in professional higher education and one-third overall. This growth trend is likely to continue in the years to come (Planning Commission, 2012). The reports of PwC titled 'Emerging Opportunities for Private and Foreign Participants in Higher Education', Grant Thornton titled 'Education in India: Securing the Demographic Dividend', the Indian Education Congress report titled 'Indian Education Investment Report, 2013', Ernst & Young report titled '40 million by 2020: Preparing for a New Paradigm in Indian Higher Education' and many such ones show the increasing potential for private investment in higher education in India; and it is likely to capture major share of all educational arena in the country by the middle of this decade.

Growth in Higher Education with Increasing Engagement of Private Providers: Though the expansion of higher educational institutions and the student enrolment therein were very slow in the preindependent and the early independent India, there has been phenomenal expansion in the higher education institution, and increase of student enrolment in this sector in very recent years.

As shown in Table 4.10, there has been phenomenal growth of higher education institutions and in the growth of student population therein. In 1970–1971, there were only 107 universities in India. In 1980–1981, it grew up to 133, in 1990–1991 to 190, in 2000–2001 to 256, in 2006–2007 to 387 and in 2011–2012 to 664. Similarly, in 1970–1971, there were only 3604 colleges; it increased to 4722 in 1980–1981, 7346 in 1990–1991, 12,806 in 2000–2001, 21,170 in 2006–2007 and 33,023 in 2011–2012. The student population has grown from 20 lakhs in 1970–1971, 28 lakhs in 1980–1981, 49 lakhs in 1990–1991, 84 lakhs in 2000–2001, 116 lakhs in 2006–2007 and 259 lakhs in 2011–2012. The GER in higher education was to the extent of 6.0 per cent in 1990–1991 and it increased to 8.1 per cent in 2000–2001, 12.3 per cent in 1990–1991 and 18.8 per cent in 2011–2012. It is important that the proliferation of higher education institutions and student enrolment therein has been conspicuously faster in the last one decade than those of the previous decades.

Table 4.10 *Expansion of Higher Education Institutions and Students in Higher Education Institutions*

	1970–1971	1980–1981	1990–1991	2000–2001	2006–2007	2011–2012
No. of universities	103	133	190	256	387	664
No. of colleges	3604	4722	7346	12,806	21,170	33,023
No. of students (in lakhs)	20.0	28.0	49.0	84.0	166.0	259.0
GER	NA	NA	6.0	8.1	12.3	18.8

Source: Planning Commission, 2013; Ernst & Young, 2012

In India, the growth rate and absolute presence of the private sector in higher education has surpassed those of the state-owned sectors in recent years. It is shown in Table 4.11 in India today that 63.9 per cent of the higher education institutions are occupied by the private sector, and the remaining by the government sector with the state government controlling 35.6 per cent and central government only 5 per cent; and that the growth rate for the private institutions has been faster than that of the government-run institutions. Again among the government-run institutions, the state government institutions have got higher share and at places higher growth rate than the central

Table 4.11 *Growth of Institutions in the Eleventh Plan (Student Numbers in Lakhs)*

Category	2006–2007	2011–2012	Increase	%	Growth Rate (%)
Central Institutions					
Degree Awarding Institutions	87	152	65		11.8
Colleges	58	69	11		3.5
Subtotal	145	221	76	0.5	8.8
State Institutions					
Degree Awarding Institutions	227	316	89		6.8
Colleges	9000	13,024	4024		7.7
Diploma Institutions	1867	3207	1340		11.4
Subtotal	11,094	16,547	5453	35.6	8.3
Private Institutions					
Degree Awarding Institutions	73	191	118		21.2
Colleges	12,112	19,930	7818		10.5
Diploma Institutions	5960	9541	3581		9.9
Subtotal	18,145	29,662	11,517	63.9	10.3
Total	29,384	46,430	17,046	100.00	9.6

Source: Planning Commission 2013.

government institutions. In 2011–2012, there were 152 central degree awarding institutes growing at the rate of 11.8 per cent, 316 state institutes growing at the rate of 6.8 per cent and 191 private institutes growing at the rate of 21.2 per cent in the period between 2006–2007 and 2011–2012. In 2011–2012, there were only 69 central government colleges that grew at the rate of 3.5 per cent, 13,024 state government colleges grew at the rate of 7.7 per cent and 19,930 private colleges grew at the rate of 10.5 per cent in the period between 2006–2007 and 2011–2012. Again, in 2011–2012, there were 3207 state government diploma awarding institutes growing at the rate of 11.4 per cent and 9541 private diploma awarding institutes growing at the rate of 9.9 per cent in this period between 2006–2007 and 2011–2012. It is important that while the overall growth rate of higher education institutions for the central government has been 8.8 per cent, state government institutes 8.3 per cent, for the private institutions it has been 10.3 per cent during the period under consideration. In fact, market penetration in the higher education has not only been higher but also faster than the government institutions in recent decades. Significantly, the state private universities have witnessed an annual growth rate of 33.8 per cent since 1995. While there was only one private university in the country in 1995, it increased to 28 in 2007 and shot up to 142 in 2012 (Twelfth Five Year Plan, Ernst & Young, 2012).

In recent years, there has been significant expansion in student enrolment in the private higher education institutions in India. As shown in Table 4.12 in 2006–2007, a total of 13,850 lakhs students were enrolled with the higher education institutions of which as high as 54.2 per cent were with the private institutions while 45.8 per cent were with the

Table 4.12 *Growth of Enrolment in the Eleventh Plan (Enrolment in Lakhs)*

Category	2006–2007		2011–2012		Increase	Growth Rate (%)	2016–2017	
	Total	%	Total	%			Total	%
Government	63.38	45.8	89.63	41.1	26.25	7.2	122.4	39.81
Central	3.10	2.2	5.63	2.6	2.53	12.7	12.0	9.80
State	60.28	43.6	84.00	38.5	23.72	6.9	110.4	90.19
Private	75.12	54.2	128.23	58.9	53.11	11.3	185.0	60.18
Total	138.5	100	217.86	100			307.4	

Source: Planning Commission 2013.

government institutions. In 2011–2012, the share of enrolment with the private institutions has gone up again to 58.9 per cent while the share for the government institutions declined to 41.1 per cent. It is again that enrolment with the private institutions has grown at the rate of 53.11 per cent while for the government institutions at the rate of 26.25 per cent in the period between 2006–2007 and 2011–2012. It is projected that by the end the Twelfth Five Year Plan, the share of enrolment with government institutions will reduce to 39.81 per cent, while for the private institutions it will grow to the extent of 60.18 per cent.

The market penetration in higher education has been marked by increasing demand and expansion of professional and market-driven sectors of education. Table 4.13 shows that though arts education still accommodates highest share of students enrolled in higher education amounting to a total of 65.78 lakhs of the total student strength of 217.86 lakhs in 2011–2012, there is a declining student share from 39.6 per cent to 30.2 per cent during the same period. On the contrary, there has been high expansion of enrolment in engineering from 18.06 lakhs with 13 per cent share to 54.68 lakhs students having 25 per cent share, followed by commerce and management from 22.87 lakhs students with 16.5 per cent share to 34.4 lakhs students with 15.8 per cent share, general science from 25.43 lakhs students lakhs with 18.4 per cent share to 30.57 lakhs students with 14 per cent share, education from 6.21 lakh students with 4.5 per cent share to 13 lakhs students with 6 per cent share, medicine, nursing and pharmacy from 5.98 lakhs students with 4.3 per cent share to 12.02 lakhs students with 5.5 per cent share, law from 3.0 lakhs students with 2.2 per cent share to 3.48 lakhs students with 1.6 per cent share, agriculture and veterinary sciences from 0.93 lakhs students with 0.7 per cent share to 1.21 per cent lakhs students with 0.6 per cent share, and other types of education from 1.16 lakhs students with 0.8 per cent share to 2.78 lakhs students with 1.3 per cent share during the period between 2006–2007 and 2011–2012. In fact, a fast shift of students from liberal to professional and technical education has become very explicit in contemporary India.

Knowledge society needs highly qualified manpower and accordingly the state has to develop a strategy to ensure the availability of such manpower in a futuristic perspective. As shown in Table 4.14, the

Table 4.13 *Growth of Enrolment by Field of Study during the Eleventh Plan (in Lakhs)*

Faculty	2006–2007		2011–2012		Growth Rate (%)
	Total	%	Total	%	
Arts	54.86	39.6	65.78	30.2	3.7
Science	25.43	18.4	30.57	14.0	3.8
Commerce and Management	22.87	16.5	34.34	15.8	8.5
Education	6.21	4.5	13.00	6.0	15.9
Engineering	18.06	13.0	54.68	25.0	24.8
Medicine, Nursing and Pharmacy	5.98	4.3	12.02	5.5	15.0
Agriculture and Veterinary Science	0.93	0.7	1.21	0.6	5.4
Law	3.00	2.2	3.48	1.6	3.0
Others	1.16	0.8	2.78	1.3	19.1
Total	138.5	100	217.86	100	9.5

Source: Planning Commission, 2013.

state has envisaged a 7.1 per cent growth in enrolment the in higher education sector during the Twelfth Five Year Plan with an increase from 217.9 lakhs enrolment in higher education in 2011–2012 to 307.4 lakhs in 2016–2017 (see Table 4.14). It is projected that the number of PhD students will increase from 1 to 3 lakhs with 24.6 per cent growth rate, PG General from 17.3 to 33.2 lakhs with a growth of 13.9 per cent, PG Technical from 5 lakhs to 12.2 lakhs with a growth rate of 19.5 per cent, UG General 116.6 lakhs to 128 lakhs with a growth rate of 1.9 per cent, UG Technical 45 lakhs to 66 lakhs with a growth rate of 8 per cent, Diploma 33 lakhs to 65 lakhs with a growth rate of 14.5 per cent, ODL from 42 lakhs to 52 lakhs with a growth of 4.4 per cent during the period between 2011–2012 and 2016–2017. It has also targeted the GER in higher education to grow from 17.9 per cent to 25.2 per cent during the same period. It has been envisioned that PhD students who formed only 0.38 per cent of the total enrolment in 2011–2012 would be forming 0.83 per cent of the total enrolment in 2016–2017. Similarly, the proportion of the PG General students would increase from 6.6 per cent to 13.9 per

Table 4.14 *Enrolment Targets by Level Type for the Twelfth Plan (Student Numbers in Lakhs)*

Level/Type	2011–2012 (Estimates)		2016–2017 (Targets)		Growth Rate
	No. in lakhs	%	No. in lakhs	%	
PhD	1	0.38	3	0.83%	24.6
PG General	17.3	6.6	33.2	9.2	13.9
PG Technical	5.0	1.9	12.2	3.4	19.5
UG General	116.6	44.8	128.0	35.6	1.9
UG Technical	45.0	17.3	66.0	18.4	8.0
Subtotal	184.9		242.4		5.6
Diploma	33.0	12.7	65.0	18.1	14.5
Total	217.9	–	307.4	–	7.1
ODL	42.0	16.6	52.0	14.5	4.4
Grand Total 3	259.9	100	359.4	100	6.7
Population 18–23 years	1451.2	–	1427.4	–	–0.1
GER %	17.9	–	25.2	–	–

Note: UG = Undergraduate, PG = Postgraduate, ODL = Open and Distance Learning.
Source: Planning Commission 2013.

cent, PG Technical from 1.9 per cent to 3.4 per cent, UG Technical from 17.3 per cent to 18.4 per cent, Diploma holders from 12.7 per cent to 18.1 per cent during the same period. However, the proportion of the UG General and the ODL students would decline from 44.8 per cent and 16.6 per cent to 35.6 per cent and 14.5 per cent, respectively, during this period.

The growth in education is crucial to sustain the growth of knowledge economy and these would reinforce each other. The mutual growth is possible not only by promoting elite but also mass higher education in the country that would be based on the principle of quality and access simultaneously.

VI Mass Education: Open and Distance Learning

To Drucker (1968), the knowledge society needs both the great men who create knowledge and the journeymen who can convert new knowledge into everyday action. To him 'There is no conflict between mass education and quality education. We need to educate large mass of people to get the large amount of quality we need... to get large number of competent journeyman and stimulate large number of future masters.' He however cautions that 'mass education should be quality education' (Drucker, 1968).

Should the quality of highly educated and skilled human capital need to be developed at a mass scale for mass production and use of knowledge in the country, a flexible and open arrangement is rather imperative to suffice the purpose. Such quality mass education needs an engagement with lifelong, quality, innovative, flexible and autonomous learning arrangement, which functions in conjunction with the existing arrangement to promote and sustain the knowledge base of society among the cross-section of population especially among the disadvantaged social group. Herein, the significance of the ODL has been emphasised in India by the planners, educationists, politicians and administrators alike. Because of their capacity to be flexible and open to accommodate diverse need of the learners, to integrate advanced technologies such as ICTs, audio, videos, new media, to provide educational opportunities to attract huge number of students to suffice their knowledge needs through alternative/parallel modes of learning and to get high economic returns the Open University (OU) system in particular and the distance education system in general have occupied a place of significance in contemporary educational discourse and practise in India. From a marginal position, these systems have emerged to be major players in the contemporary educational scenario of India and have emerged to be a haven of hope to the vast majority of learners who for one reason or the other have not got an entry in the convention system, looking for second chance entry in higher education, or skill upgradation, through a flexible arrangement for learning. In view of the fast expansion of higher educational arrangements and its move from 'elite' to be 'mass' based (with the crossing of threshold of 15 per cent GER and is now moving towards universal higher education for the threshold of 50 per cent GER), the Planning Commission (2012) has reinforced the state's commitment to ODL to widen access in a cost-effective and flexible manner to provide better access to the poor and disadvantaged social groups and first-generation learners from backward areas (Planning Commission, 2012).

Over the years, there has been phenomenal growth in the ODL

system in the country. From a mere one OU to 33 distance education institutions (DEIs) and in March 2012 there were 14 Open Universities (OUs) and about 200 DEIs in the country. The growth of DEIs is given in Table 4.15. The numerical strength of distance learners has also increased over the decades from an enrolment of 1112 in 1962 to

Table 4.15 *Institutional Growth of Distance Education*

Year	Open Universities	Distance Education Institutions	Total Distance Teaching Institutions
1962	–	1	1
1980–1980	1	33	34
2009–2010	14	186	200
2012	14	200	214

Source: Menon 2012, DEC, 2013

1,66,428 students in 1980–1981 to 36,36,744 in the year 2009–2010. Distribution of enrolment in OUs and DEIs is given in Table 4.16.

In 1962–1963, the share of total distance education enrolment was only to the extent of 0.15 per cent. It increased to 5.7 per

Table 4.16 *Growth of Enrolment in Open Universities (OUs) and DEIs*

S. No.	Year	OUs	DEIs	Total
1	1962–1963	–	1112	1112
2	1980–1981	–	1,66,428	1,66,428
3	2009–2010	16,29,732	20,07,012	36,36,744
4	2011–2012	17.77	24,24,000	42,11,000

Source: Menon 2012.

cent in 1980–1981 with a growth rate of 31.8 per cent over the decade. In 2008–2009, the share of ODL to total enrolment increased to 20.56 per cent and its growth rate to 18.52 per cent (Madhava Menon Committee, 2010). According to the Report to the People on Education 2012, MHRD, Government of India, of the 146.25 lakhs people admitted in the higher education institutions in 2010–2011, 55.8 lakhs amounting to 37 per cent are enrolled with the ODL systems in the country.

During the last five years, as shown in Table 4.17, the DEIs have grown at the rate of 8.9 per cent. In 2006–2007, there were altogether 27.41 lakhs enrolment in the ODL educational institutions in the

Table 4.17 *Growth of Enrolment in ODL Programme in the Eleventh Plan (Enrolment in Lakhs)*

Enrolment	2011–2012	Increase	Growth Rate (%)
Indira Gandhi National Open University (IGNOU)	6.97	2.29	8.3
State Open Universities (SOU)	10.80	3.03	6.8
Distance Education Institutions (DEI)	24.24	9.28	10.1
Total	42.01	14.60	8.9

Source: Planning Commission 2013.

country that increased to 42.01 lakhs in 2011–2012. Among the major providers in ODL system, the Indira Gandhi National Open University (IGNOU) alone has enrolled 6.97 lakhs, all thirteen SOUs provided 10.80 lakhs and the DEIs 24.24 lakhs students in 2011–2012. IGNOU has experienced 8.3 per cent growth rate, the SOU altogether 6.8 per cent and the other DEIs 10.1 per cent growth rate in enrolment in the period between 2006–2007 and 2011–2012.

VII Emerging Challenges in Higher Education

While contemporary India experiences the proliferation of new varieties of higher educational institutions, and host of media hype and publicity of these institutions, these are seldom matched by the societal and quality concerns. While the market takeover of education has been an emerging phenomenon, the state apathy, unwarranted state intervention and intent to control the educational arrangement by the bureaucrats make the government-run educational institutions a site for market-driven consumption, power play and extended local and regional and national politics. These problems are again compounded for the state-run educational institution by resource crunch, lack of adequate faculty, research facility and host of related issues.

Resource Crunch

Higher education in India has been posited with a paradoxical situation: while there has been increasing emphasis to maintain a high standard, be globally competitive, there has been inadequate funding to encounter the challenges faced by these institutions. Though in absolute terms, the allocation in higher education has increased from ₹ one million in the First Five Year Plan to ₹ 84,940 million in the Eleventh Five Year Plan, in view of the increase of the number of the educational institutions, student strength, research need and price escalation, most of the educational experts consider such allocation to be inadequate to meet the need of a growing knowledge economy. Even the Planning Commission argues that:

> there is an urgent need to step up both public and private investment in higher education (including technical), and increase in the efficiency of its utilisation. About 18.0% of all government education spending or about 1.12% of GDP is spent on higher education today. This should be raised to 25.0% and 1.5%, respectively. An increase of 0.38% of GDP means an additional allocation of about ₹ 25,000 crore to higher education for the Centre and the States taken together. (Planning Commission, 2012)

Massive Faculty Crunch

The higher education system in the country suffers from the problem of adequate strength of faculty. While, on the one hand, there has been a decline in the quantum of committed faculty, on the other hand, there has been nonfilling of available position. A recent report of MHRD presented to Parliamentary Consultative Committee shows that of the 16,602 sanctioned positions in the 42 Central universities in the country, 6542 positions have remained vacant for one reason or the other. Again, in the 15 Indian Institutes of Information Technologies (IIITs), of the 5092 sanctioned faculty positions 1611 remained vacant, and in 13 IIMs, of the 638 positions 111 remained vacant; in the four IITs, 104 remained vacant out of 224 sanctioned positions, in the National Institute of Technologies (NITs), 1487 sanctioned positions remained vacant out of 4291 positions, and in the Indian Institutes of Science Education and Research, 131 vacant positions remained vacant out of 518 sanctioned positions (*Times of India*, 03 August 2012). In a reply to the questions in the Lok Sabha in March 2013, it has been revealed that in old IITs 2198 (41 per cent), new IITs 410 (57 per cent), old NITs 2808 (48 per cent), new NITs 226 (100 per cent) positions remained vacant. The ministry has noted a lack of PhD candidates and students' preference for corporate jobs over teaching jobs as the main reasons (*Times of India*, 13 March 2013). In general, however, this crunch has resulted from nonavailability of suitable candidates, bureaucratic red tapism leading to the delay in selection process, migration of faculty to other countries due to lack of research facilities and condusive working conditions in India, etc. Such faculty crunch in higher education, very often than not, contributes to overall performance in the higher education system. This problem has again been compounded by political interference and nepotism in selection process in higher education. Hence, the institutes are resorting to contract, adjunct, visiting faculty, part time, and online, etc., modes of teaching to make up for the faculty shortage.

This situation is precarious in many of the state universities and the local colleges, which are only institutions to get access to higher education for the local students. For example, in the state of Orissa, since the 1990s, there has been no recruitment of lecturers (assistant professors) at the degree colleges except for 1997 when only 30 lecturers were recruited only in few disciplines/areas. In this state, there are approximately 1200 private colleges and 90 government colleges. In the private colleges, teaching is conducted by engaging temporary/part time lecturers who are paid a very minimal salary. Similarly, even in the government colleges, there are no regular recruitment; and classes predominantly conducted by the part time or guest lecturers/faculties. Even though as per the UGC norm a professor is to take 12 classes, associate professor 14 classes and assistant professor 16 classes of 45 minutes each per week, they end up taking more than 28 classes per week. For example, in the G.M. Autonomous (Government) College in Sambalpur District of Orissa, the total number of teaching positions was slashed down from 149 to 119 in 1999 even though students' strength doubled. As a large number of teachers have retired without new recruitment, the college authority is largely dependent on 35 temporary teachers who are paid ₹ 500 per class, and 8 guest faculties who are paid ₹ 14,000 per month to conduct the regular classes along with another 76 regular faculties. Similar is the situation of most of the colleges where the faculty members are to work without proper library, research and faculty development facilities adversely affecting the quality of teaching and research in the country. Such a situation is rampant in most parts of contemporary semi urban and urban India.

Lack of Quality Assurance and Absence of Students Choice

In view of this growing demand for professional education, the educational space of India is flooded with the proliferation of institutions that are predominantly private in nature to provide professional education programmes in computer sciences, biotechnology, health care, engineering, nursing, etc., and managerial courses in various areas. However, the process of manufacturing managers and engineers is taking shape in an unequal footing and at times is devoid of the concern for quality assurance and social relevance. Such expansion of professional education has been encountering the challenge of untimely closure of educational institutions by a section of private providers of such education due to relevance and quality deficit. In 2011–2013, the AICTE received 231 applications for closure from the management and 84 other colleges offering Master of Computer Application. The Times of India reports that 'Growing in a professional college was once the pinnacle of an Indian student's career. Aspirants far outnumbered the seats available. Hence students, left with little choice, would join anonymous professional colleges. However, a section of these students are now withdrawing from these institutions mostly due to poor quality of teaching, lack of adequate faculty or no job offers at the end' (*Times of India*, 1 July 2013). Many also add this to the economic boom and recession in the country in particular and of the globe in general. Many experts however feel that this temporary phase will be overcome; and Indian professional education institutions should be ready with good faculty and innovative/competitive/quality educational environment on campus.

There is no denying the fact that the knowledge society needs more knowledge managers than anything else; and the higher educational institutions, especially the universities, are to be preoccupied in producing managers: we need managers (Drucker, 1968). In the society, there is as much need of professional skill as much as critical knowledge. The Planning Commission (2012) observes that in India, while the general education often fails to equip graduates with necessary work skills due to its poor quality, professional education is often expensive, lengthy and usually imparted in narrowly specialised areas. The private institutions that impart professional education again seldom inculcate critical thinking, which is essential for the development of intelligent able-minded citizens (Planning Commission, 2012).

Though the New Education Policy 1986 of the GOI has provided an elaborate framework to enhance quality, access, equity and democratise education, and the Planning Commission of India emphasised on the expansion, excellence and equity in education, the issue of criticality, quality and democracy seldom privilege over expansion. Thus, despite having a phenomenal expansion, none of the Indian education institutions come within the first 100 in ranking among the educational institutions in the world. Indian politicians very often forcefully comment on the issue; but do too little to redress the scenerio.

Though the educational institutions in India are supposedly autonomies bodies, these are in effect under the tight control of the government. It is not only through the allocation of budgets, policy directives, appointment of the Vice-Chancellors and the crucial Committee/Board/Senate members that the government exercises its control over these institutions, but also by deciding day-to-day internal functioning in many ways. At times, many of these institutions become victims of administrative apathy and lack of clarity from the administration. For example, many institutions in India started offering engineering programmes through distance mode getting recognition from the Distance Education Council. However, the AICTE came up with the notice of nonrecognition of Engineering Programme through distance mode and derecognised many of the institutions causing hardship for the innocent learners. However, very recently, the GOI has come up with a notification allowing the institutions to offer engineering programmes through distance mode as the previous order was against the spirit and directives of New Education Policy 1986. In fact, contradictory policy decisions, especially on the issue of recognition on part of the knowledgeable who decide the educational destiny of the nation, cost very much to the ordinary learners.

Crisis in the ODL system

The ODL system in India is also undergoing a phenomenal crisis widely caused by shift in priority of the state to use this system as instruments to enhance GER in higher education, extract revenue for the state from learners, accommodate a host of nonformal arrangement in the name of experimentation and openness, provide recognition to an alternative structure than to enhance quality by motivating the distance education providers by providing research and development facilities. This crisis has again been compounded by insensitivity of a section of the ODL leaders to the cause of the students and their tendency to throw open this arrangement to the market forces than to adhere to the mandate given to this arrangement to perform. As the ODL system provides high economic returns because of its one time/periodic investment, profitable scale of operation, it has become an attractive site for economic investment and political engagement both by the market and the political forces alike, many a times devoid of social commitment and concern for quality. Despite its capacity to become the potential vehicle for the empowerment of socially deprived motivated learners, it has been subject to commercialisation and dilution of its mandate.

Experts have widely pointed out the issue of neglect of distance learners by the ODL system itself. It is pointed out that money paid by the highly motivated distance learners, many of them belong to the deprived sections of society, is used for the purpose rather than meeting requirement of these students and enhancing quality of this education system. Money collected from the students of poor families is also diverted to subside education of students who are better off and belong to the conventional system that is already subsidised (Ansari, 2012).

In fact, the revenues generated by the ODL system are seldom used either for the academic wellbeing of the distance learners or for the research and innovation in and of the system itself. Significantly, a vast amount of money generated out of students' fee has been diverted increasing for publicity and advertisement than towards research and development. For example, IGNOU that spent to the tune of ₹ 12.5 million towards advertisement in 2006–2007, sharply increased its spending on advertisement to ₹ 320 million in 2010–2011, while during the same period it spent only to the tune of ₹ 0.5 million per annum for faculty research and development. In the open education system, the skill and knowledge of the faculty are required to be updated so as to enable them to provide the student with quality self-instructional materials that are to be periodically updated with latest knowledge. However, when sincere engagement of the faculty with course designing and development activities becomes an imperative, the administration takes all initiative to low prioritise research and faculty development activity in the ODL system. Though a small section of teachers made a mark in their own areas through their own initiatives and commitment, the ODL system in India seldom comes forward to encourage and fund such research.

The administrative strategy to discourse research and to encourage recycling of pre-existing knowledge, and the delaying tactics to frame a faculty development programme, are in essence ideological in nature. While the tendency to recognise the ODL system is industrial and to designate the ODL 'teachers' as 'academic managers' is very explicit in the ODL system in India, the intersectionality between the market-driven education and faculty's limited choice for research within the given structure make the teacher withdraw from research activities. The administrators, on the contrary, do not promote the research culture within the system to suffice the purpose of immediate administrative need ever though at the cost of long term interest of the ODL. They in one way of the other discourage the culture of criticality against the control and the command system of administration. The market needs stability, depoliticisation and unquestioned compliance from the teachers. As market penetration and industrial tendency in the ODL system have been made very explicit, stereotyping and unquestioned submission to power structure is being privileged over well-informed, well-articulated critical knowledge. Research and knowledge production seldom privileged over recycling strategy that is guided by the command of market forces. In fact, 'to be market driven' has become the mantra of ODL success today, with quick fix, repackaging and use of borrowed text being privileged over generation of a new body of knowledge emerging out of committed research of the teaching faculty in the ODL system. This widely contributed to the stigmatised and marginal identity of both the teacher and taught and of the ODL system in the country.

The OUs in India have emerged out of a political commitment of the state especially to cater to the educational need of the disadvantaged section of population. Under the IGNOU Act 1985, the government has instituted the DEC to monitor the progression provided by the ODL system. However, in view of success proliferation and growing market penetration in the ODL system, efforts have been made by the government not to strengthen the DEC, but to dissolve it and to empower the UGC and other bodies to look after the activities mandated to take care of by the DEC. In a neoliberal state, collective resistance and democratic voice of teachers of the ODL system seldom gives credence. It is widely apprehended that such initiative would only pave the way for market triumph over the philosophy of open education in the country.

In the changing technoeconomic environment, caused by economic globalisation, the ODL system faces a paradoxical situation. Indeed, a part of this paradox emanates from its commitment for enhancing mass and quality of higher education, on the one hand, and its response to market forces, on the other. The OU system, which is essentially industrial in nature (Peters, 2002), now has been encountering several challenges and competitions from new providers, experiencing a shift from supply-driven to a demand-driven education (Latchem and Hanna, 2002), growing hegemony of the corporate world and the bureaucrat over the academics, a top-down approach and commodification of the educational function of the university (Noble, 1997). Again, with the phenomenal introduction of ICTs in this system, there is the growth of industrial capitalism (Fox, 1989; Javis, 1993), triumph of ideologies of market forces and 'technicisation of education' (Harris, 1987), increase in the Fordist trend and an urge for 'a quick fix' academic course to trade through available materials (Evans and King, 1991). These developments have implicitly or explicitly diminished the power of learners (Edwards, 1991). There has also been an increasing use of the OUs by the state as mainstream educational endeavour to serve its political purposes and in the process this system has lost its innocence (Tait, 1994). These processes, issues and directions are widely replicated in the Indian context.

Unequal Social and Regional Spread of Higher Education in India

Social and regional divides are widely depicted in the spread of higher education system and in the GER therein in India. These divides carry significant social ramifications for the emergence of knowledge society in India. Table 4.18 shows that though higher education GER is increasing among the disadvantaged social categories and even in the rural areas, this increase is yet to be in proportion to their representation in total population except for the scheduled tribes. Again, this disparity remains in relation to the advanced and backward social categories and rural and urban divides. During the period between 2004–2005 and 2007–2008, the GER for the scheduled caste has increased from 8.72 per cent to 11.54 per cent showing an increase of 32.33 per cent, Other Backward Classes (OBCs) 11.48 per cent to 14.72 per cent with an increase of 28.22 per cent, Muslim 8.5 per cent to 9.51 per cent with an increase of 11.88 per cent, rural areas 8.42 per cent to 16.18 per cent with an

Table 4.18 *Gross Enrolment Ratio in Higher Education by Social Categories*

Categories (%)	2004–2005	2007–2008	% Increase
SC (16)	8.72	11.54	32.33
ST (8)	8.44	7.67	–9.12
OBC (52)	11.48	14.72	28.22
Muslim (14)	8.5	9.51	11.88
Others (10)	22.52	26.64	18.29
Rural (65)	8.42	11.06	31.35
Urban (35)	16.18	19.03	17.61
Total	14.19	17.21	21.28

Source: NSS 61st and 64th Round.

increase of 31.35 per cent and urban areas 16.18 per cent to 19.03 per cent with an increase of 17.61 per cent and for the scheduled tribes, it has declined from 8.44 per cent to 7.67 per cent with a decline of 9.12 per cent. In fact, scheduled tribes have least GER followed by the Muslims, scheduled castes and the OBCs and the others in ascending order. Low GER is historically rooted, socioeconomically conditioned and has adverse implications for their integration and mobility in the knowledge economy. Significantly, however, the increasing growth rates of GER, especially those that have been higher for the rural than the urban areas and higher among the scheduled castes and the OBCs than the 'others', show a break in the stagnation in excess to higher education by a section of the marginalised people and the backward areas of the country.

The spread of university and university-level institutions has also been very uneven in the country. A comparison, as shown in Table 4.19, explicitly depicts that Delhi has 26 university/university-level institutions and 180 colleges, Maharashtra has 44 and 5970, Tamil Nadu 59 and 2885, Uttar Pradesh 56 and 4268, and West Bengal 26 and 817, respectively,

Table 4.19 Number of Recognised Educational Institutions in India and Population–Institution Ratio

States/ Union Territories	Population (2011)	Pre-Degree/ Junior Colleges/ Higher Sec. Schools (per Lakh)	High/ Post Basic Schools (per Lakh)	Middle/ Sr. Basic Schools (per Lakh)	Primary/ Jr. Basic Schools (per Lakh)	Universities/ Deemed Universities (per Lakh)	Colleges for Professional Education (per Lakh)
Maharashtra	11,23,72,972	5019	16,455	27,654	49,095	44	5970
Tamil Nadu	7,21,38,958	3660	3112	9610	28,218	59	2885
Uttar Pradesh	19,95,81,477	9751	7893	53,281	1,47,376	56	4268
West Bengal	9,13,47,736	4341	4454	2623	49,908	26	817
Delhi	1,67,53,235	1392	480	588	2563	26	180

Source: 1. Statistics of School Education 2010–2011. 2. Statistics of Higher & Technical Education 2009–2010, Planning Commission, 2013, http://indiabudget.nic.in.

as of 2011. The number of students enrolled in these institutions are 20,60,334 for Delhi, 18,28,341 for Maharashtra, 10,60,543 for Tamil Nadu, 22,18,243 for Uttar Pradesh and 9,13,722 for West Bengal. However, in terms of population, student and institution ratio, there are severe variations among these states from North, South East and West as shown in Table 4.19. For 1 lakh population Delhi and Tamil Nadu have higher population educational institutions than Maharashtra, West Bengal and Uttar Pradesh. In fact, the higher extent of urbanisation is linked to higher population educational institution ratio in the country.

In view of the non-uniformity in the expansion of higher and technical education in India, the Planning Commission (2012) has suggested a holistic and balanced expansion approach to target underrepresented sections of society; and accordingly to set up new institutions to bridge regional imbalances and disparities across disciplines and to address special economic, social and technological needs of the country.

VIII. Changing Educational Background of Work Force

Despite the above-mentioned challenges for the education system, India now experiences a paradigm shift in the educational background of its population, and a qualitative change in the knowledge and skill component of its manpower.

In India, the proportion of illiterates is in the decline among the workforce. Table 4.20 shows that in 1983, of the total workers 43.4 per cent were illiterates. The proportion of this category of workers declined to 36.83 per cent in 1993–1994, to 30 per cent in 2004–2005

Table 4.20 *Percentage Distribution of Rural Labour Force by Levels of Education*

Level of Education	1983	1993–1994	2004–2005	2009–2010
Illiterate	43.40	36.83	30.00	29.14
Primary and below	31.50	34.34	37.92	24.23
Illiterates and Least Educated	83.56	78.17	74.58	53.37
Middle Level	8.38	12.39	13.13	17.64
Sec. & Hr. Secondary	6.22	6.75	8.89	20.34
Graduation and above	1.76	2.69	3.12	8.67

Source: NSSO 38th, 50th and 61st, 64th round.

and further to 29.4 per cent in 2009–2010. The proportion of workers with primary and below level education has increased from 31.5 per cent in 1983 to 34.4 per cent in 1993–1994, 37.92 per cent in 2004–2005 and declined to 24.33 in 2009–2010. It is important that the proportion of illiterate and least educated labour force declined from 83 per cent to 56 per cent in 1983 to 53.3 in 2009–2010. This has been simultaneously marked by an increase in the attainment of middle, secondary and higher secondary level education among the work force. The proportion of workers with middle level of education background has increased from 8.38 per cent in 1983 to 17.64 per cent in 2009–2010, secondary and higher secondary education background from 6.22 per cent to 20.34 per cent and graduation and above level of education from only 1.79 per cent to 8.67 per cent during the same period.

The general interface between education and work participation as shown in Tables 4.19, 4.20, 4.21 and 4.22 indicates that increasing work participation is linked to increase in the literacy rate. In general, males have significantly higher rates of work participation, due to the higher rates of literacy; and also there is the cultural factor whereby males are considered to be the breadwinners of the family. The gender gap in literacy and in work participation has remained highly explicit in India. Higher the extent of gender gap in literacy rate, higher is the extent of the gender gap in work participation.

Table 4.21 *Male–Female Literacy, Work Participation and the Gender Gap (1991–2001) in India*

Changing Literacy and Work Participation								
Year	Literacy Rate				Work Participation			
	Male	Female	Gender Gap	Total	Male	Female	Gender Gap	Total
1971	45.95	21.93	23.98	34.45	52.6	12.11	40.49	33.8
1991	64.1	39.3	24.71	52.2	51.5	22.7	28.8	37.7
2011	82.14	64.46	17.68	74.04	51.7	25.6	26.1	39.1

Source: Population Census, 2001; Office of the Registrar General, India.

Table 4.22 *Literacy Rate and Work Participation by Gender 2011*

State	Literacy Rate			Work Participation			Population	
	Male	Female	Gender Gap	Male	Female	Gender Gap	SC	ST
Delhi	91.03	80.93	10.10	52.98	10.57	42.41	16.76	Nil
Maharashtra	89.82	75.48	14.34	56.0	31.05	24.95	18.08	9.35
Tamil Nadu	86.81	73.86	12.97	59.31	31.79	27.52	20.01	1.10
Uttar Pradesh	79.24	59.26	19.98	47.51	16.75	30.76	20.69	0.56
West Bengal	82.67	71.16	11.51	57.07	18.08	38.99	23.5	5.8
India	82.14	65.46	16.68	53.25	25.51	27.74	16.63	8.61

Source: Census of India 2011.

Majority of Indian work force still work in agriculture. Significantly work participation in agriculture has remained socioculturally conditioned. High concentration of the scheduled castes and the scheduled tribes in agriculture is positively linked to higher degree of illiteracy among these groups. Again, women's work participation in agriculture, is very common among these groups as work participation in the extra mural manual activities is customarily permitted for women among these caste and ethnic groups. It is simultaneously important that the spread of literacy and education is positively linked to withdrawal from the extra mural manual activities and upward social mobility among all social groups including those of the scheduled castes and tribes. This is also linked to the shift of work force from the agricultural to nonagricultural sector (to be discussed in Chapter 6).

Both at the all India and the state levels, rural women have a higher rate of work participation than their urban counterparts despite having low level of literacy and education among them. It is because of the fact that women especially from the scheduled castes, tribes and OBC backgrounds still overwhelmingly participate in agricultural activities in rural areas. Maharashtra and Tamil Nadu have significantly high rates of rural women's work participation than those of Delhi, Uttar Pradesh and West Bengal.

The general trends suggest that at the all-India level, the extent of work participation has increased among all categories of literate and educated workers cutting across the rural and urban divide. Though the literate and educated male workers of both the rural and urban areas have substantially higher rate of work participation than those of their female counterparts, the work participation of the literate and educated female work force has also increased substantially both in rural and in urban areas. Significantly, the work participation rate of the rural literate and educated female work force has increased at a faster rate than their urban counterparts. This crucial change indicates the potential of a shift in the work participation from agricultural to the nonagricultural sector of the economy.

As indicated earlier, males having a higher rate of literacy have a higher rate of work participation than females who have a relatively lower rate of work participation with low rate of literacy. However, this work participation rate is also locally and socioculturally conditioned. Delhi, despite having a high rate of female literacy with 80.93 per cent, has only 10.57 per cent rate of female work participation. It is widely pointed out that gender-hostile working environment discourages women's work participation despite having a higher degree of literacy.

Maharashtra has 75.48 per cent and Tamil Nadu 73.86 per cent literacy rate for female and has got 31.05 per cent and 31.79 per cent rate of female work participation, respectively. Both the states have relatively lower gender gap in work participation than the other states. Uttar Pradesh has 59.26 per cent and West Bengal 71.16 per cent female literacy rate with 16.75 per cent and 18.08 per cent female work participation rate, respectively. Both the states have got significant gender gap in work participation rate. At the all-India level, while the female literacy rate is 65.46 per cent, female work participation is to the extent of 25.51 per cent. It is important that the increased rate of literacy and conducive working environment are important to ensure high rate of work participation.

While India enters the knowledge society, its educated labour force encounters the problem of increasing unemployment. The unemployment rate in present India has become increasingly higher among the educated than the illiterate; and higher the level of education, the higher is the extent of unemployment (The Employment and Unemployment Survey of India 2012).

Table 4.23 shows that the unemployment rate among the illiterates is to the extent of 1.2 per cent while the rate among the overall is 3.8 per cent. The unemployment rate among the primary level educated is 1.7 per cent and for the urban and rural areas these are 2.1 per cent and 1.6 per cent, respectively. Among the workers with secondary level education, this rate is 5.4 per cent with the urban and rural rates being 4.4 per cent and 5.8 per cent. Among the workers with

Table 4.23 *Educated Unemployed in India 2012*

Level	Urban	Rural	Total
Illiterate	1.3	1.1	1.2
Primary	2.1	1.6	1.7
Secondary	4.4	5.8	5.4
Higher Secondary	7.3	7.8	7.3
Graduate	8.2	11.0	9.4
Postgraduate	7.7	13.9	10.0
All	5.1	3.5	3.8

Source: *Labour Bureau 2012. Cf. Times of India, 18 July 2012, p. 1.*

higher secondary level of education, unemployment rate is 7.3 per cent with the rural and urban rates 7.8 per cent and 7.3 per cent. The unemployment rate among the workers with graduate level education is 9.4 per cent and postgraduate level is 10 per cent. For the urban graduates and postgraduates, unemployment rates are to the extent of 8.2 per cent and 7.7 per cent and for their rural counterparts these are to the extent of 11 per cent and 13.9 per cent, respectively. It is also shown that unemployment rate among the rural educated is higher than the urban educated as avenues for their employment in rural areas are conspicuously less than the urban areas and many of them lack proper information about the proper avenues for their employment. Again, a mismatch between the acquired educational qualification and available avenue of employment is another important factor for increasing unemployment among the educated youths. Significantly, the scheduled castes, scheduled tribes and OBCs have a low rate of unemployment than the general categories till the secondary levels of education (see Table 4.24). However, these categories with graduate and postgraduate degrees have higher levels of unemployment than the general categories. All these have composite bearing on the work participation patterns in the emerging knowledge society.

Indian education system is placed in the intersection of great demographic, economic and ideological shifts today; and to respond to these shifts India today experiences the emergence of multiple

Table 4.24 *Unemployment and Education by Caste*

Level	SC	ST	OBC	General	All
Illiterate	1.1	1.2	1.2	1.2	1.2
Primary	1.4	1.3	1.8	2.0	1.7
Secondary	4.9	4.6	3.9	7.7	5.4
Higher Secondary	8.4	7.5	7.1	7.5	7.3
Graduate	11.3	3.9	9.5	9.0	9.4
Postgraduate	12.7	2.5*	10.5	9.7	10.0
All	3.2	2.7	3.2	5.4	3.8

*Note: *No. of ST PG is very low.*
Source: Labour Bureau 2012. Cf. Times of India, 18 July 2012, p. 1.

educational processes widely facilitated by market liberalisation, on the one hand, and state control, on the other. At the ground level, these shifts are accompanied by faster expansion of private providers than the state providers of education and phenomenal proliferation of open and distance educational arrangements, fast expansion of educational infrastructure for professional education, increasing students' enrolment in the higher and technical and professional education, development of skilled and trained manpower in the country and a growing demand for technical and professional education. These have widely paved the way for mass production and use of knowledge at all levels and types of activities. Though these expansions have been uneven both in social and spatial terms, India today experiences a visible improvement in the educational background of the workers, increasing literacy rates among all sections of people, declining gender and rural-urban divides in educational attainment of people and workers. These shifts are again augmented by the fast interpenetration of ICTs in the country by creating a new environment of social being and becoming, and by bringing new possibilities and challenges for a new society in India. These shifts however have brought a host of paradoxes in society that swing between state commitment for educational expansion, on the one hand, and phenomenal market intervention and liberalisation, on the other; increasing rates of literacy, on the one hand, and persisting social and spatial disparities, on the other; growing need of technical and skilled manpower, on the one hand, and lack of quality assurance on education, on the other; improved educational background of the labour force, on the one hand, and prevalence of the high degree of unemployment among the educated work force, on the other; occupational diversification, mobility and choice for a section of workforce, on the one hand, and stagnation of a vast section of people in utter poverty and insecurity, on the other. Along with the proliferation of such education arrangements and contradictions therein, India enters into the domain of a knowledge society that is posited to be the hope of young India.

5

Information and Communication Technologies for Knowledge Society

I. ICTs: The Ever Greatest Mobiliser

Notwithstanding the debate as to whether technology shapes social progression or vice versa, it is widely acknowledged that technology has always remained a crucial component of development all through the progression of human society. Importantly, each stage of society is marked by the significance of specific type of technology, as plough was for the agrarian and steam engine for industrial, in recent decades Information and Communication Technologies (ICTs) have been for the knowledge society. Each of these technologies again functions in specific socioeconomic and political contexts as the agrarian technologies work in localised rural contexts, industrial technologies in the urban and national contexts, while ICTs in the global contexts cutting across the boundaries of geographical contextualisation, as knowledge does.

ICTs as the prime constituents of knowledge society along with globalisation have paved the way for the emergence of new waves of economy, culture and politics across the world. These waves are widely globalised and have brought into being phenomenal time–space compression in all areas of human activities, and have injected considerable new orientation, on the one hand, and disorientations in the preexisting institutional arrangements, values and norms, social interaction and behavioural and cultural practises, on the other. Though ICT, like any other technology, is a product of human brain, it works in association with human brain to generate power, knowledge, wealth, connectivity and new social and cultural dynamics. It works as both a cause and a function to the knowledge society allowing it to be manoeuvred and newly configured through the use of human intelligence at each and every moment. Moreover, all over the world it has brought a new economic order that is globally interlinked and locally intimidating and transformative.

Growth of ICTs in the World Scenario

Though all mass communication technologies, television, radio, newspaper, Internet, mobile phones and landline telephone form the broad foundation of the ICTs, in recent years Internet, mobile telephone and landline telephone have got privilege over the rest because of the multifaceted social, economic and political use of these technologies. Again amongst all these technologies Internet and mobile have occupied the key positions as the ever greatest communicators to revolutionise the process of production, storage, processing, transference of knowledge and the forms and intensity of social interconnectivity across the globe. This revolution has reached the doorsteps of trillions of millions of humanity in an unparalleled and unprecedented speed. Though the developed countries have reached a high-level penetration of these technologies, the developing nations are also endeavouring to catch up with the momentum.

Internet is the game changer of modern civilisation. The multi-dimensional use of Internet has not only interconnected the world with an alternate mode of economic order, but also a new sense of being and becoming. The unprecedented social adaptability of Internet has been delineated in its high rate of penetration across the world. In 1995, all over the world, there were only 16 million Internet users who constitute only 0.4 per cent of the world population. In December 2000, this increased to 361 million users constituting 5.8 per cent of the world population. In June 2012, it increased to 2405 million constituting 34.3 per cent of the world population to be Internet users. During the period between 2000 and 2012 June, there was a growth of 566.4 per cent in Internet users across the world. The number of Internet users is increasing every moment. As per the March 2013 world level data, there are 2749 million Internet users in the globe who altogether constitute 38.8 per cent of the world population. However, it has been observed that the nature and extent of growth and penetration of Internet has been highly oclectic among the nations even though it is growing phenomenally across the globe. In general, it has been linked to the state of economic and educational development, on the one hand, and population size, on the other. In recent years, the developing areas of the world are getting a faster rate of penetration than the developed areas. Many now occupy the position within the first 20 users of Internet in the world.

As shown in Table 5.1, most of the developed countries with high rate of penetration and absolute number of users belong to the first

Table 5.1 *Top 20 Countries with Highest Number of Internet Users – 30 June 2012*

S. No.	Country or Region	Population, 2012 (million)	Internet Users Year 2000 (million)	Internet Users Year 2012 (million)	Penetration (% Population)	Growth Rate 2000–2012	Users % World
1	China	1343.2	22.5	538.0	40.1	2291.1	22.4
2	United States	313.8	95.4	245.2	78.1	157.2	10.2
3	India	1205.1	5.0	137.0	11.4	2640.0	5.7
4	Japan	127.4	47.1	101.2	79.5	115.0	4.2
5	Brazil	194.0	5.0	88.5	45.6	1669.9	3.7
6	Russia	142.5	3.1	68.0	47.7	2093.0	2.8
7	Germany	81.3	24.0	67.5	83.0	181.2	2.8
8	Indonesia	248.6	2.0	55.0	22.1	2650.0	2.3
9	United Kingdom	63.0	15.4	52.7	83.6	242.4	2.2
10	France	65.6	8.5	52.2	79.6	514.5	2.2
11	Nigeria	170.1	0.2	48.4	28.4	24,083.1	2.0
12	Mexico	115.0	2.7	42.0	36.5	1448.4	1.7
13	Iran	78.9	0.3	42.0	53.3	16,700.0	1.7
14	Korea	48.9	19.0	40.3	82.5	111.8	1.7
15	Turkey	79.7	2.0	36.5	45.7	1722.8	1.5
16	Italy	61.3	13.2	35.8	58.4	171.2	1.5
17	Philippines	103.8	2.0	33.6	32.4	1580.0	1.4
18	Spain	47.0	5.4	31.6	67.2	486.6	1.3
19	Vietnam	91.5	0.2	31.0	33.9	15,417.5	1.3
20	Egypt	83.7	0.5	29.8	35.6	6524.4	1.2
	TOP 20 Countries	4664.5	273.4	1776.4	38.1	549.8	73.8
	Rest of the World	2353.4	87.6	629.2	26.7	618.1	26.2
	Total World Users	7017.8	361.0	2405.5	34.3	566.4	100.0

Source: http://www.internetworldstats.com/top20.htm

20 users of Internet. The United States with more than 245.2 million users and 78.1 per cent rate of penetration occupies the second position, Japan with 101.2 million users and 79.5 per cent penetration occupies the fourth, Germany with 67.5 million users and 83 per cent penetration occupies the seventh, United Kingdom with 52.7 million users and 83.6 per cent penetration occupies the ninth, France with 52.2 million users and 79.6 per cent penetration occupies the 10th, Korea with 40.3 million users and 82.5 per cent penetration users occupies the 14th, Italy with 35.8 million users and 58.4 per cent penetration occupies the 16th, Spain with 31.6 million users and 67.2 per cent penetration occupies the 18th among the top 20 users of Internet across the globe. However, the numerical strength of human population is a big asset in the contemporary world. China with 538.0 million users and 40 per cent rate of penetration occupies the first position, India with 137 million users and only 11.4 per cent penetration occupies the second, Brazil with 88.5 million users and 45.6 per cent penetration occupies the third, Russia with 68 million users and 47.7 per cent rate of penetration occupies the sixth, Indonesia with 55 million Internet users and 21.1 per cent penetration rate occupies the eighth, Nigeria with 48.4 million users and 28.4 per cent rate of penetration occupies the 11th, Mexico with 42 million users and 36.5 per cent rate of penetration occupies the 12th, Iran with 42 million users and 53.3 per cent penetration occupies the 13th, Turkey with 36.4 million users and 45.7 per cent penetration occupies the 15th, Philippines with 33.6 per cent users and 32.4 per cent penetration occupies the 17th, Vietnam with 31 million users and 33.9 per cent penetration occupies the 19th and Egypt with 29.8 million users and 35.6 per cent penetration occupies the 20th of the top 20 users of Internet in the contemporary world. The top 20 countries altogether control 73.3 per cent internet users of the world.

The nations such as Canada, Australia, Denmark and many other countries though have more than 80 per cent rate of penetration of Internet; significantly in terms of absolute number of users and their world share they are yet to be the part of top 20 users of Internet in the world. The Asian countries in general and India and China in particular have higher number of users of Internet, higher world share and high growth rate of Internet penetration. For example, India has recorded 2640 per cent growth rate in the penetration of Internet in the period between 2000 and 2012 even though has only 5.7 per cent world share and China has 22.4 per cent world share and 2291.1 per cent growth rate during this period. Such variations are widely among the continents.

Globally, the ICTs are also spreading very fast across the continents though in an unequal speed. Among the continents/subcontinents, North America that had got the highest rate of penetration in 2009 with 76.2 per cent has increased to 78.6 per cent rate of penetration in 2012, followed by Oceania/Australia from 60.8 per cent in 2009 to 67.6 per cent in 2012, Europe from 53.8 per cent in 2009 to 63.2 per cent in 2012, Latin America/Caribbean from 31.9 per cent in 2009 to 42.9 per cent in 2012, Middle East from 28.8 per cent in 2009 to 40.20 per cent in 2012, Asia from 21.1 per cent in 2009 to 27.5 per cent in 2012 and Africa from 8.7 per cent in 2009 to 15.6 per cent in 2012.

Significantly, the African region has registered 3606.7 per cent growth in Internet users during 2000–2012. However, this region constituted only 7 per cent of the Internet users of the world in 2012. Similarly, though the Middle East exhibited 2639.9 per cent growth during 2000–2012 contributed only 3.7 per cent of the world users of Internet in 2012. Latin America has also registered a very high growth rate with 1301.8 per cent during 2000–2012 with a world share of 10.6 per cent in 2012.

Though Europe, North America and Oceania/Australia have got a high rate of penetration, their world shares are relatively low because of their population size. Their present Internet growth rates are relatively moderate as they have already achieved very high rates of penetration in the previous years. In Europe, during 2000–2012, the Internet penetration has registered growth rates of 393.4 per cent. However, Europe's world share has declined from 23.6 per cent in 2009 to 21.5 per cent in 2012. Similarly, North America has got a penetration growth rate of 153.3 per cent in 2012 with declining world shares from 14.4 per cent in 2009 to 11.4 per cent in 2012. The Internet penetration in Oceania/Australia regions also experienced a growth of 218.7 per cent during 2000–2012 with declining world shares from 1.2 per cent in 2009 to 1.0 per cent in 2012.

Significantly, while the developed parts of the world are showing moderate growth rates, and declining world shares, the developing world of Asia retained its high growth rates and registered an increase world share in Internet usage. During 2000–2012, Internet penetration has shown a growth of 841.9 per cent in Asia; and its world share has increased from 42.4 per cent in 2009 to 44.8 per cent in 2012. The high rates of Internet penetration and increase in world share are linked to high rates of economic growth and occupational mobility in this region of the world in recent years (Table 5.2).

Table 5.2 *World Internet Usage and Population Statistics, 30 June 2012*

Continents	Population (2012 Est.) (million)	Internet Users (million)		Penetration (%)		Growth 2000–2012	Users % of Table	
		December 2000	June 2012	2009	2012		2009	2012
Africa	1073.4	4.5	167.3	8.7	15.6	3606.7	4.8	7.0
Asia	3922.1	114.3	1076.7	21.1	27.5	841.9	42.4	44.8
Europe	820.9	105.1	518.5	53.8	63.2	393.4	23.6	21.5
Middle East	223.6	3.3	90.0	28.8	40.2	2639.9	3.2	3.7
North America	348.3	108.1	273.8	76.2	78.6	153.3	14.4	11.4
Latin America/ Caribbean	593.7	18.1	254.9	31.9	42.9	1310.8	10.4	10.6
Oceania/ Australia	35.9	7.6	24.3	60.8	67.6	218.7	1.2	1.0
World Total	7017.8	361.0	2405.5	26.6	34.3	566.4		100

Source: www.internetworldstats.com

In terms of absolute number, the Asian region has the highest number of users in 2000 with 114.3 million that has increased to 1076.7 million in 2012. It is followed by Europe with 105.1 million in 2000, which has increased to 518.5 million in 2012, North America with 108.1 million in 2000 that increased to 273.8 million in 2012, Latin America and the Caribbean 18.1 million in 2000 that increased to 254.9 million in 2012, Africa with 4.5 million in 2000 that increased to 167.3 million in 2012, Middle East with 3.3 million in 2000 that increased to 90.0 million in 2012 and Oceania/Australia with 7.6 million in 2011 that increased to 24.3 million in 2012.

ICTs in Asia

Within the Asian region China, Japan and India occupy the leading position in Internet usage. Table 5.3 shows that India had the third highest number of Internet users with 81 million to follow Japan with 96 million and China with 384 million in 2009. India however now occupies the second position within Asia in Internet usage, which substantially increased to 137 million in 2012 to follow China that still occupies the first position with 538 million users. In 2012, Indonesia occupied the fourth position with 55 million users followed by South Korea with 40.3 million, Vietnam 31 million, Philippines 33.6 million, Pakistan 29.1 million, Thailand 20.1 million and Malaysia 17.7 million. However, this order was somewhat different in 2009 wherein South Korea occupied the fourth position with 37.6 million, followed by Indonesia with 30 million, Philippines 24 million, Vietnam 22.8 million, Pakistan 18.5 million, Malaysia 16.9 million and Thailand 16.1 million users.

Table 5.3 *Internet Use among Top 10 Nations in Asia in 2009 and 2012 (in Millions)*

Country	Popula- tion 2012 (million)	2009 (million)	Position within the Top 10 in 2009	Users 2012 (million)	Position within the Top 10 in 2012	Growth Rate 2009– 2012	Penetra- tion 2012 (%)
China	1343.2	384	1	538	1	40.1	40.1
Japan	127.3	96	2	101.2	3	5.4	79.5
India	1205.0	81	3	137	2	69.1	11.4
South Korea	48.8	37.6	4	40.3	5	7.1	82.6
Indonesia	248.6	30	5	55	4	83.3	22.1
Philippines	103.7	24	6	33.6	6	40	32.4
Vietnam	91.5	22.8	7	31	7	36	33.9
Pakistan	190.2	18.5	8	29.1	8	57.2	15.3
Malaysia	29.1	16.9	9	17.7	10	4.7	60.8
Thailand	67.0	16.1	10	20.1	9	24.8	30

Source: www.internetworldstats.com/stats3.htm 2009, 2012.

India has got the second highest growth rate of Internet penetration during 2009–2012 with 69.1 per cent to follow only Indonesia with 83.3 per cent having the highest growth rate in Asia. On the other hand, China has got 40.1 per cent, Japan 5.4 per cent, South Korea 7.1 per cent, Philippines 40 per cent, Vietnam 36 per cent, Pakistan 57.2 per cent, Malaysia 4.7 per cent and Thailand 24.8 per cent growth rate during the same period. With the high growth rate in Internet penetration, Internet users of India constitute 12 per cent of the Asian and 5.7 per cent of the world users of Internet in 2012. India now occupies a distinctive position in Internet use among the South Asian Association of Regional Cooperation (SAARC) countries. The details of Internet penetration in SAARC countries are given in Table 5.4.

Table 5.4 *Internet Usage in SAARC Countries*

ASIA	Population (2012 Est.)	Internet Users (Year 2000)	Internet Users 30 June 2012	Pen- etra- tion 2012	SAARC	Facebook 31 December 2011	Facebook 31 December 2012	Growth Rate 2011– 2012
Afghanistan	30,41,9928	1000	15,20,996	5.0	0.84	2,57,180	3,84,220	49.4
Bangladesh	16,10,83,804	1,00,000	80,54,190	5.0	4.43	22,52,800	33,52,680	48.8
Bhutan	7,16,896	500	1,50,548	21	0.08	64,000	82,040	28.2
India	120,50,73,612	50,00,000	13,70,00,000	11.4	75.32	4,13,99,720	6,27,13,680	51.5
Maldives	3,94,451	6000	1,34,860	34.2	0.07	1,14,100	1,36,760	19.9
Nepal	2,98,90,686	50,000	26,90,162	9.0	1.48	14,03,420	19,40,820	38.3
Pakistan	19,02,91,129	1,33,900	2,91,28,970	15.3	16.01	58,87,400	79,84,880	35.6
Sri Lanka	2,14,81,334	1,21,500	32,22,200	15.0	1.77	11,82,720	15,15,720	28.2
Total	163,93,51,840	54,12,900	18,19,01,926	11.1	100	5,25,61,340	7,81,10,800	48.6

Source: http://www.internetworldstats.com/stats3.htm#asia

Among the SAARC countries, India has the highest share in the total number of Internet users with 75.32 per cent followed by Pakistan 16.01 per cent, Bangladesh 4.43 per cent, Sri Lanka 1.77 per cent, Nepal 1.48 per cent, Afghanistan 0.84 per cent, Bhutan 0.08 per cent and Maldives 0.07 per cent. In the SAARC countries, the overall rate of Internet penetration was 11.1 per cent in 2012. Though Maldives with 34.2 per cent, Pakistan 15.3 per cent, Bhutan 21 per cent and Sri Lanka 15 per cent have higher degree of penetration in Internet than India with 11.4 per cent, in terms of absolute number of users India stands well ahead of all other SARRAC countries.

Along with the increasing access to Internet not only the regular communication through email, but also through social media such as blogs, Twitter, Facebook is spreading like wild fire across the globe. The SAARC nations are not an exception to it. Over a period of only one year, December 2011 and December 2012, Facebook has registered 49.6 per cent growth in the SAARC countries. India is again the leading country in terms of both absolute number and the growth rate in the Facebook usage among the SAARC countries. During the last one year, Facebook usage has increased by 51.5 per cent in India followed by 49.4 per cent in Afghanistan, 48.8 per cent in Bangladesh, 38.3 per cent in Nepal, 35.6 per cent in Pakistan, 28.2 per cent in Sri Lanka and Bhutan and 19.9 per cent in Maldives.

II. The Patterns of Expansion of ICTs in India

Within India along with the high speed of penetration of Internet, there has been phenomenal expansion of mobile phone, landline telephone, television, radio newspaper and other related communication devices. However, the form and extent of expansion of these technologies have been very eclectic within the country in terms of their social relevance, economic affordability of the people and market accessibility following the global trend.

Growth of Telecom in India

In recent years, the telecom sector of India has achieved phenomenal growth in view of both increase in the size of subscribers and generation of revenue. According to the Telecommunication Regulatory Authority of India (TRAI, 2011) in the telecom sector while the number of subscribers reached the first 1 million mark only 25 years after independence, 100 million in April 2005, 500 million in September 2009, it is set to surpass the 1 billion mark much before December 2014. This sector, on an average, has added about 18.8 million subscribers during the last year; and the total number of subscribers has crossed 826 million by the end of February 2011, 926.53 million at the end of December 2011 and 965.52 million by June 2012. Thus, India surpassed the number of telephone connections in the United States in March 2008 and has grown to be the world's second largest market after China (TRAI, 2011, 2012).

Internet and Broadband

Though access to Internet and broadband access has become a precondition to foster economic development and meaningful social transformation, their growth has so far been modest in India. The net broadband addition per month is just 0.2–0.3 million in contrast to around 18 million mobile connections per month in the country (TRAI, 2011). The Internet subscriber base in the country stood at 23.01 million at the end of June 12 in comparison to 6.70 million in December 2005, registering a growth rate of about 234.17 million during this period. The number of broadband subscribers increased to 13.35 million at the end of December 2011, and again to 14.57 million in 2012 (TRAI, 2011, 2012).

Though India has acquired the distinction to be one of the fastest growing telecommunication markets of the world and there has been quantum increase in the telecommunication service users in the recent years, the spread of these technologies has been very uneven in terms of both types (mobile and fixed line, etc.) of this technology and rural–urban penetration rate of the same (see Table 5.5). In the wake of ICTs

Table 5.5 *Telephone Subscribers Base, Village Public Telephone, Internet*

Bases	December 2005	June 2012	Percentage Change
Total Subscribers (Million)	116.94	965.52	725.7
Rural Subscribers (Million)		343.76	
Rural Teledensity		40.66%	
Urban Subscribers (Million)		621.76	
Urban Teledensity		169.03%	
Wireline Total (Million)	41.00	31.43	−23.3
Wireline Teledensity	4.47%	2.59%	−42.1
Wireline Rural (Million)	12.56	7.25	−42.3
Wireline Urban (Million)	28.44	24.17	−15.0
Wireless Total (Million)	75.94	934.09	1130.0
Wireless Teledensity	6.95%	76.99%	1007.8
Wireless Rural (Million)		336.51	
Wireless Urban (Million)		597.59	
Village Public Telephone VPTs (Million)	5.39	0.58	−89.24
Public Call Office (PCOs) (Million)	3.73	1.71	−54.2
Internet (Million)	6.70	23.01	243.4
Broadband Subscribers (Million)		14.57	

Source: TRAI, 2006, 2012 Indian Telecom Services Performance Indicator, April–June 2006, June 2012

revolution India has been experiencing the ever fastest expansion of mobile (wireless) users, quantum increase in the Internet subscribers and a decline in the fixed line (wireline) users across the country. In June 2012, the overall size of telephone (both the wireline and wireless) subscribers has increased to 965.52 million from 116.94 million in December 2005 registering 725.7 per cent growth over a period of six years. Of these total subscribers in 2012, 621.76 million are from urban and 343.76 million from rural areas. In 2012, the rural and urban overall teledensities (both wireline and wireless) were to the extent of 40.66 per cent and 169.03 per cent, respectively. India, however, has witnessed differential growth in the wireline and wireless telephony. Importantly, the wireline subscribers have declined from 41.00 million in December 2005 to 31.43 million in June 2012 and its teledensity from 4.47 per cent to 2.59 per cent during the same period. The wireline has simultaneously declined in both rural and the urban areas. In the rural areas, it declined from 12.56 million to 7.25 million and in the urban areas from 28.44 million to 24.17 million during the same period under reference. The wireless sector, on the other hand, has grown phenomenally from only 75.94 million with a teledensity of 6.95 per cent in 2005 to 934.09 million with a teledensity of 76.99 per cent in 2012. Of the total wireless subscribers in 2012, 336.50 million belong to the rural and 579.59 million to the urban areas.

With the increase in the use of wireless telephone, the Village Public Telephone (VPT) centres and Public Call Office (PCOs) have significantly declined from 5.39 million and 3.73 million in 2005 to 0.58 million and 1.71 million, respectively, in 2012. The decline of wireline subscribers, VPTs and PCOs, is accompanied by the increase in mobile/ wireless subscribers and increase in Internet and broadband users as indicated above.

Increasing Take Over of Telecom Services by Private Sector

Economic liberalisation and globalisation provide the wider contexts for the ICTs' penetration in contemporary India. The changing extent of telecom penetration in the country is linked to changing state policy in this sector, and the consequent privatisation of a large part of this service. Though with the increasing involvement of private operators in this sector there has been phenomenal expansion of telephone services across the country, their involvement has been higher in wireless than in the wireline services. On the other hand, though the private operator's penetration has increased in the Internet services in the recent years, the public sector undertaking still controls two-thirds of this market share. As shown in Table 5.6 in June 2012 in the wireless connection, the market share of private operator has been to the extent of 88.9 per cent and that of the Public Sector Undertaking (PSUs) only 11.1 per cent. While

Table 5.6 *Market Share of Operators in June 2012*

	Private Operator	PSU Operator	Teledensity
Wireless (%)	88.9	11.1	79.58
Wireline (%)	19.93	80.1	2.59
Internet (%)	33.7	66.3	

Source: TRAI, 2013 Indian Telecom Services Performance Indicator, 2012 (ITSPI).

in the wireline and Internet connections, the share of PSUs has been to the extent of 80.1 per cent and 66.3 per cent, the share of private sector has been to the extent of 19.93 per cent and 33.7 per cent, respectively. In general, however, the presence of the private operators has increased wireline, wireless and Internet density in the country.

Significantly, along with the private penetration in the tele-communication sector, there have been significant proliferations of private satellite channels, pay channels, FM private radio stations, DTC subscribers and set-top boxes uses in notified areas. The details are given in Table 5.7.

Table 5.7 *Private Operator's Penetration in Broadcasting, Cable, Satellite, Pay Channel, FM Radio, DTH Services*

Broadcasting and Cable Services	Number
Number of private satellite TV channels registered with Ministry of I&B (as on 6 March 2012)	831
Number of pay channels	184
Number of private FM radio stations	245
DTH Subscribers registered with Pvt. SPs	48.45 million
Number of set-top boxes in CAS-notified areas	10,01,033

Source: TRAI, 2012.

Mass Media and Communication Technology

According to United Nations, the journey of any country to the knowledge-based economy has to be accompanied by fast expansion of the mass media and communication technology. In 1981 (a period unaffected by globalisation), while only 2.2 per cent of the population had access to newspaper, this access increased to 2.75 per cent in 1991, 5.7 per cent in 2001 and 8.7 per cent in 2009. In 1981, only 26 per cent of country population was covered by radio. This coverage increased for 79 per cent population in 1991, 89 per cent in 2001 and 99 per cent in 2009. India has got high degree of television coverage since 1980s with 89 per cent coverage in 1982, which has increased to 99 per cent in 2009. However, with increasing people's access to television, VCD, VCP, etc., the number of cinema halls has declined in recent years. In 1981, there were 10,813 cinema halls in the country that increased to 13,181 in 1991. However, it has subsequently declined to 11,898 in 2001 and again to 8521 in 2009 (Table 5.8).

Table 5.8 *Access to Telephone, Newspaper, Cinema Hall in India over the Decades*

	1981	1991	2001	2009
Newspaper Per 100 population	2.2	2.75	5.7	8.7
No. of Cinema Hall	10,813	13,181	11,898	8521
Percentage of population covered by radio	26	79	89	99
Percentage of population covered by television	89	95	99	92

Source: Office of the Registrar of Newspapers for India, and Ministry of Information and Broadcasting.

The broadcasting sector consisting of television and radio services has facilitated the expansion of knowledge society in diverse ways. According to the TRAI (2012), India has become the world's third largest TV market after China and the United States. During the year 2010–2011, the TV owning households in India have grown from 136 million to 143 million, which amounts to an increase in penetration of TV services from 58 per cent to 61 per cent in the Indian households. During the same period, total number of registered TV channels grew from 524 to 649 including the pay channels whose number increased from 147 to 155.

III. Regional Divides in ICT Access in India

The expansion of ICTs in India has been widely influenced by preexisting social, regional and spatial divides. Such divides are visible even in the context of the selected five states that belong to the category of top 10 ICT users of the country. Following the national trend in all the selected states from East (West Bengal), West (Maharashtra), North (Uttar Pradesh) and South (Tamil Nadu) and in all four metro cities of Delhi, Kolkata, Mumbai and Chennai, the number of wireline subscribers has been lower to that of wireless subscribers (Table 5.9). In Maharashtra state, of the total subscribers of 113.0 million, 107.36 million are wireless while only 5.63 million are the wireline subscribers. Significantly, Maharashtra has acquired 96.97 per cent teledensity, of which 92.14 per cent are of wireless and only 4.83 per cent are of wireline teledensity. Again, there are 42.92 million Internet subscribers in Maharashtra.

In Tamil Nadu, of the 80.70 million subscribers, 79.53 million are of wireless and the remaining 3.17 millions are wireline subscribers. This state also has 25.26 million Internet subscribers. Uttar Pradesh has only 9.98 million Internet subscribers. Of the total 134.66 million telecommunication subscribers in Uttar Pradesh, 132.89 million are wireless and only 1.98 million are wireline subscribers. West Bengal has 74.61 million telecommunication subscribers, of which 72.83 are wireless and the remaining 1.78 million are wireline subscribers. This state has 8.81 millions of Internet subscribers. Delhi has a total of 45.4 million telecommunication subscribers of which 42.81 million are wireless and the remaining 2.92 million are wireline subscribers. So far as the Internet is concerned, in Delhi there are 22.66 million Internet subscribers. Similarly, in Mumbai, of the total 40.24 million telecommunication subscribers, 37.62 millions are wireless and the remaining 2.62 million are wireline subscribers. In Kolkata, of the 26.74 millions telecommunication subscribers, 25.58 millions are wireless and the remaining 1.16 are wireline subscribers.

Rural–Urban Divide

At the all-India level, the overall teledensity is to the extent of 79.58 per cent with the rural being 40.66 per cent and the urban 169.03 per cent registering a rural–urban gap by 128.37 per cent. The wireless

Table 5.9 *Wireline, Wireless and Internet/Broadband Users in Selected States and Metros in India as on 31 December 2012*

State	Tele Access (in Millions)			Internet/ Broadband (in Million)
	Wireline & Wireless	Wireless	Wireline	
Maharashtra including Mumbai	113.00	107.36	5.63	42.92
Tamil Nadu including Chennai	80.70	79.53	3.17	26.26
Uttar Pradesh	134.66	132.89	1.98	9.98
West Bengal including Kolkata	74.61	72.83	1.78	8.81
Delhi	45.4	42.81	2.92	22.66
Mumbai	40.24	37.62	2.62	
Kolkata	26.74	25.58	1.16	
All India	965.52	934.09	31.43	

Note: Ratio to be worked out.
Source: TRAI, 2011 December, The Indian Telecom Services Performance Indicator (ITSPI).

teledensity of India is to the extent of 76.99 per cent with 39.40 per cent for rural and 162.46 per cent for the urban areas with a rural–urban gap by 123.06 per cent. The wireline teledensity of India is only to the extent of 2.59 per cent while the urban wireline teledensity 6.57 per cent and the rural being only 0.86 per cent (Table 5.10).

Among the selected states again there have been sharp rural urban

Table 5.10 *Rural–Urban Teledensity among Selected States as on June 2012*

State	Wireline + Wireless (Million)	Teledensity			Wireless Density			Wireline Density		
		Rural	Urban	Overall	Rural	Urban	Overall	Rural	Urban	Overall
Maharashtra + Mumbai		53.81	145.71	96.97	26.32	136.66	92.14	1.09	9.05	4.83
Tamil Nadu + Chennai		57.20	167.47	119.05	67.29	160.80	114.49	1.86	6.67	4.56
Uttar Pradesh (E + W)		33.99	161.05	62.48	16.99	157.82	61.56	0.25	3.23	0.92
West Bengal + Kolkata		43.77	175.55	81.35	41.70	169.82	79.40	0.44	5.73	1.95
Delhi				235.34			220.27			15.27
All India		40.66	169.03	79.58	39.40	162.46	76.99	0.86	6.57	2.59

Note: Figure in the parenthesis is the rural–urban gap.
Source: TRAI, 2012 (ITSPI).

divides. For Maharashtra, while the overall teledensity is 96.97 per cent, the teledensity for rural and urban areas are 53.81 per cent and 145.71 per cent, respectively, showing a rural–urban gap of around 91.90 per cent. Again while wireless teledensity is 92.14 per cent, for the rural and urban areas, these are 26.32 per cent and 136.66 per cent, respectively, showing a rural–urban gap of 110.34 per cent. Similarly, for wireline, the overall, rural and urban teledensities are 4.83 per cent, 1.09 per cent and 9.05 per cent, respectively. Thus, the rural areas substantially lag behind in teledensity. Such scenario is also reflected for Tamil Nadu, West Bengal and Uttar Pradesh. Tamil Nadu has a total of 119.05 per cent overall teledensity with the rural and urban densities being 57.20 per cent and 167.47 per cent, respectively. Here, the rural and urban gap is to the extent of 110.27 per cent. The overall wireless teledensity for the state is 114.49 per cent, with rural and urban wireless teledensities becoming 67.29 per cent and 160.80 per cent, respectively. Here, the rural–urban gap is to the extent of 93.51 per cent. On the other hand, the wireline teledensity of the state is only to the extent of 4.56 per cent with rural being 1.86 per cent, and urban 6.67 per cent.

In Uttar Pradesh, the total teledensity is to the extent of 62.48 per cent with the rural being 33.99 per cent and urban 161.05 per cent, showing a rural–urban gap of around 127.06 per cent. In this state, wireless teledensity is to extent of 61.56 per cent with rural wireless teledensity being 16.99 per cent and urban 157.82 per cent that shows a rural–urban gap of 140.83 per cent. On the other hand, wireline teledensity is only to the extent of 0.92 per cent with urban being 3.23 per cent and the rural being 0.25 per cent.

The overall teledensity of West Bengal is to the extent of 81.35 per cent with the rural being 43.77 per cent and the urban to extent of 175.55 per cent. The wireless teledensity of West Bengal is to the extent of 79.40 per cent with the rural being 41.70 per cent and the urban to the extent of 169.82 per cent. The rural and urban gaps in overall and wireless teledensities are to the extent of 131.78 per cent and 128.12 per cent, respectively. The wireline teledensity of the state is only to the extent of 1.95 per cent, the urban being 5.73 per cent while the rural only to the extent of 0.44 per cent. The metropolitan city of the Delhi has 235.54 per cent teledensity wherein the wireless teledensity is to the extent of 220.27 per cent and wireline 15.27 per cent.

However, despite these gaps, the overall teledensity of India has increased with the induction of wireless telecommunication in general. More importantly in the rural areas despite the tele-divide, the quantum of telecommunication services has been increased with the penetration of the wireless/mobile services. This penetration has been facilitated by anywhere and everywhere availability, low cost, user friendliness and increasing use of this technology by the customers.

Pattern of Usage of Internet

With the fast spread of Internet interactive social media like those of the Facebook, Twitter, Google+, LinkedIn, YouTube, Skype and all other such platforms have emerged to occupy crucial space in social networking in contemporary India. Opinions and information are given on all issues of everyday concern. These are used not only to exchange ideas, but also to form groups and identities and at times to develop contestation to power structure. According to Internet World Stats 2012, Facebook subscribers are spread all across the world in 210 countries and territories; and it is spreading phenomenally. In March 2011, 664.0 million, that is, 9.6 per cent of the world population used Facebook and in March 2012, it increased to 835.6 million constituting 12.2 per cent of the world population. In India social media, especially Facebook, Google+, Blog, Twitter etc have become an important site to exchange ideas of all sorts. Among the SAARC countries, India occupies the prime position in the use of social networking sites.

ICTs are used in various extents and forms. These are again varied by the rural–urban, ethnic and gender considerations. According to a survey by Justconsult India (2010) in 2005, urban India had a total 17.63 million of regular Internet users. It has increased to 30.03 million in 2008. During the same period, the occasional Internet users were 5.20 and 10.31 million. Thus, altogether there has been an increase from 22.83 million to 40.34 million Internet users during this period under reference. In rural India, in 2008, there were altogether 9.06 million Internet users of which 5.06 were regular and 4.0 million were occasional. Though altogether 12.0 per cent of the urban population has access over Internet, only 1.2 per cent of their rural counterparts have got access to Internet. Thus, altogether only 4.5 per cent of Indian population had access over Internet as either regular or occasional users (Table 5.11).

Table 5.11 *Urban–Rural Internet Users in India (in Millions)*

Internet User-ship in India (Rural–Urban)	2005	2006	2007	2008
Urban-Internet using individuals (Regular)	17.63	21.95	25.17	30.03
Urban-Internet using individuals (Occasional)	5.20	1.65	5.15	10.31
Urban-Internet using individuals (Total)	22.83	23.60	30.32	40.34
Rural-Internet using individuals (Regular)				5.06
Rural-Internet using individuals (Occasional)				4.00
Rural-Internet using individuals (Total)				9.06
All India-Internet using individuals (Regular)				35.09
All India-Internet using individuals (Occasional)				14.34
All India-Internet using individuals (Total)				49.40
All Urban Internet users as % of Indian population	7%	7%	9%	12%
All Rural Internet users as % of Indian population				1.2%
All India Internet users as % of Indian population				4.5%

Source: Juxtconsult India.

According to data provided by Juxtconsult India, 77 per cent of all online users belong to the 19–35 age group category, 70 per cent of the total users belong to the A, B and C towns, 51 per cent users are salaried employees, 63 per cent users own an automobile and English is the most preferred language of reading for only 28 per cent of Internet users.

The top 10 online activities undertaken by net users are: emailing 91 per cent, job search 72 per cent, instant messaging/chatting 70 per cent, check news 63 per cent, check sports 57 per cent, download music/movies 54 per cent, check cricket score 50 per cent, dating/friendship 50 per cent, matrimonial search 49 per cent.

In India, though the process of expansion of ICTs has been very fast, it has been very uneven wherein the urban area, economically advanced and urbanised and socially developed areas of the country have relatively got more access than the rural, economically and socially backward areas. It has also formed a basis for a new economic and social foundation and mobility more for the advanced than for the backward areas. Significantly, notwithstanding these variations, there has emerged an amount of uniformity across India on the usage of ICTs in both the rural and the urban areas and among the cross sections of the population. This uniformity can be delineated by the dominant patterns of usages of these technologies between the pre-globalisation and the globalising periods as shown in Table 5.12.

Table 5.12 *Changing Usage of Technology*

Name of Technology	Pre-globalisation Period	Globalising Period
Radio	Mostly entertainment and information (guided by limited choice)	Entertainment, information, changing cultural style (multiple choice)
Television	Entertainment, information (guided by limited choice)	Entertainment, information, changing life style, consumerist information, health and spiritualism (multiple choice)
Newspaper, Limited Choice	Information, social networking	Information, developing world views (multiple choice)
Telephone	Inter-personal information, status symbol, limited social networking	Interaction, information, social networking
Mobile	–	Interaction, information, social network, forming opinion, new lifestyle
Internet	–	Interaction, information, social network, forming opinion, new lifestyle
Computer	Information processing, status symbol	Information processing, platform for social network, lifestyle, integrate part of daily life

Mass media and ICTs today are no more the simple instruments of entertainment and interpersonal communication, rather are viable media for imparting education, dissemination of information, social networking, formation of social capital, construction of new associations, groups and identities, promotion of new ideas, thoughts and actions and transformation of human structures into agencies in the globalising world. Thus, mass communication and ICTs deprivation not only amounts to denial of alternative choices for one's social, economic and political elevation in society, but also denial of the possibilities of integration with an informed and networked world and getting transformed into a change agent. In the Indian context, inequality in access to ICTs not only breeds inequality in both social and economic terms by denying knowledge and prohibiting the scope and conditions for equal access to the world of information and for equal upward social mobility, but also reinforces traditional social segregation and deprivations cumulatively.

IV. The IT Economy in India

The expansion of ICTs has paved the way for an economic foundation based on the development, usage and expansion of Information Technology (IT) and the IT-enabled services (ITeS) that function through four major subcomponents, namely IT services, business processing organisation (BPO), engineering services and research and development (R&D) and software products for the expansion of knowledge economy in the country. According to Government of India Economic Survey 2011–2012, these industries have given India not only 'the image of a young and resilient global knowledge power'. (Government of India Economic Survey, 2011–2012), but also contribute significantly to earning from export. In 2011–2012, the software exports were to the extent of estimated US$ 69 billion as compared to US$ 59 billion in 2010–2011. Indeed, exports continue to dominate the IT–ITeS industry with 78.4 per cent of its total revenue generated through exports. The growth rate of the domestic sector in 2010–2011 was 20.6 per cent as compared to 18.8 per cent for the export sector. In 2012–2013, as per NASSCOM estimates, export revenues are expected to grow by 11–14 per cent and domestic revenues by 13–16 per cent. IT–ITeS industry's share to the total export has been to the extent of 62 per cent in 2011–2012 due to consistent demands from abroad (Government of India, Economic Survey, 2011–2012, p. 241).

The IT–ITeS industry market in India is spread over various segments of the economy starting from the traditional segments such as banking, financial services and insurance to the new emerging ventures such as retail, health care, media, utilities and others. The Business Processing Organisations (BPO) have emerged to be the immediate focal points of IT–ITeS industries in India. It is undergoing regular process of renewal and innovation. According to the Annual Report of the Ministry of Communications & Information Technology, GOI, Department of Information Technology, 2012, despite the slowing down of growth of the Indian economy, the Indian IT-BPO Industry (including hardware), continued to exhibit resilience. Its share in global sourcing stands at 58 per cent in 2011. It is estimated that India-based resources account for about 60–70 per cent of the offshore delivery capacities available across the leading multinational IT-BPO players.

This report points out that this sector is responsible for creating significant employment opportunities in the economy. Direct employment within the IT-BPO sector is expected to grow by over 9 per cent to reach 2.77 million, with over 230,000 jobs being added in 2011–2012. IT services exports (including Engineering Research and Design (ER&D) and software products) continue to be the largest employer within the industry with nearly 47 per cent share of total 'direct employment, BPO exports generate about 32 per cent of the total industry's employment and the remaining 22 per cent is accounted for by the domestic IT-BPO sector. The sector is responsible for enabling employment to an additional 8.9 million people in various associated sectors – catering, security, transportation housekeeping, etc. – many of whom belong to rural areas/small towns of India'.... 'In 2011–2012, the IT-BPO industry's contribution to GDP is estimated to be 7.5 per cent as compared to 7.1 per cent in 2010–2011' (Ministry of Communications & Information Technology, 2012).

V. Future Direction

The scope of ICTs has phenomenally increased in India in all sectors and levels of activities for creating the right governance, forming new institutional mechanisms, developing core infrastructure, framing new policies and standards, developing the necessary legal framework, etc., in the country. Towards this endeavour, there has also been initiative 'for establishing State Wide Area Networks across the country to connect all State/UT Headquarters' up to the Block level via District/ Sub-Divisional Headquarters. Interestingly, the Central Government has approved a scheme in the country for establishing 1,00,000 Common Services Centres (CSCs) in over 6,00,000 villages in the country as the front-end delivery points to provide government services through development schemes such as Mahatma Gandhi National Rural Employment Guarantee, National Rural Health Mission, Sarva Shiksha Abhiyan and many others in rural areas. Again there is a proposal to establish a National Knowledge Network to connect all universities, research institutions, libraries, laboratories, hospitals and agricultural institutions across the country to enable the end users get access to latest information for their optimal use in the given context (Government of India, 2010 a).

In view of the immense potential of ICTs, the education providers of the country are seized with the idea of e-learning and web-based educational arrangements for a border-less education developing public–private partnership. Several international players are also seized with this endeavour. The Government of India has framed a National Mission on Education through ICT during the Eleventh Five Year Plan. This mission has been 'envisaged as a centrally sponsored scheme to leverage the potential of ICT, in providing high-quality personalised and interactive knowledge modules over the Internet/Intranet for all the learners in higher education institutions in any time any where mode'. This programme aims for:

- enhancing the GER in higher education, ensuring access and equity,

- generating e-content,

- enhancing connectivity along with provision for access devices for institutions and learners,

- bridging the digital divide in teaching and learning among urban and rural teachers/learners,

- empowering these who have hitherto remained untouched by the digital revolution and have not been able to join the mainstream of knowledge society,

- extending computer infrastructure and connectivity to over 18,000 colleges in the country including each of the departments of all universities/deemed universities and institutions of national importance,

- enhancing the standards of education, in government as well as in private colleges,

- enhancing access to quality education, making available knowledge modules in cyberspace and optimal utilisation of available resources by using ICT for educating the masses, especially those inhibited in remotely located areas and places at disadvantage.

It plans to focus on appropriate pedagogy for e-learning, providing facility of performing experiments through virtual laboratories, online testing and certification, online availability of teachers to guide and mentor learners, utilisation of available Education Satellite and Direct to Home platform, training and empowerment of teachers to effectively use the new method of teaching learning, etc. (http://pib.nic.in/newsite/erelease.aspx?relid=46323).

New Policy Framework

As the expansion of ICTs is largely dependent on the liberal economic order to smoothen the process, 'an outward looking and liberal trade policy' is initiated by the state as one of the main features of India's economic reforms. Allowing foreign direct investment up to 100 per cent in the electronics hardware-manufacturing, allowing import liberalisation capital goods for pre-production, production and post-production of computer software systems and promoting, schemes like Zero Duty Export Promotion Capital Goods, Electronics Hardware Technology Park, Export-Oriented Unit/Special Economic Zone, etc. To convert India into a good host of IT-driven economy (Annual Report 2009–2010, Government of India, Ministry of Communications & Information Technology Department of Electronics and Information Technology: New Delhi).

By accepting ICTs as the key enabler of development, the government of India has drafted a long-term National Policy on Electronics to achieve multifold its growth in production and investment, enhance its capacity to generate more and more employment. This policy aims to empower the software industry to achieve global leadership by promoting export and to enhance the availability of skilled manpower through active participation of the private sector and thrust on higher education. This policy also aims to set up National Electronic Mission as an institutional mechanism to formulate policy and to promote 'Brand India' in electronics by developing core competencies in automotive avionics, LED industrial, medical electronics, solar photovoltaic and information and broadcasting Ministry of Communications & Information Technology, 2012).

Significantly, these policies are taking shape against the backdrop of expansion of education, globalisation and phenomenal growth of ICTs as the key enabler of knowledge economy in India in a global context.

Computer and TV Industry

The PC market in India has grown around 10.3 million units in 2011–2012. For Printers and MFDs, the market is of 2.8 million units. Production of computer hardware is estimated to increase to ₹ 16,500 crore in 2011–2012 (Ministry of Communications & Information Technology, 2012). Significantly, the market size of India's TV industry has increased from ₹ 25,700 crore in the year 2009 to ₹ 29,700 crore in the year 2010, registering a growth of 15 per cent (TARI, 2012).

ICTs and its Increasing Application

India has been widely depicted as essentially a nation of low-end service provider to global corporations based in the United States or Europe; and that the country is bereft of product-oriented companies and India cannot call itself a technology powerhouse despite employing two million professionals in this sector; that India is yet to show cause a company like Microsoft or Google, and that Infosys or Wipro, etc., are the creatures of global demands. However, notwithstanding these criticisms, several technology companies have emerged in India with innovations made in India, by and for India to meet the demands of local business for helping capture finger print and iris data for the Aadhar Card to crunching numbers so that chicken live healthier and longer; they use cutting-edge technology to provide tailor-made solutions for Indian needs: for example, the Sugunar Food based on Hyderabad has deployed an enterprise IT system from one largest software makers to find solutions to local poultry problems. Similarly, the Indore-based

Anaxee Technologies is engaged in the Unique Identification Number Project of Nandan Nilekani; Nirmalab is engaged in the local biometric systems. Similarly, Noida-based Setelling Technologies and Bangalore-based Byoma Technologies are engaged in providing personalised information to the travellers. Similarly, several organisations are also working in the area of banking, rural development and education (Abrar, 2013).

Knowledge has never been such a potential source of power in the human society as in knowledge society today. It is the form and extent of one's capacity to get access over information and capacity to process this information through ICTs that provide the basis of one's empowerment and mobility in society. Expansion of ICT is significantly linked to the state of educational and economic development of society. It is not autonomous of education as were the cases of agricultural and industrial technologies. Higher extent of education is linked to higher degree of penetration of ICTs and knowledge, which are in turn linked to the state of economic development. Herein, the expansion of ICTs is linked to economic development both as a cause and function and vice versa; and simultaneously ICTs are linked to occupational mobility both as a cause and as a function and vice versa; and there has emerged an intrinsic cyclical relationship among education, ICTs economic transition and occupational mobility. These relationships are again largely conditioned by inherited sociocultural dynamics of society from the below, on the one hand, and those of the forces of economic, social and political transition from the above, on the other. These dynamics are posited within neoliberal state policies and broad processes of economic transition in contemporary India.

ICTs have helped globalise Indian economy not only by exposing the country with new technological arrangements, but also by bringing in a new way of doing business, generating employment, organising social, political and cultural events and new lifestyles and ideals and thoughts. It has provided the foundation for new varieties of knowledge job, helped erect the foundation of knowledge economy and has emerged to be a crucial vehicle to transform knowledge a tradable commodity across the globe. In the process, ICTs have paved the way for integrating their economic, social and cultural fabrics with the wider world. Though ICTs are penetrated in a given social context and operate within it, they also create a social context with their own dynamics. Such dynamics are intertwined with the demographic, educational, ideological and broad economic shifts in society.

Though fast expansion of ICTs has paved the way for the emergence of a vibrant knowledge society in India, this expansion has been eclectic. Significantly, the expansion of ICTs has been facilitated by the shifting state policy on information and telecommunication that has widely encouraged private investment in this sector increasing private and foreign direct investment and promotion of public–private partnership in this sector. The neoliberal state of India has walked extra miles to make ICTs available to the largest segments of population not only by providing connectivity even in the remotest part of the country, but also by providing required technologies at a cheap rate among the end users of these technologies. It is not only that political parties are competing to provide cheap kerosene oil, rice, sugar, etc., among the poor, but to distribute free coloured television, free cable connections among people, free laptop computers, cheap tablets, etc., among the young students. These political initiatives again are supplemented by the initiatives of computer, mobile phone and Internet service providing private companies to provide interest-free loans to lure public towards these items. Along with the fast penetration of ICTs, the emerging India not only experiences a paradigm shift in it technological base, but also a host of contradiction in its social set-up that are delineated in the form of unprecedented proliferation of ICTs, on the one hand, and persisting knowledge and digital gaps in society: on the other, interpenetration of new sociocultural milieu, on the one hand, and resurgence of traditional identities, on the other and enhances flow of information and occupational and delinquency in society, on the other. As against these contradictions, questions are usually raised as to how does a preexisting social context in India get redefined with the interpenetration of ICTs and its intertwined dynamics. How does it foster a knowledge society by replacing its agricultural and industrial technological foundation? Or has there been coexistence of all these sectors together? Have all segments of society got equal access to ICTs? How do ICTs enable people to break the barriers of marginality and help formation of new social identities? How do the

ICTs negotiate with global market and local culture simultaneously to construct a new cultural milieu in society? These issues would be addressed while dealing with the changing trajectory of Indian economy, emergence of new work and work relations, sociocultural milieu in India in the subsequent chapters of this book with empirical evidences.

6

Indian Growth Story
Service and Knowledge Dynamics

The economic fundamentals of India that was guided by a socialist and welfare state philosophy, institutionalised centralised planning, state-controlled industrialisation and market mechanisms and a strategic framework of mixed economy till the 1980s bore witness to a paradigm shift since the 1990s in the wake of introduction of economic neoliberalisation by the state. Such a paradigm shift in the nature of the state has been accompanied by dismantling of state control on market mechanism, opening up gates for multinational and foreign investment in domestic market and articulation of public–private partnership for mobilisation of resources and execution of plans and policies of the state. The society has also simultaneously experienced fast expansion of educational arrangements and Information and Communication Technology (ICT) networks, increasing flow of goods and services, movement of migrant workforce and their interactions across the globe. This neoliberal economic framework has brought about speedy transformation in organisation of production through economic integration with global market forces, increasing occupational diversification, fast rate of economic growth, on the one hand; it has also generated a host of anomalies and inconsistencies by retaining poverty, unemployment, casualisation and informalisation in work participation, livelihood/food insecurity, social and spatial divides for a vast section of people, on the other. This chapter besides discussing the economic development and the anomalies arising out of it also positions the process of emergence of knowledge economy of India and the related economic dynamics arising out of it at a macro level.

I. Transformation in the Organisation of Production

With the speedy expansion of educated and skilled manpower, improvement in the literacy rate and educational status of the workforce, fast penetration of ICTs and initiation of new economic policy of India stands today in the threshold of a new economic order. Most importantly, this emerging new economic order is widely characterised by a fast rate of economic growth and encompassing occupational diversification, a sharp decline of agriculture, a moderate rate of expansion of industry and a fast expansion of the service sector with its increasing significance in national economy both as a producer of wealth and a provider of employment.

Fast Economic Growth

The growth rate of Indian economy that was to the extent of 2.8 per cent in the Third Five Year Plan (1960–1965), and 5.5 per cent during the Seventh Plan (1985–1989), had shot up to 7.7 per cent during the Tenth Five Year Plan (2002–2006), and again to 8.0 per cent during the Eleventh Five Year Plan (2007–2012). Significantly, in 2006–2007, India achieved the ever highest i.e. 9.7 per cent rate of economic growth. Though in the last five years, the growth rate of India has slowed down to around 6 per cent and that the International rating agency Standard & Poor's has awarded India the lowest investment rating in 2012 and has warned India of a downgrade to junk category, Indian experts foresaw the possibility of Indian economy bouncing back soon notwithstanding global slowdown. Indeed, the bouncing back process has happened as the Standard & Poor's has withdrawn its warning within six months of issuing the same in view of the strong fundamental of Indian economy. The Gross National Income (GNI) of India has grown over the years from US$ 442.2 billion in 1999 to US$ 1566.6 billion in 2010 and in terms of international dollars using purchasing power parity, the GNI of India has been US$ 4170.9 billion in 2010 showing a quantum increase in the GDI by 166.2 per cent during this period between 1999 and 2010 (UNDP, 2000; World Bank, 2012). According to a press release of the Press Information Bureau, Government of India, dated 31 May 2012, the Gross National Income (GNI) at factor cost at 2004–2005 prices is now estimated to be ₹ 51,50,686 crore during 2011–2012, as against the previous year's Quick Estimate of ₹ 48,33,178 crore. In terms of growth rates, the Gross National Income is estimated to have risen by 6.6 per cent during 2011–2012, in comparison with the growth rate of 7.9 per cent in 2010–2011 (http://mospi.nic.in/Mospi_New/upload/ NAD_Press_Note_31may12.pdf). India has also been experiencing increasing arrival of foreign direct investment and remittance inflows. According to UNDP in 2009, the foreign direct investment inflows formed 2.5 per cent and the remittance inflow 3.6 per cent of the GDP in India (UNDP, 2011).

Service Sector Growth Rate Surpassing Agriculture and Industry

The increasing growth rate as indicated above, however, has not been uniform for all sectors of the economy. Table 6.1 shows that the

Table 6.1 Growth Rate of Various Sectors of the Economy since 1980

Year	Agriculture (Agriculture, Fishing and Forestry)	Industry (Mining and Quarrying Manufacturing, Electricity, Water, Construction)	Service (Trade, Hotel, Restaurant, Transport, Storage and Communication, Financial, Insurance, Real Estate and Business Services, Community, Social and Personal Services)	Total
1980–1990	2.9	7.1	6.9	5.6
1992–1996 (Eight Plan)	4.72	7.29	7.28	6.54
1997–2001 (Ninth Plan)	2.44	4.29	7.87	5.52
2002–2006) (Tenth Plan)	2.30	9.17	9.30	7.74
2006–2007	4.0	11.0	11.2	9.74
2008–2009	2.6	4.8	9.6	7.1
2009–2010	1.0	8.4	10.5	8.0
2010–2011	5.4	8.1	9.65	8.6
2011–2012	2.8	3.4	8.95	6.5
2012–2013 (Mid Year)	2.1	3.2	7.7	5.4
2007–2012 (Eleventh Plan)	3.7	7.2	9.7	8.0
2013–2017 (Twelfth Plan as Envisaged)	4.0	7.6	9.0	8.0

Source: Department of Economic Affairs, Economic Division, 4(5)/Ec. Dn. /2010, Monthly Economic Report, January 2011, March 2012, Planning Commission 2013.

growth rate of the Indian service sector has surpassed those of the industry and the agriculture over the decades despite the recent year's downward slide of the economy. During the Seventh Five Year Plan (1980–1990), the growth of Indian service sector was to the extent of 6.9 per cent while for the industry it was 7.1 per cent, and for the agriculture the growth rate was to the extent of 2.9 per cent only, while the overall growth rate was 5.6 per cent. During the Tenth Five Year Plan (2002–2006), the growth rate of the service sector increased to 9.3 per cent, industry to 9.17 per cent and agriculture declined to 2.3 per cent, while the overall growth rate was 7.74 per cent. In 2006–2007, the service sector registered a phenomenal rate of growth with 11.2 per cent, the industry grew at the rate of 11 per cent and agriculture only 4.0 per cent. Significantly, the overall growth of economy in 2006–2007 was 9.74 per cent. With economic 'slow down' becoming a global phenomenon in 2008–2009, the growth rate in agriculture declined to 2.6 per cent, industry to 4.8 per cent and the overall economic growth rate to 7.1 per cent; the service sectors of India withstood this challenge maintaining a growth rate of 9.6 per cent. In 2009–2010, while the growth rate of agriculture declined to 1 per cent, for industry it increased to 8.4 per cent and service to 10.5 per cent and the overall growth rate became 8.0 per cent. In 2010–2011, the service sector has registered a marginal decline in growth rate to 9.6 per cent, industry to 8.1 per cent, the overall economic growth also declined to 8.6 per cent, while agriculture grew at the rate of 4.5 per cent showing an increasing trend. All these show that though the service sector has had a steady growth from 6.9 per cent in 1980–1990 to 11.2 per cent in 2006–2007, it declined to 9.65 per cent in 2010–2011 and again to 8.95 per cent in 2011–2012. Though the growth of the service sector is widely impacted by global slowdown, the service sector has got a comparative edge over the other sectors of economy. In 2011–2012, though the annual growth rate of agriculture, industry and service sector has further declined to 2.8 per cent and 3.4 per cent and 8.95 per cent from the previous growth rate, the service sector has remained substantially higher than those of the other sectors. The mid-year review of 2012–2013 shows that economic growth rate slowed down to 5.4 per cent with agriculture showing 2.1 per cent, industry 3.2 per cent and service 7.7 per cent growth rates. It is significant that despite the overall economic slowdown in post 2006–2007 periods, the service sector has retained highest growth rate among all other sectors of the economy. The Eleventh Plan has seen altogether 8 per cent growth with 9.7 per cent growth rate in the service sector, 3.7 per cent for the agriculture and 7.2 per cent for the industry. The Twelfth Plan has targeted 8 per cent growth of the economy with 4 per cent and 7.6 per cent for agriculture and industry and significantly 9.6 per cent growth rate for the service sector.

Increasing Contribution of Service Sector to GDP

With the changing growth rate in different sectors of the economy, contribution of each of the sector to the national GDP has also got significantly altered and the service sector has emerged to be the single longest contributor to national GDP over the decades. As shown in Table 6.2, the contribution of agriculture to the total GDP of the

Table 6.2 Gross Domestic Product of India at Factor Cost by Industry of Origin

Year	Agriculture (%)	Industry (%)	Service (%)	Total (%)
1950–1951	56.70	13.66	29.64	100
1960–1961	52.48	17.09	30.43	100
1970–1971	46.00	20.41	33.58	100
1980–1981	39.93	22.03	38.04	100
1990–1991	34.05	23.24	42.70	100
2000–2001	26.18	23.51	50.32	100
2006–2007	20.55	24.71	54.75	100
2008–2008	17.1	25.9	57.0	100
2009–2010	14.6	28.1	57.3	100
2010–2011	14.2	28.0	57.8	100
2011–2012	13.9	27.0	59.1	100
2012–2013(Mid Year)	12.0	27.1	61.0	100

Source: 1. Economic Survey, Government of India, 2. Ministry of Finance Ministry of Finance, Department of Economic Affairs, Economic Division, 4(5)/Ec. Dn. /2010,· Monthly Economic Report, January 2011, Mid-year Economic Analysis, Ministry of Finance, 2013.

country has phenomenally declined from 56.7 per cent in 1950–1951 to a meagre 12 per cent in 2012–2013.

The contribution of the industrial sector to the GDP has increased from 13.66 per cent to 27.1 per cent during this period. Most significantly, the contribution of the service sector has increased from 29.64 per cent in 1950–1951 to 61 per cent in 2012–2013. It shows that over the periods under consideration, the contribution of agriculture to GDP has declined by 78 per cent, while for industry it has increased by 98.4 per cent and most importantly for service sector it has increased by 105.8 per cent. These phenomena have an intertwining with varied growth patterns within the various sectors of economy and with the changing patterns of work participation therein.

As shown in Table 6.3, the growth rate in agriculture, forestry, fishing, mining and quarrying (Primary Sector) has been relatively slower

Table 6.3 *Annual Growth Rates of Real Gross Domestic Product at Factor Cost by Industry of Origin*

Type of Industry	1951–1952	1961–1962	1971–1972	1981–1982	1991–1992	2001–2002	2011–2012 (1R)
Agriculture, Forestry & Fishing, Mining and Quarrying	1.9	0.3	–1.7	5.2	–1.4	5.5	3.1
Manufacturing, Construction, Electricity, Gas and Water Supply	4.6	6.9	–2.5	7.4	–0.1	2.7	3.8
Trade, Hotels, Transport & Communication	2.6	6.5	2.3	6.1	2.3	8.6	7.0
Financing, Insurance, Real Estate and Business Services	2.3	4.3	5.2	8.1	10.8	7.1	11.7
Community, Social & Personal Services	3.0	4.7	4.5	2.1	2.6	4.1	6.0
Gross Domestic Product at Factor Cost (2–8)	2.3	3.1	1.0	5.6	1.4	5.5	6.2

Source: Central Statistics Office. 1R: 1st Revised Estimates, Hhttp://indiabudget.nic.in.

than the other sectors of the economic activities. The slow growth rate is also reflected in the manufacturing, construction, electricity, gas and water supply (Secondary Sector), even though this has registered high rate of growth in 1961–1962 and 1981–1982. The decadal variation shows that agricultural activities acquired a growth rate of 1.9 per cent in 1951–1952, it increased to 0.3 per cent in 1961–1962, declined to 1.7 per cent in 1971–1971, increased to 5.2 per cent in 1981–1982, again declined to 1.4 per cent in 1991–1992, improved to 5.5 per cent in 2001–2002, again declined 3.1 per cent in 2011–2012. The industrial activities increased at the rate of 4.6 per cent in 1951–1952, increased to 6.9 per cent in 1961–1962, declined to 2.5 per cent in 1971–1972, again increased to 7.4 per cent in 1981–1988, declined to 0.1 per cent in 1991–1992, increased to 2.7 per cent in 2001–2002, and again to 3.8 per cent in 2011–2012.

The service sector includes a host of activities such as trade, hotels, transport, communication, financing, insurance, real estate and business services, community, social and personal services. Most of these activities have shown constant growth with some variations in between these decades. For example, the activities such as financial, insurance, real estate and business services increased from 2.3 per cent in 1951–1952 to 4.3 per cent in 1961–1962 again increased to 5.2 per cent in 1971–1972, again increased to 8.1 per cent in 1981–1982, again increased 10.8 per cent in 1991–1992, again to 11.7 per cent in 2011–2012 after declining to 7.1 per cent in 2001–2002. Similarly, community, social and personal services also increased from 3 per cent in 1951–1952 to 6 per cent in 2011–2012 with minor variation in between; trade, hotels, transport and communications also increased from 2.6 per cent in 1951–1952 to 7 per cent in 2011–2012 with some variations in between the decade under reference.

Table 6.4 shows the share and growth of the Indian service sector at factor cost in the period between 2000–2001 and 2012–2013 in the total share of the service sector to GDP. The share of Indian service in trade, hotel and restaurant, transport, storage and communication that was 22.2 per cent in 2000–2001 increased to 28.5 per cent in 2012–2013, financing, insurance, real estate and business services increased from 13.8 per cent in 2000–2001 to 19.3 per cent in 2012–2013. The

Table 6.4 *Share and Growth of India's Services Sector at Factor Cost (%)*

Services Sector	2000–2001	2012–2013
Trade, Hotels, & Restaurants, Transport, Storage and Communication	22.2	28.5
Financing, Insurance, Real Estate and Business Services	13.8	19.3
Community, Social and Personal Services	14.8	13.2
Total Services	50.8	61.0

Source: Central Statistics Office (CSO), Mid Year Economic Analysis, Ministry of Finance, 2013

share of community, social and personal services, however, marginally declined from 14.8 per cent to 13.2 per cent during the period under reference. Significantly, the knowledge sector of India is located within the service. The growth and transition of this sector of economy affected the process of emergence of knowledge economy in particular and in the patterns of work participation in general in all sectors of economy.

II. Work Participation

The shift in the Indian economy has been accompanied by an increasing rate and changing patterns of work participation. With the increase in population, increasing level of knowledge and skill and emergence of new avenues of employment, work participation has also increased in India. Consequently, the size of labour force has also increased both in the rural and urban areas. The size of Indian labour force that was of 307.4 million in 1983 increased to 379.9 million in 1993–1994, 466.8 million in 2004–2005 and 522.8 million in 2009–2010. In terms of spatial distribution, the strength of rural labour increased from 245.6 million in 1983 to 347.1 million in 2004–2005 and 395.9 million in 2009–2010 and the urban labour from 61.8 million in 1983 to 119.7 million in 2004–2005 and 126.9 million in 2009–2010. Significantly rural labour force still constitute 75.7 per cent of India labour force. Though the average annual growth rate of urban labour force has been much higher with 4.9 per cent as against the rural labour growth rate of 2.35 per cent and the overall growth rate of 2.69 per cent during the same period, the rural areas still provide more employment to people than the urban areas in India (see Table 6.5). India today stands in the threshold of the emergence of huge young labour force because of its demographic transition. As a large section of this work force is confined

Table 6.5 *Size and Growth of Labour Force by the Rural and Urban Areas (in Millions)*

Areas	1983	1993–1994	2004–2005	2009–2010	Average Growth Rate (%) 1983–2009–2010
Rural	245.6 (79.9)	294.4(77.5)	347.1 (74.4)	395.9 (75.7)	2.35
Urban	61.8 (20.1)	85.8 (22.5)	119.7 (25.6)	126.9 (24.3)	4.05
Total	307.4 (100)	379.9 (100)	466.8 (100)	522.8 (100)	2.69

Source: NSSO 38th, 50th, 61st and 66th Round

to the education system, India is yet to see the arrival of this labour force in the labour market. It is obvious that their arrival will make a qualitative and quantitative difference in the labour market of India. Significantly, the Census of 2011 shows the size of Indian total labour force to be 481.7 million. The National Sample Survey Organisation (NSSO) 2011–2012 shows a decline in the size of labour force in India clearly indicating a scenario of job loss for rural areas, especially for rural women and job gain for urban women. While in 2009–2010, 81.2 million rural women were in the work force, it declined to 72.1 million in 2011–2012. For the urban women, it increased from 19.8 million to 23.3 million during the same period. Similarly, in the subsidiary work, 104.5 million rural women participated in 2009–2010; this work participation declined to 101.8 million in 2011–2012. However, for the urban women, it improved from 22.8 million to 27.3 million during the same period. The lack of employment security, low wage in agriculture, un/underemployment and also withdrawal from manual agricultural activities after acquiring literacy and education and migration to urban areas widely caused such decline in rural women's work participation.

Changing Patterns of Work Participation

India has also witnessed a phenomenal change in the work participation patterns among these broad sectors of the economy. As shown in Table 6.6, in 1971, more than 72.05 per cent of the workforce was

Table 6.6 *Changing Nature of Work Participation in Various Sectors of the Economy*

Year	Agriculture: (Agriculture, Fishing and Forestry)	Industry(Mining and Quarrying Manufacturing, Electricity, Water, Construction)	Service (Trade, Hotel, Restaurant, Transport, Storage and Communication, Financial, Insurance, Real Estate and Business Services, Community, Social and Personal Services)	Total (%)
1971	72.05	11.20	16.75	100
1983	65.42	14.83	19.74	100
1993–1994	61.03	15.92	23.06	100
1999–2000	56.64	17.58	25.78	100
2004–2005	52.06	19.45	28.47	100
2009–2010	53.2	21.5	25.4	100
2011–2012	48.9	24.3	26.8	100

Sources: Census, 1971; Planning Commission, 2009; NSSO, 2011, 2013.

engaged in the agricultural sector, and 11.20 per cent and 16.75 per cent were in the industrial and in the service sectors of the economy, respectively. With the change in the economy over the decades, there has been a decline in the work participation rate in agriculture, and increase in industry and service sectors. In 2004–2005, of the total workforce in India, 52.06 per cent were employed in agriculture, 19.45 per cent and 28.47 per cent were employed in industry and service sectors, respectively. However, in 2009–2010, the declining trend in work participation in agriculture halted with a marginal increase to 53.2 per cent and it has again declined to 48.9 per cent in 2011–2012. The work participation in industry has increased to 21.5 per cent in 2009–2010 and again to 24.3 per cent in 2011–2012. Importantly, the service sector that showed a declining trend to 25.4 per cent in 2004–2005 has improved to 26.8 per cent in 2011–2012. In the wake of increasing interconnectedness of global economy, macro-level work participation has been widely impacted. The decline in the work participation in the service sector during 2009–2010 was positively linked to global slowdown indicating the interconnected nature of global economy in which the service sector is located today. The increasing work participation in industry is widely caused by increasing work participation in the manufacturing, construction and related jobs both in the rural and urban areas as set in motion by new economic forces.

According to NSSO (2011–2012), more than 51 per cent of the total workforce and 40 per cent of rural workforce today are engaged in the nonagricultural sector with 40.6 per cent rural male and 25 per cent rural female work force are engaged in nonagricultural activities as their principal engagement. In fact, nonagricultural activities have increased the principal activity in the rural areas and simultaneously a large chunk of this workforce has got association with nonfarm activities as subsidiary sources of their income. As land–man ratio has declined, marginal and semimarginal land holdings have been the dominant modes of land ownership for the majority of these rural populations, a sizeable section of them either migrates out of the village or looks for alternative avenues of livelihood security outside agriculture. Herein, self-employment in rural areas has emerged to be an immediate alternative venture for a vast section of these people. Besides, withdrawal from manual agricultural activities with the penetration of literacy and education has also been a phenomenon to reckon with.

Work Participation, Employment, Underemployment and Selfemployment

The Census of India has shown a marginal increase in the work participation rate from 36.8 per cent in 1981 to 39.1 in 2001 to 39.8 per cent in 2011. According to NSSO (2011–2012), around 40 per cent of the Indian population belongs to the workforce by its usual working status. In India again, there has been increasing presence of marginal workers, who do not get more than 180 days (for 2011 Census not more than 90 days as well) of employment in a year, in the workforce. As pointed out in the previous chapter, in 1981, only 9 per cent of total workers were the marginal workers. In the 2001 Census marginal workers constituted 22 per cent of total workers; in 2011, their presence has shot up to 24.8 per cent of the total workers (Census of India 1981, 2001, 2011). In fact, ratio of marginal labour within the total workers indicates the scenario of un/underemployment in the country.

In India, unemployment rate had gone up despite phenomenal economic growth during the period between 1993–1994 and 2004. During this period, the unemployment rate for male increased from 5.6 per cent to 9.0 per cent in rural areas and from 6.7 per cent to 8.1 per cent in urban areas by the current daily status of the workers. In the financial year 2004–2005, unemployment grew at the rate of 8.3 per cent and the GDP growth rate was hovering around 8 per cent indicating a job unfriendly growth story for India. Subsequently, the 2009–2010 NSSO report, however, shows a declining trend in the unemployment rate to 6.6 per cent and the 2011–2012 reports a further decline to around 3 per cent by usual status. The unemployment rate in rural areas was lower with 2 per cent and higher in the urban areas with 4 per cent in 2011–2012. Significantly, in recent years, India has experienced a decline in wage/salaried employment and increase in selfemployment in the wake of increasing rate of literacy and global economic slowdown. This trend is shown in Table 6.7.

In 2004–2005, while 55.4 per cent of the workers were wage employees or salaried person, their proportion to total workforce has declined to 49 per cent in 2009 2010 and further to 47.8 per cent in

Table 6.7 *Changing Patterns of Employment in Rural and Urban Areas*

Year	Rural		Urban		Total	
	Selfem-ployed	Labour Salaried	Selfem-ployed	Labour Salaried	Selfem-ployed	Labour Salaried
2004–2005	51.7	49.3	37.5	62.5	44.6	55.4
2009–2010	54.2	46.8	41.1	58.9	51.0	49.0
2011–2012	55.9	44.1	41.9	58.1	52.2	47.8

Source: NSS 2004–2005 and 2009–2010. NSSO, 2013.

2011–2012. During the same period, the proportion of self-employed to total workforce has increased from 44.6 per cent to 51 per cent and further to 52.2 per cent, respectively. The proportion of self-employed person has increased in rural areas from 51.7 per cent in 2004–2005 to 54.2 per cent in 2009–2010 and further to 55.9 per cent in 2011–2012 and urban areas from 37.5 per cent to 41.1 per cent and further to 41.9 per cent during the same period. Simultaneously, there has been a decline in work participation in the labourer/salaried category in rural areas from 49.3 per cent in 2004–2005 to 46.8 per cent in 2009–2010 and further to 44.1 in 2011–2012; in the urban areas, this has been from 62.5 to 58.9 per cent and further to 58.1 per cent during the same period. This decline has been attributed to the growing inability of the industrial and service sectors to absorb the available potential labourers as workers and salaried persons and also a growing tendency among the literate and educated workforce to be engaged in self-employment than to be engaged in low-paid, insecure jobs in the wake of global recession.

Informalisation of Workforce

In India, an overwhelming segment of workforce is engaged in the informal sector of the economy. In 2004–2005, of the total work force (455.7 million) in India, 92.3 per cent belongs to the informal sector of the economic activities whose work participation is governed by the lack of rules and regulations to ensure proper wage, working hours, health care, maternity and social security benefits, job security and scope for upward mobility (National Commission for Unorganised Sector, 2009). Despite the fast expansion of the service and the industrial sectors of the economy concentration of the workforce in the informal sector continues. Based on the consumption criteria, the National Commission for Enterprises in the Unorganised Sector, Government of India (2008), by examining the NSS 2004–2005 data pointed out that 77 per cent of this working population in India population do not have even ₹ 20 per day for consumption. Significantly, the unorganised sector of India is conspicuously marked by a high rate of work participation from the marginalised section of society. It is shown that 87.8 per cent of the schedule castes, 79.9 per cent of other backward classes, 84.5 per cent of the Muslims and 54.8 per cent of the general category of workers are engaged in the unorganised sector (Government of India, 2007).

Casualisation of Rural Labour Force

The process of casualisation of labour force is also linked to declining rate of work participation in agriculture and again decline of the category of cultivators and an increase in agricultural labourers; and shifting of labour force from agriculture to nonagricultural sector through a process of casualisation of rural labour force.

Table 6.8 shows that along with declining work participation in agriculture, the proportion of cultivators has declined from around 50 per cent in 1951 to 31.7 per cent in 2001 and further to 24.65 in 2011 showing a decline of the category of cultivator by 50.65 per cent. On

Table 6.8 *Changing Patterns of Work Participation in Agriculture in India since 1951*

Year	Work Participation in Agriculture		Nonagriculture
	Cultivator	Agricultural Labourers	
1951	49.9	19.5	30.6
2001	31.7	30.8	37.5
2011	24.65	30.0	45.4

Source: Census of India, 1971, 2001, 2011.

the contrary, the proportion of agricultural labourers has increased from 19.5 per cent in 1951 to 30.8 per cent in 2001 with a marginal decline to 30 per cent in 2011. The agricultural labourers are mainly the casual labourers who work in precarious working conditions without getting job security, scope of upward mobility and adequate wage, legal and social security protection. The marginal decline in the category of agricultural labour is linked to a shift of the labourforce to the non agricultural sector. Thus it shows that the category of non-agricultural labourers has also increased from 30.6 per cent to 37.5 per cent and further to 45.4 per cent during the same period. Decline of the category of cultivators and increase in the category of labourers are related to increasing underemployment in rural areas and informalisation of Indian economy and a quantum increase in rural–urban migration. This has a bearing on the presence of higher number of casual workforce in the country especially in the rural areas (Table 6.9).

Table 6.9 *Percentage Distribution of Usual Status of Workers by Status in Employment in 2011–12*

| Place | Category of Persons | Status of Employment | | |
		Self-employed	Regular Wage/ Salaried	Casual
Rural	Male	54.5	10.0	35.5
	Female	59.3	5.6	35.1
	Total	55.9	8.7	35.4
Urban	Male	41.7	43.4	14.9
	Female	42.8	42.8	14.3
	Total	41.9	43.3	14.8
Total	Male	50.7	19.8	29.4
	Female	56.1	12.7	31.2
	Total	52.2	17.9	29.9

Source: NSSO, 2011–2012.

As indicated earlier India has a high rate of work participation as self-employed persons than the salaried and the wage earners. Again among the salaried and the wage earners, there are more casual labourers than the salaried labourers. At the all-India level, 52.2 per cent of the total workforce is self-employed, 17.9 per cent is regular/ salaried and the remaining 29.9 per cent are casual labourers. For female, these are to the extent of 56.1 per cent, 12.7 per cent and 31.2 per cent and for male these are 50.7 per cent, 19.8 per cent and 29.4 per cent, respectively. Rural areas have more self-employed persons with 55.9 per cent than urban areas with 41.9 per cent. Rural areas again have a higher level of casual labourers with 35.4 per cent than the urban areas with 14.8 per cent. The gender difference in work participation as casual labourers is insignificant as most of the casual labourers are illiterates and are from the lower caste or tribal backgrounds; for them gender difference seldom comes in the way of work participation as labourers. Though the urban areas have more regular/salaried workers with 43.3 per cent than that of the all-India with 17.9 per cent and rural levels with 8.7 per cent, it is in no way to deny the fact that the vast majority of Indian workforce is employed in the unorganised sector whose work condition seldom ensure job security and social and legal protection.

As against these backdrops, the increasing incidences of job insecurity, unemployment and poverty among the workers, on the one hand, the increasing rate of literacy and the enhanced communication networks therein on the other, contribute to the increasing incidence of rural-to-urban migration in India. Rural workers who are unable to get accommodated either in agriculture or in the emerging new avenues of employment in rural areas tend to migrate to urban areas subject to the availability of appropriate communication networks, and a minimum assurance of employment in the area of arrival. In many ways, migration of rural labourers is symptomatic of extension of rural underemployment and poverty in the urban areas. According to the NSSO (2010) report on Migration, 'migration of households in both the rural and urban areas was dominated by the migration of households from rural areas. Nearly 57 per cent of urban migrant households migrated from rural areas whereas 29 per cent of rural migrant households migrated from urban areas'. According to this report, *employment is the major reason for migration and that nearly* 55 per cent of the households in rural areas and 67 per cent of the households in the urban areas have migrated for employment-related reasons (NSSO, 2010).

In the wake of globalisation and increasing local–global connectivity, migration is as preponderant in the rural as in urban areas. However, the rate of migration (proportion of migrants in population) is 35 per cent in urban areas and 26 per cent in rural areas. Significantly, the quantum of male migration rate was far lower than female migration rate, in both rural and urban areas. In the rural areas, migration rate among females is 48 per cent, while for males it is only 5 per cent, in the urban areas female and male migration rates are 48 per cent and 26 per cent, respectively (NSSO, 2010).

In the rural areas, *migration rate* is lowest among the scheduled tribe with 24 per cent and highest among those classified in the social group 'others', with 28 per cent. Significantly, the migration rate is lowest among the illiterates. For a rural illiterate male, it is 4 per cent and for an urban illiterate male it is 17 per cent.

Migration and shifting of workforce from agricultural to non-agricultural sector, in substantive terms, has neither been for the upward social mobility in rural areas and nor for integration with industrialisation or healthy urbanisation with secured livelihood and employment. Rather, this scenario has been caused by destabilisation in traditional sources of livelihood, low levels of capacity building for integration with industrial and service sectors and uneven economic growth, erosion of the traditional bases of the economy, persistent social disparity and marginalisation and inconsistencies between economic growth and social development.

III. Erosion of the Bases of Traditional Economy

Traditionally, India lives in villages and agriculture has remained to be the main means of livelihood to a majority of its population. However, the agrarian societies in India are undergoing a fast process of disorientation in recent years. The first waves of land reforms of the 1950s, 1960s and 1970s, and Green Revolution of the 1970s and 1980s are behind us now. The occasional political outburst for the second phase of Green Revolution does not hold much of a zeal among the ruralites as it has not emerged as an attractive avenue of career promotion for the educated workforce. Rural societies in India, in general, are now characterised by decline in the traditional bases of natural resources and decline in the land–man ratio, stagnation of a vast section of rural workforce in subsistence and below subsistence living and their increasing downward and horizontal social mobility for vast segment of population. The phenomenon of declining land-man ratio over the last half century is shown in Table 6.10:

Table 6.10 *Decline in Availability of Per Capita Land in India 1951, 1981, 2003*

Year	Population (Density in Per Sq Km)	Cultivable Land Including Forest (in hectare)	Total Cultivable Land Excluding Forest (in hectare)
1951	36.1 cr. (117)	0.89	0.48
1981	68.4 cr. (216)	0.50	0.20
2001	102.7cr. (324)	0.33	0.15
2011	121cr. (382)	—	0.13

Source: Indian Council of Agricultural Research (WWW.india.stat.com.), Census of India, World Bank 2012

India has got a phenomenal population growth from 36.1 crore with the density of 117 persons per sq km in 1951 to 68.4 crore with 216 density of population per sq km in 1981. It has increased to 102.7 crore with the density of 324 persons per sq km in 2001 and to 121 crore with a density of 382 population per sq km in 2011. Such quantum increase of population has created enormous pressure on the limited natural resource like land and contributed to the declining land–man ratio in the country. In 1951, per capita cultivable land including forest was 0.89 ha and that of the cultivable land only was 0.48 ha in India. This per capita land holding of cultivable land including forest land has declined to 0.50 ha in 1981 and further to 0.33 ha in 2001. The cultivable land excluding forest land declined to 0.20 ha in 1981 and further to 0.15 ha in 2001 due to sharp population growth in the country. In 2011 it has declined to 0.13 hectare per person. The emerging phenomenon has significantly contributed to a significant increase in the category of semimarginal (having less than 0.04 ha of land) and marginal (owing less than 1.00 ha land) owning households and a decline in the category of landless, medium (owning between 2.01 and 4.0 ha), semi-medium (owning between 4.01 and 10 ha) and large category (owning10+ ha) of land-owning households.

As shown in Table 6.11, in 1971–1972, around 46 per cent of the

Table 6.11 *Percentage Distribution of Rural Household by the Size of Landholding and Covered Area in 1962, 1971–72, 1982, 1992, 2003 in India*

Categories of Households	1971–1972	1982	1992	2003
Marginal (0–1.00)	45.8 (9.2)	56.0 (11.5)	62.8 (15.6)	69.8 (22.6)
Small (1.01–2.00)	22.4 (14.8)	19.3 (16.6)	17.8 (18.7)	16.2 (20.9)
Semimedium (2.01–4.00)	17.7 (22.5)	14.2 (23.6)	12.0 (24.1)	9.0 (22.5)
Medium (4.01–10.00)	11.1 (30.5)	8.6 (30.02)	6.1 (26.4)	4.2 (22.2)
Large (10.00+)	3.1 (23.0)	1.9 (18.2)	1.3 (15.2)	0.8 (11.8)
Total	100 (100)	100 (100)	100 (100)	100 (100)

Note: Figures in the parentheses are the percentage distribution of the area owned by each category.
Source: NSS, 1961–62, 1971–72, 1982, 1992 and 2003.

rural household belonged to the category of marginal cultivators. In 2003, the proportion of marginal cultivators phenomenally increased to around 70 per cent of the total rural households. There has also been significant increase in the area occupied by these categories of the landowners from 9.2 per cent to 22.6 per cent of the total cultivable areas. On the contrary, the proportion of the semi-medium landowners has declined from 17.7 per cent to 9 per cent, medium cultivators from 11.1 per cent to 4.2 per cent and large cultivators from 3.1 per cent to 0.80 per cent of the rural households during the same period. There was a corresponding decline in the area of the land occupied by the medium and the large categories of land owners from 30.5 per cent and 23 per cent of the total area, respectively, in 1971–1972 to 22.2 per cent and 11.8 per cent of the total area respectively in 2003.

There, however, has not been a noticeable change in the quantum of landholding among the semi-medium category of landowners as it has remained fixed to 22.5 per cent during the period under reference despite a decline in the proportion of this category of agrarian household in rural areas from 17.7 per cent to 9.0 per cent during the period under reference. Very significantly, the quantum of land occupied by the small cultivators has significantly increased from 14.8 per cent to around 21 per cent during this period, though the proportion of the small cultivators has decreased from 22.4 per cent to 16.2 per cent. A holistic scenario suggests that in 1971–1972 less than 32 per cent of rural upper category land-owning households (semi-medium, medium and large) had occupied around 74 per cent of the land, while around 68 per cent of lower category land-owning households (marginal and the small) occupied 26 per cent of the land. In contemporary India, a total of 14 per cent rural households (semi-medium, medium and large) occupy 56.5 per cent of the rural land while 86 per cent of the (marginal and small) households occupied 43.5 per cent of the rural land in 2003. The increasing proportion of marginal landholding has brought significant instability in rural economic order. Marginal and small holding is unable to provide livelihood and employment security to a vast segment of rural people. Hence, search for alternative livelihood and employment both inside and outside the village has emerged to be very explicit in rural India.

As the pattern of agricultural development has been very uneven spatially and socially, only limited segments of the population from the agriculturally advanced areas of the country could yield benefit out of this development. Since the caste and class nexus has remained obvious in agricultural modernisation, the affluent upper caste cum class of agrarian society could get further upwardly mobilised – economically, educationally, politically and technologically – through all phases of the Green Revolution. They have got access to advanced education, knowledge and skill and got a greater scope and condition to get integrated with ICT-based education and skill-driven knowledge economy because of their pre-existing social and economic advantage than the remaining sections of society. They pave the way to usher knowledge economy in rural areas, experience relatively more upward mobility than the rest. They migrate to urban areas exercising their economic, social, educational and occupational choice, while the other would migrate out of economic and social compulsion. The lower strata of agrarian hierarchy are most likely to experience a very limited choice because of their pre-existing economic, technological and education/skill deprivation. However, within pre-existing agrarian and rural economy, the low strata and caste of rural work force find themselves decontextualised as labourers and experience growing insecurity and sharp downward mobility.

Increasing Downward Mobility and Marginalisation of Rural Workforce

Currently, 10.5 per cent of rural household are landless. The landless and semi-landless households (having less than 0.04 ha of land that are mostly for residential purposes) altogether form 40.2 per cent of the rural households. In rural India, the landless, the semi-marginal and the marginal cultivators, who altogether formed 62 per cent of the rural households in 1981, constituted 80 per cent of rural holds in 2003 and have emerged to be highly economically vulnerable (NSSO, 2003). Due to meagre size of landholding, a majority of these households either opt for wage earning as agricultural labourers or switch over to nonagricultural avenues of employment to augment household income causing a decline in work participation as cultivators, increase in the category of agricultural labourers and marginal workers, and increasing participation in nonagricultural activities. Lack of proper education and skill makes their mobility circumscribed in manual works of all sorts. Though a section of them got access to functional literacy, this is of seldom help to get an employment security in the rural set-up. Consequently, a section of them migrate to urban areas and joins the army of unorganised labour force experiencing an amount of immediate horizontal mobility without any substantive alternation in their life situation in terms of housing, health, education and livelihood security.

Increasing Use of Agricultural Land for Nonagricultural Purposes

The crisis in agriculture has been compounded by the acquiring of agricultural land from the unwilling and willing landowners both by the government and the private businessmen houses for non-agricultural purposes. Starting from metro cities to district towns, there have been unprecedented activities to acquire and convert agricultural land for building office complexes, industrial set-ups, shopping malls, banquet and cinema halls, housing projects, recreation centres, roads and expressways, varieties of service centres, special economic zones and many such activities that have got priority in the wake of economic liberalisation. An estimate from Uttar Pradesh shows that out of the total area of 19.8 million hectares under food grain cultivation, 6.6 million hectares (roughly one-third) is being shifted for the nonagricultural sector. Such conversion of agricultural land for nonagricultural purpose is underway in many other states under the auspice of the state with the expectation that such initiative would accelerate to economic growth and generate unprecedented flow of employment and wealth. However, in many places, these initiatives have brought economic and cultural shock. Many of these initiatives are executed without taking the farmers into confidence and without fulfilling their basic needs. The agitation by cultivators in Mangalore (Karnataka), Noida and Aligarh (Uttar Pradesh), Hyderabad (Andhra Pradesh), Ambala (Hariyana), Mansa (Punjab), Singur and Nandigram (West Bengal), Goa, Orissa and many other places of the country only reveal economic uncertainty generated among the agriculturalists across the country out of the state sponsored land acquisition initiative.

Large sections of the rural work force who are mostly illiterate, semiliterate, unskilled or semiskilled and lack social capital also find it difficult to get integrated with the current process of industrialisation and emerging new avenues of employment in the service sector. In view of their available skill, capacity, traditional and cultural resources, a large section of them still considers its labour power to remain best suited to agriculture as the main source of livelihood security. A vast section of these people are culturally and emotionally attached to land. Herein the attempt of forceful acquisition of agricultural land by the state has met with organised people's resistance in many parts of the country. In fact, such resistance depicts underneath contradiction between traditional bases of economic, social and cultural security and the perceived threat from market forces of globalisation.

IV. Economic Transition and Anomalies

Poverty: The economic transition of India has been accompanied by high incidence of poverty even though the criteria for the measurement of poverty have varied over the decades. Based on income data of 2005, the World Bank (2012) has calculated that 41.6 per cent of the population lives *below earning poverty line* in India with less than $1.25 per day income while cumulatively 75.6 per cent of the population lives *below earning poverty line* with less than $2 per day income (World Bank, 2012). The Planning Commission of India further reduced poverty line to ₹ 28.65 per capita daily consumption in cities and ₹ 22.42 in rural areas bringing the overall poverty ratio to 29.8 per cent.

According to the NSSO, the ratio of population living below the poverty line has declined from 37.2 per cent in 2004–2005 to 29.8 per cent in 2009–2010 and the rural poverty has declined from 41.8 per cent to 33.8 per cent and urban poverty from 25.7 per cent to 20.9 per cent during the same period. The scheduled tribes of India have the highest extent of poverty with 47.4 per cent followed by scheduled castes 42.3 per cent, other backward classes 31.9 per cent. The poverty ratio among the agricultural labourers in rural areas is to the extent of 50 per cent and among the casual labourers in the urban area is 47.1 per cent. Though the poverty ratio has declined in the country, it has remained significantly higher in the rural areas, among the agricultural labourers and casual labourers especially belonging to the socially marginalised sections of the population (Table 6.12)

Table 6.12 *Changing Poverty Ratio in Contemporary India*

Place	2004–2005			2009–2010				Overall
				Rural		Urban		
	Rural	Urban	Over all	Per Capita con. Ex. Per day	Poverty Ratio	Per Capital con. Ex. Per day	Poverty Ratio	Poverty Ratio
India	42.0	25.5	37.2	22.42	33.8	28.65	20.9	29.8
Maharashtra	47.9	25.6	38.2	24.79	29.5	32.0	18.3	24.5 (13.7)
Tamil Nadu	37.5	19.7	29.4	21.21	21.2	26.7	12.8	17.1 (12.3)
Uttar Pradesh	42.7	34.1	40.9	22.1	39.4	26.6	31.7	37.7 (3.2)
West Bengal	38.2	24.4	34.2	21.4	28.8	27.7	22.0	26.7 (7.5)

Note: Figures in the parentheses are the poverty gap between decadal variations.
Source: Planning Commission, Government of India, Press Information Bureau 19 March 2012.

It is again that poverty has got a regional variation. Among the selected states, Uttar Pradesh has the highest poverty ratio with 37.7 per cent and Tamil Nadu has the lowest poverty ratio with 17.1 per cent; for West Bengal the poverty ratio is 26.7 per cent and Maharashtra 24.5 per cent in 2009–2010. Among these states in the period between 2004–2005 and 2009–2010, decline in poverty has been the highest in Maharashtra with 13.7 per cent, followed by Tamil Nadu 12.3 per cent, West Bengal 7.5 per cent and Uttar Pradesh 3.2 per cent. Despite a decline in the overall poverty ratio across the country, rural poverty has remained significantly higher than the urban areas. In Maharashtra, rural and urban poverty ratios are 29.5 per cent and 18.3 per cent, Tamil Nadu 21.2 per cent and 12.8 per cent, Uttar Pradesh 39.4 per cent and 31.7 per cent, West Bengal 28.8 per cent and 22 per cent, respectively, in 2009–2010.

Slow Pace of Urbanisation and Growing Slums

In India, the extent of urbanisation has substantially increased with a decadal growth rate of around 33.0 per cent during 2001–2011. Now, of the total 1210 million population in this country 377 million (31.16 per cent) live in urban areas. According to 2011 Census, Greater Mumbai has 41.3 per cent, Delhi 14.6 per cent, Kolkata 29.6 per cent and Chennai 28.5 per cent slum households to the total households of these metros. Simultaneously, India's slum-dwelling population has been more than doubled rising from 27.9 million in 1981 to 65.4 million in 2011. They altogether form 22.4 per cent of the total urban areas reported slums in 2011. The growth of slums is widely recognised as the extension of rural poverty, declining land–man ratio, resourcelessness and unemployment and livelihood insecurity in the rural areas. Significantly, more than 91 per cent of the slum population belongs to the other category of workers who mostly work in the unorganised sector.

Lack of Integration of the Marginalised with Emerging Economic Processes

Scheduled tribes, scheduled castes and other backward classes who form 8.2 per cent, 16.2 per cent and 27 per cent of the total population of the country represent not only the lower rung of Hindu caste order but also concentrate on the low paying economic activities in the unorganised sectors. Significantly, of all the agricultural labourers' households, 14.1 per cent are represented by the scheduled tribes, 34.1 per cent by the scheduled castes and 36.4 per cent by the other backward classes (Census, 2001). Around 88 per cent of the scheduled tribes and scheduled castes, 79.9 per cent of other backward classes and 84.5 per cent of the Muslims workers working in the unorganised sector are economically poor and vulnerable (National Commission for Enterprises in the Unorganised Sector, Government of India, 2008). School dropout rates among the scheduled tribes at the primary level is to the extent of 41 per cent and the high school levels 77 per cent; and those for the scheduled castes are to the extent of 37 per cent and 71 per cent, respectively. The incidence of poverty as indicated earlier is also highest among scheduled tribes with more than 47.4 per cent followed by scheduled castes with 42.3 per cent and the other backward classes 31.9 per cent.

In the agrarian society, the submarginal and marginal holdings have become very preponderant among the scheduled castes and scheduled tribes (see Table 6.13) as despite downward mobility they are constrained to remain integrated with agriculture due to the high incidence of illiteracy and lack of alternative skill among them.

Table 6.13 *Landholding and Employment among SC, ST, OBC and Others in Rural Areas*

Social Categories	Average Size of Landholders	Landless and Semilandless (0–04 ha)	Nature of Employment		
			Self-employed	Labour	Others
ST	0.77	34.51	45.7	45.3	8.9
SC	0.30	56.9	34.2	56.0	9.8
OBC	0.75	38.2	56.2	32.7	11.0
Others	100.00	31.1	61.4	23.7	15.3
All			51.7	36.7	11.6

Source: NSSO, 2003.

While the average size of per household landholding for 'other' social categories is 1.00 hectare, for the scheduled castes, scheduled tribes and other backward classes households these are to the extent of 0.30 hectare, 0.77 and 0.75 hectare. For the scheduled castes, 56.9 per cent households are either landless or semi-landless; such types of households among the scheduled tribes are to the extent of 34.51 per cent, other backward classes 38.2 per cent while for 'others' 31.1 per cent. They have a high concentration of illiterates among them and higher extent of work participation as labourers. While among the 'other' social categories, only 23.7 per cent of the workers are employed as labourers, among the scheduled castes, scheduled tribes and other backward classes 56 per cent, 45.3 per cent and 32.7 per cent of workers are employed as labourers. Consequently, they have lower extent of work participation as self-employed. 'Other' social categories have higher ratio of work participation as self-employed with 61.4 per cent. While among the scheduled castes 45.7 per cent, scheduled castes 34.2 per cent and other backward classes 56.2 per cent workers are self-employed.

Besides the above-mentioned social groups, there are more than 360 million illiterates (constituting 35 per cent of the population), more than 60 million primary- and middle-level school drop-outs (constituting 26.45 per cent of the drop outs at the primary level and 49.95 per cent at the middle level, respectively) (MHRD, Government of India, 2008), 21.9 million physically handicapped (constituting 2.13 per cent of the population), 77 million-aged population (constituting around 8 per cent of the total population) from the cross section of the population to be socially vulnerable. All these categories of population suffer from several immediate economic, social and political deprivations and are either denied or deprived of economic, social and political opportunities of mobility in society. Moreover, these categories have explicit intertwining with caste, ethnic and gender divisions of society.

The developmental pathways of India are being confronted with a host of contradictions and anomalies. These are reflected in persistent hunger, poverty, lack of health care, emerging, scare of corruption and many other such issues. Despite 'India Shining', India Leadership; twenty-first century hope, Bharat Nirman, etc., campaign and frequent description of India as an emerging country with high economic growth, 77 per cent of the population cannot afford more than ₹ 14.6 daily for consumption (The Report of the National Commission for Enterprises in the Unorganised Sector, Government of India). In India, there has been phenomenal increase in agricultural production since the 1970s. The average per hectare yield has increased from less than 10 quintals in the 1960s to over 24 quintals in many parts of the country in 2004 (CMIE, 2004). However, this growth does not ensure food security of the rural poor. According to the NSSO (2005) report, the proportion of the rural population unable to access required calories of 2400 a day has climbed from 75 per cent in 1994–1995 to a record of 87 per cent by 2004–2005. In the urban area as well, where the nutritional norms are lower at 2100 calories a day, the proportion rose from 57 per cent to 65 per cent. According to the Global Hunger Index, India ranks 94 among 119 countries of the world with 230 million of rural people being undernourished: the highest for any country in the world. More than 27 per cent of the world's undernourished people live in India, and 20 per cent of India's population is undernourished. Significantly, inflation in food prices continues to rise from 5 to 11 per cent during July 2008–January 2009 even though the general inflation rate has reported to have come down significantly. Again this economic growth has not been able to provide social security to the farmers. According to a report presented in the Lok Shaba, 137,621 farmers committed suicide in 2006 because of indebtedness, crop failure, food insecurity and so on. The farmers' suicide constitutes more than 15 per cent of the total suicide in the country. The fast economic development has also been accompanied by high incidences of corruption at all levels. According to Transparency International, India occupies 94th position at the bottom of 177 nations of the world in the practice of fairness in the public domain (Transperancy International 2013).

Economic Transformation, Regional Disparities and Uniqueness

The story of economic and occupational transformation of India is again marked by regional and rural–urban disparities in India. There have remained variations among the selected states from north, south, east and west in the form and extent of occupational diversification, and these variations have got extended within the state in terms of rural and urban divides and by the sectors of economy therein. Some districts have achieved higher levels of occupational diversification than the state and national average. However, despite these variations, the general trends suggest that in the urban areas service sector provides more employment than the industry, that the service sector has emerged to be the single largest employer, that in rural areas agriculture has remained the single largest employer and industry has remained the second-largest employer in most of the states, that the service sector has been emerging very fast and has surpassed the industrial sector in rural areas in some states (e.g. Maharashtra and West Bengal). These variations are linked to the state of education and extent of urbanisation and technological advancement in the states/regions concerned.

In comparison to 1981, India now has got a higher rate of literacy, an improved level of access to ICTs, higher rate of work participation and occupational diversification and with more people now living in the urban areas in 2011. Importantly, the relation between urbanisation, literacy, ICT penetration and work participation has emerged to be positively interlinked. Table 6.13 shows that while India as a whole has achieved a moderate level of urbanisation with 31.6 per cent in 2011, Maharashtra and Tamil Nadu have achieved a relatively higher level of urbanisation with 45.33 per cent and 48.45 per cent population living in the urban areas, respectively. On the contrary, West Bengal with 31.89 per cent has achieved a relatively moderate level of urbanisation and Uttar Pradesh with 22.8 per cent a low level of urbanisation. Significantly, along with high rate of urbanisation, Maharashtra has also achieved high rate of literacy with 82.91 per cent, high rate of tele-density with 96.34 per cent, high coverage of Internet connectivity with 42.10 per cent, high rate of work participation with 44.0 per cent and high rate of occupational diversification with 30.5 per cent of the workers in service, 17.1 per cent in industry and 52.4 per cent in agriculture (see Table 6.14). These developments are positively linked to a declining rate of work participation as marginal workers and increasing rate of participation in the nonagricultural activities. As shown in Table 6.15 in the period between 2001 and 2011, the proportion of marginal workers to the total workers of Maharashtra has declined from 15.6

Table 6.14 *Trends of Urbanisation, Spread of Literacy, ICTs and Work Participation in India*

States	Urbanisation (%)		Literacy (%)		ICTs (%)		Work Participation Rate (%)		Work Participation in Agriculture (%)		
					Tele Density	Internet Density					
	1991	2011	2011	2011	2010	2010	1991	2011	1991	2011	Change
Maharashtra	35.0	45.33	64.9	82.91	96.34	42.10	42.84	44.0	62.15	52.7	−9.45
Tamil Nadu	33.0	48.45	62.7	80.33	114.28	25.26	44.13	45.5	61.17	42.12	−19.05
Uttar Pradesh	18.0	22.8	41.6	69.72	58.97	9.98	31.27	32.9	74.2	59.2	−15.0
West Bengal	16.5	31.89	57.7	77.08	77.67	12.20	32.37	38.1	54.25	44.3	−9.95
All India	25.7	31.6	52.2	74.04	76.86	12.10	37.68	39.8	67.13	54.6	−12.53

Source: Census of India, 1971, 2001, 2011. TRAI 2011–12

per cent to 11.46 per cent and work participation in nonagricultural activities has increased from 37.85 per cent to 47.3 per cent.

Besides having high rate of urbanisation, Tamil Nadu has also high rate of literacy with 80.33 per cent, high rate of tele-density with 114.28 per cent, high rate of penetration with ICTs with 25.26 per cent and high rate of work participation with 45.5 per cent. Tamil Nadu has also got very high levels of occupational diversification with 4.2 per cent in the household industry, 53.68 per cent in other category of works and 42.12 per cent engaging in agriculture. Like Maharashtra, Tamil Nadu's developmental trajectory has also positively linked to an increasing rate of work participation in the nonagricultural activities.

As shown in Table 6.15 in the period between 2001 and 2011, the proportion of marginal workers to the total workers of Tamil Nadu has only marginally increased from 14.6 per cent to 15.5 per cent and work participation in nonagricultural activities has increased from 38.3 per cent to 57.9 per cent.

The low level of urbanisation with 22.8 per cent in Uttar Pradesh is linked to its relatively low rate of literacy with 69.72 per cent, lower rate of tele-density with 58.97 per cent, low level of Internet coverage with 9.98 per cent and low rate of work participation with 32.5 per cent. Uttar Pradesh has also got relatively slower rate of occupational diversification with more than 59.2 per cent workforce still engaged in agriculture, and the remaining engaged in nonagricultural occupation. These low rates of development are linked to high rates of work participation as marginal workers and low rate of work participation in the nonagricultural activities. As described in Table 6.15 in the period between 2001 and 2011, the proportion of marginal workers to the total workers of Uttar Pradesh has increased from 27.1 per cent to 32 per cent. Work participation in nonagricultural activities has increased from 25.8 per cent to 40 per cent. Though Uttar Pradesh experienced sharp increase in nonagricultural occupation in the last decade, agricultural occupation still predominates in the state.

West Bengal, on the contrary, besides having a relatively moderate level of urbanisation with 31.9 per cent, has a moderate rate of literacy with 77 per cent, tele-density of 77.67 per cent and low level of ICT penetration with 12.20 per cent and a moderate level of work participation with 36.8 per cent. West Bengal, however, has a very high level of occupational diversification with declining work participation in agriculture to 43.8 per cent, increasing work participation in the nonagricultural sector. Significantly, high rate of population growth and declining land–man ratio has compelled a vast section of the workforce to move out of agriculture. There has been a significant increase in the quantum of marginal workers and simultaneously non-agricultural work participation in the state in recent years. In the period between 2001 and 2011, the proportion of marginal workers to the total workers in West Bengal has increased from 21.9 per cent to 26.1 per cent and work participation in non-agricultural activities has increased from 45.47 per cent to 56 per cent.

Table 6.15 *Changing Patterns of Work Participation Selected States Update*

State	Size of Work Force (in Million)	Marginal Workers Within Total Workers			Other than Agricultural		
	2011	1991	2001	2011	1991	2011	% Change
All India	481.7	9.0	22.2	24.8	32.87	45.6	12.73
Maharashtra	34.78	8.5	15.6	11.46	37.85	47.3	9.45
Tamil Nadu	32.88	5.7	14.6	15.5	38.83	57.9	19.07
Uttar Pradesh	65.81	7.7	27.1	32.8	25.8	40.8	15.0
West Bengal	43.75	6.1	21.9	26.1	45.75	56.0	10.25

Work participation has also increased in urban areas from 36.8 per cent in 1981 to 39.3 per cent 2001 in all India level, 35.21 per cent to 36.49 per cent in Mumbai, 28.3 per cent to 34.3 per cent in Chennai, 32.2 per cent to 32.8 per cent in Delhi and 35.2 per cent to 37.6 per cent in Kolkata during the same period. Though the proportion of marginal workers to total workers is lower in metro cities in comparison to the overall trend, there has also been an increase of this category of workers over the decade from 1.5 per cent in 1981 to 5.7 per cent in 2001 in Mumbai, 1.5 per cent to 7.2 per cent in Chennai, 0.78 per cent to 5 per cent in Delhi and 0.91 per cent to 5.5 per cent in Kolkata.

VI. The Shifting Horizon and Its Social Complexities

The Structural Adjustment Programme and economic neoliberalism that have brought phenomenal shift in the economic fundamental of the state, insinuated the processes of economic transition, extent and patterns of work participation by repositioning the significance of education and technology in it. The shift in the economic arrangement has been accompanied by a shift in the educational and ICT perspectives of the state resulting in increasing market take-over of education and ICTs and their phenomenal expansion across the space. The shift that has been reflected in the economic, educational and ICT arrangements in the country and in their phenomenal expansion. These have been accompanied by new economic, social and cultural momentum in society. India has shifted towards an era of fast economic growth (notwithstanding recent economic slowdown) with new avenues of employment and occupational diversifications and by producing high-quality manpower.

These shifts experience positive co-relationships between increasing literacy with declining gender gap in literacy rates and increasing rates of work participation both for men and for women, increasing rate of urbanisation, access to literacy and ICTs with high rates of occupational diversification and increasing work participation in the non-agricultural sector along with an increase in work participation as marginal workers. In the process of such repositioning, the traditional sector of economy that has provided livelihood, employment and sociocultural sustenance to the dominant majority experiences a shift whereby the new expanding service sector has been experiencing the highest rate of economic growth and has got a place of privilege over the traditional one. Despite agriculture remaining the highest provider of employment in the country and rural areas providing more employment in comparison to the urban areas, there has been phenomenal occupational diversification and expansion of the non-agricultural sector of economy. This growth story is marked by a decline of contribution of agriculture to the national GDP and a decline in work participation in agriculture, a relative increase in the contribution to GDP by the industrial sector and an increase in work participation and significantly fast expansion of the service sector of economy surpassing the growth rate of agriculture and industry and producing the highest GDP.

The phenomenal expansion of occupational diversification and occupational diversification is accompanied by the declining land–man ratio and erosion in the traditional source of economy in the country, on the one hand, and increasing level of education, skill and literacy in the country, ICTs and knowledge revolution and the changing political and economic environment across the globe on the other. This growth trajectory, however, is marked by regional and spatial disparities, poverty, rampant illiteracy, low level of skill development among a section of workers, increasing presence of marginal workers as a significant category, overwhelming employment in the informal sector both in rural and in urban areas, and casualisation of work force, increasing the presence of self-employed workers due to the inability of industrial and service sector to provide salaried employment.

Though this new momentum has widened the space both for horizontal and for vertical occupational mobility for a vast section of the people, there have remained severe disconnects between prosperity and poverty, economic growth and livelihood insecurity, new occupational proliferation and occupational diversification and casualisation and marginalisation of workforce, increasing foreign direct investment and un/under-employment, increasing rate of migration and inadequate spread of urbanisation, ICT revolution and digital divides across the country. In fact, these social and economic disconnects have remained ingrained with inherited social realities, lives.

The economic transition is taking shape in India within the given spatial diversities and the coexistence of multiple economic and social realities. These realities are part agricultural, part industrial and part service driven. These are again posited within the complexities of spatial (rural, urban and metropolitan) and social (caste, ethnic, and gender) divides and the diverse access to education and ICTs by different segments of people therein. The economic and the occupational dynamics of contemporary India are located within these composite multiple realities, on the one hand, and the neoliberal economic drive of the state, on the other. The combination of these realities has simultaneously conditioned the emergence of knowledge society to be layered and segregated, but rejuvenating and resurgent in India.

7

Education, ICTs and Work

The Divergent Empirical Reality

I. Knowledge Society in the Making with Inequality in Access as Social Reality

The emergence of knowledge society as a global phenomenon in the contemporary world is augmented ideologically by the expansion of the political philosophy of neoliberalism, socially strengthened by the expansion of skill and education, technologically furthered by the penetration of ICTs and mass communication networks and economically enhanced by the emergence of knowledge workers and new avenues of employment as promoted by the neoliberal globalisation. The neoliberal states have initiated new and modified old institutional mechanisms paving the way for fast transition in the economy, educational arrangements, ICTs usage and work participation patterns and in the broad social and cultural edifice of society. The foundation of knowledge society is in the making in India and the potential of such making has been marked by the phenomenal increase in the rate of literacy; increase in the average age of retention of youth in the education system; enlargement of numerical strength of trained and educated manpower; expansion of educational arrangements at all levels; increasing use of knowledge and ICTs; phenomenal state support for the promotion of ICTs; ICT-enabled industries and its usage; emergence of knowledge work and knowledge workers as a distinct social category; increasing occupational mobility and diversification of economy and declining significance of agriculture, rising contribution of service sector in economy; growing significance of knowledge workers in the economic life of the state and society; increasing flow of foreign investment especially in the service sector of economy; escalating collaboration in offshore trading with multinational agencies; emergence of new avenues of employment both in rural and in urban areas; increasing speed of urbanisation and rural-to-urban migration; and many such conspicious changes in the techno-economical, demographic and socio-cultural dynamics of society. In fact, the emerging technoeconomic environment of the country has now provided the required space for the mass production of knowledge, ushering of opportunities for knowledge works and knowledge workers and their integration with economy and culture of society. The new economic momentum has set in motion with new policy initiatives of the governments and active participation of international agencies and the multinational corporations. These altogether have provided the space and possibilities of shaping up of a new society and economy founded on knowledge. This environment has taken a leap forward by willingness of the people, cross-cutting the boundary of all social divides, to invest on education and training, to get access to ICTs and to contribute to the mass production and use of knowledge in their day-to-day life, on the one hand, and huge concentration of young population in the country who would be available as the educated and trained manpower to the world knowledge market in years to come.

In recent years, the scope and condition for the development of required potential for integration with knowledge society has been furthered, and new patterns of social mobility have been initiated. However these processes have got widely conditioned by the pre-existing societal arrangements along with their inherited dynamics of social segregation, hierarchy, divisions and exclusions. These traditional divisive forces have got reinforced or reoriented to keep their hold in many ways on the present society. In essence, the social foundation of Indian society, which is intrinsically linked to varieties of social inequalities and divides based on caste, class, gender, religion, region and ethnicity, has profoundly influenced, in all likelihood, the arrival of any new order. The unequal access to productive and social resources remain the basis for unequal social integration; and the previously induced economic transformations have bred more social inequality than inclusion. The pre-existing social and economic divides by conditioning people's access to recognised bodies of skill or knowledge are likely to provide people only equal opportunities to develop skill and knowledge to get integrated with the knowledge society. Though philosophically the knowledge society is expected to break the barriers of pre-existing social and economic unevenness, the historical experience only restricts us from making a sweeping conclusion. It indeed needs a critical scrutiny of the emerging facets of knowledge society that is being shaped within these pre-existing social divides, on the one hand, and the spatial rifts among the villages, district towns and the metropolitan cities, on the other.

The Empirical Scheme: The Village, the District Town and the Metro City Continuity or Disconnect?

India has posited itself since the last six decades in a state of economic and social flux resulting from the complementary coexistence of diverse forces of tradition and modernity, enlightenment and ignorance, indigeneity and exogeneity, agrarianism and industrialism and industrialism and postindustrialism within the transitional ambit of its society. This flux has been accentuated in view of sustained spatial diversities and social divides in contemporary India causing unequal space and pace for integration of people with the emerging social and economic momentums. As against this backdrop focusing empirically on the access to education, ICTs, patterns of work participation, ratio of participation in knowledge work, position in occupational hierarchy and emerging patterns of social interaction of 2946 working people, of which 989 are from metro cities, 1004 from district towns and 953 from villages, engaged in all varieties of occupations and organisations including knowledge-based ones, this study delineates the form and extent of emergence of knowledge society, and the patterns of integration of various segments of population with this emerging society in India. This study besides focusing on work participation has examined the key dimensions of the emergence of knowledge society and has also elaborated the sociocultural dynamics as generated out of the penetrations of education, ICTs and the new market forces and the formation of new sociocultural milieu, fluidities and identities across the space.

Occupational Categorisation

India now experiences the proliferation of varieties of workers across the social space – the metro cities, the district towns and the villages.

This proliferation has been widely distinctive for a large section of the workforce and has been facilitated by their skill and knowledge improvisation, technological enabling and occupational and spatial mobility. For example, rural agricultural labourer has got exposed to parallel avenues of employment as construction labourer or a manual cart or rickshaw puller. A section of the marginal peasants also exploits the opportunity of becoming a petty shop owner, small vendor, vegetable seller and even a construction labourer seasonally. Thus, a condition has emerged for a section of the agricultural labour force to be released from agriculture for other avenues of manual work. Similarly, the scope of mobility has become a possibility for other sections of workers as well, for example, a manual typist now upgrades his or her skill to become a computer operator, or an office peon upgrades his or her qualification to become a clerk or to be a multitask/multiskilled worker or the like. Many traders and departmental store owners open chains of business outlets. Many newly educated youth become simultaneously property dealers and manufacturers of localised items, transporters and take advantage of emerging new avenues of economic engagement being self-employed. Similarly, many engineers become managers. Many of these sections of workers practise seasonal secondary occupation and take advantage to immediate economic opportunities. Despite such inclusiveness major sectors of activities are classified into five types keeping in view the parameter of major source of yearly earning from specific occupational engagement.

- *Cultivator/farmer*: Big, medium, small and marginal landowners who spend majority of their time in agriculture and whose major source of earning is agriculture and who engage either in self-cultivation or hiring labourers for cultivation of own land are categorised as cultivators/farmers.

- *Agricultural labourers*: Semi-marginal cultivators, share croppers, tenants (who do not find agriculture as their major source of their earning; and combine cultivation with wage earning), agricultural labourers, construction labourers, fishermen, gardeners', etc., engaged in wage earning through manual activities are categorised as 'agricultural labourers'.

- *Other nonagricultural manual labourers/workers*: 'Workers such as plumbers, carpenters, cycle or automechanics, mechanics, drivers, rickshaw pullers, security guard, sweepers, cobblers, petty vendors, hawkers, etc., are included in the category of 'other nonagricultural manual labourers/workers.'

- *Business or self-employed:* In the 'business or self employed' category, persons occupied as traders, manufacturers, agricultural or nonagricultural product processors, petty shop owners with varieties of activities are included.

- *Service:* In general, the respondents working as teachers, researchers, laboratory assistants, government employees and private sector employees, artists, media workers, tourist guides, accountants, civil society activists, property and tax consultants, property dealers, lawyers, personnel in the tourism and travel industry and courier services, data operator and health workers, *anganwadi* workers, doctors, nurses, salesmen, BPO workers, private tutors, typists, computer operators, service providers of all electronic and electrical equipment and any such category who provide services based on specialised knowledge and skills are included in the category of 'service'.

II. Caste, Ethnicity and Occupation

The traditional social framework of Indian society that is deeply interwoven with traditional caste, ethnic and gender hierarchy while, on the one hand, influences the course of proliferation of new avenues of employment, people's association with these emerging avenues, it also gets influenced by interpenetration of education and skill development opportunities and ICTs in society, arrival of new avenues of occupational mobility and interpenetration of new cultural milieu on its members, on the other. However, the emerging intersectionality between these forces is again widely spatially conditioned. Does it produce new occupational categories or reproduce the old ones in a new context?

The Metro Phenomenon

In terms of caste composition, 56.3 per cent of the respondent of metro cities belong to the general category (members from Hindu, Muslims, Christians, Buddhists, Jains and others who are not included in the reserved category), 23 per cent to the other backward classes, 19.4 per cent to the scheduled castes and only 1 per cent to the scheduled tribes (see Table 7.1). Of the total respondents in metro cities, 41.6 per cent are in service, 22.7 per cent in business/self-employment, 34.8 per cent in wage earning as labourers in all categories and only

Table 7.1 *Social and Occupational Backgrounds of the Respondents*

Place	Social Background					Occupation Background				
	Total	Gen	OBC	SC	ST	Culti-vators	Agri-cultural Labour	Nonagri-cultural (Manual Labour-ers and Workers)	Business	Service
Delhi	278	56.8	15.2	27.0	1.0	3.8	–	43.8	20.1	32.3
Mumbai	210	70.6	7.9	21.5	–	–	–	32.0	32.0	36.0
Chennai	227	15.7	68.6	15.7	–	–	–	20.5	19.1	60.4
Kolkata	274	82.0	1.5	13.5	3.0	–	–	42.6	19.7	37.7
Metro Cities	989	56.3	23.3	19.4	1.0	0.9	0.0	34.8	22.7	41.6
Meerut	277	62.4	23.8	13.8	–	8.0	2.8	31.5	19.9	37.8
Thane	180	71.4	5.9	22.7	–	2.3	–	30.7	27.0	40.0
Balurghat	217	61.7	7.0	22.3	9.0	10.5	13.2	36.9	10.4	29.0
Nagercoil	330	8.6	84.6	6.8	–	2.7	8.3	17.8	24.8	46.4
District Towns	1004	51.0	30.3	16.4	2.3	5.9	6.1	29.2	20.5	38.3
Bhagwanpur	144	45.5	32.0	22.5	–	30.5	20.0	15.0	22.2	12.3
Dangarhat-Mamudpur	262	51.1	8.9	28.9	11.1	20.6	24.0	25.4	18.0	12.0
Killiyur	347	–	88.0	10.7	1.3	4.0	28.3	30.4	20.8	16.5
Villages	753	32.2	43.0	20.7	4.1	18.4	24.1	23.6	20.3	13.6

Source: Data Collected by the Research Team in 2010–11.

0.9 per cent in cultivating/farming activities. However, the localised variations are important in the emerging socioeconomic formations of these metro cities as these have social bearings on the penetration of knowledge society therein.

Of the 278 respondents selected from Karol Bagh, Govindpuri, Ayanagar areas covering middle class and lower middle class and the slum areas of Delhi, 56.8 per cent belongs to the general category, 15.5 per cent to the other backward classes, 27 per cent to the scheduled castes and one per cent to the scheduled tribes. So far as the occupational distribution of these respondents are concerned, 3.8 per cent is engaged in cultivation, 43.8 per cent in wage earning and manual activities as labourers, 20.1 per cent in business and 32.3 per cent in service. Of the total 227 respondents from Chennai, 15.7 per cent belongs to the general category, 68.6 per cent to the other backward classes and 15.7 per cent to the scheduled castes. There has been high concentration of working population in service sector in Chennai with 60.4 per cent followed by wage labour of all categories with 20.5 per cent and business with 19.1 per cent. In Kolkata, of the 274 respondents 82 per cent belong to the general category, 1.5 per cent to the other backward classes, 13.5 per cent to the scheduled castes and 3 per cent to the scheduled tribes. Of these selected respondents, 42.6 per cent is in wage labour and related activities, 37.7 per cent in service and 19.7 per cent in business as their major economic pursuits. Of the total 210 respondents from Dharavi slums, Kalina and adjacent areas with middle-class and lower-middle-class areas of Mumbai, 70.6 per cent belong to the general category, 7.9 per cent to other backward classes and 21.5 per cent to the scheduled castes. Of the total respondents, 36 per cent is in services, 32 per cent each is engaged in wage earning as labourers and in related activities and in business.

The District Towns

In India district towns are growing fast. Significantly, relatively less people are engaged here in business and service than that of the metro cities; and simultaneously more people have retained their agricultural occupation than found in the metro cities. In general, in the district towns, 38.3 per cent of the population are engaged in service, 20.5 per cent in business, 29.2 per cent in wage earning and related activities and 12 per cent in agriculture either as cultivators or agricultural labourers. Socially of the total population, 51 per cent belong to the general category, 30.3 per cent to the other backward classes, 16.4 per cent to the scheduled castes and 2.3 per cent to the scheduled tribes. However, there are a few socioeconomic specialties of these district towns as well that are linked to their varied educational backgrounds, occupational structures and caste compositions.

In Meerut, of the 277 respondents from Shastri Nagar, Saket and adjacent areas, 62.4 per cent belong to the general category, 23.8 per cent to the other backward classes and the remaining 13.8 per cent to the scheduled castes. Of the total, 10.8 per cent are engaged in agriculture either as cultivator or agricultural labour, 31.5 per cent are labourers or manual workers, 19.9 per cent in business and 37.8 per cent in service. Out of the 180 respondents from Thane, 71.4 per cent belong to the general category, 5.9 per cent to the other backward classes and 22.7 per cent to the scheduled castes. Of these selected respondents, 30.7 per cent are labourers or manual workers, 27 per cent in business, 40 per cent in service and only 2.3 per cent are engaged in farming/cultivation as their main economic activity. Of the 330 respondents in Nagercoil, 84.6 per cent belong to the other backward classes while 8.6 per cent to general category and 6.8 per cent to the scheduled castes. Occupationally, 11 per cent population are engaged in agriculture, 17.8 per cent in the activities as labourers or manual workers and 24.8 per cent in business and as high as 46.4 per cent in service. In the district town of Balurghat, of the 217 respondents 61.7 per cent belong to the category of general population, 7 per cent to the other backward classes, 22.3 per cent to the scheduled castes and 9 per cent to the scheduled tribes. Though this is a growing town, a majority of the population, that is, 36.9 per cent is engaged in economic activities as labourers or manual workers, 10.4 per cent in business, 29 per cent in service and 23.7 per cent in agricultural occupation. A significant section of the respondents, especially from low-caste and tribal background who are occupationally engaged labourers and others, migrate to this town seasonally while remaining occupied in agriculture in their native places.

The Villages

Though India still lives in villages, the socioeconomic framework of Indian villages has undergone phenomenal change in recent decades. However, these changes are taking shape in the pre-existing societal arrangements where caste system largely conditions social and economic frameworks of society and its organisation of production. Of the 753 respondents from the village areas, 32.2 per cent belong to general category, 43 per cent to the other backward classes, 20.7 per cent to the scheduled castes and 4.1 per cent to the scheduled tribes. Economically, of all these respondents, 18.4 per cent are cultivators, 24.1 per cent are agricultural labourers, 23.6 per cent are nonagricultural labourers, 20.3 per cent are in business and 13.6 per cent are in service. Significantly, a total of 57.5 per cent of these respondents are engaged in nonagricultural activities to indicate that rural India now is in the process of fast occupational diversification. However, the pattern of this development is socioculturally distinctive and locally specific that delineates variations between the villages from east, west, north and south.

In the Bhagwanpur village of Meerut District, Uttar Pradesh, 45.5 per cent of the respondents are from the general category, 32 per cent the other backward classes and 22.5 per cent the scheduled castes. Occupationally, 30.5 per cent of them are farmers/cultivators, 20 per cent agricultural labourers, 22.2 per cent in business and 12.3 per cent in service. The villages of Dangarhat and Mamudpur in the Kumarganj Development Block of South Dinajpur district, West Bengal, are marked by multiethnicity and occupational diversification. Among the selected respondents, 51.1 per cent belong to the general category, 8.9 per cent to the other backward classes, and 28.9 per cent to scheduled castes and 11.1 per cent to scheduled tribes. Occupationally, 20.6 per cent are engaged in farming/cultivation, 24 per cent belong to the category of agricultural labourers, 25.4 per cent to nonagricultural labourers and 18 per cent to business and 12 per cent to service.

Killiyur is predominantly a fishing village located in the Kanyakumari District of Tamil Nadu. Of the total respondent, 88 per cent belong to the category of other backward classes, 10.7 per cent to the Schedule Castes and 1.3 per cent to the Schedule Tribes. Only 4 per cent respondents from this village are engaged in economic activities as cultivator, 28.3 per cent as agricultural labours, 30.4 in fishing as non-agricultural labourers, 20.8 per cent in business and 16.5 per cent in service.

Line of Commonality

However, despite all these variations, the patterns of caste/ethnic concentration in the metro cities, district towns and villages are widely linked to the overall population composition of the state concerned. The metropolitan and the district towns such as Delhi, Kolkata, Mumbai, Meerut, Thane and Balurghat and the adjacent villages have high concentration of general category population while the metropolitan city of Chennai, district town Nagercoil and the adjacent villages to it have a high concentration of other backward classes population. This phenomenon in Tamil Nadu is linked to the sociohistorical background of anti-Brahmin movements in the state as during these movements many upper caste households left the villages for cities forever.

Though there has been significant representation of the scheduled caste population in the metropolitan cities and district towns across the regions, there have been very marginal representations of scheduled tribal population in most of the metropolitan cities. The representation of scheduled tribe population in the urban areas is widely linked to their low-level educational attainment and low access to information about alternative avenues of livelihood, and low extent of their occupational mobility, on the one hand, and their sociocultural orientation, on the other. While a section of the educated tribal population come to the urban areas by availing the opportunity of reservation in government jobs, a very few of the illiterate and manual labourers from this category chose to migrate to urban areas predominantly because of cultural contrast and lack of social networks. While for the other backward classes and the scheduled castes spatial and occupationally mobility has been higher with relatively higher degree of educational attainment and increasing flexibility among them to move from one occupation and space to others.

III. Educational Background

Though education is the key enabler for integration in knowledge society, it has got unevenly spread in society and among the population both from the rural and from urban areas. Vast sections of social groups, who have suffered historically and have remained subject of social negligence and injustice in contemporary India, find themselves unevenly posited vis-à-vis the others for getting integrated with knowledge society directly through education. Even though the urban areas of India have emerged to be educational hubs, providing necessary opportunities for capacity development and integration with knowledge society, within this set-up itself these segments have got varied extent of access to education and the skill development opportunities and capability for integration with knowledge society. As the intensity of urbanisation decreases such capability also declines in general and for the marginalised segments of population in particular. The technical and higher educational qualifications that play a key role in getting integrated with the core activities of a knowledge society have been diversely acquired by different segments of population; and thus though contemporary India has emerged to be a hub of highly trained manpower, the form and extent of such emergence have been highly layered and widely conditioned by social and spatial divides.

The General Trend

Both the micro and macro-level data suggest that illiteracy in general has remained concentrated among the scheduled caste and scheduled tribe and in rural areas, while higher and technical education mostly among the general categories and a small section of the other backward classes both in rural and in the urban areas. Again, rural areas have more concentration of population with the general category of education, while the urban ones have more population with technical and higher levels of education than those of the rural areas. There have also been gender divides among the respondents in terms of their level and types of educational backgrounds. Higher the caste and ethnic background of women worker, higher is their educational status. Significantly, the patterns of work participation in general and work participation as knowledge workers in particular have widely been conditioned by historically inherited and situationally accumulated disparities in India.

Literacy, Education and Metro town and Village Divides

As discussed in Table 7.2, the increasing extent of urbanisation has remained positively linked to the higher level of educational backgrounds of the workers. Indian villages have higher extent of illiterate workers and workers with secondary and below levels of educational background than the district towns; and district towns have more workers with such educational background than the metro cities. Again, the villages have lesser proportion of workers with under- and postgraduate and technical educational background than district towns and the district towns have lesser proportion of workers with such higher educational background than the metro cities. The slum areas in the district towns and the metro cities in particular have

Table 7.2 *Levels of Education, Access to ICTs and Occupational Patterns in the Metro Cities, District Towns and Villages*

		Metro Cities	District Towns	Villages
Levels of Education	Illiterate	3.6	7.2	15.5
	I–XII	47.0	50.8	63.2
	UG & PG (liberal)	32.8	31.4	19.8
	Technical	16.6	10.6	1.5
Access to ICTs	Telephone	80	55.5	22.0
	Mobile	98.0	82.5	83.3
	Computer	38.0	29.0	6.1
	Internet	31.0	20.8	2.9
	Radio/TV	100	100	100
Occupational Patterns	Farming	0.9	5.9	18.4
	Agricultural Laboural	-	6.1	24.1
	Nonagriculture Laboratory and Others	34.8	29.2	23.6
	Business	22.7	20.5	20.3
	Service	41.6	38.3	13.6

Source: Data Collected by the Research Team in 2010–11.

been lagging behind in the overall achievements in literacy rate in the urban areas. Of the total selected working population from the rural areas, 15.5 per cent are illiterates while in the metro cities and district town their proportions are to the extent of 3.6 per cent and 7.2 per cent only. More than 63.2 per cent of rural workers have pre-primary to senior secondary levels of education, while 47 per cent from metro cities and 50.8 per cent of district towns have such educational backgrounds. The high representation of rural workers in this educational cohort is predominantly because of expansion of adult literacy and total literacy programmes in the rural areas. Though these have brought them to the above the illiteracy level, they are yet to have a big leap forward for the graduation and technical levels of education. Only 19.8 per cent rural working population have under and postgraduate levels of education, while in the metro cities and district town 32.8 per cent and 31.4 per cent workers have such educational background, respectively. Technical education plays a crucial role for skill upgradation and upward social mobility. Only 1.5 per cent of the rural workers, while 10.6 per cent district town and 16.6 per cent from metro cities, have technical educational background.

It is again that higher the extent of highly qualified and technical manpower, the lesser is the participation in agriculture; and more is the participation in business- and service-related activities. The high concentration of highly qualified and technically educated manpower in the metro cities and district towns has been positively linked with higher participation of the workforce in the service and business pursuits. While low-level educational and technical background is positively linked to the high extent of participation in agriculture-related activities or manual activities in rural areas.

Deep Down Social Divides across the Space

The general trend of unequal access to literacy and education is not only linked to the degree of urbanisation, but also to the caste, ethnic and the gender hierarchy. Higher the place in the caste and gender hierarchy, higher is the access to literacy and education. This has again been influenced by the degree of urbanisation.

Illiteracy: At the village level, 18 per cent of women workers are illiterate; it declines to 14.25 per cent in the district towns (see Table 7.3). The lower the social status, higher is the rate of illiteracy among the social groups; and again illiteracy declines as the degree of urbanisation increases. 50 per cent of the scheduled tribal workers at the village level are illiterate and it declines to 40 per cent in district towns and becomes zero per cent in metro cities. Among the scheduled castes, 19.7 per cent are illiterate at the village level; 4.8 per cent at the level of district towns and 13 per cent in the metro cities. The high degree of illiteracy among the scheduled caste workers in the metro cities is due to the higher extent of illiterate migrants among them. The general category workers have no illiteracy at any level.

Secondary and below level: Secondary level of education has been spreading very fast in the country and accordingly more workers have educational background up to secondary level than the higher ones. At the village level, around 70 per cent of the general category

Table 7.3 Level of Education of Respondents

Place	Gen				OBC				SC				ST				Women			
	Nil	I–XII	UG+PG	Tech	Nil	I–XII	UG+PG	Tech	Nil	I–XII	UG+PG	Tech	Nil	I–XII	UG+PG	Tech	Nil	I–XII	UG+PG	Tech
Delhi	–	53.0	25.0	22.0	–	46.0	30.0	16.0	12.0	78.0	8.0	2.0	–	50.0	50.0	–	–	30.0	40.0	30.0
Mumbai	–	52.0	32.0	16.0	–	58.0	26.0	10.0	21.0	55.0	13.0	11.0	–	–	–	–	–	33.0	41.0	26.0
Chennai	–	–	50.0	50.0	–	60.0	23.0	17.0	–	65.0	20.0	15.0	–	–	–	–	–	23.0	59.0	18.0
Kolkata	–	50.0	39.0	11.0	–	100.0	–	–	19.0	61.0	10.0	10.0	–	33.0	67.0	–	–	7.0	57.0	36.0
Metro Cities	0.0	38.8	36.5	24.7	3.5	66.0	19.7	10.8	13.0	64.7	12.8	9.5	0.0	41.5	58.5	0.0	0.0	23.3	49.2	27.5
Meerut	–	35.0	55.0	10.0	5.0	22.0	66.0	7.0	19.0	48.0	24.0	9.0	–	–	–	–	15.0	26.0	43.0	16.0
Thane	–	38.0	41.0	21.0	–	58.0	33.0	9.0	–	58.0	29.0	13.0	–	–	–	–	12.0	40.0	33.0	15.0
Balurghat	–	72.0	20.0	8.0	7.0	66.0	15.0	12.0	–	90.0	7.0	3.0	40.0	50.0	10.0	–	20.0	42.0	30.0	8.0
Nagercoil	–	56.0	35.0	9.0	–	51.0	31.0	18.0	–	64.0	25.0	11.0	–	–	–	–	10.0	61.0	22.0	7.0
District Towns	0.0	50.2	37.8	12.0	3.0	49.2	36.3	11.5	4.8	65.0	21.2	9.0	40.0	50.0	10.0	0.0	14.3	42.2	32.0	11.5
Bhagwanpur	–	63.0	34.0	3.0	15.0	48.0	34.0	3.0	23.0	63.0	14.0	0.0	–	–	–	–	16.0	80.0	4.0	–
Dangarhat-Mamudpur	–	86.0	10.0	4.0	5.0	78.0	15.0	2.0	13.0	77.0	8.0	2.0	50.0	30.0	20.0	–	20.0	55.0	25.0	
Killiyur	–	60.0	37.0	3.0	20.0	43.0	34.0	3.0	23.0	63.0	14.0	0.0	–	–	–	–	18.0	78.0	4.0	–
Villages	0.0	69.7	27.0	3.3	13.3	56.3	27.7	2.7	19.7	67.6	12.0	0.7	50.0	30.0	20.0	0.0	18.0	71.0	11.0	0.0

Note: Percentage is calculated to nearest round figure.
Source: Data Collected by the Research Team in 2010–2011.

workers have secondary or lower levels of education; at the district level, it declines to 50.2 per cent and metro cities to 38.8 per cent. For the other backward classes at the village level 56.3 per cent, district towns 49.2 per cent and metro cities 66 per cent have such educational background. For the scheduled castes, these are 67.6 per cent at the village level, 65 per cent at the district and 64.7 per cent at the metro city levels. For the scheduled tribes at the village level 10.6 per cent, district town 12.5 per cent and metro city 20.6 per cent and for women workers at the village 71 per cent, town level 42.25 per cent and metro city level 23.3 per cent have secondary or below level of education.

Under-and postgraduate: At the village level, the other backward classes have highest with 27.7 per cent of workers with under- and postgraduate educational backgrounds, closely followed by the general category with 27 per cent, scheduled castes 12 per cent, women 11 per cent and scheduled tribes 6.7 per cent. At the district level, 37.8 per cent general category workers are with such high educational background followed by the other backward classes with 36.3 per cent, women 32 per cent, scheduled castes are far behind with 21.2 per cent and the scheduled tribes 2.5 per cent only. In the metro cities, women have 49.2 per cent workers with such educational qualification, followed by the general category with 36.5 per cent, the scheduled tribes 29.3 per cent, other backward classes 19.75 per cent and the scheduled castes 12.8 per cent. The high extent of women's representation in high educational background is reflective of the fact that more and more women are now entering the job market than ever before in India. Similarly, in the metro cities the scheduled tribe workers have got a higher educational background even though their numerical strength is very limited. In fact, most of them joined the job with a higher educational qualification.

Technical education: Though among all social categories, respondents with technical educational backgrounds are proportionately low, respondents from urban areas and general caste background and other backward classes have got an edge over the rest. Only 3.3 per cent of general category workers at the village level, 12 per cent in district and 24.7 per cent in metro cities possess such technical qualification. Among the other backward classes and the proportion of workers with such technical educational background are to the extent of 2.7 per cent at the village, 11.5 per cent at the district and 10.8 per cent at the metro city levels. The scheduled castes and the scheduled tribes substantially lag behind the general category and the other backward classes. Among the scheduled castes, these are .7 per cent at the village, 9 per cent at the district town and 9.5 per cent at the metro town levels, respectively. In our sampling, no scheduled tribal worker has a technical educational background. At the village level, the women workers with technical educational background are conspicuously missing while at the district and the metro cities, 11.5 per cent and 27.5 per cent of them, respectively, have such educational qualifications. Women from the general categories and other backward classes have high access to technical education than those of the scheduled castes.

Education by providing the impetus for acquiring knowledge has paved the way for occupational and upward social mobility. There has been the tendency, which is but natural, among the educated population to switch over from agriculture and manual activities to nonagriculture and nonmanual activities. In fact, with increasing access to education, quest for alternative avenues of nonagricultural employment both in rural and in urban areas has substantially increased. Hence, business and service have been generous hosts to accommodate the aspiration of this upwardly mobile skilled and educated population and have been playing a crucial role in the occupational mobility and in the emergence of knowledge job in society.

IV. Access to ICTs

ICTs have emerged to be a vital factor for integration of workers with the knowledge society widely affecting their occupational mobility, social networking and patterns of engagement with the wider world. However, their access has also been conditioned by several of the social and economic factors. The low level of literacy and educational background is positively linked to low level of access to ICTs especially landline telephone, computer and Internet and a high rate of participation in agricultural activities in the villages. On the other hand, high rates of literacy and higher educational level have been positively linked to higher levels of access to ICTs and mass communication systems and higher extent of participation in nonagricultural activities, especially in the business-and service-related activities in urban areas. The variation in this relation is again circumscribed by the caste and ethnic backgrounds of the respondents and spatial divide in society.

The Comparative Trend

In recent years, the process of shifting of working population from agriculture to nonagriculture and also migration of people from rural to urban areas has been facilitated by the spread of ICTs and mass communication networks. Though ICTs are spreading very fast, villages phenomenally lag behind the district towns and the metro cities in this regard. However, the gap in the access to mobile phone and radio/ TV has been substantially lower than to the access in other ICTs such as landline telephone, computer and Internet. In the rural areas, 22 per cent of the workers have got access landline telephone, while for the metro cities and district towns this is to the extent of 80 per cent and 55.5 per cent, respectively. Among the rural workers, (as shown in Table 7.2) only 6.1 per cent have access to computer and 2.9 per cent to Internet, while for the metro cities 38 per cent and 31 per cent and the district towns 29 per cent and 20.8 per cent, respectively, have access over these ICTs. However, in the case of mobile phone, population from the village and the district town have more or less similar extent of access with 83.3 per cent and 82.5 per cent respectively while the workers from metro cities have higher extent of access with 98 per cent. Though people across the villages, district towns and in the metro cities make extensive use of both landline and mobile telephones, the use of mobile phones, has been very extensive than the landline because of easy accessibility and cost effectiveness. Significantly, all respondents from rural areas, metro cities and district towns have access over either radio or a TV.

Telephone and Mobile Connections

Working people from metro cities still have higher usage of landline telephone than their counterparts in the district towns and the villages. In Delhi, the penetration rate of telephone and mobile among these people is to the extent of 66.2 per cent and 90 per cent, respectively.

Table 7.4 *ICTs Penetration in the Selected Metros, District Towns and Villages*

Place	Telephone	Mobile	Computer	Internet	Radio and/or Telivision
Delhi	66.2	90.0	21.1	10.2	87.0
Mumbai	51.0	92.0	17.2	9.3	75.0
Chennai	63.0	94.0	25.6	13.0	82.0
Kolkata	55.0	95.0	18.4	10.6	85.0
Metro Cities	58.8	92.7	20.6	10.7	82.3
Meerut	41.0	70.0	9.1	6.6	70.0
Thane	55.0	80.0	10.6	8.2	75.0
Balurghat	47.0	75.0	7.2	2.1	80.0
Nagercoil	13.2	69.6	12.3	6.3	76.7
District Towns	39.0	76.15	9.8	5.8	75.4
Bhagwanpur	15.2	86.3	4.0	2.2	75.6
Dangarhat-Mamudpur	13.0	72.0	2.0	0.5	76.0
Killiyur	15.2	74.0	1.5	1.0	92.0
Villages	14.5	77.4	2.5	1.2	81.2

Source: Data Collected by the Research Team in 2010–11.

For Mumbai, these densities are to the extent of 51 per cent and 92 per cent, Chennai 63 per cent and 94 per cent and Kolkata 55 per cent and 95 per cent.

The gap between telephone and mobile densities among the working population in the district towns is higher with 37.15 per cent than the metro cities where the gap is to the extent of 33.9 per cent. In the district towns of Meerut, the telephone and mobile densities among these people are 41 per cent and 70 per cent, for Thane 55 per cent and 80 per cent, Balurghat 47 per cent and 75 per cent and Nagercoil 13.2 per cent and 69.6 per cent, respectively.

The gap in teledensity in telephone and mobile phone among the workers is highest in the rural areas with 62.9 per cent. Significantly, the higher gap between landline telephone and mobile phone shows a higher extent of the use of latest communication tool, that is, the mobile phone.

For the Bhagwanpur village, telephone and mobile densities among the working population are to the extent of 15.2 per cent and 86.3 per cent, Dangerhat-Mamudpur 13 per cent and 72 per cent and Killiyur 15.2 per cent and 74 per cent, respectively. It is important that the rural–urban divide is in the decline so far as access to mobile telephone is concerned. Such divide has also declined over access to radio and television.

Computer and Internet

Computer and Internet as the potential social transformers have been penetrating at a high speed all over the country. However, the spatial disparities are sharp for the access in computer and internet technologies across the space. The extent of penetration of computer and internet increases along with the increasing intensity of urbanisation and educational development in the country. For metro cities such as Delhi 21.1 per cent and 10.2 per cent working people have got access over computer and internet, for Mumbai, Chennai and Kolkata these are to the extent of 17.2 per cent and 9.3 per cent, 25.6 per cent and 13 per cent, and 18.4 per cent and 10.6 per cent, respectively. For the district towns of Meerut, Thane, Balurghat and Nagercoil, these penetrations among these people are 9.1 per cent and 6.6 per cent, 10.6 per cent and 8.2 per cent, 7.2 per cent and 2.1 per cent, and 12.3 per cent and 6.3 per cent, respectively. The village workers lag behind substantively in having such access to computer and Internet. In Bhagwanpur, Dangarhat-Mamudpur and Killiyur villages, these are to the extent of 4 per cent and 2.2 per cent, 2 per cent and 0.5 per cent and 1.5 per cent and 1 per cent, respectively.

Though there are internal variations within the selected villages, district towns and the metro cities in terms of their access to ICTs, these overall variations are tending to be minimal except for a few cases. These variations are again minimal among the working population engaged with new avenues of employment across the space. This phenomenon will be explicit as we discuss the changing occupational landscape in society.

V. The Changing Occupational Landscape and Pre-existing Social Divides

Increasing access to literacy and education, ICTs and wider social and economic networks have brought a phenomenal change in the occupational landscape of the country. Traditionally, work participation in rural India has long been described in terms of predominance of agriculture while occupational diversification has been a feature of urban areas. However, in contemporary India, occupational diversification has characterised the pattern of work participation across the space: village, district towns and metro cities with diversity though. The metropolitan cities are usually dominated by service, business and varieties of nonagricultural activities. Such trends are also preponderous for the district towns such as Meerut, Thane, Nagercoil and Balurghat. Because of its proximity to Mumbai, Thane has absolute concentration of nonagricultural occupation. The spread of nonagricultural occupation is reflected even in the villages of Uttar Pradesh, Tamil Nadu and West Bengal as well.

The general trend in the occupation transition in India shows that there has been significant penetration of nonagricultural activities even in the rural areas, that the district towns and metropolitan cities have more workers engaged in business and services than in the rural areas and that rural areas have more population engaged in manual activities as labourer than that of the district town and the metropolitan cities. However, the patterns of occupational transition have not been the same for all caste groups and also for men and women equally (see Table 7.5).

Work Participation in the Village, Towns and Metro Cities by Caste, Ethnicity and Gender

The emergence of knowledge society and its functioning is linked to the proliferation of nonagricultural activities in general and service and business activities in particular. This emergence is significantly conditioned by the preexisting spatial and social divides in the country as these have played crucial roles in getting one's access to education and technology.

The overall trend: All over India across the metro cities, the district towns and the villages, the general category of population has higher extent of participation in the business and service followed by the other backward classes. On the other hand, the scheduled caste has highest concentration in all categories of 'labour' followed by the scheduled tribes. However, the extent of such work participation for these social categories has been varied by their spatial location. Significantly, the

Table 7.5 *Patterns of Work Participation (%) by Caste and Gender*

Place	Gen				OBC				SC				ST				Women (Form all these Groups)			
	Total	Farm	Lab and other	Bus and Ser	Total	Farm	Lab and other	Bus and Ser	Total	Farm	Lab and other	Bus and Ser	Total	Farm	Lab and other	Bus and Ser	Total	Farm	Lab and other	Bus and Ser
Delhi	120	1.0	14.0	85.0	32	12.0	42.0	46.0	57	6.0	65.0	29.0	2	–	50.0	50.0	67	–	48.0	52.0
Mumbai	108	–	2.0	98.0	12	–	38.0	62.0	33	–	53.0	47.0	–	–	–	–	57	–	35.0	65.0
Chennai	24	–	25.0	75.0	104	–	30.0	70.0	24	–	12.0	88.0	–	–	–	–	75	–	15.0	85.0
Kolkata	162	–	18.0	82.0	3	–	33.4	66.6	27	–	78.0	22.0	6	–	50.0	50.0	76	–	33.4	66.6
Metro Cities	414	.25	14.7	85.0	151	3.0	35.8	61.2	141	1.5	52.0	46.5	8	0.0	50.0	50.0	275	0.0	32.8	67.2
Meerut	126	–	–	100.0	48	18.0	27.0	55.0	28	14.0	71.0	15.0	–	–	–	–	75	–	39.0	61.0
Thane	85	–	6.0	94.0	7	–	24.0	76.0	27	9.0	48.0	43.0	–	–	–	–	61	–	45.0	55.0
Balurghat	97	10.2	2.6	87.2	11	5.0	52.0	43.0	35	20.0	45.0	35.0	14	9.0	80.0	11.0	60	8.0	71.0	21.0
Nagercoil	19	–	–	100.0	186	8.0	45.0	47.0	15	3.0	26.0	71.0	–	–	–	–	110	–	33.4	66.6
District Towns	327	2.5	2.2	95.3	252	7.8	37.0	55.2	105	11.5	47.5	41.0	14	9.0	80.0	11.0	306	2.0	47.1	50.9
Bhagwanpur	50	21.0	4.0	75.0	35	48.0	11.0	41.0	25	34.0	61.0	5.0	–	–	–	–	34	19.0	64.0	17.0
Dangarhat-Mamudpur	92	11.0	4.0	85.0	16	32.0	60.0	8.0	52	29.0	43.0	28.0	20	10.0	72.0	18.0	82	21.0	68.0	11.0
Killiyur	–	–	–	–	213	6.0	37.0	57.0	26	–	60.0	40.0	3	–	100.0	–	105	10.0	38.0	52.0
Villages	142	16.0	4.0	80.0	264	28.7	36.0	35.3	103	21.0	54.7	24.3	23	5.0	86.0	9.0	221	16.7	56.7	26.6

Note: Lab stands for labour, bus for business, ser for services.
Sources: Data collected by research team in 2010–11

scheduled castes and the tribes are more in workforce as labourers in the rural areas and in district town than in the metro towns. Women's work participation in business and service is least in rural and sequentially more in the district town and in metro cities. It is due to the fact that the metro cities and district towns with more educational facilities provide relatively more space for occupational mobility to the scheduled castes, tribes and the other backward classes and women than their counterparts in the rural areas.

Work Participation Patterns of the General Category and the Other Backward Classless

As shown in Table 7.5, as the levels of urbanisation increase the extent of participation in the business and service also increases for all. However, the general category and the other backward class people have got higher participation in these occupations than the other social categories. In the villages, 80 per cent of the general category people are engaged in business and service. In the district town and in metro cities, their participation in business and service is to the extent of 95.3 per cent and 85 per cent, respectively. Now the general category people have a significantly higher rate of work participation as labourers than ever before in the urban areas. Their participation in the cultivation and labour category job is to the extent of 16 per cent and 4 per cent in the rural areas, 2.5 per cent and 2.2 per cent in the district towns and .25 per cent and 14.7 per cent in the metro cities. While in the rural areas and even in the district towns, the general category people are reluctant to accept labour category job, in the metro cities such social reluctance seldom gets a place of prominence over economic necessity. Again many migrants from the general category, who were reluctant to work in rural areas as labourers, accepted this category of jobs in urban areas without much hesitation. Many respondents reveal that anonymity helps to get them associated with manual work in the urban, especially in the metro cities. Among the other backward classes 28.7 per cent are farmers, 36 per cent are labourers and 35.3 per cent are in service and in business in rural areas. However, in the district towns and in the metro cities, 55.2 per cent and 65.2 per cent are in business and service, 37 per cent and 35.8 per cent In labour category jobs of all sorts and 7.8 per cent and 3 per cent in farm-related activities. Higher degree of urbanisation and access to education provide them the space for upward occupational mobility.

Work Participation Patterns of the Scheduled Castes and Scheduled Tribes

Though work participation in the business- and service-related activities have significantly penetrated, the predominant form of work participation for these social categories has remained confined to labour-type activities. Of the total scheduled caste working population in rural areas, 21 per cent are in farming, 54.7 per cent are labourers and 24.3 per cent are in business and service. While in the district towns and metro cities among the scheduled castes 11.5 per cent and 1.5 per cent are in farming, 47.5 per cent and 52 per cent in labour-type activities and 41 per cent and 46.5 per cent in business and service activities. Among the scheduled tribes 5 per cent of the working population are in cultivation/farming, 86 per cent in labour category jobs and 9 per cent in business and service in the rural areas. In the district towns 80 per cent of them are in labour category activities, 11 per cent in service and business and 9 per cent in cultivation/farming activities. Not all metro cities have scheduled tribal working proportion. However in these metros where ever their presence is available 50 per cent of them are in the labour and other categories of jobs and the remaining 50 per cent in service. Though for the scheduled castes along with the increased intensity of urbanisation, participation in the business- and service-related activities have increased, such increase has been minimal for the scheduled tribes. In fact, capacity deprivation holds a large section of workforce from these social categories to remain associated predominantly with manual labour.

Women and their Work Participation

The localised values and conditions have widely circumscribed the interplay of several indigenous and exogenous forces affecting women's work participation. In general, women from the general category have more representation in business and service than the scheduled castes, tribes and backward classes who have more representation in labour category activities. At the village level, working women are predominantly engaged in agriculture with 56.7 per cent occupied as agricultural and other labour and 16.7 per cent engaged in farming as cultivators while 26.6 per cent women are in business and service. In the district towns and metro cities, 47.1 per cent and 32.8 per cent are in labour category activities, and 50.9 per cent and 67.2 per cent in business- and service-related activities, respectively. Again 2 per cent district town women are also engaged in farming activities. In general, intensity of urbanisation and access to education have provided women opportunities for occupational mobility in the nonagricultural activities. Across the urban space, the urge to prove the intellectual and creative worth has been very explicit among educated women.

Work Participation among Social Groups in Individual Metro Cities

In Delhi, of the total general category respondents only 14 per cent are in the category of labour and other activities while 85 per cent are in business and service, and only 1 per cent of them is involved in cultivation. Among the other backward classes, 42 per cent are engaged in labour and other activities, 46 per cent in business and service while 12 per cent of them are in farming. Of the total SC population, the overwhelming majority with 65 per cent are engaged in labour and other activities, 29 per cent in service and business and 6 per cent in farming. Among the scheduled tribes, 50 per cent are in labour and other activities while 50 per cent are in service. Among the working women, 48 per cent are employed as labour and other related activities and remaining 52 per cent are in business and service. Delhi depicts the association of lower social status of women with their higher participation in the labour and other types of activities. It is also linked to low educational status of a section of women workforce who predominantly work in the construction activities or as the domestic help, etc.

In Mumbai, 98 per cent of the working population from the general category are in business and service and only 2 per cent are in labour and other activities. Among the other backward classes 62 per cent are in business and service while 38 per cent are in labour and other related activities; and among the scheduled castes 88 per cent are in business and service and only 12 per cent in labour and other categories. Among the women 85 per cent are in business and service while 15 per cent are in labour and other activities.

In Chennai, 75 per cent of the working population of general category are engaged in business and service while 25 per cent in labour and related activity. Among the other backward classes, 70 per cent are in business and service and remaining 30 per cent are in labour and other related activities. Among the scheduled castes also 88 per cent are in business and service while 12 per cent are in labour and other related activities. Among the women respondents, 15 per cent are in labour and other related activities while 85 per cent in business and service. The higher extent of women's participation in business and service is linked to the higher extent of their participation in teaching, and in new avenues of employment such as the ICT-BPO sector and in retail shop, etc.

In Kolkata, 82 per cent of the general category workers are engaged in business and service while 18 per cent are in labour and other related activities. About 66.6 per cent of the other backward classes workers are in business and service and 33.3 per cent are in labour and other related activities. While for the scheduled caste workers, 78 per cent are in labour and other related activities and 22 per cent are in business and service. About 50 per cent of the scheduled tribe workers in Kolkata are in business and service and 50 per cent are in labour and other related activities. Among the women respondents, 33.4 per cent are in labour and other activities while 66.6 per cent are in business and service.

Work Participation among Social Groups in Individual District Towns

In the case of Meerut, cent per cent workers from the general category belong to the occupational group in business and service. Among the other backward classes, 55 per cent of the workers are in business and service, 27 per cent in labour and other activities and 18 per cent in cultivation. So far as the scheduled castes are concerned, 78 per cent of them are in labour and other activities, while only 22 per cent in business and service activities. Among the women workers, 61 per cent are in business and service activities and 39 per cent are in labour and other related activities. The increasing participation of women in business and service is linked to the expansion of education among women and emerging nature of middle class aspiration of the city.

In Thane, 94 per cent general category working women are in business and service and only 6 per cent are engaged in labour and other related activities. Among the other backward classes, 76 per cent are in business and service and remaining 24 per cent are in labour and other related activities. Among the schedule caste respondents, 48 per cent are in labour and other related activities, 43 per cent are in business and service and 9 per cent in cultivation. Among the women workers, while 55 per cent are in business and service 45 per cent are in labour and other activities.

In Nagercoil, of all the general category workers, 47 per cent of the other backward classes and 71 per cent of the scheduled castes are engaged in business and service. About 45 per cent of the other backward classes and 26 per cent of the scheduled caste workers are engaged in labour and other related activities. Women workers also have a high rate of work participation in business and service with 66.6 per cent, while 33.4 per cent workers are in labour and other related activities. The other backward classes and scheduled castes in Nagercoil and Chennai have high access to education and simultaneously have the opportunity of employment in business and services due to the expanding new educational and economic institutional networks in these areas. Again the long traditions of anti-Brahmin movement have made the other backward classes and the scheduled castes equally aware of the new avenues of social mobility.

Among the general category workers of Balurghat, 87.2 per cent are in business and service, 2.6 per cent are in labour and other related activities and 10.2 per cent are in the cultivation. Of the total other backward class workers, 52 per cent are in labour and other related activities, 43 per cent in business and service and 5 per cent in cultivation. Among the scheduled castes, 35 per cent are in business and service, 45 per cent are in labour and other related activities and 20 per cent in cultivation. While among the scheduled tribe workers 80 per cent are in labour and other related activities, 11 per cent in business and service and 9 per cent in cultivation. Among the female workers, 71 per cent are engaged in labour and other related activities, 21 per cent in business and service and 8 per cent in cultivation. In the district towns, the number of agriculturalists is relatively more because of the fact that (a) a section of agricultural labourers seasonally migrate to urban areas for employment as peddlers or construction labourers, (b) many landowning households have migrated and settled in towns for educational purpose of their children while their main source of earning has remained agriculture and (c) the city is surrounded by agriculture.

Work Participation among Social Groups in Individual Villages

Occupational diversification is also taking place in the villages in the caste line. In the Bhagwanpur village in Meerut district, while 75 per cent of the working population among the general caste are in business and service, only 4 per cent of them are in labour and other related activities. Agriculture is less preferred by them over business and service and thus only 21 per cent of them are in the farming activities. Among the other backward classes, 41 per cent are in business and service, 48 per cent are in cultivation and only 11 per cent in labour and other activities. Among the scheduled castes, only 5 per cent are in business and service, 34 per cent are in cultivation and 61 per cent are in labour and other activities. Among the women workers from the village, only 17 per cent are in service and business, 19 per cent are in cultivation and 66 per cent in labour and related activities. Business and service activities have emerged to be fast-expanding revenues of economic engagement in this village. However, because of higher access to education, social capital and existing awareness, the upper caste and the other backward classes have been able to take greater access to the emerging avenues of nonagricultural activities than the lower castes. Though women are also making an onward march towards service economy with expansion of education, they lag behind in comparison with men due to the pre-existing social bearing.

In the Dangarht-Mamudpur villages in Kumargang block, 85 per cent of the general category workers are in business and service, 4 per cent are in labour and other activities while 11 per cent are in cultivation. Among the other backward classes, 60 per cent are in labour and other related activities, 32 per cent in cultivation and only 8 per cent in business and services. Among the scheduled caste, 29 per cent are in farming, 43 per cent in labour and other related activities and 28 per cent in business and service. Among the scheduled tribes, 10 per cent are in cultivation, 72 per cent are in labour and other activities while only 18 per cent in business and service. Among 82 female workers,

68 per cent is in labour and other related activities, 21 per cent are in farming and 11 per cent are in service and business.

In the Killiyur village of Nagercoil District, there is no general category working people. Among the other backward classes, 57 per cent are in business and service, 37 per cent are in labour and other activities and 6 per cent are in cultivation. All the scheduled tribe workers are engaged in labour and related activities. Among women workers, 10 per cent are in farming, 38 per cent are in labour and other related activities while 52 per cent are in business and service. In these villages, as the overwhelming section of workers are engaged in fishing, women have higher extent of participation in the marketing of fishing than in other activities.

Table 7.6 *Levels of Education and Occupational Diversification*

Places	Level of Education				Types of Occupation				
	Illit-erate	I–XII	UG + PG	Tech-nical	Farm-ing	Agri-cultural Labourer	Nonagri-cultural + Others	Business	Service
Delhi	4.0	51.4	30.6	14.0	3.8	–	43.8	20.1	32.3
Mumbai	6.8	49.5	28.0	15.7	–	–	32.0	32.0	36.0
Chennai	–	37.0	38.0	25.0	–	–	20.5	19.1	60.4
Kolkata	3.8	50.2	34.6	11.4	–	–	42.6	19.7	37.7
Metro Cities	3.6	47.0	32.8	16.6	0.9	0.0	34.8	22.7	41.6
Meerut	9.8	32.7	47.0	10.5	8.0	2.8	31.5	19.9	37.8
Thane	3	48.5	34.0	14.5	2.3	–	30.7	27.0	40.0
Balurghat	13.4	64.0	16.4	6.2	10.5	13.2	36.9	10.4	29.0
Nagercoil	2.5	58.0	28.2	11.3	2.7	8.3	17.8	24.8	46.4
District Towns	7.2	50.8	31.4	10.6	5.9	6.1	29.2	20.5	38.3
Bhagwanpur	13.5	63.5	21.5	1.5	30.5	20.0	15.0	22.2	12.3
Dangarhat-Mamudpur	17.6	65.2	15.6	1.6	20.6	24.0	25.4	18.0	12.0
Killiyur	15.3	61.0	22.2	1.5	4.0	28.3	30.4	20.8	16.5
Villages	15.5	63.2	19.8	1.5	18.4	24.1	23.6	20.3	13.6

Source: Data Collected by the Research Team in 2010–11

In all it shows that higher degree of urbanisaion is linked to higher level of educational attainment among the working population, and higher level of occupational diversification therein. As it is again a part of this sequence, as shown in Table 7.6, higher level of urbanisation and education is linked to higher degree of work participation in the non-agricultural activities. Thus, as the degree of urbanisation increases work participation in service and business activities also increases, paving the way for the emergence of knowledge work with diverse intensity across the space.

Empirical Trends of Diversity

The spread of higher and technical education, literacy and penetration of ICTs notwithstanding its unequal access, brought changes not only in the work condition but also in the patterns of work participation and in occupational mobility. Within these whole processes across the space, India has posited phenomenal occupational diversification through the emergence of nonagricultural avenues of employment at all levels. These show varieties of correlations between education technologies and pre-existing social arrangements, social and spatial divides. Hence, the identified empirical trends show that:

- The quantum of educated and trained manpower has phenomenally increased all over India. However, this increase has been faster in the metro cities and in the district towns than in the villages.

- Human resources with higher and technical education background mostly remained confined in the district town and the metro cities, while illiterate and semieducated or semiskilled manpower have remained proportionally higher in the rural areas than in the urban areas.

- Though the spread of technical education has been slower than other education, and the general categories have got greater access over this education than the other social groups across the space, this situation is undergoing a change. While the upper castes have dominance over higher and technical education in the rural areas and the upper castes along with the other backward classes dominate over such education in the district towns, much of their domination is in the decline in the metro cities.

- Though ICTs have been spreading very fast all over the country, the spread of such technologies has been layered. The rural areas significantly lag behind the district towns and the district towns in relation to the metro cities in terms of their access to Internet, computer and landline telephone. Again, the general category population has a higher quantum of access over these ICTs than the other backward classes and the other backward classes have higher access than the scheduled castes, scheduled tribes and women. Women from higher caste groups have higher access over ICTs than women from the lower caste groups.

- Though the people from metro cities have higher access over mobile than the district towns and villages, the difference between the district town and village respondents has become minimal so far as the access to mobile phone is concerned. Again, caste divide has become minimal as far as the penetration of mobile telephone is concerned.

- The penetration of radio and television has been significantly high both in the rural and in urban areas.

- The expansion of education and ICTs has been accompanied by a high level of occupational diversification and emergence of new avenues of employment across the country. Service business and manufacturing activities of various sorts have contributed predominantly to this occupational diversification.

- Positive corelationships have been explicit between higher educational achievement, higher access to ICTs and higher degree of occupational diversification.

- These correlations are also having caste, gender and spatial orientation that depicts that the working people from metro areas due to higher access to higher and technical education have got higher access to ICTs and experience higher degree of occupational diversification than those of village and district towns.

- The general category because of their higher access to higher and technical education and ICTs experience higher degree of occupational mobility diversification. The education and ICT-driven occupation mobility to business and service is higher in the metro cities than the district towns and the cities. However, these opportunities have been opened up across the space with diverse intensity though.

- Women from upper general categories and middle-class background experience higher degree of occupational mobility because of their access to higher and technical education and ICTs than the rest.

- The lower caste and tribal respondents experience faster occupational mobility than ever before having access to ICTs and education. They experience mobility on the new avenues of manual jobs both in urban and in rural areas.

- A section of the general category workers also experience downward mobility because of the lack of capacity development among them.

Notwithstanding the debate as to whether people created alternative avenues of economic activities to meet their social need or people participated in these alternative economic activities as these appeared in the scene, contemporary India experiences a new momentum of work and work relations with substantive alteration in the social existence, quality of lives and social relations of people across the villages, towns and cities. This momentum is accompanied by fast occupational mobility among all sections of people and across space. However, this mobility is largely circumscribed by the contemporary state of their access to education, skill and technology especially the ICTs, on the one hand, and the varied inherited economic and social realities, on the other. With this new economic momentum, on the one hand, and continuity of multiple economic arrangements, on the other, India experiences new waves of rejuvination with the arrival of knowledge workers.

8

Knowledge Society

Work, Workers and Work Relations

I. Knowledge: Changing Contexts and Combination

Conventionally in Indian society, though there have remained a numerically thin category of intellectual or 'people of wisdom' to provide society with the required guidance, information, direction, judgement and explanation on a variety of economic, social and natural processes and events, efforts for scientific validation and commercial exploitation of these expertise were not explicit in the public domain. These bodies of knowledge, as we have discussed in chapter three, were neither processed nor certified for mass production and application at a large scale. In contemporary society, the scope and condition of economic exploitation of knowledge has become very explicit with knowledge acquiring a commodity value though with a varied intensity across the social and geographical space. In recent years, along with revolution in Information and Communication Technologies (ICTs) and globalisation of economy, large-scale commercial exploitation and mass production of knowledge, there has been phenomenal increase in use of knowledge in all domains of lives. These have altogether redefined the significance of knowledge workers of all sorts. They have acquired new cultural meaning, political power and economic validity in present-day society. Significantly, knowledge work in India is taking shape in a pre-given order that has not discarded the past. As contemporary society has become highly transitional with a high volume of swinging socially between tradition and modernity, culturally between globalisation and localisation, economically between agrarianism, industrialism and post-industrialism, technologically between hoe–hammer and microchips, operationally between multitasking and specialisation the scope of application of knowledge with all possible combinations has emerged to be a reality. Herein, there has been the process of combining old knowledge with new knowledge, old knowledge jobs with the emerging new knowledge jobs and continuation of old knowledge workers with the emerging body of new knowledge workers.

The Knowledge Workers

In the changing trajectory of Indian society there have been:

- the old/conventional knowledge workers such as the teachers, lawyers, judge, doctors, health workers, etc., and also

- the new knowledge workers who are dealing with information and communication technologies, media, business processing and a host of related activities that have emerged especially in the wake of globalisation and information revolution in recent decades.

In general, metro cities have a high concentration of knowledge workers followed by the district towns and the villages. Again, the villages have a higher ratio of old knowledge workers than the new knowledge workers among them, even though there has been a gradual emergence of new knowledge workers in the rural space. The urban space, on the other hand, has borne witness to the fast proliferation of new knowledge workers. Significantly, many of the old knowledge jobs have either got redefined or got added new value with application of new technology or new knowledge both in rural and urban space. For example, local *aya* (midwife) after undergoing training now uses modern techniques of child delivery or a village *Patwri* (land record official) now uses computer to maintain their land records. Most conventional typists now use computer and new software for word/data processing. Most of the old knowledge workers are now also posited to apply and use ICTs and new body of knowledge emerging through interpenetration of ICTs in recent years. Though a vast category of knowledge jobs is exclusive in nature, there are a number of jobs whose scope has expanded in recent years getting indirectly linked to knowledge jobs.

As the knowledge job cannot sustain in isolation, it creates the condition for its support services and accordingly provides employment opportunity to a large number of people as support service providers. Thus, in India across the social and spatial divides, there have emerged categories of core knowledge workers, workers indirectly linked to knowledge work and the manual workers. Hence, these major categories are again posited in a hierarchical order.

• *Core:* A host of jobs are identified to be knowledge jobs directly like those of teachers, researchers, managers and executives, judges, lawyers, doctors, entrepreneurs, nurses and health workers, professionals engaged in ICTs, software and hardware engineers, banking and retail services providers, media, business processing, real estate, share market, etc., brokers, consultants, event managers, lobbyists, journalists, planners, architects, editors, designers, typists, computer operators, telephone operators, proof readers and agricultural extension workers, intelligence and intellectual service providers and so on. They are highly specialised, predominantly occupy fixed positions and experience sharp occupational and frequent spatial mobility.

• *Linked to the core:* A variety of jobs such as that of office peons, laboratory assistants, security service managers, human resource providers, labour contractors, suppliers dealing with computer hardware, ICTs and other electronic media devices, transport providers, floor assistants, make-up man/woman in a film studio, electronic and electrical technicians and so on are indirectly linked for the promotion of knowledge jobs. Many of them are the intermediaries and arrange support services for the knowledge industries. While many of these services pre-existed, the nature and extent of those activities are in the increase with expansion of new knowledge jobs. The workers engaged in these jobs are highly flexible and transitional categories, and experience vertical occupational mobility. A section of this category gets upwardly mobilised after acquiring skill, knowledge and specialisation as knowledge workers.

• *Manual worker:* They are the direct support service providers who include both semiskilled such as fitters, carpenters, drivers, rickshaw pullers, security guards, mechanics, etc., and unskilled manual workers of all sorts such as construction labourers whose quantum of activities have increased with expanding knowledge economy. They have pre-existed as manual workers in agricultural and in varieties of non-agricultural/part manual activities. The manual content of their work prevails over their knowledge and skill even though many of them work in association with machine. They are predominantly the migrants in urban space, marginal workers in the villages and experience occupationally horizontal mobility.

Knowledge workers have differential intensity of arrival and work participation in the mega metro cities, the district towns and the villages. This differential intensity has got caste, ethnic and gender orientations and has got compounded by differential access to education and ICTs.

Knowledge Workers (Both the Core and Linked to Core) as Engaged in Business and Service Activities

Business and service have emerged to be core areas of engagement for knowledge workers amongst all non-agricultural activities. Significantly, a proportion of self-employed among the knowledge workers is in the increase in recent years. Hence, as the knowledge workers are directly engaged in the activities of production, dissemination and exploitation of knowledge through their association in the varieties of business and service activities, it would be restricting but reasonable to identify knowledge workers through their engagement in business and service in metro cities, district towns and villages in India. The available trends suggest that higher the extent of participation in the business and service activities, irrespective of social and spatial divides, higher is the extent of engagement with knowledge-based activities therein. Consequently, upon the increase in the proportion of the direct knowledge workers in the service and business activities, the proportion of workers providing support services for knowledge jobs through various kinds of semi- and unskilled activities has also increased significantly. Again importantly, the proportion of knowledge workers within business and service categories is higher across India among the general category of population followed by the other backward classes than among the scheduled castes and scheduled tribes. Women have higher representation as knowledge workers than the schedule castes and other backward classes, and scheduled tribes. Again women from general category have a higher presence in knowledge jobs than those of the rest. On the contrary, the proportion of support service providers in knowledge jobs is higher among scheduled castes and scheduled tribes.

Knowledge Workers in Metro Cities

In general, metro cities have the highest concentration of knowledge workers followed by the district towns and the villages. In the metro cities, among the total working population 64 per cent is in business and service and the proportion of knowledge workers among the business and service categories is to the extent of 73 per cent, while the proportion of knowledge workers among the total workers is 49.8 per cent (see Table 8.1). In the district towns, these are to the extent

Table 8.1 *Proportion of Knowledge Workers in Relation to the Service/Business and Total Workers*

Place	Gen % of Work-ers in Bus + Ser	OBC % of Work-ers in Bus + Ser	SC % of Work-ers in Bus + Ser	ST % of Work-ers in Bus + Ser	Women % of Work-ers in Bus + Ser	Total		
						% of Work-ers in Bus + Ser	% of Knowl-edge Workers in Bus + Ser	% of Knowl-edge Workers to Total Workers
Delhi	85.0	46.0	29.0	50.0	52.0	63.0	78.0	59.0
Mumbai	98.0	62.0	47.0	-	42.0	62.0	72.0	47.0
Chennai	87.0	70.0	88.0	-	85.0	78.0	81.0	49.0
Kolkata	82.0	66.0	22.0	50.0	36.0	53.0	61.0	44.0
Metro Cities	88 .0	61.0	46.5	25.0	53.8	64.0	73.0	49.8
Meerut	100.0	55.0	15.0	-	61.0	57.0	56.0	40.0
Thane	94.0	76.0	43.0	-	65.0	67.0	70.0	55.0
Nagercoil	100.0	47.0	71.0	-	62.0	68.0	72.0	41.0
Balurghat	87.0	97.0	35.0	11.0	21.0	51.0	48.0	39.0
District Towns	95.3	68.8	41.0	02.7	52.3	60.8	61.5	39.5
Bhagwanpur	75.0	41.0	5.0	-	17.0	32.0	40.0	33.0
Killiyur	-	57.0	40.0	-	52.0	46.0	48.0	21.0
Dangarhat–Mamudpur	85.0	92.0	28.0	18.0	11.0	48.0	41.0	21.0
All villages	53.3	63.3	24.3	6.0	26.7	42.0	43.0	25.0
Average of Total	78.86	64.36	37.26	11.23	44.26	55.6	59.16	38.1

Source: Data collected by the Study Team in 2010–2011.

of 60.8 per cent, 61.5 per cent and 39.5 per cent and for the villages 42 per cent, 43 per cent and 25 per cent. These are indicative of the fact that the quantum of knowledge workers declines with the decline of the quantum of urbanisation and vice versa.

Of the total working population in Delhi, 63 per cent are in business and service; again, of the total workers engaged in business and service, 78 per cent are the knowledge workers and the knowledge workers altogether constitutes 59 per cent of the total workers in Delhi. In Mumbai, 62 per cent of the total working population are engaged in business and service categories; and 70 per cent of them are knowledge workers, and these workers altogether form 47 per cent of the total working population of Mumbai. Chennai has a very high intensity of occupational diversity with 78 per cent of the workers engaged in business and service. The knowledge workers of Chennai form 81 per cent of the workers engaged in business and service; and 49 per cent of the total workers. In Kolkata, 53 per cent of the total working population are engaged in business and service. The knowledge workers form 61 per cent of these categories of workers and 44 per cent of the total workers.

District Towns

At the district town level, this scenario is substantially different. In Meerut city, 57 per cent of the total working population are engaged in business and service, the knowledge workers form 56 per cent of these categories of workers and 40 per cent of the total workers. In Balurghat town, 51 per cent of the total workers are engaged in business and service, the knowledge workers form 48 per cent of these workers and 39 per cent of the total workers. In Thane, 67 per cent of the total workers are in business and service and 70 per cent of them are in knowledge job and they form 55 per cent of the total workers. In Nagercoil, 68 per cent of the workers are engaged in business and service, 72 per cent of them are the knowledge workers who altogether form 41 per cent of the total workers.

The Villages

In the Dangerhat–Moudpur village of West Bengal, 48 per cent of working population are engaged in business and service and 41 per cent of these workers are knowledge workers who form 21 per cent of the total workers. In the Bhagwanpur village, the proportion of the workers engaged in business and service are significantly lower with 32 per cent and 40 per cent of them are the knowledge workers who form 33 per cent of total workers. Indeed, the proportion of the knowledge workers increased in recent years as knowledge-based services and business are penetrating fast in this village. In Killiyur, 46 per cent of the total workers are engaged in business and service and 48 per cent of these workers are engaged in knowledge category jobs forming 21 per cent of the total workers.

Ratio of knowledge workers within the social groups: In view of varied access to education and ICTs, the ratio of penetration of knowledge jobs has been eclectic among the social groups. In fact, higher the caste, gender and ethnic status, higher has been the ratio of knowledge workers across the space. In the metro cities, the overall ratio of knowledge workers is 49.8 per cent; while among the general categories this is as high as 70 per cent followed by the other backward classes with 52 per cent, scheduled tribes 50 per cent, women 48 per cent and scheduled castes 28 per cent (see Table 8.2). In the district towns again, while

Table 8.2 *Proportion of Knowledge Workers in Relation to Total Workers in Metro Cities, District Towns and Villages by Caste and Gender*

Place	General	OBC	SC	ST	Women	Overall
Metro city	70.0	52.0	28.0	50.0	48.0	49.8
District town	58.0	48.0	25.0	20.0	45.0	39.5
Villages	50.0	30.0	20.0	8.0	18.0	25.0

Source: Data Collected by the Study Team in 2010–2011.

the overall penetration of knowledge jobs is 39.5 per cent, it is to the extent of 58 per cent among the general categories, followed by other backward classes with 48 per cent, women 45 per cent, scheduled castes 25 per cent and scheduled tribes 20 per cent. In the villages, the overall ratio of knowledge jobs is quite low with 25 per cent, while among the general categories this ratio is 50 per cent, other backward classes 30 per cent, scheduled castes 20 per cent, women 18 per cent and scheduled tribes only 8 per cent. In the metro cities, the scheduled tribes have a higher ratio in knowledge jobs even though their numbers are very few as a vast section of them entered these types of cities with knowledge jobs getting higher level of education and benefits of the reservation policies of the state. Again, the low caste and tribal women have low representations in knowledge jobs than the general category women across the space because of their accumulated capacity deprivation in society. However, as indicated earlier, despite these variations higher ratio in knowledge jobs have been linked to a higher degree of urbanisation across social groups.

II. Educational Background of Knowledge Workers

It is evident that higher the extent of higher and technical education among the workers, higher is the proportion of IT workers among them. It is again that while the old knowledge workers capitalise on the conventional educational background, the dominant section of new knowledge workers have professional and technical educational backgrounds and have an edge over the rest socially, economically and technologically. Most importantly, higher and high technical educational background is linked to higher degree of participation in the core category of knowledge jobs in general and in the managerial level of knowledge jobs in particular. However, the educational levels of knowledge workers across the space have remained linked to their caste, ethnic and gender backgrounds (Table 8.3).

Metro Cities

Among the general categories in metro cities, 32 per cent of the knowledge workers have technical educational background, 56.7 per cent undergraduate or postgraduate and the remaining 11.3 per cent up to senior secondary levels of educational background. Among the other backward classes, these backgrounds are to the extent of 11.5 per cent, 66.8 per cent and 21.7 per cent, scheduled castes 41.2 per cent, 45 per cent and 13.8 per cent and among women 19.3 per cent, 52.2 per cent and 28.5 per cent. Among the metro cities, only Kolkata and Delhi have knowledge workers from the scheduled tribal background. Putting together, 50 per cent of knowledge workers from those categories have technical education and the remaining 50 per cent have up to senior secondary levels of education.

In Delhi, of the total general category of knowledge workers,

Table 8.3 *Educational Backgrounds of the Knowledge Workers*

Place	Gen			OBC			SC			ST			Women		
	1–XII	UG+PG	Tech	1–XII	UG+PG	Tech	1–XII	UG+PG	Tech	1–XII	UG+PG	Tech	1–XII	UG+PG	Tech
Delhi	19.0	57.0	24.0	10.0	57.0	33.0	8.0	42.0	50.0	-	-	100	19.0	51.0	30.0
Mumbai	12.0	60.0	28.0	14.0	85.0	1.0	17.0	40.0	43.0	-	-	-	40.0	41.0	19.0
Chennai	-	50.0	50.0	13.0	75.0	12.0	20.0	38.0	42.0	-	-	-	30.0	62.0	8.0
Kolkata	14.0	60.0	26.0	50.0	50.0	-	10.0	60.0	30.0	100	-	-	25.0	55.0	20.0
Metro Cities	11.3	56.7	32.0	21.7	66.8	11.5	13.8	45.0	41.2	50.0	0	50.0	28.5	52.2	19.3
Meerut	11.0	71.0	18.0	17.0	63.0	20.0	15.0	55.0	30.0	-	-	-	8.0	81.0	11.0
Thane	25.0	57.0	18.0	22.0	75.0	3.0	24.0	41.0	35.0	-	-	-	59.0	34.0	7.0
Nagercoil	15.0	69.0	16.0	26.0	67.0	7.0	16.0	62.0	22.0	-	-	-	41.0	53.0	6.0
Balurghat	24.0	57.0	19.0	-	100	-	70.0	20.0	10.0	-	100	-	31.0	52.0	17.0
District Towns	18.7	63.5	17.8	16.3	76.2	7.5	31.3	44.5	24.2	0	100	0	34.8	55.0	10.2
Killiyur	-	-	-	47.0	45.0	8.0	57.0	43.0	-	-	-	-	46.0	53.0	1.0
Bhagwanpur	41.0	55.0	4.0	20.0	78.0	2.0	24.0	66.0	10.0	-	-	-	59.0	38.0	3.0
Dangarhat-Mamudpur	49.0	49.0	2.0	44.0	50.0	6.0	25.0	60.0	15.0	80.0	20.0	-	40.0	50.0	10.0
Villages	45.0	52.0	3.0	37.0	57.6	5.3	35.3	56.3	8.4	80.0	20.0	0	48.3	47.0	4.7

Source: Data Collected by the Research Team in 2010–2011.

19 per cent have education up to secondary level, 57 per cent are undergraduates and postgraduates and 24 per cent have technical education, 33 per cent of the other backward class workers have technical education, 57 per cent undergraduate and postgraduate and 10 per cent up to secondary level of education. Among the schedule castes, 50 per cent have technical education, 42 per cent undergraduate and postgraduate and 8 per cent up to secondary level of education. All the knowledge workers from the scheduled tribes have technical education here. Among women, 30 per cent have technical education, 51 per cent undergraduate and postgraduate and 19 per cent up to secondary level of education. It is important to note that in Delhi,

the knowledge workers from other backward classes, schedule castes, schedule tribes and women categories have higher extent of technical education than knowledge workers of the general category. Importantly, most of the knowledge workers from these categories have certificate or diploma level qualification in technical education. It is again that there are more knowledge workers among all categories with undergraduate, postgraduate and technical education than the rest indicating that higher the degree of penetration of higher/technical education higher is the participation in the knowledge jobs.

In Mumbai, among knowledge workers from the general categories, 12 per cent have up to secondary level of education, 60 per cent undergraduate and postgraduate level of education and 28 per cent technical education. Among the other backward classes, 14 per cent have upto secondary level of education, 85 per cent undergraduate and postgraduate while only 1 per cent has technical education. Among the schedule castes, on the other hand, 43 per cent have technical education, 40 per cent with undergraduate and postgraduate and 17 per cent have up to secondary levels of education. Among the women knowledge workers, 40 per cent have below secondary level, 42 per cent are undergraduates and postgraduates and 19 per cent have technical education.

In Chennai, among the knowledge workers from general category, 50 per cent are undergraduate and postgraduate and the remaining 50 per cent have technical education. Among the knowledge workers from other backward classes, 75 per cent are undergraduate and postgraduate, 13 per cent up to secondary level and 12 per cent are with technical education. Among the schedule castes knowledge workers, 38 per cent are undergraduate and postgraduate, 42 per cent technical and 20 per cent up to secondary level education. Among the women knowledge workers, 62 per cent are undergraduate and postgraduate, 32 per cent have upto secondary and 8 per cent technical education.

In Kolkata, of the total general category knowledge workers, 14 per cent have up to secondary level education, 60 per cent undergraduate and postgraduate and 26 per cent technical education. 50 per cent of the knowledge workers from the other backward classes have up to secondary level and another 50 per cent undergraduate and postgraduate. Among the scheduled caste knowledge workers, 10 per cent have up to secondary level, 60 per cent undergraduate and postgraduate and 30 per cent technical education. Of the total women knowledge workers in Kolkata, 25 per cent have up to secondary level, 55 per cent undergraduate and postgraduate and 20 per cent technical education. All scheduled tribe knowledge workers have below secondary level of education.

District Towns

In the district towns, though there have been high proportions of knowledge workers with under- and postgraduate degrees, it has been of varied nature according to caste and gender. Among other backward classes 76.25 per cent, general category 63.5 per cent, women 55 per cent and scheduled castes 44.5 per cent knowledge workers have graduate and postgraduate level education. Significantly, in the districts, the proportion of knowledge workers with technical educational background is relatively lower than that in the metro cities. Only 10.2 per cent of the knowledge workers among women, 24.2 per cent among scheduled castes, 7.5 per cent among other backward classes and 17.8 per cent among the general categories have technical education. Many scheduled caste youths have acquired certificate or diploma level degrees in the technical and professional subjects for getting knowledge jobs in the district towns. Around 34.8 per cent women, 18.7 per cent general categories, 16.3 per cent other backward classes and 31.3 per cent scheduled caste knowledge workers have below secondary level education in these towns.

In Meerut, among the knowledge workers from general categories, 71 per cent are with undergraduate and postgraduate, 18 per cent with technical education and 11 per cent upto secondary level of education. Among the other backward classes, 63 per cent knowledge workers are undergraduate and postgraduate, 20 per cent have technical education and 17 per cent up to secondary level of education. Among the schedule castes, 55 per cent are with undergraduate and postgraduate, 30 per cent technical education and 15 per cent up to secondary level of education. Among the women, 81 per cent are undergraduate and postgraduate, 11 per cent with technical and 8 per cent up to secondary level of education.

In Thane, among the knowledge workers from the general category, 25 per cent have upto secondary level education, 57 per cent postgraduate and undergraduate and 18 per cent technical education.

Twenty-two per cent of knowledge workers from other backward classes have education up to secondary level, 75 per cent undergraduate and postgraduate and only 3 per cent with technical education. Among the knowledge workers from the scheduled castes, 35 per cent have technical education, 41 per cent are undergraduate and postgraduate and 24 per cent up to secondary levels of education. Among the women knowledge workers, 59 per cent have below secondary level, 34 per cent undergraduates and postgraduates and 7 per cent have technical education.

In Nagercoil, among the knowledge workers from the general category, 15 per cent have up to secondary level, 69 per cent undergraduate and postgraduate and 16 per cent technical education. Among the knowledge workers from other backward classes, these are to the extent of 26 per cent, 67 per cent, and 7 per cent; scheduled castes 16 per cent, 62 per cent and 22 per cent; and women knowledge workers 41 per cent, 53 per cent and 6 per cent respectively.

The Village

The rural areas have more knowledge workers with educational background up to senior secondary followed by under- and postgraduate educational backgrounds. Indeed, the rural areas have very limited proportion of knowledge workers with technical educational background. Among the knowledge workers from the general category, 45 per cent possess up to secondary levels of education, 52 per cent undergraduate and postgraduate and only 3 per cent technical education. Among the knowledge workers from other backward classes, such educational backgrounds are to the extent of 37 per cent, 57.6 per cent and 5.3 per cent, scheduled castes 35.3 per cent, 56.3 per cent and 8.4 per cent, women 48.3 per cent, 47 per cent and 4.7 per cent respectively. Among the knowledge workers from scheduled tribes 80 per cent have up to secondary level of education and the remaining 20 per cent undergraduates and postgraduates. Bhagwanpur village has more knowledge workers among all social categories with up to secondary level of education than those of undergraduate, postgraduate and with technical education. Thus, among the knowledge workers from general category, 41 per cent have up to secondary level of education, 55 per cent are undergraduate and postgraduate and only 4 per cent with technical education. Among the knowledge workers from other backward classes, 22 per cent have up to secondary level of education, 78 per cent undergraduate and postgraduate and 2 per cent with technical education. Among the knowledge workers from the schedule castes, 24 per cent have up to secondary level of education, 66 per cent are undergraduates and postgraduates and 10 per cent with technical education. Among the women knowledge workers, 59 per cent have up to secondary level of education, 38 per cent are undergraduate and postgraduate and 3 per cent with technical education. In the Killiyur village, there are no general or tribal social categories. Among the knowledge workers from other backward classes, only 8 per cent have technical, 45 per cent undergraduate and postgraduate and 47 per cent upto secondary levels of education. For woman knowledge workers such education backgrounds are to the extent of 1 per cent, 53 per cent and 46 per cent, respectively. Among the scheduled castes, 43 per cent are undergraduate and postgraduate and 57 per cent up to secondary levels of education.

In the Dangarhat–Mamudpur village, among the general categories only two per cent knowledge workers have technical, 52 per cent are undergraduate and postgraduate and 45 per cent have up to secondary level of education. The corresponding educational background for the other backward classes are 5.3 per cent, 57.6 per cent and 37 per cent, scheduled castes 8.4 per cent, 56.3 per cent and 35.3 per cent, scheduled tribes 0 per cent, 20 per cent and 80 per cent, and for women 4.7 per cent, 47 per cent and 48.3 per cent, respectively.

Significantly, in all the villages, with the expansion of education, the proportion of knowledge workers to the total working population has increased in recent years. Among all social groups, knowledge workers represent a distinctive category with distinguishing educational qualification. However educational differences among the knowledge workers is linked to social divides; and the extent of their proportional representation in knowledge jobs only depicts the pre-existing patterns of social inequality. In fact, the social and economic differences among the various caste and ethnic groups have got compounded with educational differences and the extent of availability of knowledge workers therein. It is established that the lower castes and tribal groups have low representation in knowledge jobs because of their low level of educational attainment in rural areas. This is also linked to unequal access to ICTs and thereafter their representation in the organisational hierarchy of knowledge-based industries.

III. The Knowledge Workers and the ICTs: Access and Use

Like education, the access to ICTs among knowledge workers in general is eclectic and conditioned by spatial, caste, tribe and gender divides in society. Knowledge workers across the towns and cities have more access to mobile than landline telephone among all social categories. However, though the knowledge workers in rural areas have good access to telephone and mobile and radio and TV, they lagged behind in terms of access to PCs and Internet.

Among the knowledge workers from metro cities, 80 per cent have access to telephone, 98 per cent to mobile, 38 per cent computer, 31.8 per cent Internet and 100 per cent to radio and television. All the knowledge workers across the caste, tribe and gender groups here have high access to ICTs. Among the general category knowledge workers, 84 per cent have telephone, 97 per cent have mobile, 41.5 per cent have personal computer and 38.5 per cent have internet connectivity (see Table 8.4 and 8.5). Similarly, among the knowledge workers from

Table 8.4 *ICTs Penetration among the Knowledge Workers*

Place	Telephone	Mobile	Computer	Internet	TV/Radio
Delhi	87.6	93.4	47.8	38.6	100
Mumbai	69.0	99.0	33.4	25.8	100
Chennai	77.8	100	35.4	33.8	100
Kolkata	85.6	99.5	35.6	29.0	100
Metro Cities	80.0	98.0	38.0	31.8	100
Meerut	63.6	78.6	28.6	18.6	100
Thane	69.0	80.0	37.6	28.8	100
Balurghat	72.4	96.0	13.4	5.8	100
Nagarcoil	16.6	74.4	36.7	30.0	100
District Towns	55.5	82.5	29.0	20.8	100
Bhagwanpur	38.4	98.0	9.2	4.2	100
Dangarhat-Mamudpur	38.5	77.4	5.1	1.2	100
Killiyur	47.2	74.6	4.2	3.2	100
Villages	41.3	83.3	6.1	2.9	100
Total					

Source: Data Collected by the Study Team in 2010–2011.

other backward classes, the access to these ICTs are to the extent of 84.5 per cent, 95.5 per cent, 40.8 per cent and 35.3 per cent; for the scheduled castes 81.5 per cent, 94.8 per cent, 44 per cent and 35 per cent; among scheduled tribes 100 per cent, 100 per cent, 66.3 per cent and 66.3 per cent and among women knowledge to the extent of 99.5 per cent, 100 per cent, 40.8 per cent and 32.8 per cent, respectively. Knowledge workers from all these social groups have 100 per cent coverage of radio and television.

In Delhi, 80 per cent of the knowledge workers belonging to general category have telephone landlines, 92 per cent mobile phones, 34 per cent computers, 27 per cent Internet and 100 per cent have TV and radio. Among the knowledge workers from other backward classes, 78 per cent have telephone, 88 per cent have mobile phones, 35 per cent have computers, 22 per cent have Internet and 100 per cent have TV and radio. Among the knowledge workers from scheduled caste, 80 per cent have telephone, 87 per cent mobile phone, 35 per cent computer, 19 per cent Internet and 100 per cent have access to TV and radio. Among the knowledge workers from scheduled tribe, possession of telephone, mobile, computer, Internet, TV and radio is to the extent of 100 per cent, among the women knowledge workers 100 per cent have telephone and mobile, 35 per cent have computers, 30 per cent Internet and 100 per cent have TV and radio. Similar trend is also visible among other metro cities as shown in Table 8.5. Significantly among the knowledge workers in metro cities caste, tribe and gender divides in access to ICTs shows a fast-declining trend.

Importantly, the access to ICTs declines as the degree of urbanisation decreases, and inequality becomes vivid in ICT access in caste and gender line in less urbanised areas. In the district towns, as shown in Table 8.4, 55.5 per cent have telephone, 82.5 per cent have mobile, 29 per cent have computer, 20.8 per cent have Internet and 100 per cent have radio and television. The *district towns* lag behind in terms of the knowledge workers' access over ICTs, except for mobile phone. Among the knowledge workers from general categories, (see Table 8.5) 71.2 per cent have access over telephone, 96.2 per cent mobile, 34 per cent computer and 25 per cent over Internet. For the knowledge workers among other backward classes, these are to the extent of 70.5 per cent, 95 per cent, 29.3 per cent and 25 per cent, scheduled tribes 75 per cent, 100 per cent, 8.5 per cent and nil, and for women 88.3 per cent, 100 per cent, 32.8 per cent and 17.8 per cent, respectively. Through the knowledge workers from the general category, other backward classes and the scheduled castes have more or less similar level of access to ICTs, the scheduled tribes and women significantly lag behind so far as their access to Internet is concerned. Among the general category knowledge workers in Meerut, 75 per cent have landline telephones, 100 per cent have mobile, 41 per cent have computers, 21 per cent have Internet and 100 per cent have radio and TV. Among the knowledge workers from other backward classes, 66 per cent have telephone, 100 per cent have mobile, 30 per cent have computers, 28 per cent have internet and 100 per cent have radio and TV. Among the knowledge workers from scheduled caste, 71 per cent have landline telephone, 98 per cent have mobile, 32 per cent have computers, 29 per cent have internet, 100 per cent have radio and TV. Among the women knowledge workers, 100 per cent have landline and mobile, 40 per cent have computer, 26 per cent have Internet and 100 per cent have TV and radio. Such specificities of individual district towns are provided in Table 8.5.

Though the *village* knowledge workers are distinctive social categories in rural space, they conspicuously lag behind in terms of their access to ICTs in comparison to their urban counterparts. This phenomenon is very explicit so far as their access to computer and Internet are concerned. In an average, villages have access to these technologies to the extent of 41.3 per cent, 83.3 per cent, 6.1 per cent, 2.9 per cent and 100 per cent, respectively (see Table 8.4). While depicting the social variation in access to ICTs Table 8.5 shows that among the knowledge workers from general category, 33.3 per cent have access to landline telephone, 66.6 per cent mobile, only 8 per cent computer and 7 per cent Internet; among the knowledge workers from other backward classes, 38.3 per cent have access to telephone, 91.3 per cent mobile, 9.67 per cent computer and 3.3 per cent Internet. For the knowledge workers from scheduled castes, these are 100 per cent, 40 per cent, 92 per cent, 7.3 per cent and 4 per cent; among women knowledge workers, 70.6 per cent, 100 per cent, 7.33 per cent and 1.5 per cent, respectively. The knowledge workers from the scheduled tribe have no access to computer and Internet, though 22 per cent have landline telephone and 33.3 per cent have mobile phone. Though mobile phone has penetrated very fast in the rural areas among all sections of population, computer and Internet access have remained restricted among a limited few. In fact, limited access has also been conditioned by the social divide.

In the Bhagwanpur village, of the total general category of knowledge workers, 60 per cent have access to telephone, 100 per cent have to mobile, 17 per cent have computers, 19 per cent have Internet and 100 per cent have TV and radio. Among the knowledge workers from other backward classes 35 per cent have access to telephone, 100 per cent have mobile, 10 per cent have computers, 3 per cent have Internet and 100 per cent have TV and radio. Among the knowledge workers from scheduled caste, 31 per cent have telephone, 90 per cent have mobile, 7 per cent have computers, 3 per cent Internet and 100 per cent have radio and TVs. Among the women knowledge workers, 66 per cent have telephone, 100 per cent have mobiles, 15 per cent have computers, 5 per cent have Internet and 100 per cent have radio and TV. Similar trend of other villages in provided in Table 8.5.

Though there have been caste-based divisions over the access to ICTs and mass communication technologies, knowledge workers from within all castes and in the villages as well distinguish themselves from the rest of the society with the higher extent of possession and use of these resources.

The higher and technical educational background and high degree of access to ICTs gives the knowledge workers a distinctive position in society. In general, the knowledge workers in metro cities have higher access to ICTs than the district towns and the district towns have higher access than the villages, even though mobile and telephone have emerged to be the greatest equalisers between the rural–urban ICT divides. Again, the knowledge workers form the upwardly mobile segments of the society not only have access over high level of education and training and new avenues of employment but also have access to state-of-the-art communication and information technologies. In fact having a very high degree of access to technology, high and technical education, command over the skill for exploitation of new body of information the knowledge workers occupy a distinctive position in society. Across the space they are the visible and established knowledgeable in contemporary society.

Table 8.5 ICTs and Mass Communication among per 100 Knowledge Workers

Place	Gen					OBC					SC					ST					Women				
	Tele	Mob	PC	Internet	TV/Radio	Tele	Mob	pc	Internet	TV/Radio	Tele	Mob	PC	Internet	TV/Radio	Tele	Mob	PC	Internet	TV/Radio	Tele	Mob	PC	Internet	TV/Radio
Delhi	80	92	34	27	100	78	88	35	22	100	80	87	35	19	100	100	100	100	100	100	100	100	35	30	100
Mumbai	80	96	42	42	100	85	100	40	37	100	82	100	45	39	100					100	98	100	40	32	100
Chennai	100	100	51	50	100	100	100	56	52	100	87	100	60	52	100		100	33	33	100	100	100	50	38	100
Kolkata	76	100	39	35	100	75	94	32	30	100	77	92	36	30	100					100	100	100	38	31	100
Metro Cities	84	97	41.5	38.5	100	84.5	95.5	40.8	35.3	100	81.5	94.8	44	35	100	100	100	66.3	66.3	100	99.5	100	40.8	32.8	100
Meerut	75	100	41	21	100	66	100	30	28	100	71	98	32	29	100						100	100	40	19	100
Thane	75	100	48	45	100	90	100	45	38	100	80	100	50	45	100						100	100	45	20	100
Nagercoil	65	85	36	25	100	56	92	35	28	100	66	95	40	20	100					100	75	100	36	25	100
Balurghat	70	100	11	10	100	70	90	7	6	100	69	90	6	6	100	75	100	33	–	100	78	100	10	7.0	100
District Towns	71.2	96.2	34	25.3	100	70.5	95.5	29.3	25	100	71.5	95.8	32	25	100	18.8	25	8.2	0	100	88.3	100	32.8	17.8	100
Bhawanpur	60	100	17	19	100	35	100	10	3	100	31	90	7	3	100					100	66	100	15	2.0	100
Killiyur					100	50	83	12	6	100	54	90	10	7	100	66	100			100	66	100		–	100
Dangarhat-Mamudpur	34	100	7	2	100	30	91	7	1	100	35	96	5	2	100					100	80	100	7	–	100
Villages	33.3	66.6	8	7	100	38.3	91.3	9.67	3.3	100	40	92	7.3	4	100	22	33.3	0	0	100	70.7	100	7.3	.66	100

Source: Data Collected by Research Team in 2010–2011.

IV. Knowledge Workers in Emerging Social Structure

Conventionally, Indian society is hierarchical and one's position in this hierarchy is shaped by traditional position to specific caste, ethnic and gender hierarchy, on the one hand, and educational achievements, spatial location and access to ICTs, social networks, economic resources and authority structure in organisational hierarchy, on the other. The social framework of knowledge society is being shaped through intertwining with these arrangements. Unlike the social framework of agrarian society and the industrial society, those are conventionally situated in the rural and the urban/industrial contexts, respectively, and through circumscribed employer–employee relationships therein, the emergence of knowledge society and its social frameworks in a wider context encompass the spatial divides between the rural and urban areas, economic divides between various sectors of economy and social divides among various sections of people. Unlike its agrarian and industrial society, where social structures are evolved based on a well-defined context and the work relations are structured within given orders, social structure of knowledge society has emerged to be more diffused than consolidated. Being expert and creative in their own areas of engagement in the interconnected world, the knowledge workers are self-centred and circumscribed, on the one hand, and diffused and mobile, on the other. However, despite this wide horizon for the knowledge workers and their increasing presence in all sectors of activities in India, a vast majority of them are to work through organisational arrangements as knowledge culture is mass nurtured, promoted, used and exploited through organisational set-ups. Hence, it is rather imperative that social relations of knowledge workers within these organisations should be understood in relation to their social backgrounds, on the one hand, and their position in the emerging organisational hierarchy, on the other.

Knowledge Worker and the Organisational Structure

The emergence of knowledge society has brought significant change in the formal organisational structures. While, on the one hand, it has increased the significance of the traditional variety of the knowledge workers, it has also included highly trained professional workers in the system to meet to the emerging needs of the organisation. A vast majority of the old knowledge workers are now in the process of getting introduced to the ICTs' culture either through their own or organisational initiative by undertaking required skill and training. As the tendency to remain ignorant of ICTs now incurs a high opportunity and social cost, most workers now adopt it as an important aspect of professional life. Data collected from an educational institution and a data processing unit (private) in Delhi, four (private) Internet Kiosks in the district towns and two in the villages have observed that these knowledge-based organisations, though work as an integrated whole, are essentially hierarchical in nature; and that the conventional hierarchical dynamics have got extended in these organisations.

Like the conventional organisation, these are top heavy in terms of concentration of authority and bottom heavy for the concentration of ICT workers. While in the educational institution, the old knowledge workers – the teachers, administrators and a thin layer of new knowledge workers – are employed against the permanent position, the majority of the new knowledge workers in these institutions are employed on a contractual basis. In the government institution, they are employed through the hiring agencies. Within the organisational structure, they are recruited at the lower level of the hierarchy, conditioned by job insecurity, low salary and high work pressure. Though the new knowledge workers are relatively young in the organisational set-up and they experience a higher mobility and higher quantum choice, their entry in the organisation begins with an exploitative term. Being young and non-permanent, they accept the condition as dictated by the organisation and are seldom able to express their discontent. Significantly, knowledge workers are bound by these common characterisations across the metro cities, the district towns and the villages within these organisational arrangements.

These organisational arrangements are built up on formal foundations to recruit and to govern knowledge workers in many ways contributing to casualisation and informalisation of knowledge workers within this arrangement. Their work situation is widely characterised by:

Smart working condition: The knowledge workers work in a smart working environment, which is mostly air conditioned, dust-free environment, surrounded by good furniture and with smart people around. They command a good status in society through their association to knowledge jobs.

Job insecurity: Insecurity in their employment situation that is conditioned by world economic boom or recession. Both in the public and in the private sector, new variety of knowledge workers suffers from the problems of job insecurity. Significantly, the old variety of knowledge workers enjoys better degree of job security than that of the new ones. Significantly, part time and contract work has been the emerging mode of employment both in the public and in the private sector as far as the employment in the ICT-related work is concerned. While in the private educational institutions the culture of working through part time, ad-hoc and guest faculty is rampant, this has also become an emerging phenomenon in the government-run educational institutions. We have elaborated this issue in Chapter IV in detail.

Inappropriate social security measures: Many are compelled to accept these jobs as this arrangement gives them immediate relief from unemployment. In the private, data processing centres and rural kiosks social security is a myth. In the government sector also because of the predominance of contractual employment these knowledge workers seldom get advantage of social security as prescribed by law. Many employers apprehend legal complicacy, growth of trade unionism and possible demand for permannent position by these recruits.

High turnover ratio: Though the organisation prefers the casual staff, many also leave such a job by getting an alternative. The employers also prefer to replace the workers frequently in one plea or the other.

Educational mismatch between acquired qualification and position held: Many highly qualified and trained workers engage them with a low-position job with the aim to gain experience. Large sections are also compelled to accept the given arrangement due to global slowdown and non-availability of suitable options. In metro cities, many MBA and MCA degree holders are found to opt for data processing jobs as no other employment is available to them immediately. Employers also blame the quality of education and question the employability of many technically qualified graduates in their firms.

Lack of unity and union activity: As a rule, trade unionism is never encouraged by the management; and these workers have least desire to form an association because of thinness of their strength, contractual nature of employment and a high turnover rate of the workers.

Casual or short-term employment: In the villages and the district towns, most of the new knowledge workers work in the computer kiosks through informal arrangement and without proper written communication. Many of these professionals are to render personalised services to employer even unwillingly.

High stress: The work situation of most of knowledge workers is conditioned by high stress in the work place due to pressure for ontime delivery, ensuring customer's satisfaction, irregular work shifts, late night duty, lack of child care, housing and recreation facilities. Many a time, these are again compounded by long hours of travel and daily commuting. Significantly, women and young recruits suffer the most out of this stress. It is usually observed that lower is the age and educational qualification higher is the stress in the work place.

Encountering traditional role expectation and stereotyping in the workplace: Though the knowledge workers are the most educated and enlightened lots of society with less caste prejudice and higher incidences of inter-caste dowry-free marriage among them, they are to encounter a host of customers and an environment that is full of caste, region, ethnic prejudice and gender-role stereotyping. Many of them reported to have faced regular ethnic bullying, gender-centric derogatory comments and humiliating behaviour from the clients.

In the social term, these organisations have retained many of the characters of traditional set-ups, whereby the representation of marginalised communities has been very few and far between. The social dimensions of these organisational arrangements are widely characterised by:

- Substantially, low representation of the marginalised communities especially the scheduled castes and tribe in the formal structure of these organisations in comparison with those of the rest of the society.

- Very meagre representation (only to the extent of 1.5 per cent) of the marginalised communities in the private sector. While there has been marginal representation of the scheduled caste and other backward classes, there is no representation of the scheduled tribe in the private sector. It is despite the fact that the private sector is more prompt to adopt, to change and to introduce technology than that of the government sector.

- Relatively more representation of the marginalised community in the category of knowledge workers in the public sector that of the private sector wherein recruitment is guided by the principle protective discrimination. As the maintenance of the ICTs is concerned, they are mostly 'outsourced' to the private companies who are not obliged to adhere to the principle of protective discrimination, by implication through outsourcing mechanism the public sector indirectly deprives the opportunities of knowledge jobs to the marginalised communities. Largely within the public sector than the outsourcing dynamics represent a coercive semi-informal sector.

- Relatively more representation of the other backward classes in knowledge jobs than those of the schedule castes occur both in the private and in the public sectors.

- More representation of the marginalised communities in the lower levels of the organisational structure than those of the middle and the upper level with knowledge jobs.

- Availability of knowledge workers from the background of marginalised communities at the lower level of the organisational hierarchy in the public sector more or less as per the prescribed quota, while at the top level their representations are very few and far between.

- Significant representation of women in knowledge jobs of all varieties in the urban areas and women are found to be adaptive and preferred in all varieties of knowledge jobs. In the educational institutions, women have representation at all levels of knowledge work, while at the private sector women are predominantly concentrated in the lower rung of the organisational structure.

- Non-preference of women workers in the elevated position in organisational hierarchy has remained an unwritten rule. Most of the women knowledge workers reported to have problems in the workplace. Many of these problems relate to denial of promotion, biased attitude of the male superiors, non-recognition of their contribution by the employer, insufficient security, lack of child care and social security. Their work participation is not devoid of traditional role expectations and gender-role stereotyping even in interpersonal relations within the organisation. Most of these workers report to compromise between the traditional role expectation in the family and work situation in the organisation, even though they find their partners to be cooperative.

- Encountering hardship by majority of the knowledge workers from the marginalised communities to have access to education. The quantum of hardship was higher among the scheduled tribes than among the scheduled castes and the other backward classes and they recognise that reservation was of great help for their entry in education and government jobs. In fact, the scheduled caste, scheduled tribe, other backward classes and women are to overcome varieties of structural barriers in getting access to the organisational structure of knowledge society.

V. Organisational Hierarchy and the Knowledge Workers

Though the shift in the organisation of production has provided the scope for more knowledge job and employment of knowledge workers ever before in India, their arrival and increasing strength in the organisational set-up seldom remove the organisational hierarchy. The knowledge workers are highly hierarchically posited within the emerging organisational structure in particular and society at large.

Significantly within the emerging technoeconomic environment, many of the old arrangements are being redefined while new ones are being shaped. Within the organisation, the old organisational hierarchy is either strengthened or new hierarchy is evolved based on everyday need of the organisation irrespective of its size. The knowledge workers who are essentially formal professionals in their own areas of activities relate themselves to the society through these formal organisations across the country – villages, towns and cities. On the other, it is through these workers that the society largely experiences new momentum of social mobility, cultural and economic dynamism and rejuvenation. As the society is getting more and more professionalised, more and more formal organisational arrangements are being interlinked with the functioning of society at all levels. A large part of traditional organisational arrangements even in the rural areas are being formalised and reoriented with the interpenetration of new organisational arrangements.

Within the formal organisational hierarchy, the professional status of doctors, lawyers, teachers, researchers, officials working at the office, managerial, supervisory and executive etc. level have retained the position of authority. On the other hand, there are below managerial-level workers and other service providers within the organisational hierarchy. A strong hierarchy is formed within these organisations to reinforce the control and command arrangement by the management the so-called by privileging seniors over the juniors. An outline of this ideal hierarchy is placed as follows:

a. Managerial/supervisory level (Directly engaged in knowledge work): Managers, bankers, chartered accounts, ICT professionals, air hostage, architects, travel agents, lawyers, head teachers, head nurse, doctors, researchers, college, postgraduate, secondary level school teachers, university and college professors, metro planners, government officials (gazetted and non-gazetted) event managers, media organisers, lawyers, businessmen and self-employed persons, social entrepreneurs, advertising executives, artist, software and hardware engineers, marketing executives and such other officials having the authority to take decisions.

b. Below managerial level (Both directly and indirectly engaged in knowledge work): Development workers, primary school teachers, health workers, assistant and below level government officers, BPO workers at non-managerial level, nurse, tutors, sales men/women, telephone operators, receptionists, secretarial staffs, field-level media persons, computer operators, typists etc.

c. Support service providers (As semiskilled workers indirectly engaged in knowledge work): Office peons, carpenter, plumber, lift operators, xerox operators, drivers and many others.

d. Manual workers – sweepers, cleaners, security guards, etc.:
In essence, the foundation of knowledge society that has emerged through a complex relationship between skill and educational achievement, penetration of ICTs, urbanisation, proliferation of and new avenues of employment, has still remained hierarchical and this hierarchy has got linked to the traditional social structure. The occupational hierarchy in the emerging organisational arrangements has re-established the traditional interface between social and the organisational hierarchy

whereby knowledge workers in the managerial, supervisory, executive and related professional positions across the villages, district towns and with somewhat lesser degree in the metro cities are predominantly represented by the general category social groups. The predominance of the general categories among the knowledge workers has been relatively less in the metro cities as other social categories especially the other backward classes and scheduled castes have started making their mark in these jobs. In rural areas, the representation of the general category knowledge workers in the managerial supervisory jobs is to the extent of 57 per cent (See Table 8.6). While in the district

Table 8.6 *Proportion of Knowledge Workers in Managerial/Supervisory (M) Below Managerial/Supervisory (BM) and Support Service Levels by Caste, Ethnicity and Gender*

Places	General			OBC			SC			ST			Women		
	M	BM	SSP	M	BM	SSP	M	BM	SSP	M	BM	SSP	M	BM	SSP
Metro	49.0	27.0	24.0	35.0	29.0	36.0	11.0	19.0	70.0	-	50.0	50.0	22.0	62.0	16.0
District Town	58.0	24.0	18.0	28.0	30.0	42.0	10.0	16.0	74.0	2.0	35.0	63.0	30.0	60.0	10.0
Villages	57.0	29.0	14.0	11.0	38.0	51.0	7.0	12.0	81.0	-	25.0	75.0	16.0	78.0	6.0

Source: Data collect by the Study Team in 2010–2011.

towns and in the metro cities, their representations at the managerial level are to the extent of 58 per cent and 49 per cent, respectively. Though the other backward classes and the scheduled castes started making their representation in the managerial levels of knowledge jobs in recent years, they substantially lag behind the general category. In fact, the other backward classes, scheduled castes and the scheduled tribes are represented predominantly in the below managerial and in the service providing jobs. The extent of their work participation in the below managerial and service providing jobs is more intensive in rural than in district towns and metro cities. In metro cities, 35 per cent of the knowledge workers from the other backward classes are in the managerial category, 29 per cent in the below managerial and 36 per cent in the support service providing categories. At the village level only 11 per cent of them are in the managerial, 38 per cent below managerial and 51 per cent in the support service providing categories.

Among the knowledge workers from the scheduled castes 11 per cent at the metro cities, 10 per cent at the district towns and 7 per cent at the villages belong to the managerial levels. Again in the metro cities 19 per cent and 70 per cent, district towns 16 per cent and 74 per cent, and villages 12 per cent and 81 per cent of knowledge workers from the scheduled castes are engaged as below managerial and support service providing knowledge workers, respectively. The knowledge workers from scheduled tribes have no representation at the managerial level either in the village or in the metro cities. They have only 2 per cent representation at the managerial level in district towns. In metro cities, 50 per cent of them work below managerial and another 50 percent in the support service providing levels. In the district towns 35 per cent and 63 per cent, villages 25 per cent and 75 per cent of knowledge workers from the scheduled tribal groups are engaged at below managerial and support service providing levels, respectively. Lower caste, ethnic status and lower degree of urbanisation is positively linked to the higher degree of concentration in the below managerial-level knowledge jobs and support service providing activities for the scheduled castes and the scheduled tribes.

Women predominantly represent themselves in the below managerial and support service providing jobs with 62.0 per cent and 16 per cent in the metro cities, 60 per cent and 10 per cent in district towns and 78 per cent and 6 per cent in the villages, respectively. This phenomenon is linked to the lack of technical educational background among women workers. However, women knowledge workers have a relatively higher representation at the managerial level in the district towns and the metro cities than the villages. Of the total woman knowledge workers, 30 per cent from the district towns and 22 per cent from the metro cities and 16 per cent from the village belong to the managerial level. A relatively higher proposition of women knowledge workers in supervisory and managerial role in the district towns and in metro cities is due to the facts that women have a high representation in teaching, health, in tourism and travel, sales executives etc. jobs and in the emerging new avenues of employment, and that a large section of them are from the general category background who have good exposure to modern education.

Though the educational background of the knowledge workers are linked to their placement in the formal organisational hierarchy and the capacity of earning, there has emerged a high degree of mismatch between the level of education and their placement in the formal position in the organisation that specifies distinctive job norms. As discussed earlier, many of the higher education and technically qualified workers are placed in the below managerial and support service providing categories of knowledge workers. This is rampant in the metro cities and district towns mostly among the general category and the other backward classes at time due to surplus supply of these categories of workers, lack of quality and unemployability of the workers. This phenomenon is relatively less in rural areas and among the scheduled castes and scheduled tribes.

VI. Spatial and Occupational Mobility and Changing Social Relations across Space

The emerging knowledge society by intensifying the scope for employment both in the knowledge- and non-knowledge- related areas has generated unprecedented momentum for the emergence of new avenues of employment, occupational diversification, rural–urban connectivity, increasing quantum of migration and occupational mobility for a vast section of population across the space. This process has been accompanied by fast movements of refined and processes consumer goods along with computer, typewriters, televisions, radio, mobile phone, new machine, automobiles and fashion technologies, new message (both grounded and faceless), images and information from urban to the rural areas. Significantly, these new and refined objects and opportunities are injected from above, while reverse movements have predominantly been in the raw form – raw food grains, vegetables, woods, stone and even untrained and raw human power. However, the newly injected social and economic momentum has produced new employment opportunities and work relations both in the rural and in urban areas.

Generating Demand for Labour Force from Rural Areas

Vast part of rural societies in India that have already remained exposed to occupational momentum in the wake of Green Revolution, implementation of varieties of rural development schemes and increasing urban contacts have got exposed to another spell of occupational mobility both within the village and outside. With the proliferation of new avenues of employment in the government and non-government organisations in construction, repairing, maintenance etc. activities and self-employment through small business, and employment in the Mahatma Gandhi National Rural Employment Guarantee Scheme (MGNREGS), and in several rural development programmes a vast section of rural workforce experiences an amount of employment security and horizontal occupational mobility.

Simultaneously, a large section of the rural workforce now experiences fast spatial and occupationally horizontal mobility by joining the army of manual labourers and support service providers in the urban areas. The construction and maintenance of new infrastructures for government and private buildings, local and multinational corporations, business and ICTs hubs, mass communication, cable services, DTH (Direct To Home) networks, new educational institutions, hotel and tourism industries, new housing complexes, roads and transport, railways, metro rail and monorails, shopping malls, housing projects, airports and Special Economic Zones and varieties of other related activities, those are initiated in an unprecedented scale and speed in the urban and sub-urban areas have increased the need for new variety of unskilled, semiskilled and multi-skilled manpower to be engaged in these activities. There has again been increasing need of electricians, plumber, fitters, carpenters, decorators, designers, security personnel, cleaners, sweepers, drivers, peons and messengers, gardeners, such other categories for both the organisational and domestic purposes. A vast section of this workforce is drawn from rural areas, especially from lower social and economic backgrounds to suffice the need of urban areas causing shift of labour force from the agricultural to the non-agricultural sector. Under the emerging scenario, while the space for horizontal mobility of the illiterate, semiliterate and semiskilled workers has also got widened, the scope of upward occupational mobility for the educated and skilled labour force from rural areas has also got expanded. Again the voluminous increase of migration of rural youths in urban areas for higher and technical education predominantly now results in the migration of educated and trained rural workforce in urban areas.

Occupational diversification, however, has also widened the scope of horizontal and upward social mobility of the upper strata in rural areas. Business relating to transport, modern amenities, electronic and electrical goods, cable television network, telecommunication hubs, Internet kiosks etc. have not only provided them new avenues of earning but also the scope of providing employment to others. Because of their past educational, economic and social backgrounds and significant access to modern education, ICTs and social networks they not only monopolise the government jobs but are also posited to take more advantage of the new avenues of employment both in rural and in urban areas than those of the lower strata who have remained economically and educationally disadvantaged. These upper strata not only generate market for the urban produce in the rural areas, but also develop effective social networks with urban partners for new economic ventures and play the role of catalysts in bringing new socioeconomic momentum in society.

Multiple Employer–Employee Relations in Rural Areas

The new economic momentum in the urban areas and the increasing quantum of occupational and spatial mobility in rural areas has caused the emergence of multiple employer–employee relationship in rural areas. It is not only the pre-existing patterns of work participation but also the work relations that have undergone phenomenal changes. The predominant and stable forms of agrarian employer–employee relationships (landlord–tent or landlord–agricultural labourer etc.) are now being replaced by unstable, infrequent relationship with multiple employers–employee or the service providers and users relations. An agricultural labourer is now simultaneously a milkman, a construction labour, a *bidi* maker, part-time rickshaw puller and seasonally petty shop owner. Similarly, landowners are also simultaneously the village entrepreneur, ICT or IPO hub owner, transporter, teacher or a government servant or agent dealing with insurance, property transfer and many such activities. These have emerged with the penetration of new economic forces. Significantly, such relation goes beyond the boundary of predefined notion of domination and hierarchy. These workers now experience lot of choices that are more likely to be guided by a sense of freedom, even with a risk, from the pre-existing domination of fixed employer–employee relations as traditionally practised in agriculture or household industry. Sections of rural labour also migrate to the urban areas, at time seasonally to get alternative employments. The changing trajectory of new economic relations that has been widely characterised by contractuality and non-permanence, fluidity and flexibility and increasing worker's choice and freedom has injected a new outlook of criticality on the pre-existing primordial social relations.

ICTS, New Employment and Changing Landscape of Social Relations

A Tale from Below: Though access to ICTs has been uneven, for a section of population it has become a great enabler. The emerging scope of work and changing work relations are now widely mediated for them by the access to ICTs at the grassroots. The migrant and the migratory rural workers make substantive use of ICTs for the furtherance of their work opportunities and social networking that has brought time–space compression even in rural society in many areas of social and economic pursuits. This society is now in a fast process of replacing many of the old systems like those of the typewriter by computer, landline by mobile phone, physical transfer of money by e-transfer, 'money order' by ATM card, letter by SMS or phone/mobile call, even face-to-face interaction within the village by mobile phone calls.

The age-old practice of writing detailed letter by the village students studying in urban areas, requesting for money from their parents in advance and receiving that money through postal money orders with a lot of instructions about the safety of that money and its proper usage has now been replaced by extensive use of ATM and instant SMS in the mobile phone. For many these have reduced not only uncertainties, but have also bridged the gap of time and space with increased virtual interactivity. Parents now feel more secured having the ability to remain in touch with their children constantly through electronic devices, predominantly mobile phone, even though nostalgia remains.

Mobile phone has been a boon for their intensive social and economic interactions. It has been used for getting communication about employment through labour contractors, other employers, government official, civil society and political activists for increased social interactivity. Many look for the opportunities for marketability of their physical labour, fish, pottery, agricultural and forest produce, animals and birds and other resources outside the village by making use of mobile phone. Even the labourers intended to migrate out or commute to the city for employment, now get easy access to information on the available opportunities.

Indeed, mobile phone has enabled a good section of unskilled and semiskilled labourer from West Bengal and Uttar Pradesh villages to migrate to Delhi and Mumbai for employment. The labour contractors from urban areas contact the labour broker at the village through mobile phone for the labour, who in turn recruit local labourers, organise their journey, arrange bus and train tickets to cities and provide the required reformation and guidance and also at times accompany them to the cities. These labourers usually get a better rate of wage and relatively higher man-days of employment than they usually get in their native villages. For these migrant labours, mobile phone is the key livewire to remain in touch with variety of actors – the employer, middle man, family members, friends and others. After getting employed in cities, they regularly start sending money to their families in the village. Here again, they use ICTs to send money in the village through the labour contractors. Their conventional dependency on the post office for letters and money order has now declined significantly.

The case of Abdul Rashid, a 55-year-old Muslim from Mamudpur village of West Bengal is a typical one. Rashid is the head of a joint family. He has three sons and two daughters. All three of his sons are married and mostly remained unemployed in the village. Now all his sons work in Mumbai in a construction company. Rashid is the middle man at the village level. He gets regular communication form the contractors and his sons in Mumbai about the labour requirement; and accordingly arranges the labourers and their journey. He remains in constant touch through mobile phone with all the labour families at the village and also with those labourers in Mumbai. He receives remuneration for the labourers in his account and withdraws money from a local ATM and disburses among these labour families as per the oral contract and understanding. The labour families also maintain constant touch with their migrant family members by making extensive use of mobile phone. A few of them use ATM facility directly by themselves. The emerging flow of migration has brought not only spatial mobility and alternative livelihood options, but also new sense of organising life and culture, identity and existence and work and working relations. For them, the communication patterns of globalised culture are no more alien, rather there has been the urge to use these technologies to get rid of unemployment, uncertainties and localised domination.

New Works and Work Relations in Urban India

Urban India, even though characterised by the predominance of service sector and occupational diversification, in recent years these have been multifaceted with the arrival new avenues of employment in the ICT–related services, travel, retailing, real estate share market, advertisement, media, legal consultancy, education and research, market survey and analysis and intensification of many old jobs both in the knowledge- and non-knowledge- related areas. The combination of these activities and areas has brought a new momentum in the social and economic lives of urban areas. This momentum has enhanced the scope of expansion of knowledge jobs, promoted the scope for jobs in support services related to knowledge jobs, and also non-knowledge jobs in varieties of infrastructural and developmental activities as mentioned in the early parts of this chapter. Thus, in the knowledge sector the occupational dynamics of the metro cities and the district towns are predominantly characterised by the emergence of varieties of occupational categories. These are marked by the proliferation of a new brand of knowledge workers who are highly educated and trained, globally interconnected and well informed, ICTs enabled and enriched, intellectually capable and morally inclusive, increasing expansion of old variety of knowledge workers with redefined role and increasing significance. It also experiences powerful resurgence and proliferation of a section of entrepreneurs taking advantage of new avenues of economic enterprise. They are the medium and big businessmen who make flourishing business in ICTs, construction, infrastructural development, education, media, stock market brokerage, retail services, transport, tourism, advertisement and as intermediaries of service providers in all emerging areas at time putting both the knowledge and non-knowledge sectors together.

These knowledge-based workers and entrepreneurs have not only emerged from within the urban areas, but also added to its volumes from among the neo-migrants from rural areas and sister urban areas. They occupy the core of the social and cultural lives in the urban space. The service providing workers and the manual labour force that are predominantly drawn from the rural areas, in social and cultural terms they have remained in the periphery of the urban space, even though they lend their muddy hands and dirty legs to keep the emerging knowledge society growing and sustainable. While the work relations within the organisational set-up has been reinforced to be formal, on time, demand based, it has also integrated a host of informal arrangements especially at the lower middle and at the bottom level of organisational hierarchy through the engagement of casual and contractual labourers. The mix of the formal and the informal working arrangements even within the formal sector has made the work relation in urban India quite fluid that swings between stability, on the one hand, and insecurity, on the other. Thus, knowledge society while on the one hand brought the forces of liberation; on the other hand, strengthened the processes of insecurity and non-formalisation of jobs through its own economic dynamism.

VII. Integration with Knowledge Society and Its Varied Patterns

The knowledge society, besides making a space social for mobility and introducing new social and economic momentum in society, has also developed new logics of inclusion, exclusion and marginality in society. While access to higher and technical education, ICTs, knowledge jobs and managerial/supervisory position in the organisational hierarchy are key dimensions of integration with knowledge society, these are diversely acquired by the members of society. Though the process of penetration of the forces of knowledge society has been substantially uneven among the village, district towns and the metro cities, social groups who have traditionally got command over education and skill, new technology and economic wealth and social status have got an added advantage to get access over the major forces of knowledge society. However, the social groups who have historically remained marginalised in Indian society are yet to get fully integrated with the forces of knowledge society.

As shown in Table 8.7, the general category population has got 'high' degree of integration with knowledge society in metro cities, district towns and in villages. In the metro cities, they have got a very high degree of access over high and technical education, ICTs, non-managerial knowledge jobs and high degree of access over managerial positions in knowledge jobs. They have also got a very high degree of access to ICTs and non-managerial knowledge jobs, high-level access to managerial positions in the knowledge jobs and a moderate level of access over higher and technical education and an overall high level

Table 8.7 *Dominant Patterns of Integration with Knowledge Society by Various Social Groups across the Metro Cities, District Towns and Villages*

Place	Indicators	General	OBC	SC	ST	Women
Metro Cities	Post-Secondary Education	Very High	Moderate	Low	High	Very High
	Access to ICTs	Very High	Very High	Very High	High	Very High
	Knowledge Job (Non managerial)	Very High	Very High	Moderate	High	High
	Managerial/ Supervisory Position in Knowledge Job	Moderate	Moderate	Very Low	-	Low
	Over All	High	High	Moderate	High	High
District Towns	Post-Secondary Education	Moderate	Moderate	Moderate	Very low	Moderate
	Access to ICTs	Very High	Very High	Very High	Moderate	Very High
	Knowledge Job (Non managerial)	Very High	Very High	Moderate	Very Low	High
	Managerial/ Supervisory Position in Knowledge Job	High	Low	Very Low	Low	Moderate
	Over All	High	High	Moderate	Low	High
Villages	Post-Secondary education	Moderate	Moderate	Very Low	Low	Very low
	Access to ICTs	Moderate	Moderate	Moderate	Low	Moderate
	Knowledge Job (Nonmanagerial)	Very High	Very High	Low	Low	Low
	Managerial/ Supervisory Position in Knowledge Job	High	Very Low	Very Low	Low	Very Low
	Over All	High	Moderate	Low	Low	Low

Notes: *Very High: 60 per cent and above, High: 50–59 per cent, Moderate: 30–49 per cent, Low: 20–29 per cent, Very Low: 19 per cent and below.*

of access to the major indicators of knowledge society in the district towns. At the village level, this category of population has got an overall high degree of access to the major indicators of knowledge society with very high access to non-managerial knowledge jobs, high access to managerial positions in knowledge jobs and moderate access to higher and technical education and ICTs.

The other backward classes have got overall high level of integration in metro cities and district towns and a modern level of integration in villages. They have got a high degree of access to all major indicators of knowledge society in metro cities and relatively moderate level of access to these indications in district towns and villages. In metro cities, they have got moderate level of access to high and technical education and managerial positions in knowledge jobs and very high level of access to ICTs and non-managerial knowledge jobs. In the district towns, they have very high level of access to ICTs and non-managerial knowledge jobs but low level of access to managerial positions in the knowledge jobs with a moderate access to higher and technical education. In the villages, they have got a very high level of access to non-managerial knowledge jobs but a very low level of access over managerial positions in these jobs. In fact, they have moderate level access to technical and higher education and ICTs in villages. However, despite all these variations the other backward classes are in the process of fast integration with knowledge society.

The scheduled castes have got a moderate level of integration with all the indicators of the knowledge society in metro cities and district towns and a low level of integration in the villages. In the metro cities, they have got low level of access to technical and higher education, moderate level of access to non-managerial knowledge jobs and a very low level of access to the managerial positions in knowledge jobs, though they have a very high level of access to ICTs. In the district towns, they have got moderate levels of access to higher and technical education and non-managerial knowledge jobs. However, they have very low levels of access to managerial positions in knowledge jobs even though they have got a very high degree of access to ICTs. In the villages, they have got a very low level of access to higher and technical education, low access to non-managerial knowledge jobs and very low level of access to the managerial positions in those jobs, even though they have got moderate level of access to ICTs. In fact, access to technical and higher education has remained positively linked to the access to non-managerial knowledge jobs, but not with the managerial positions therein.

The scheduled tribes have in all high level of integration in knowledge society in the metro cities even though they are thinly present in these cities. They have got low level of integration in the district towns and villages in terms of materialist indicators of integration with knowledge society. In the metro cities, though they have got high degree of access over higher and technical education, ICTs and knowledge jobs, have got no access over managerial positions in knowledge jobs. In the district towns, they have got very low level of access over higher and technical education, and knowledge jobs, low level of access of managerial position even though they have got a moderate level of access to ICTs. In the villages, they have got low level of access to higher and technical education, low level of access to ICTs and nil representation in the managerial positions of knowledge jobs.

Women, on the other hand, have got high level of integration in the metro cities and district towns and a low level of integration in the villages. They have got high degree of access to all indices of knowledge society in the metro cities with very high degree of access to higher and technical education, and ICTs, and high degree of access to knowledge jobs, but low level of access to managerial positions in general. In the district towns as well they have got in all high degree of access to all indices of knowledge society with moderate access to high and technical education, managerial position in knowledge jobs, but a high degree of access to non-managerial knowledge jobs and a very high access to ICTs. However, in the rural areas, women have got overall low level of access to the major indices of knowledge society with very low degree of access to higher and technical education and managerial positions in knowledge jobs, moderate access to ICTs and low access to knowledge jobs. Though the emerging dynamics of knowledge society has brought into being new choices for women, it is yet to demolish the traditional gender barrier in workplaces and in society. However a new beginning is the making through the arrival of knowledge society.

The emergence of knowledge society in India has been eclectic and hierarchical in terms of work participation, work relations and organisation arrangements in society. It has created the core and peripheral, workers in society by providing unequal access to education and ICTs. Process of mass production of knowledge and knowledge revolution is yet to alter the pre-existing social inequality that has remained grounded in traditional caste, gender, ethnic and spatial divides in India. Within the prevalent inequality, it has injected social and economic insecurity for vast section of the workforce. Besides, it has framed new processes of social integration wherein a vast segment of population which has been the victim of traditional social injustice has remained yet to be fully integrated with the flow of emerging knowledge society in India. All these have contributed to the production of new and reproduction of old cultures and work relations in new form in the emerging society.

Work and work relation in India are experiencing a phenomenal change in the wake of the penetration of education, ICTs emergence of knowledge jobs and new avenues of employment. These have brought a phenomenal shift in the pre-existing socioeconomic arrangements across India and varieties of contradiction in society by enhancing the scope of vertical occupational mobility of the knowledgeable on the one hand and horizontal mobility of non-knowledgeable on the other, integration of pre-existing dominant section of society with the global flow of wealth, resources and opportunities on the one hand and non-integration of vast majority in the emerging flows on the other, bringing new source of knowledge on the one hand and enforcing pre-existing social hierarchies on the other, enhancing the space for occupational mobility and migration on the one hand and bringing in occupational uncertainty and social insecurity on the other, reinforcing prevalent domination on the one hand and bringing new hope of liberation on the other. Herein, within these emerging contradictions a new socio-cultural milieu is in the making in India.

9

Knowledge Society

Culture, Continuity and Contradictions

The emergence of knowledge society with globalisation and ICTs as its major co-constituents has generated a new momentum in the social, economic, cultural and political lives in contemporary India. Locating itself within an emerging globally interdependent economic order and increasing ICT-driven interconnectivity the knowledge society has redefined in many ways the pre-existing ways of living by bringing in new avenues of economic and occupational mobility and ideals of existential well-being and fulfilment of life, new processes of socialisation, patterns of imparting education, processes of engagement with varieties of cultural practices, formation of social networks, developing friendship and redefining the pre-existing sense of 'space' and 'pace' in society.

I. New Sociocultural Milieu in the Making

ICT-Driven New Social Milieu

The knowledge society has revolutionised and intensified social interaction with increased speed and frequency through text messaging, voice mailing, commercial advertising, emailing, e-charting, Facebook posting, blogging, twitting, skyping, wave casting and host of such new media activities. These have brought into play a new milieu of organising social interaction locally, regionally, nationally and globally. The ICT-mediated interactions, which were either minimal or remained un/under preferred for economic or technical or infrastructural reasons, have now occupied the centrestage for exchange of ideas and information, for generating opinions and debates, for intensification of social issues and concerns, for seeking information on employment and education, professional enrichment and career counselling, physical therapy and medicine, art and music, travel and tourism, real estate and housing, for religion and spirituality, share market and corporate world, live-in and marriage partners, friends and companions, in fact for each and everything on Earth at a high speed as ever across the space. This has not only reduced distance and brought in speed unprecedentedly in social interaction cutting across the geographical boundaries but also brought new worldviews to redefine the social context. It has created a social milieu of closeness, a large part of which is not to be described in terms of physical proximity and visibility, which was conventionally described as 'out of sight is out of mind'. Rather, it is constructed and reconstructed through everyday kind of intensive interactivity in a virtual world independent of physical proximity or visibility: the ideal expression being 'out of (web) site out of mind'. Being active and visible in the virtual world is widely described to be active in the social world. It is posited to be described as a symbol of high modernity, forward-looking worldview, cosmopolitanism, universality, globality and knowledgability.

The Varied Intensity

However, the intensity of engagement with the emerging social milieu has been varied and layered based on varied penetration of ICTs and education, on the one hand, and the pre-exiting social, spatial, age and gender considerations, on the other. Though there have emerged social categories who are not only highly adoptive to this cultural milieu, help reproduce it through their regular engagement and are addicted to it, there are also social categories who use it very selectively and observe it critically.

In general, the intensity of acceptance and inculcation of these milieu has been higher among the younger generation than among the older generation, more among the educated than among the illiterate, more in the metro/urban than in the rural, more among the knowledge workers than among the other varieties of workers, more among new than among old knowledge workers and more among the knowledgeable than among the non-knowledgeable. Notwithstanding these divides, there has emerged continuity in the adaptation to this milieu across social categories having high degree of access over ICTs, education, social networks and knowledge jobs that have been highly instrumental for them in getting accommodated to the new frontier of social interactions, articulating new identities and exercising alternative choices in social and economic lives.

This social milieu widely contributes to the formation of a host of dichotomies by liberating various creative potentials, at one end, and rejuvenating stance of conservatism, on the other. While the daily exchange of a vast body of information, new vocabulary, symbol, image, photography, poetry, joke, satire, proverbs, exciting feeling, emotion, views, ideas and opinion help constructing new identities, on the one hand, these also entrap a vast segment of society with a predominant sense of exclusivity. Again, within each of the existing socially and spatially divided social groups, there has emerged a strong generational divide in terms of old versus new generation: a new breed of creed with deep down association with e-culture whom I prefer to call the 'e-Gen', the electronic credo who are highly pro-adaptive to the ICT-driven culture.

The Techno Adaptive Community: The e-Gen

The emerging cultural milieu has created a new community of knowledgeable who exist not only in the virtual but also in real life forming varieties of community within a community. A leading segment of this community cutting across the gender, caste, class and ethnic divides are the youth and young in urban India who are born and socialised in the culture of economic globalisation and the ICT-driven sociocultural milieu that have been set in motion in the post-economic liberalisation period of the 1990s. This e-Gen in essence is the product of ICT resolution that extensively uses ICTs to communicate, socialise and engage meaningfully across the space to produce a youth-centric social milieu sustainably. They practise new cultural idioms preferring 'Yo' handshake over hello or 'namaste', prefer western fast food – pizza, burger, pasta over local dishes – use innovative and different vocabularies and abbreviations such as 'pop' for papa, 'mom' for mummy, 'sis' for sister, 'bro' for brother, 'princy' for school principal, 'LOL' for nonsense, 'IDK' for 'I don't know' and varieties of quickly picked up new age words/vocabularies as the language of interaction.

They decorate their bodies with tattoos, adorn distinctive branded attire and keep themselves ready with the state-of-the-art electronic gadgets and have a smart and confident body language to make their presence felt in the public domain distinctively different from the rest. They are ready to be socially sensitive and make a huge hue and cry in the virtual world that has emerged to be a powerful force to reckon with. They form the core of the new smart community that is highly adaptive to the emerging socio-cultural milieu set in motion by the knowledge society whose orientation to life is widely guided by the understanding that 'you only live once' (YoLo). A section of the rural youth is also getting introduced to this smart e-Gen very fast.

They prefer to make mobile calls or send text message and make use of Facebook and email even to the next door neighbour than to interact with them directly. For them, the world has become a small virtual entity for identifying life options in the areas of profession, friendship, giving and taking opinions, organising opinions and demonstrating protests. They make use of ICTs in every areas of their life: for social networking, e-booking, e-ticketing, e-conferencing, e-marketing, e-shopping, e-business, e-learning and in fact 'e-vizing' each and every domain of life. They redefine the traditionality in a new context, place laptop, notepad, i-pod, pen drive and mobile phone in front of goddess Saraswati for blessings instead of notebook, book and pen. They prefer to make their world 'exciting' in every moment of their existence through ICT-driven innovation and its multidimensional application while most of such applications remain unused or unknown to the elderly. They prefer to use western accent, style and exhibit western body language in daily social interaction. Their attire, fashion, hair dressing, body ornaments, electronic gadgets and other accessories of life represent a global standing that gets renewed, replaced and improvised very fast along with changes as shown in the latest advertisements of these products.

Their choices of foods and clothes are more likely to be conditioned by worldly externality and less likely by localised sensitivity. They are ready to spend a high amount on consumption, fashion and comfort to be acceptable to the emerging visible social milieu without a guilt feeling. They are ready to live at present even at the cost of future and stand apart from their parents and the seniors who try to live in future at the cost of the present. They are apparently secured, smart and in favour of developing a lifestyle, which is yet to be structured. Their dominant value is instant self-gratification. They are the dominant crowd of fast food outlets, evening pubs and night clubs, which are being proliferated in the metro cities very recently. They live in the family without imbibing traditional family values; look for life partner based on choices widely available in the virtual world; seldom visit religious places but are attached to shopping malls and consider them, as mentioned by Manual Castells (1997), the cathedral of their everyday life. They are represented as P++ in Chart 9.1 as they are highly integrated with the emerging cultural milieu.

The upwardly mobile-educated youths have emerged to be engulfed with a new cultural milieu generated by ICTs, have become the reference point and the face of core group for the usage of ICTs to further and sustain the emerging new social and cultural milieu of knowledge society. Though their numerical strength is not very high, they form a powerful segment of the society whose number is increasing unprecedentedly especially in the metro towns to be followed simultaneously in the district towns and in the villages with lower intensity though. This section of the population is largely represented by the public school, college and university-going students, newly employed (both salaried and selfemployed) youth. They have been connected to universal citizenship or netizenship through similar global culture of consumerism, fashion, music, art, love, hate and threat concern and apathy. They make extensive use of ICTs in every active moment of their daily life and at times as *the techno-addicts*.

This e-Gen are indeed the children of economic liberalisation and information age and have emerged to be the 'desi zippies' of Indian society and have conditioned them and their surroundings through ICT-driven culture, are apparently liberated from traditionalities, its role expectation, and uncalled for localised bondage. Though they are located within the overburden of information flow, their world view is focused on cosmopolitanism and on being globally inclusive. They construct and reconstruct virtual communities on their own terms based on their daily experience and interactions in the cyber space.

In view of phenomenal proliferation of this brand of youth in Indian society, many experts have observed the arrival of the age of 'desi zippies' in India as those of yuppies of the United States of the 1980s. Friedman (2005) is of the view that in the globalised world the global economy from here forward will be shaped less by the ponderous deliberations of finance ministers and more by the spontaneous explosion of energy from zippies as Americans grew up with the hippies in the 1960s, and due to the high-tech revolution, many became 'yuppies' in the 1980s in the United States. *Outlook India* has described them as the Liberalisation Children, characterised by a complete absence of guilt about making money and spending it. India has 54 per cent population below 19 years. Even the oldest of them were just seven when liberalisation happened. 60 per cent Indian households have at least one Liberalisation Child who now boosts the economic growth of India that is posited in the thick of information revolution, connectivity boom, coalition politics, IT-enabled social network and the rise of the service economy. They boost economic growth with rising demand for cell phones, TVs, cars, consumer credit, etc., as symbols of rising income. They have a totally different attitude to consumption versus saving, accessing credit versus living within your means, consumption priorities and the difference between necessity and luxury. This story is also about rural India that has reduced its dependence on agriculture. This is creating a different kind of rural market (Friedman, 2005, Outlook India, 2004).

ICTs have brought a phenomenal change in the behaviour pattern, lifestyle and learning process of young students of this generation. This is somewhat closer to Prensky's (2001) reflexion on American students in contemporary era, which delineates that American students today represent the first generations to grow up with digital technology. Their live experience is surrounded by and using of computers, computer games, email, the Internet, cell phones and instant messaging, video games, digital music players, video cams and all the other toys and tools of the digital age. His calculation shows that 'average college graduates spend less than 5000 hours of their lives reading, but over 10,000 hours playing video games, and 20,000 hours watching TV'. He shows that as a result of 'this ubiquitous environment and the sheer volume of their interaction with it, today's students think and process information fundamentally differently from their predecessors'. To him, they are 'Digital Natives' who speak in the digital language of computers, video games and the Internet and 'those of us who were not born into the digital world but have, at some later point in our lives, become fascinated by and adopted many or most aspects of the new technology are, and always will be compared to them, Digital Immigrants'.

Characteristically, the digital natives as Prensky observes are used to receiving information really fast. They prefer parallel process and multitask, prefer random access (like hypertext), function best when networked, thrive on instant gratification and frequent rewards, prefer games to 'serious' work, are used to the instantaneity hypertext, downloaded music, phones in their pockets, a library on their laptops, beamed messages and instant messaging and have little patience for lectures, step-by-step logic and 'tell-test' instruction. To him, it is highly unlikely that the digital natives will go backwards despite efforts after efforts are made by immigrants because 'their brains may already be different and they have undergone a cultural migration'. Kids born into any new culture, learn the new language easily, and forcefully resist using the old. Smart adult immigrants accept that they do not know about their new world and take advantage of their kids to help them learn and integrate. Not-so-smart (or not-so-flexible) immigrants spend most of their time grousing about how good things were in the 'old country' (Prensky, 2001).

In India, e-Gen are the native variety of these digital natives or the zippes. Despite several limitations, a large chunk of this Indian youth is a part of emerging networking and consumption culture as set in motion by the interconnected world. The life pattern and cultural values of these youths are more akin to the American Zippie as emerged in the 1960s than to those of the average traditional Indian youth. In fact, they have emerged to be the vanguards of IT revolution in India. The country stands today in the threshold of mass arrival of this 'e-Gen' across the country whose initiation has just began in the metro cities and district towns and spread fast among a section of youth in the rural areas as well. While they are confident of their casual approach to life and carefully preserve this unpremeditated orientation to life, the digital immigrants – the elderly parents – find it difficult to socialise them within their own frame and to keep the belt of their children tight above the waist so as to ensure that the trouser does not fall to the ground.

Significantly, even middle-aged professionals, academicians, entrepreneurs and others who have both the desire and capacity are profoundly tended to be integrated with this sociocultural milieu. As indicated earlier, the metropolitan cities and towns have been linked much more to the forces of knowledge society effectively than the rural areas. Again the younger is the age, higher has been the attachment to ICTs, electronic gadgets and higher has been the manifestation of global outlooks. While, on the other hand, higher the age lower has been the intensity of attachments to the above. In between these two, the middle segment of the population has been more inclined to the outlooks of the younger generation than the elderly. In essence, the dominant majority of urban India tilts in favour of a youth-centric outlook that has emerged out of the interpenetration of globalised market forces and the ICTs. As against these backdrops, the twenty-first century urban India is posited with the velocity of the e-gen who are fashioned to lead the ICT age. The patterns of penetration of new cultural milieu and its adaptation however have acquired varied intensity both in rural and in urban areas. Again, this varied intensity has been conditioned by caste, ethnic and gender and generated considerations.

Urban Tale of Cultural Divide and Varied Integration

As mentioned earlier, the usage of ICTs has been layered in the urban areas. While the upwardly mobile-educated sections are linked to the multiple dimensions of knowledge society through ICTs, new culture and market-oriented consumption, the traditional marginalised sections and a small segment of general category people who concentrate themselves in the lower-middle-class cluster, slums and are employed in the low paid jobs in the unorganised sector are only partly integrated to the knowledge society. The overall pattern of integration with the sociocultural milieu knowledge society is circumscribed by class and caste divides, generational and gender gaps.

A large section of general category and the other backward classes, because of their pre-existing higher educational and training backgrounds, have got higher degree of awareness of new economic opportunities. They are culturally integrated with the forces of globalisation and the milieu of emerging knowledge society (represented by P+). The younger generation of these groups is more akin to the core of the knowledge society in India (represented by P++), while the elderly generation has casual or infrequent linkages with these forces (represented by P). Significantly, the middle-aged section of this group is more akin to the life choices of the younger generation than the elderly (represented by P++).

The youths from other backward classes and the scheduled caste background because of their recently acquired educational and economic wellbeing are more prone to get integrated with emerging culture than their elderly generation. In terms of dress, language, ICT use and fashion, they stand apart from the rest of the community. Indeed, at times they are aggressively consumerist. Many of the households of these segments of the society have lived for many centuries together. While the elderly generation tends to stick to old technology, dress, food, language, culture, art, music and patterns of social networking (represented by P−) predominantly with a sense of indifference but not negation, the young generation adheres to new social and cultural codes (represented by P++). The Jat caste household in Delhi is a typical example to this case. Women, especially the elderly and the married, are found to adhere to the principles of 'pardha' (represented by −P) and the new generation maintain the same inside the house. Significantly, the young generation boys and girls are more attached to the emerging culture outside their home due to the prevailing customs and traditional authority structures. They are, however, the effective harbingers of change in traditional ways of living inside the home and the neighbourhood. These school-college and university-going youths and the new entrants in job market significantly influence the technological and consumerist options of their family. A vast majority of this middle strata experiences economic prosperity caused by price escalation of their landed property and increasing earning from the rent. Though they have adapted to all high cost modern amenities in their house, their cultural practices and orientation to life have remained predominantly traditional. Thus, the middle segments of the urban areas are in a flux by the mix of integration with the knowledge society with its technology, culture and outlook, on the one hand, and the traditionality, on the other. These segments, however, are the most dynamic in nature as they have acquired the potential for upward social, technological and cultural mobility (they twist between P and P+).

The Rural Tale of Social Divide

In the rural areas, there has been a layered use of these technologies and a corresponding segregated flow of new social milieu and sociocultural orientations. A section of educated upwardly mobile *youth* who are predominantly from general categories, followed by a small section of the other backward classes and the scheduled castes with access to education and mass media, have got acquainted with ICT-driven culture. They are now connected with the wider world through ICTs for fashion, further studies, job opportunities, new frontiers of social contacts and communication. Though their numerical strength is small in size, they indeed represent the smart generation with fresh outlook for a new future. Their size is increasing very fast and gradually penetrating among all segments in rural areas. Within dillydally rural life, they project themselves as the smart people with smart branded mobile phones and other electronic gadgets, fashionable clothes and other accessories of daily life, which were earlier considered to be the privilege of the urban youth. They are quick to adapt to change. They are knowledgeable about the ICTs and alert about the happenings taking shape globally and locally, use vocabularies and language that are frequently used in social media, SMS and MMS. In appearance and interaction, they are more akin to their urban counterparts than the rural ones. Though many of them may not be owning personal computers or have personal Internet access, they predominantly use the public Internet facility available within the village or outside and their mobile handsets. They acquire information about transport, banking, medicine, health, education, employment, entertainment and all other relevant areas. A small number of youth also makes extensive commercial use of this information and the ICT-induced opportunities (represented by P++).

The social media used by these youth has put many of the remote villages in World Wide Web with detailed information about the images of uniqueness of their areas, developing association of village school alumina and contact with the outside world. This generation of ICT shabby youth is in a process of developing a bridge between the people who migrated out of the village and the villagers through the use of social media. They are the 'parents' pride' by all conventional indicators of acceptance in the wider society. Significantly, they are a generation without a deep sense of caste prejudice and are good agents of accommodation of globalised culture in the localised context and of change in society. The emergence of these segments of the youth and also gradual increase in the number of knowledge workers especially of new ones in the rural area has posed severe threat to the conventional structure of authority in many ways. They prefer to respond to mobile calls and even listen to music and also to dance to its tune or have ear phones hanging on their neck than to remain silent in front of the elders as a traditional mark of respect.

The Moderates

Similar new vistas of interactions are also being shaped in their lifestyle and professional world of upwardly mobile sections of the society who have been able to take advantage of the proliferation of knowledge economy. The *middle-aged* literati who are predominantly from the urban areas and a thin upwardly mobile section of population from the rural areas are in the process of getting acquainted with identities, interests and ideas that are articulated by global market forces cutting across the boundary of territoriality. Herein, many of their personalised choices for car, housing, living standards, food, drinks, cloth, art, music, attire and fashion get widely influenced by these new orientations to life. They are not so young but try to remain young taking care of their physical appearance and fitness, join the fitness club, go to the beauty parlour and pay handsomely to remain presentable as per the latest fashion magazine. They have acquired the capacity to be a part of conspicuous consumerism and have the desire to be techno savvy (represented by P++).

While a section of them is predominantly represented by the old and new knowledge workers and develop a global secular outlook, another section of them is predominantly represented by the traditional entrepreneurs. These traditional entrepreneurs take recourse to ICTs and the consumption culture to reinforce their traditional worldview. They seldom participate in consumption injudiciously. They combine new cultural milieu with the pre-existing old ones. They are predominantly from traditional social and business background, and are economically enterprising but socially conservative, educated yet intellectually business oriented, politically ambitious but morally self-centred. They are globalised for their economic enterprise, use ICTs for economic venture, develop nexus with politicians to promote and protect their mutual interest. They are highly exclusive in their social orientation, celebrate the traditionality, mourn for the women's liberation and autonomy and tend to compartmentalise their personal lives from public lives. Their preference for caste-gender and ethnicity-based social segregation continues unabated. They publicise caste-based matrimonial and are ready to spend lavishly on dowry and go for extravaganza for marriage and other social ceremonies. Though they are predominantly represented by the elderly generation, the younger generation of these communities are yet to come out of these worldviews. They try to compartmentalise their public appearance through modernity and secularism, but their private commitment for traditionality prevails over their overall orientation to life. These successful entrepreneurs use their newly acquired economic power to reinforce their traditional hegemony in society, donate for religious purposes, feed people on special days for religious significance and also donate for several social causes to enhance their public image. Though their strength is numerically very thin, they represent a powerful group that reproduces traditionality through modern means. They use ICTs for caste-based match selection, develop and use everyday horoscope (ICT based) and make use of religious and traditional rituals to form communities of their own. For them, viewing of regular social programmes in the religious or spiritual TV channels are more appealing than debates on generation gap or gender justice or poverty or unemployment in society. They are represented as P+ being moderately adaptive and integrative of modernity and tradition in the emerging context.

The Part Adaptive

In the midst of this emerging social milieu, there has remained a vast majority of the Indian population widely represented by the *marginalised sections* and a section of the general category of Indian population, both from the rural and from the urban areas, who are either illiterate or semiliterate and have inadequate access to ICTs, and are yet to be integrated effectively with the forces of knowledge economy. The predominant patterns of their social, economic and cultural interactions are guided by traditionality, even though a thin section of them has got indirectly or partly introduced to knowledge society. A vast section of them has the desire for a change. They use the limited segment of technology for both social interaction and economic betterment. Significantly, the young generation of this segment of population are more prone to get adapted, in a limited form though, to the emerging cultural milieu than the elderly generation. They are, however, the intermediate category who stand between the two worlds of tradition and transition mostly by compulsion than by choice. They are shown as P, as they have been only partly adaptive.

The penetration of new information technology, however, has not replaced the old patterns of social networking. Though telephones and mobiles are used in regular social networking, the *middle-aged* and *elderly generations* still like face-to-face interaction. In all the village areas, elderly people are still fond of regularly visiting each other's place. For them, it is more satisfying to meet old friends, relatives and acquaintances in a leisurely way than to talk for few minutes over telephone or the mobile phones. As a village elder says, 'there is no fun in dry talk over phone unless we share a *bidi* or a *huckka* or a glass of Lachhi or cup of tea together and see each other's face'. Though the ICT-driven cultural milieu touches their lives, the elderly are more prone to keep themselves anchored in traditional arrangement. The middle aged, especially from the higher caste/class and educated background, is more adaptive to the ICT-driven culture than the low caste and the uneducated. The adaptive behaviour in both the cases is circumscribed by the extent of access over ICTs.

Women in rural areas are less techno savvy and have relatively less access over the ICTs and are relatively more inclined to face-to-face interactions and upholding traditional practises than the male folk. However, in general, the frequency of interaction of general category rural women with their relatives and friends has increased with the arrival of mobile phones. This is also gradually getting penetrated among the women from the other backward classes and to a little extent among a few scheduled castes. In general, younger girls prefer more telephonic conversations than the elderly women in daily interaction. Significantly, among a small section of young women from the general categories, other backward classes and scheduled castes, ICT-based social interaction has also started taking place especially for occupational purpose. A good number of educated young women from these categories visit ICT hubs or kiosks for information about education and employment. The ICTs, which were initially a tool for social interaction and connectivity, have emerged to be potential social change in rural India. The elected representatives in the Village Panchayet or members of self-help groups, from these backgrounds, are more inclined to ICTs driven culture than the others in these social groups.

The Indifferent

Beyond the highly integrated, moderately and partially integrated segments, there are vast segments of population who are passive observers of the emerging ICTs driven culture. Though a section of them has the desire, they are incapacitated to be integrated due to educational, technological and economic and geographical limitations.

These indifferent people, in fact, are located far away from the glitters of new sociocultural milieu and are yet to be integrated with the emerging cultural milieu of knowledge society due to inadequate access to education and ICTs, and predominant mode of horizontal occupational mobility among them. Though they have the highest numerical strength, they are devoid of the proper educational opportunity and concentrate in the low-paid unorganised sectors of the economy, live in the slums or small tenements. The predominant segment of this population comprises the schedule castes, a small section of the other backward classes and general categories, and the migrants from rural areas. Many of them are unaware of the usage of computer and Internet even though they extensively use mobile phone. They are regularly engaged in the manual activities as construction workers, domestic help, rickshaw puller, small vendor, small mechanics, tailors, hawker, gardener, helper, sweeper, scavenger and varieties of unorganised activities in the industrial units. A small portion of them are the child labourers who work in tea stalls, grocery and other processing units, cycle or motor repairing shops. In the real sense, these segments of society have remained nonintegrated with the knowledge society.

They represent the character of marginal man in the urban set-up and are conditioned to live with substandard, at times inhuman, state of life by compulsion. Though through dressing patterns, food habits, social interaction, language and life style they are predominantly attached to the traditional societies, they are also simultaneously localised in the urban way of life. Lack of economic and social resources condition them to remain attached to traditionability. They present themselves predominantly as a continuum of rural and urban life, and an extension of rural poverty and under/unemployment in urban areas. Though they provide support service to the knowledge society, they are far from being integrated in the knowledge society due to their prevalent capacity derivation.

Mohammad Karim is a 22-year-old, semiliterate migrant from West Midnapur District of West Bengal living in Shahpur Jat Village in South Delhi and works there for a multinational garment company as a tailor. He has been living along with other seven boys from his village in a small dark room of around 10 × 12 feet size since the last four-and- a-half years. The room is without water and toilet facility. Before shifting to a new accommodation, he was to share these facilities with another half a dozen boys who lived in an adjacent room. Most of his roommates frequently developed skin disease and respiratory problems. However, they preferred to stay there as it was cheap and full of Bengali migrants around.

Now, Karim has taken a separate room with the arrival of his wife and two daughters from the village to stay with him permanently. He earns approximately ₹ 5000 per month. Karim repents as he has not been able to pay a visit to the Jama Masjid to offer a 'namaz' even though he is in Delhi since the last four-and-a-half years because of his preoccupation with daily activities. His wife, Salma, works as a domestic help. The eldest daughter is of school-going age but they are unable to send her. To Karim and Salma, it is more important to arrange food and shelter for the children than to look for their education immediately. Karim works overtime and Salma works in four houses as part-time domestic help and their eldest daughter takes care of her sister while they are at work. Karim maintains a strong bond with his ageing parents and sends a sum regularly for their maintenance in the native village. Karim's family is alien to the cultural and social life of Delhi like most of the migrant labour families. Salma is interested in movies. They are yet to purchase a TV set. At times, movies are shown free of cost in the Siri Fort Auditorium. Salma is hesitant to go there with the apprehension that the security guard may not allow her an entry into the auditorium. She has never visited a shopping mall, but has used the metro train once only as a lifetime experience. Similar is the story of thousands of migrants in major cities who are pushed to migrate there more out of livelihood compulsion and less of choice. Besides these segments of urban people, the 'ICTs indifferents' are also widely represented by a vast section of marginalised people, rural poor, beggars, street children, a section of the slum dwellers, migrant labours, etc. For them this is an alien culture, even though they are regularly impacted with the wider processes of the emergence of knowledge society. They are shown as P−.

II. New Drive for Education and Socialisation: Contradiction and Adjustment

India now encounters a host of tensions emerging out of stereotypical parental attitudes, role expectations and their social image, on the one hand, and the proliferation of knowledge economy, ICTs and knowledge revolution, on the other. This tension is again compounded with increasing competition for higher and technical education and their commoditisation, on the one hand, and the capacity of the parents to finance such educational processes, on the other. This has mounted an increasing pressure on the school-going students not only to be successful in their educational pursuits, but also to be successful in getting a place in the 'reputed' professional or technical educational institutions. These have caused unbridled competition not only among students but also among parents. The competition has got multiplied with the availability of limited number of seats in the reputed professional institutions in the country. Though the private educational entrepreneurs across the country have opened up new professional and technical educational institutions and introduced varieties of professional programmes, converted the educational arena as a market place for producing and providing academic degrees, most of the institutions are yet to acquire a 'status of reputation'. Again, the fee structure of many of these institutions are too high to reach the level of affordability of poor parents. As the seats in state-funded engineering colleges such as IITs, ITIs, IIMs, etc., are very limited, parents and students alike have to make extra efforts from early childhood for securing a seat in good government-run institutions as a first choice. These have made

Table 9.1 Trends of Association with Emerging Cultural Patterns

Place	Social Class/Categories	Young — Boys			Young — Girls			Middle Aged — Men			Middle Aged — Women			Elderly — Men			Elderly — Women		
		ICT	Branded Fashion Items – Clothes, Shoe, Watch, Perfumes etc.	Fast Foods	ICT	Branded Fashion Items – Clothes, Shoe, Watch, Perfumes	Fast Foods	ICT	Branded Fashion Items – Clothes, Shoe, Watch, Perfumes	Fast Foods	ICT	Branded Fashion Items – Clothes, Shoe, Watch, Perfumes	Fast Foods	ICT	Branded Fashion Items – Clothes, Shoe, Watch, Perfumes	Fast Foods	ICT	Branded Fashion Items – Clothes, Shoe, Watch, Perfumes	Fast Foods
Villages	Upper, Upper Middle	P++	P++	P	P+	P+	P	P-	P-	P-	P-	P-	P-	P-	P-	P-	P-	P-	P-
	Middle	P++	P++	P+	P+	P+	P+	P-	P-	P-	P-	P-	P-	P-	P-	P-	P-	P-	P-
	Lower	P-	P-	P-	P-	P-	P-	P-	P-	P-	P-	P-	P-	P-	P-	P-	P-	P-	P-
District Towns	Upper, Upper Middle	P++	P++	P++	P++	P++	P++	P+	P+	P+	P+	P+	P+	P+	P	P	P	P	P
	Middle	P++	P++	P++	P++	P++	P++	P+	P+	P+	P+	P+	P+	P	P	P-	P	P	P
	Lower	P-	P-	P++	P++	P-	P++	P++	P-	P++	P++	P-	P-	P+	P+	P+	P-	P-	P-
Metro Cities	Upper, Upper Middle	P++	P++	P++	P++	P++	P++	P++	P++	P++	P++	P++	P++	P+	P+	P	P+	P	P
	Middle	P++	P++	P++	P++	P++	P-	P++	P++	P++	P++	P++	P++	P+	P+	P-	P	P	P
	Lower	P-	P-	P-	P-	P-	P-	P-	P-	P-	P-	P-	P-	P-	P-	P-	P-	P-	P-

Note: P++ stands for highly adaptive and addicted; P+ stands for moderate adaptive and mixing old with new; P stands for only partly adaptive due to social and economic limitation; P– stands for indifferent.

the parents to be extra caring in nurturing the future of their children, arranging viable options to secure their future and to socialise them within the frame of old societal mechanisms and emotional bondage. While market-driven education has created the culture of competition and consumption, it is not only the parent, but also the students who develop competitors out of classmates.

While the child finds himself/herself within the flow of ICT-driven cultural milieu and multiple learning arrangements and future career/ academic choices, parents feel themselves insecure in view of the arrival of new economic arrangements that is globally competitive. These insecurities are again compounded with new initiatives and experiments of the state, on the one hand, and emergent need for the articulation and alternative strategy by the parents to match these initiatives, on the other. In the wake of globalisation the state has been vigorously experimenting varieties of curriculum, pedagogic and evaluation techniques on the students (mostly without a stable framework and frequently inviting alterations of the same) to suffice the emerging educational need of the market varying between comprehensive continuous evaluation to one-time evaluation, common test to specific tests for professional course, e-learning to face to face learning etc. In response, parents however try to make the future of their children secure by remaining anchored in the conventional roots of socialising the children and pushing them to undertake all possible hard work for securing a place in 'good' educational programmes (usually in medicine, engineering, law, management, commerce and other processional courses) in elite educational institutions and passing examinations with high grades even at social and cultural cost.

Children's success is defined in terms of consistency in good results in their academic career, admission in good professional and technical education and thereafter getting a secure and good salaried job. Hierarchy in education and knowledge is systematically made and injected in the mind of the child from an early stage of childhood and children are conditioned to achieve the top place in this hierarchy. Accordingly medical, engineering, management and computer-related disciplines are thought to have preference independent of children's choice. For many, children's life is conditioned from an early stage through hour-to-hour tuition, subject-wise tutorial and coaching classes and no-go to sports and extracurricular activities with the sole aim to get a place in the preferred discipline and cherished institution. The professional tutorial homes or coaching classes located mostly in the metro cities attract parents' and students' attention from all over the country. Some coaching centres have emerged to be more successful than the others and have acquired elite status. In fact, there have emerged chains and circles of coaching centres with several branches.

Many students first join special coaching or tutorial classes to be successfully enrolled in these elite coaching centres. Once getting enrolled, their efforts are again supplemented by individual tuition in subject-specific areas at home. The average middle-class parents not only keep watch on their children's daily movements and use of social media, Internet, mobile phone and watching of television programme, but also restrict it through all possible means. The cumulative parental pressure, which was a predominant phenomenon of urban India, has started spreading very fast even in rural areas.

A vast body of the student population gets entrapped within this circle more by parental, peer group and other societal pressure and compulsion than by their own choice. Rare are the parents from both the rural and the urban areas who do not advocate professional education for their children today. In India, students besides appearing for national level tests for All Indian Engineering Entrance Exam (AIEEE), Indian Institute of Technology Joint Entrance Exam, All India Pre Medical Test (AIPMT), Armed Forces Medical College Entrance Exam (AFMC), National Institute of Fashion Technology Entrance Exam (NIFT), National Entrance Examination for Design (NEED), Common Law Admission Test (CLAT), Birla Institute of Technology and Science Admission Test (BITSAT), National Council for Hotel Management and Catering Technology Joint Entrance Exam (NCHMCT), National Defence Academy & Naval Academy Examination (NDA & NA), etc., appear in state-level exams for admissions in the professional courses separately conducted by 31 states and union territories, and also by several private institutions, universities and deemed-to-be universities across the country. In India, an average of 12.5 million students appear for the entrance tests to be qualified for admission in the professional programmes available in medicine, engineering, law, management, etc., areas. For example the Entrance Test for IITs is one of such common grounds for competition in India whereby over 5 lakhs students appeared in the IIT entrance test in 2013, of which 1,50,000 qualified for the advanced test and only 9885 were selected for the final admission. Similar is the position of medical, para-medical, law and other professional programmes.

As the number of seats available in the elite institutions is very few and only a small section of the children make a balance and become successful in getting seats in reputed institutions, the others get frustrated if no immediate options are available. Despite increasing incidences of suicide by students, competition for scoring a higher percentage in education and parental aggressiveness for technical and professional education continues unabated in India. Once competition for education is over, students have to be prepared for competition for services such as Indian Administrative, Banking, Railways, Revenue, Judicial, Air Force, Army and Navy, Economic, Engineering and a host of other services until and unless somebody opts for self-employment either by compulsion or by choice. Increasing culture of competition, low performance, failure, peer group and parental pressure frustrates a section of youths. According to a new study, India has the highest suicide rates in the world with maximum number of young people on the brink, and worse still, it may soon turn out to be the biggest killer in the country. According to the National Crime Bureau Report in 2011, 1,34,599 people committed suicides in India, of which 35.38 per cent belonged to the age group of 15–19 years (NCRB, 2011).

The Shaky and Sacrificial Generation

In India, the average middle class parents have emerged to be very insecure and nervous with the increasing competition for success of their children on the one hand and growing instability in society on the other. Many parents want their own dream to be fulfilled through the success of their children. Average parents now realise the power of education and their own powerlessness in the wake of power getting concentrated in the hands of politicians, bureaucrats and ruling class, businessmen and brokers. They want to encounter their powerlessness by making their children powerful by providing good education. The lower strata want their social status to be elevated to those of the upper strata of society, while the upper strata wants to improvise their status and reproduce and retain the status quo through their children's success.

Common parents now use education as a tool for their empowerment in society, through educational attainment and success of their children. They make all possible sacrifices for the purpose of the same. Parents want to be socially recognised as powerful not as much through their sacrifice as much through the success of their children. Many parents tend to live in the future at the cost of the present. They earn and save not as much for themselves as much for their children. They seldom spend on extravaganza, but rather carry a guilt feeling on spending conspicuously on themselves. Even though these middle-class groups experience an economic boom in the middle or the later ages of their life, they continue their 'simple living and high thinking' old lifestyle in a new economic age that is usually guided by hope for a bright future of their children. The growing craze for English medium public school and professional education for the child has made the parents be extra laborious, alert and competitive. Social network, political influence and donation are frequently put into work for a child's admission in educational institutions. Such efforts are preponderant not only among the economically affordable middle class, but also among several of the poor parents. They are ready to sell property, ornament and cattle, take bank loans, loan from Employees Provident Funds (EPFs) and even from local money lenders at a high rate of interest, do part-time or extra job for good education of their children.

The dream for a successful future of their children has made many of the rural parents invest a huge part of their time, money and energy on children's education. Amol Roy, a schedule caste semiliterate cultivator cum betel shop owner in Kumarganj, West Bengal, regularly takes his VIIth standard son in a bicycle for science tuition to a suburban area that is 6 km away from his home. He gets up early morning at 5.30 am and leaves with his son for tuition and returns by 8.30 am. He saves an amount of ₹ 500 per month for the tuition, avoids purchasing new cloth for himself or for his wife as this may affect the tuition of his son. His dream is to make his son a doctor. He has only one acre of land. He has kept this land reserved to be used for his son's future tuition fee, course fee and other related expenditure in the medical education programme. To him life is fulfilled only with the success of the children and his future 'will be taken care of by God'.

III. Constructing Social Choice and Critiquing from Below

In the wake of growing denial and deprivations, and increasing hardship of vast segments of people, on the one hand, and increasing interactivity with the wider world and exposure to mass media, on the other, critiquing of the power structure and the political hegemony of the dominant section is in the making at the grassroots in both the rural and urban areas.

An important segment of the rural population is increasingly exposed to television and radio and newspaper besides getting interconnected with the wider world through spatial and occupational mobility and virtual connectivity. While popular serials and movies in the television channel give them regular entertainment, news and advertisements largely help them construct alternative views and choices. Though a section of the economically well-off population especially from the general categories construct their consumerist need and choice, select attire and vocabulary being influenced by television serial and advertisement, many from nongeneral categories have now become aware of the happenings taking shape outside their given world and about their rights and entitlements. A section of rural women have been alert enough to ascertain the maximum retail price of grocery items and their date of expiry, assert the need for toilets in the house and the cooking gas connection instead of old hearth, and have been active in the activities of Panchayat Raj Institutions. A large section of rural labourers now make alternative employment choice within the village itself especially through the MGNREGS schemes, etc. Village elders develop opinion about the correctness of Anna Hazare's Jan Lokpal Bill, misuse of public funds during the construction of Commonwealth Games Village, distribution of 2G, 3G licences, and scams widely influenced by mass media, etc. However, despite visible impact of television and newspaper on them, a section of the village elders are very categorical about the distinction between the 'real' and 'reel' life. Though they consider the ICTs to be a boon, they are very protective of their own cultural practises, dressing style, food habits and other localised norms and values. They strictly keep a watch over the movement and ICT usage by the young generation. As a 55-year-old educated woman from Dangarhat says,

> our clothes, skin and appearances are different and out habits are unique. The TV and mobile phone are making the youth to forget these difference and uniqueness. We should make them to know ourselves first. Now there are perversions and threats in society because of TV and mobile phone. We get absence calls in the mid nights and also threats... I allow my daughter only to have limited access to TV and mobile phone... It is good to talk big in public... But in reality things are different. In case of mishaps everybody will criticise but nobody will come for help. It is better that we should step out cautiously.

In fact, her own articulation has come out of her increasing access to television programmes. 'I watch television programme without fail.... Now there is big change in my husband. He shares a lot of household chores with me'.

For the upper caste or general category people while access to education, television, radio and ICTs help concentrate their domination in the rural areas, for the low-caste people, especially the young generation, such access and increasing quantum of migration to urban areas help construct resistance against such domination. Many urban-returned and techno-inclined low-caste rural migrant workers, and school and college-going students decline to pay traditional respect through 'Namaste' to upper-caste village elders; many of them question the cause of their economic and social plight and status in society; get networked with the wider world to articulate views on their marginal identity and to develop a visible contestation against their subordinate position in society that is partly implicit and partly explicit in their body language and in collective action. Many rural Dalit youths now network among themselves, and with civil society activists, social movement actors and also with political parties to reconstruct their marginal position as a united political weapon against age-old domination. Significantly, their networking that was predominantly local, is now being widely connected with the wider world through ICTs.

The traditional structure of authority and the primordial form of domination has been widely questioned with the emergence of a new brand of mobile techno-savvy members of marginalised communities. Educated rural youth do not want to lag behind their urban counterparts and want to be compatible in all possible means. Localised issues of women, religious minorities, scheduled castes, scheduled tribes and other backward classes have no more remained local, rather these are now articulated in a wider context being well informed and interconnected through ICTs against the hostile forces of patriarchy, feudalism and caste and ethnic hegemony. Their increasing participation in the localised protest is shaped by their interconnectivity with the wider world.

The new sociocultural flow has not remained confined only among the knowledge workers, the ICTs users and the educated lots, but has also got expanded among cross sections of population. This expansion has been 'apparently' double edged. While, on the one hand, it has promoted the secular identity of common citizenship and netizenship, on the other hand, it has reinforced many of the primordial identities. While the Rajbansi youths of Dangarhat-Mamudpur and Dalit and Jat youths of Bhagwanpur village express common concern on several social issues, they also simultaneously assert their caste identities to protect their political and economic interests and develop individual and collective critique against the traditional domination and their sustained marginalisation in society. However, these formulations are not contradictory, rather complimentary as both the articulations help to question bases of subordination locally and globally constructing simultaneously secular and primordial identities. As the knowledge society is yet to be fully formed, it has emerged to be partly transformative and partly restorative. However, for these sections of rural population, the transformative dynamics of knowledge society prevails over the restorative one. Though economic neoliberalism aims to condition knowledge society to be restorative of stability, the inner dynamics of this society that is founded on knowledge and education have opened up the possibility of questioning the bases of domination. It has created the condition of insurrection of knowledge and identity of the oppressed through mobility, migration, interconnectivity and education.

IV. Networks: Exclusion and Inclusion

Knowledge society has paved the way for a contradiction in the society by integrating a limited few of the metro city, district towns and villages through ICT-based network culture, social mobility and economic prosperity, on the one hand, and excluding or ineffectively integrating marginalised segments of population, because of their limited access to education, ICTs and occupational mobility with the dominant domain of social network, on the other. In the process of such emergence, knowledge society in India has bred a variety of inequality.

Unequal Integration through Consumerism

The emerging sociocultural milieu of knowledge society in many ways has threatened the pre-existing processes of formation of social solidarity, inbuilt social security and traditional interdependence among social groups by a host of new and virtual relations and networks. The educated, occupationally mobilised and relatively urbanised segments of population, due to their pre-existing social advantage, has been part of these borderless, limitless social networks and relations that have enhanced their economic, social and political mobility and interests. These have helped them construct a dominant social network and to reproduce a cultural milieu of conspicuous consumption. The euphoria for this consumption is constructed globally through media and ICTs that have converted society to be a site for consumption. Here, market-driven relations with consumers, purchasers, borrowers, users, communicators, etc., are privileged over the nonconsuming producers or persons who save. A section of the population getting adequate access to ICTs and economic resources under their command has emerged to be global consumerists by adopting the internationally manufactured clothes, perfumes, watches, latest brands of mobile phone, laptop, car, music and other attires. Through the extensive use of SMS, MMS, Facebook, YouTube and host of other applications, they help construct a global consumerist image and become active agents of this culture even deliberately. Through physical and virtual mobility and enhanced consumerism, they are integrated into the dominant network while the rest remain to be the immigrant to the emerging flow. The pre-existing identities that are conventionally framed in the name of nation, citizenship, countryman, caste, ethnicity, gender, village and family now encounter challenges from the consumerist identities that take shape at times globally in diverse direction through ICTs very often decontextualising subject from reality. This virtual world that is essentially commercial and hegemonic, transnational and global seldom keeps identities rooted in reality and therefore makes them liable to frequent deconstruction. Though globalisation has harmonised the world by injecting culture of consumerism, it has also brought multiple choices in all areas: food, drinks, clothes, automobile, and ornaments – in each and everything.

These cultural flows also help commoditise religion, ritual and host of cultural idioms to suffice the economic need of market. The major religious trusts now have their online and media-based propagation to attract visitors and followers from across the globe. With the extensive use of ICTs, religious entrepreneurs have also initiated new vocabularies and slogans to integrate them with real-life problems and politics. They produce and sell alternative goods and services, starting from food to soap, medicine to perfume, touch therapy to yoga, obviously at a higher cost by producing communities of consumers out of spiritual followers.

Exclusion and Alternative Network and Worldview of the Marginalised

Within the consumerist flow, while a small section of society has got networked, a vast majority has remained either unequally posited or excluded. Though a vast section of marginalised population is excluded from the dominant network, they frame their alternative networks using mobile phone at least based on their day-to-day experience, to ensure their job and livelihood security. Once the manual labourers migrate from rural to urban, they switch over from one activity to another, shuffle between one job market to another due to employment insecurity. The mobile phone-enabled network now helps them significantly to come out of this insecurity. Many of them have formed their own social networks to remain informed about alternative employment opportunity, to maintain social relations and also to explore and exercise options, even though these have limited potential to break the barrier of marginalisation in society immediately. The story of Ramji Lal, a migrant labourer from Bihar, is a typical one who came to Delhi around 10 years back along with six members of his extended family. They look for work in the construction site. Previously, all of them used to assemble in the Neb Sarai Chauk of IGNOU,

New Delhi, for employment. Earlier, many a days they returned home without getting any employment as they had no immediate information about employment opportunity even in the nearby places. They used to move from one market to another in vain, as it was too late to be employed for the day. Now they are connected by mobile phones. If no employment is available in Neb Sarai Chauk, they come to know about the possibility in Malaviya Nagar or elsewhere quickly through mobile phone. Now they are aware of the market rate of their wages. Through mobile phone they are also simultaneously linked to several labour vendors and exercise their own option. However, Ramji strongly feels that in Delhi, even though he gets a higher wage and more man-days of employment here than in his native village, he is not treated here as an 'Admi' (human being). He also concedes that he was not treated as a human being in his native village either and that pushed him to come out of his village. To him, his indignity and devaluation continues despite his migration to Delhi as he is an 'unpad'- an illiterate.

Despite being digitally, educationally, occupationally, spatially and socially segregated, mobile phone has become an effective tool to keep these marginal men connected within his own group and also with the outside world. The newly acquired interconnectivity helps them to rejuvenate their primordial culture, idioms and choices to construct their identity in terms of region, religion, caste and language. Primordial cultural practices are again reinforced by popular regional and linguistic media that occupy a significant public space among them. Within the emerging fluidity, the primordiality keeps them grounded in society and helps them develop a criticality of the emerging order. Thus, despite being in Hindi-dominated culture among the Bengali and Bihari domestic helps in Delhi, Bangla and Bhojpuri channels are still popular in giving them an essence of traditional culture and lifestyle. The emerging dominant ICT and new media-driven networks in many ways help reconstruct identity of the young marginalised people by injecting new ways of looking at their existence in the emerging society.

Sustained Exclusion

Thus, within this emerging knowledge society, one segment of workers gets devaluated even though they relentlessly contribute for the progression and sustenance of knowledge society by providing varieties of support services. The emerging labour process has kept this vast segment of the population in the margin and away from the waves of prosperity and possible upward social mobility; and it has made the support service providers sub-servants to their own needs. This segment of labour force has remained to be the cheap pool of labour for the global economy. They have also simultaneously emerged to be the bearers of the brunt of environmental pollution, global warming and climate change caused by the fast expansion of knowledge economy even though they are not the end users or immediate beneficiaries of the same. Again within the emerging consumerist culture, the core knowledge workers in particular and the affluent segments of knowledge society in general accept and promote environment-degrading lifestyle by deliberate choice while the poor and the marginalised passively bear the brunt of this emerging lifestyle by compulsion.

Ramkishan is an old 'Thelawala' (cart puller) from Eastern Uttar Pradesh in Delhi and currently lives in a slum in Gobindpuri. He has been pulling his cart full of furniture and hardware items in Old Delhi and transporting to several parts of Delhi since last the 20 years or so. In summer, he exposes himself not only to the unbearable heat of sun in congested Old Delhi road, but also to the accumulated pollution and CO_2 emission from the bus, cars, ACs, generators from all directions on the street. He drinks MCD pipe water, which is seldom found to be pure. Though ageing and with ill health, Ramkishan claims to have high immunity and good health with an artificial smile on his face, but his physical appearance and frequent coughing would make everybody think otherwise. Ramkishan, however, is well connected to his village and relatives though mobile phone. He makes extensive use of it to get new work on a daily basis in Delhi and remain connected socially.

V. The Emerging Challenges

The knowledge society has brought into being a host of challenges in contemporary India, the most prominent of which are unequal occupational mobility, devaluation of educational qualification, new form of delinquency, ineffective traditional parenting, resurgence of primordiality and increasing fluidity in society.

Unequal Occupational Mobility

Though the powerful forces of knowledge economy have brought into being several opportunities of social and economic mobility in the lives of important segments (the emerging knowledge haves) and have compressed the time and space considerations by providing varieties of opportunities to them, these have also reinforced the pre-existing processes and evolved new forms of marginalisation for a vast segment of the population in both the rural and the urban areas.

As advancement of knowledge economy has not been able to replace the agricultural and industrial economy, the process of informalisation and casualisation of labour force with low pay has not only remained unabated but has also generated a momentum by way of increasing the demand for informal support services for the knowledge economy. While it has provided the scope of upward social mobility of sections of young population of the marginalised sections, this mobility has been widely horizontal, and has not altered the pre-existing patterns of their deprivation and inequality. Rather, this has uprooted them from many parts of their own art, culture, music, values and lifestyle through hybridisation. Social relations have merged to be more fluid than consolidated both within and between social groups through the devaluation of traditional occupational specialisation and spatial and horizontal occupational mobility.

Strengthening Intermediary Agencies at the Cost of Interests of Workers: Significantly within the emerging knowledge society, a category of entrepreneurs has emerged to take advantage of increasing informalisation and casualisation of work force and 'sourcing out' and contractual appointments strategy for formal bodies or for knowledge industries. There has been mushrooming growth of agencies providing security services, sweepers, office attendants/peons, drivers, computer operators and many such categories of workers. These agencies are empanelled predominantly by the government organisations, by private bodies and by multinational agencies to supply workers of above categories as per prescribed guidelines and time-to-time requirements. A huge chunk of the workers recruited through these agencies allege that unless there is a recommendation from the officials of service-seeking bodies, or a bribe is given, it is nearly impossible to get enrolled with these agencies to get a job. Even after recruitment, they do not get their salary on the last day on the month or even in the first week of the next month. They rather get it in the third or fourth week of the subsequent months. Though a fixed amount is regularly deducted from their salary towards provident fund and medical care, they seldom know the future of this fund. They are never provided a salary slip. Inquisitive and dissenting voices are ruthlessly crushed by publicly humiliating and instantly suspending them by the hiring agencies in the name of indiscipline. Most interestingly, though the service providing agencies are changed periodically, as publicly visible with the changed uniform of these workers, the workers and their working conditions remain the same. Many of these workers have been working for decades with government organisations, even though their hiring agencies have changed, without job security. Though regularly a part of their salary is deducted towards Employees Provident Fund (EPF) and Employees State Insurance (ESI), these agencies seldom deposit these funds to Employees Provident Fund Organisation and Employees State Insurance Corporation. At times, in connivance with the internal staff member, the service-providing agencies overcharge from the hiring agencies in the name of EPF and ESI. Ironically, these benefits are never provided to the workers. As most of these workers are migrants, not united among themselves and there is no trade union to take up their cause, they are to accept these terms and conditions of insecurity without any protest. For example in IGNOU, in 2008, as a section of *Safai Karmachari* (Sweepers) protested against their low pay, they were instantly removed from service in the name of indiscipline. When a group of teachers protested against such removal, an institutional inquiry was also instituted against these teachers for alleged attempt to violate law and order situation in the university campus. Though some political activists from outside made some intervention, it was in vain. The action of the administration functioned as deterrent against the initiative for political mobilization of such workers. In fact, in the wake of emerging market domination over employment, informalisation and casualisation of workforce has become an effective tool for workers' discipline and containment.

Devolution and Under Utilisation of Educational Qualification

The urge for non-manual jobs, which are conventionally preferred in Indian society as a status symbol, has increased phenomenally in contemporary India with the increasing quantum of educated manpower among all social groups across the country. With the surplus supply of educated and highly qualified manpower, competition in the job market has escalated phenomenally forcing many of the highly qualified manpower to accept jobs lower than the status of their acquired educational qualification or remain unemployed. These educated youths are not interested in the traditional occupation of fishing, cultivation and animal raising, pottery, carpentry, iron smithy, etc., of their family as these manual activities are in variance with their acquired educational background; and also leads the devaluation of the perceived status which they have acquired through educational qualification in the public eyes. A graduate from a rural landowning family now prefers to join a government job even as an office attendant or a lower-level office assistant if other avenues are not available, than to remain in a village as a cultivator. Many graduate and postgraduate youths prefer to have these lower-level jobs than to remain unemployed or to go for self-employment venture. This situation is precarious in rural areas especially for the highly educated youth in the absence of adequate opportunity structure for the educated youth. Cases are rampant where donation, bribe and political pressure are put into play to get jobs in government offices and in local schools. Hence, many well-qualified candidates feel dejected and devaluated.

Challenge to Parenting

As the ICTs have helped question the traditional authority, it has also invited reactionary response from the traditionalists. The traditional parents try to keep the new generation away from the misuse of Internet and the mobile phone. Though the new age children are smart enough to keep their secret hidden from their parents by availing several technological means, parents are also too concerned to hide their traditional-role expectation. The traditional parents and their conventional style of parenting have emerged to be highly inadequate to nurture the young minds who are posited today within massive flow of information and communication. Many parents find it difficult to restrict the child's interaction within the limit of their own choice and to inculcate the behaviour patterns, norms and values that they have Inherited from their forefathers. Even in nuclear families the choice of popular TV programme is seldom guided by the desire of the elderly generation. Many elder members in the family withdraw from watching TV jointly with young members as either there is a conflict of choice or the wish of the young members prevails over the elders or the elders find it culturally or temperamentally uncomfortable to watch some programmes jointly with the other family members. While the traditional cultural milieu prevents the elderly generation to get fully engaged with the new cultural processes as engineered by ICTS and media, the new generation finds it difficult to resist from engaging themselves in this milieu as they want a life that is to be fully enjoyed and experimented here and now. Thus, in vast parts of India, there has been a coexistence of the cultural practices with conflict, at one end, and compromise, at the other.

Reinforcing Traditionality

Contemporary India also sees the resurgence of fundamentalism to restrict the use of mobile telephone by village women. A 'village council in the eastern Indian state of Bihar has banned the use of mobile phones by women, saying the phones were "debasing the social atmosphere" by leading to elopements – a move that set off outraged protests from activists'. In addition to the ban, the Sunderbari village council in a Muslim-dominated area, some 385 km (239 miles) east of Patna, the capital of Bihar, has also imposed a fine of ₹ 10,000 ($180) if a girl is caught using a mobile phone on the streets. Married women would have to pay ₹ 2000 ($36.00) (http://www.reuters.com). Similarly, a village Panchayat in Bagpat district of Uttar Pradesh has banned love marriage, barred women below 40 years of age from going out for shopping and girls from using mobile phones on the streets. The panchayat at Asara village in Ramala area has issued the diktat restraining women below 40 years from going to markets and using mobile in the village or outside (http://www.indianexpress.com). A khap panchayat in a Hisar village has banned mobile phones for youngsters and ordered girls not to wear jeans and T-shirts. Organising a DJ party is out of bounds and a complete prohibition on liquor has also been issued. The decision was taken by the panchayat at Khedar village. Sarpanch Shamsher Singh said, 'We have decided to ban alcohol as it is the main reason behind rapes. We have also banned jeans and T-shirts for girl students as it is not a proper dress' (timesofindia.indiatimes.com 2013).

Crime, Delinquency and its New Face

The ICTs and new media have brought a culture of physical exposure and bare body show not only in the advertisement of consumer goods, but also in music, movie and tele talks, fashion show and the like. ICTs have brought severe challenges to these pre-existing taboos and moorings that traditionally provided a good deal of stability in society and a framework for socialisation of new members in society. Many of the youths are exposed to adult/pornographic sites at an early stage of their life as clips are easily available for downloading or even for purchase from the mobile recharge shops. An account from a mobile charging stall shows that teenage boys are the major customers of such clips than the girls and the elderly people. A good number of youths has not only fictitious names and accounts on the website but also know others though fictitious names to avoid parental vigilance. Cyber bullying, instant threat, uncalled for desire and emotional blackmailing have become important segments of ICT-driven interaction in contemporary India. Though many parents both from urban and from rural areas express concern over the growing exposure of their children to the adult/mature and socially unwanted sites, they are left with little to curve these activities through the traditional means of coercion or vigil as the new age children are smart enough to find out alternative means to get access over these sites without any stretch remaining in the computer at home.

Knowledge society has also brought new varieties of delinquency and cybercrime. Though the experts have long been propagating threat of espionage against governments, businesses and human-rights activists, cyber attack on the major science and defence laboratories, at the local level day-to-day crime has taken endemic forms. These are engineered not by the young alone, but even by the matured. Crime is increasing at a high speed. According to the Crime Bureau Report of India, in 2008, only 288 cases of cybercrime was reported related to tampering computer source document, hacking with computer system, obscene publication/transmission, unauthorised access/attempt to access to transmission, fraudulent digital signature, breach of confidentiality/privacy, etc., activities. In 2011, this figure increased to 1791 (NCRB, 2012). Despite new cyber law, many people find themselves in a vulnerable position with the increasing incidence of cybercrime. For example a senior female academic from IGNOU, New Delhi reported to the police about the repeated receipt of SMS from a particular person constantly for six months; an FIR was lodged in the police station. However, the erring youth was allowed to go scot free only with minor caution by the police. Unfortunately, the youth kept on repeating the same SMS until a new mobile number was used by this academic.

Redefining Primordial Identity

The emerging ICT-driven cultural milieu constructs borderless clients, consumers, friends and users in the virtual world who are faceless. In reality, some parts of these identities are constructed ignoring the experience of real life in order to remain connected and becoming impressionistic. While a large part remains grounded in reality with surroundings conditioned by locality and primordiality. As one's own setting defines his/her identity, a netizen's world view of himself/herself and selection of friendship and followers and like-mindedness, formation of virtual groups tends to be based on these considerations. Hence, within the whole process of deconsolidation of pre-existing identities, as engineered through knowledge age, primordial and other related identities are at times being privileged at the grass roots level in real life over the rest. Accordingly, ethnic, gender, caste and other localised identities have sustained and got rejuvenated themselves both in the real and in the virtual world. These identities, however, are more resistant than legitimising in nature.

Thus, the formation of global identities through ICTs based on primordial and other localised concern at times creates 'love for within', 'hate for others' and at times 'peace for all' campaigns. It works more dangerously like an unguided missile that may be moved in both forward and backward directions simultaneously by conflicting forces. The communal riots in Assam in 2012 produced a series of love and hate campaigns and counter campaigns through extensive use of ICTs. The morphed image of physical torture of the member of one linguistic and religious community by the other provoked both love and counter hate campaigns across the world. It resulted in physical violence among the students from North Eastern part of the country in Mumbai, Pune and Nagpur and in many other parts of India, pushed a large section of these students to return home for physical and emotional security compelling the Government of India to hurriedly ban around 200 Internet sites and impose restrictions over sending of bulk SMS and MMS. In fact, this event has shown the strength of ICTs in constructing love within and hate against communitarian primordial identities as against its perceived secular image. Indeed, the formation of such identities is political in nature and the modern state has least control over it. Significantly, the interactional determinants of the emerging cultural milieu are being shaped and mediated more by the exogenous forces of globalisation and ICTs from above, and less by the indigenous forces from below. It is despite the fact that indigenous forces have provided the required base for the sustenance of these global markets and technological forces in Indian society.

Increasing Flux and Fluidity

Knowledge society has brought significant disorientations in the pre-existing economy and employment patterns, cultural practices and social interaction and in the overall orientations to life and social well-being for many. The contemporary society has posited itself in a process of decontextualisation through the enhanced movement of people from rural to urban areas, shifting of workforce from agriculture and industry to the service sector, unsettled interactional patterns from local to global and global to local, secular to primordial and primordial to secular. These processes have again got expanded with the reinforcing of traditionality in a new context, emergence of new interactional patterns among social groups, multiple and unstable work relations, and increased transference of ideas, images, objects, goods and service both within and outside the country. All these contribute more to fragmentation and decontextualisation; and less to consolidation of an average reality. This process of decontextualisation has been strengthened by faceless social interactions through MMS, SMS, Facebook, etc., social media. These have multiplied without a specific point of origin and departure. It brings new forms of collective mobilisation with a common concern, but without recognisable leadership, ideology and organisation. This emerging fluidity however has brought into being new momentum in articulating several social concerns, unable to provide a concrete direction in the absence of stable structure of this interaction.

The emerging knowledge society in India by setting in motion a new sociocultural milieu, by bringing new economic and cultural practices, new orientations to life for a section of society, on the one end, and by keeping a vast section of society only partly integrated or nonintegrated with this new sociocultural milieu, on the other, has brought into being a host of new social contradictions in society. These contradictions are multiplied with eclecticity of expansion of knowledge society that has released modernity and scientific spirit, on the one hand, and has reinforced traditionality and primordiality in a new context, on the other. By expanding the scope and condition for occupational mobility while it has brought a new sense of social critiquing, it has also helped consolidate the economic and social positions of dominant sections of society. Despite these dichotomies, the increasing sociocultural momentum as generated by the knowledge society has altered in many ways the pre-existing economic, social, cultural and political fabrics of society across the space and produced new dynamics of inclusion and exclusion, fluidity in social identity and new frontiers of solidarity. It has released a profound transformative dynamic in society, as it is based on the power of knowledge that endeavours to critique not only the pre-existing rules of domination and hegemony, but also resurge new identities, knowledge and praxis whose full potential is yet to be realised.

India stands today in the threshold of new socio-cultural order that is widely conditioned by the explosion of young population on the one hand, and knowledge and ICTs revolution, globalization and phenomenal shift in the economy and patterns of work participation in society on the other. The flag bears of this new socio-cultural order has emerged to be the knowledgeable young mind, *the e- Gen* and their adherent who with unequivocal command over information technology and social networking, not only regularly redefine their day to day cultural existence and networking choices, but also influence choice of others, its culture, economy and politics. They have brought in and simultaneously have been the part of attentive ways of 'thinking and doing' even at time in contravention of old. They are the live wire of social media- the email, Skype, face book, tweeter, blog and others for generating enormous flow of counter message that travels from below to construct a world view of dissent and protest against domination and hegemony as propagated by the conventional state and market driven mass media from the above wherein a selected few reproduces most frequently than not the stereo-type image of politics and culture of society. While the conventional politicians reproduces the culture of blame game in public domain on social issues through powerful mass media, the e-Gen and their adherent unlash huge social forces to be active in public space through the intervention of social media. They mobilize public opinion against corruption; mobilize people for demonstrations on host of social issues. They motivate and influence the larger society to be part of the huge flow of social media, be part of large mobilization, for alternative sensibility on social and political issues. These have made them a social force to be recon with that redefines the social and political space.

As the social media and ICTs posited to play the decisive role in ushering a new era of collective mobilization both by the civil society and political parties in contemporary India, contemporary society experiences a sense of rejuvenation in ideas and action. The ICT driven civil society campaign for right to information and for anti corruption or for Janlokpal Bill has given a new dimension in social mobilization culture in the country by bring in a new relationship between civil society, citizenship and politics. The public space is no more a site uni-polar domination, but a site for democratic engagement through variety views and counter views. The success of Anna Hazare's fasts for a Janlokpal Bill, the formation of an alliance of civil societies as India Against Corruption, the formation of Aam Admi Party (AAP) out of the civil society movement against corruption, and unprecedented success of the AAP the State Assembly election in Delhi in 2013 and art of seeking of public opinion by the AAP as to whether or not it should form a government with outside support form Indian National Congress etc. have not only predominantly been ICTs and new media driven, but also been driven by the power of the youth. It indicates the emergence of an era of new politics.

The extensive use of ICTs for the 16th Lok Sabha election campaign in April–May 2014 by all political parties to reach out to the voters in the nook and corner of the country has added a new chapter not only to the election process, but also to the history of ICTs usage in society. Mr Narendra Modi's use of digital Hologram for bouncing his image to create floating 3D affect via satellite in order to reach out to millions has brought in a digital mile-stone in the electioneering process. No doubt such digital usage will have long lasting impacts on the culture of mass mobilization in the country in especially for the youth.

Though e-Gen, experiences multiple ideological and political choices, in common they dream of an ideal India grounded in dignity for all common man, devoid of corruption and injustice. They dream for a new politics while the conventional politics is grounded in vote bank caste, religion, language and ethnicity, the new politics idealizes India for secular citizenship. India now visualizes the unprecedented enthusiasm for a new way politics driven by the power of new knowledgeable.. However one is to see whether this new way politics will bring Indian spring in an institutional way prevailing over the forces of corruption, social division and segregation, or it will get prevailed by the old order. Power of knowledge is irresistible. It will create its own order of rationality and freedom by developing contestation against domination of all forms. The new cultural order as ushered by the knowledge society in India has initiated this journey of liberation which is however multifaceted.

10

Conclusion

Marginality, Identity, Fluidity and Beyond

The composite framework of Indian society that has remained grounded on unequal distribution of economic resources, social status, political power and formal authority, on the one hand, and traditional division based on the principle of caste, ethnicity and gender, on the other, has retained a vast section of its population to be marginalised despite broad processes of social transition and economic transformation and varieties of state-sponsored reformative and developmental initiatives in general and agricultural modernisation and industrialisation in particular. In an unequal society where the poor, powerless and the disadvantaged people are denied and deprived of social, economic and cultural opportunities for integration with the larger society and where the traditional institutional arrangements and values have provided the legitimacy to such denials and deprivations, knowledge society has been envisaged to break these barriers to equal opportunities and social integration, to enable everybody to be powerful through their own capability and to bring a new social order founded on equality, dignity and humanity by developing their inner unlimited resource, the knowledge (UNDP, 2001). In fact, 'this mixture of justified hope, positive expectations of high quality life for all people everywhere' makes the development and application of knowledge as well as living in the knowledge-(based) society the overriding interest of society as a whole (UN, 2005). Such expeditions have brought most of the world society to have a close look and experiment with the ideals of the emerging knowledge society, and closer to the conviction that humanity has no choice but to accept it as the ultimate one for its inner progress, with collective resonance and resilience.

I. Knowledge Society and Its Upsurge

Though every human society has been using knowledge for its survival and sustenance from the very inception of its civilisational journey, and its progression is linked to the progression of knowledge, knowledge society distinguishes itself from the rest of the societies by nurturing, exploiting and integrating knowledge to all its domains of activities as its key resource. It is widely characterised by mass production and use of knowledge for generation of wealth and employment, formation of a new social order and solidarity, building of new frontiers of social networks and solidarity, shaping up of a new framework of social relations and culture, inculcation of new variety of economic interests and social meaning and creation of new space and pace of development for its members in society.

The foundation of this society is erected on the creative potentials embodied in the human mind that produces knowledge, which is harnessed by inculcating appropriate human capability through formal education and skill development; and is exploited, disseminated and put in wider use through Information and Communication Technologies (ICTs) in a globalising environment. In this society, knowledge acquires a value-added meaning that transforms the man of knowledge into a new man of power with redefined responsibilities (Drucker, 1968). It recognises each human being as the potential resource and agency of social and economic transformation having the capacity to be knowledgeable. By reinforcing human mind as the site of this power, the knowledge society makes power both identified and diffused (Castells, 1997) and registers its strong imprint on the social and occupational mobility, education and socialisation, social contradictions and conflicts, and on the dynamics of interests and identity in society.

The economic structure of knowledge society, which is founded on mass creation and accumulation of knowledge as its material base (Masuda, 1981; UN, 2005), develops global network of wealth, power and identity (Castells, 1983, 1997), ushers economic and social transformation at a global scale, creates new economic appetites, aspirations and demands (Porat, 1977) by transforming knowledge as the main means of livelihood of the largest group of the population (Drucker, 1968). By all conventional parameters, this emerging economic arrangement has been widely recognised to be a game changer, a hope of the twenty-first century that has bypassed the era of agricultural and industrial economy. It facilitates new mode of work participation through the increasing engagement of the knowledge workers, and displacement of agricultural and industrial workers as significant social categories and a new economic arrangement for production and consumption at a global scale in conjunction with market liberalisation.

The Neoliberal Context

The process of mass production of knowledge, wealth and power and its mass use and transference across the globe has become a reality in a self-regulated market under economic neoliberalism that has emerged to be a global phenomenon since the early 1990s. Though the arrival, departure and rearrival of self-regulated markets have always brought 'great transformations' in human destiny, its recent incarnation in the form of economic neoliberalism has been a unique one as it aims to cultivate, commoditise and control human mind across the globe through market homogenisation by producing common products, generating common appetite and promoting a common culture for market hegemony. The self-regulated market has arrived/re-arrived in history with specific implications for the society. For Polanyi (1957), the arrival of self-regulated – the *laissez-faire* – economy after the industrial revolution that instead of embedding economy in social relations, embedded social relations in the economic system, brought 'a complete reversal of the trend of development' leading to the whole scale commoditisation of production process and ushering of First Great Transformation in the life of humans with the nature of the society to be changed by free-market economics (Polanyi, 1957). To him 'There was nothing natural about laissez-faire; free markets could never have come into being merely by allowing things to take their course...laissez-faire was enforced by the state...'. 'Laissez-faire was planned; planning was not' (1957). This 'economic liberalism made a supreme bid to restore the selfregulation of the system by eliminating all interventionist policies which interfered with the freedom of markets for land, labor, and money. It became in effect the spearhead of a heroic attempt to restore world trade, remove all avoidable hindrances to the mobility of labor, and reconstruct stable exchanges' (1957). However, as this system started collapsing since the early twentieth century in the wake of the Great Depression in the 1930s and especially after the Second World War, the self-regulating market got replaced by the Keynesian economics of welfare states and even by 'New Deal' in the United States paving the way for the Second Great Transformation. This wave continued until the late 1970s in Europe.

Now in the wake of globalisation, Washington Consensus, World Bank and the International Monetary Bank-driven Structural Adjustment Programme, a neoliberal state is put in place and a Third Great Transformation has already taken place at a global scale. With economic globalisation in the agenda, free trade to become the philosophy, state intervention with the market to be minimal, state is getting its role redefined vis-à-vis its commitment to international bodies, the *modus operandi* of new economic order is being shaped by the neoliberal state. The economic essence of this society is founded on economic neoliberalism that is explicitly conditioned by the resurgence of self-regulated liberal market through its late twentieth century incarnation.

The contemporary world now experiences the powerful resurgence of economic neoliberalism and a retreat to state welfarism. On the reappearance of economic and political liberalism, Francis Fukuyama wrote in 1989: 'the century that began full of self confidence in ultimate triumph of Western liberal democracy seems at its close to be returning in full circle to where it started to: no to an end of history, or convergence between capitalism and socialism as earlier predicted but to an unabashed victory of economic and political liberalism'. He considered it to be 'the end point of mankind's ideological evolution and the universalisation of Western liberal democracy as the final form of human government'. In the context of the demise of socialist regime in the second world he asserts that 'The passing of Marxism-Leninism first from China and then from the Soviet Union will mean its death as a living ideology of world historical significance. And the death of this ideology means the growing "Common Marketisation" '…To him again …'The end of history will be a very sad time. The struggle for recognition, the willingness to risk one's life for a purely abstract goal, the worldwide ideological struggle that called forth daring, courage, imagination, and idealism, will be replaced by economic calculation, the endless solving of technical problems, environmental concerns, and the satisfaction of sophisticated consumer demands' (Fukuyama, 1989).

The ideology of knowledge society contributes to the triumph of market economy over the 'welfare state' philosophy (Giddens, 1999) giving away the Keynesian welfare state to a Schumpeterian Social Workfare State that promotes innovation, flexibility, competition and entrepreneurship for a knowledge-driven flexible economy (Jessop, 2003). Knowledge society in India is being shaped within this emerging neoliberal world order; and the shaping up of the Third Great Transformation of history. Herein the emergence of Knowledge Society in India need not be seen only through the spectacle of end of history, but beginning of a new one. It has brought into being a new developmental journey by generating its own dynamics of inclusion, marginality and new identity of formation, which invites a critical look.

II. India: The Shifting Perspective and New Initiatives for Knowledge Society

India has been experiencing varieties of transformations in the economic and technological orders since the days of its early independence. Most of the transformative initiatives such as land reforms, agricultural modernisation and rapid industrialisation were initiated and practised in India in the 1950s, 1960s, 1970s and 1980s aiming to usher an egalitarian society, achieve a faster economic growth rate, eradicate poverty and unemployment, ensure livelihood security, social justice and prosperity were engineered within the well-articulated state policies guided by the principles of equality, fraternity and justice as enshrined in the Indian Constitution. Until the early 1990s, economic policies in India were predominantly characterised by state-controlled planning, rigid economic discipline, predominance of state-controlled business environment, protectionism to domestic market forces, export promotion and import restriction. These policies in all possible ways put the state in command to hold the market within its sovereign limit. However, the part success in agricultural modernisation and limited industrialisation, only contributed to a sustained low rate of economic growth, regular budget deficit, inflation, high rate of unemployment, labour unrest, large-scale industrial sickness and increasing trade deficit and huge burden of indebtedness on the international agencies leading to visible credibility deficit of the state both in the national and in the international arena. While these initiatives strengthened the social and economic position of a limited section of the people who are already in social, economic and political command, it pushed the vast majority to economic uncertainty, livelihood insecurity and downward mobility. As against these backdrops, while the world had been experiencing the proliferation of new technological and economic choices, and these choices along with the new waves of knowledge revolution reached its doorstep, India's economic and technological options have been geared to a new direction. India accepted it to be a new opportunity to ignite its human resource for a new future. Significantly, in India, the traditional knowledge-based past, availability of huge pool of young population, recent achievements in science and technology, fast proliferation of quality human resource and phenomenal explosion of ICTs across the country have provided a potential platform for new developmental journey, which was hitherto unaccomplished in India.

Shift towards Economic Liberalisation

In fact, in India, the process of emergence of knowledge society is embedded with the emergence of neoliberal state. While the agrarian and the industrial transformation was promoted under the auspice of a welfare state with a tilt towards socialism and nationalistic forces, the transformation to knowledge era is promoted and propagated by a neoliberal state, with a tilt towards market capitalism that is supported by international forces such as multinational corporations, IMF, World Bank and host of other such organisations. The Indian state that has laid its foundation on a 'socialist' philosophy as enshrined in the Preamble of the Constitution of India and followed the path of a 'mixed economy' for economic transformation along with the policy of market restriction till the late 1980s, has initiated a paradigm shift in its political philosophy and economic perspective in the early 1990s with the adoption of economic neoliberalism marking a sharp transformation in the nature of the state from its 'socialist' and welfarist form to a neoliberal one. In India, the state policy for the expansion of knowledge economy, as against the policy of expansion of agrarian transformation and industrialisation, has incorporated explicit and deliberate measures for market liberalisation for the promotion of education and ICTs. It has also promoted an environment for huge foreign direct investment in the key areas of economic activities and initiated cross-border trade in services to integrate its economy with the forces of global market.

Knowledge economy has been ideally visualised in India to be an effective alternative arrangement to produce abundant resources by cultivating the potential of a vast pool of population that has remained hitherto unused, to transform population from being a liability into a resource, generate wealth and employment for people through their own innovation, creativity and engagement, to empower people irrespective of economic, social and spatial divides, to augment local global connectivity through ICTs and knowledge revolution, to eradicate economic stagnation, social backwardness, inequality, illiteracy and political domination, and largely to promote the overall well-being of the nation. Herein knowledge production, capacity building, knowledge creation and knowledge dissemination have emerged to be buzzwords in the state and the civil society discourse on social policy, social change, development and transformation. The state now invariably emphasises on the need for a knowledge revolution to take place in the front yard of this transitional society to be the key enabler of social and human development. Major policy initiatives now endeavour to yield the benefits of information and knowledge revolution to usher a new society. The state now emphatically asserts 'we missed the industrial revolution but we should not miss the information and knowledge revolution.... Leap flogging into knowledge era looks eminently possible today for the societal transformation of India in the twenty-first century, which is going to be the century of hope for India' (Planning Commission of India, 2001).

In fact, the ushering in of a knowledge age is an induced process as that of the economic neoliberalism. The combination of both invites a host of proactive policy measures and policy frameworks for technological, economic and political changes for the expansion of opportunities of education and access to ICTs in consonance with emerging needs and patterns of global economic forces. All these initiatives warranted a policy shift for education and ICTs from the pre-existing position towards market determinism.

Education as an Emerging Market-driven Project

In the emerging knowledge society, the function of education is defined in terms of need of globalisation, which has emerged an economic project of industrialised nations with fundamental implications for the future shape and role of higher education systems and institutions in society (Brennan, 2008). As in the wider world, culture and education have become commodities on the globalised market economy and education has taken the form of an industry that produces and exchanges education as goods and services for profit (Merriam, 2010), educational arrangements in India have largely been shaped by the market forces as well. In the same vain, as the educational needs today call for global education towards skillful and optimal global citizenship as never before in human history (Le Roux, 2001; cf. Scally, 2013), Indian educational arrangements look for global collaborations, partnership, investments and exchanges for both recognition and profitability.

India has set in motion varieties of initiatives for the development of literacy, knowledge and skill by strengthening the educational arrangements at all levels, by encouraging research and innovation in higher education, encouraging open-distance learning, promoting vocational education and training programme for the school dropouts and the existing work force, encouraging the use of ICTs in the learning process at all levels to promote and sustain the expansion of the quality and quantity of the human resources.

There has not only been the proliferation of private school, colleges, private universities, technical and professional colleges across the country, but also significant presence of private persons, industrialists in the decision-making bodies of these educational institutions. Private educational institutions are also getting patronage through diverse are changing and have emerged to be part of governance. These are reflective of the fact that in the globalising world in general, while citizens are getting deprived of the state-sponsored welfare activities, the corporate business has emerged as the main 'neogovernmental organisations', and are getting subsidised by government for their economic well-being (Castells, 2001).

The organised private players having control over the market have more influence on the social policies of the state than the citizens. In order to make the education market oriented and profit driven, the Prime Minister's Council on Trade and Industry in India constituted a 'special subject group on policy framework for private investment in education, health and rural development' with noted industrialists,

Mukesh Ambani (Convenor) and Kumar Mangalam Birla (Member) to suggest the implementation of the World Bank prescriptions and privatisation and commercialisation of higher education in the country. Similarly, efforts are made to take away the autonomy of educational institutions, promotion of private investment in education, formulation of private university bill, etc..

In view of phenomenal increase in the demand for education and short supply of public institutions to match the growing demand, private penetration in the educational arrangement has emerged to be a reality in India. As results of these efforts now more than 62 per cent of the higher and the technical educational institutions in India are under the control of the private players. However, this reality has been strengthened undithered of quality assurance, equity and access concern as strongly propagated by the New Education Policy 1986 and the Programme of Action 1992. India now produces more engineers and MBAs than the US and China combined. India's annual output of 15 lakh engineers and 3 lakh MBAs is way ahead of the US (1 lakh engineers and 1.25 lakh MBAs) and China (11 lakh engineers and 75,000 MBAs). Though in view of India's population size and increasing local and global demand for educated and trained man power such expansion is essential, about 30 per cent of seats in the MBA and Engineering colleges remained unfilled in 2013 as 'students are unhappy with the educational package; its quality, course cost and the job outcomes. A survey by *MBAuniverse.com* estimates that out the top 20 MBA colleges only 20% of the students are employable' in India (Sabharwal, 2013). Significantly, while there has been increasing applications for opening up of new professional colleges, there have also been applications for closure. In fact, quality concern has engulfed not only the private but also the state-run educational institutions.

Parallely, the publicly funded institutions are increasingly becoming too inadequate to address the emerging educational need of society because of their resource crunch, structural limitations widely caused by inefficiency in management, undue state control or apathy, nonrecruitment of regular faculty, non-sanctioning of additional faculty, not receiving research facilities, selective co-option of a section of teaching staff for administration, etc., and also inertia of a section of the faculty for teaching, and their inefficiency. Such issues not only affect the academic environment but also the quality of education provided by these institutions. Critiquing the private sector penetration in education, at times, holds little ground as many failures and inefficiency of publicly funded organisations have made private organisations flourish. The shifting orientation of education, from those of a process to produce knowledge for nation building to a project to generate wealth through the increasing intervention of market forces has produced instability in the system itself. This instability is again supplemented by frequent policy shifts of the state on education, contradictory political and administrative measures, sustained gaps between legislative/parliamentary mandates on the one hand and their implementation; and apathy of the state apparatus in addressing immediate issues of educational institutions on the other. These altogether have one way or the other retarded the growth and efficiency of the publicly funded educational institutions. By implication, these have promoted the growth of private education.

Formal educational arrangements by and large produce the educated and trained labour force in view of the emergent and future need of various sectors of economy—agriculture, industry and service. Knowledge society under economic neoliberalism needs knowledgeable but disciplined work force that is to work under the control and command situation. The private professional education institutions in one way or the other subscribes to this function. The market orientation of the education system again has been widely devoid of critical learning. It is not only that students' union are not allowed to be formed and social science education is avoided, the critical questioning is also discouraged in the learning process so as to inculcate a mind of submission out of the learners. Though the Indian state has been emphasising on the need of inculcation of critical ability among learners, as reflected the 12th Five Year Plan, at the operation level it seldom gets a place of prominence. In fact tendencies of submission are also in the making in the government-run institutions.

The post economic liberalisation of India sees the phenomenal proliferation of private investment and private–public partnership in education leading to the fast expansion of educational institutions and increase in the Gross Enrolment Ratio and high level of retention of students from pre-primary to the higher and technical education levels. The literacy rate in India has now increased to above 75 per cent, GER in the secondary education has increased to above 65 per cent and in higher education to above 18 per cent. Significantly, such expansion has been accompanied by fast proliferations of higher and technical education institutions, establishing of several hundreds of new universities including private and deemed universities, privately funded and self-financed professional and technical colleges and universities and phenomenal increase in highly trained and skilled manpower in the country since the late 1990s. The Knowledge Commission of India has proposed to open 1500 universities by 2015 in the country, and this would be through encouragement of private investment and public–private partnership in the education system. Amidst such shifting tendencies in education, India today stands in the threshold of a knowledge economy with considerable repository of educated and trained manpower and a vast pool of young population in its command.

Enabling State Initiatives on ICT and Mass Media for a Market Drive

India has also been experiencing phenomenal investment in the information and telecommunication sector both by the public and the private investors and by the multinational companies. These are accompanied by increasing proliferation and use of telephone, mobile phone and Internet, listenership of radio, viewership of television, readership of newspapers, magazines and journals in both rural and urban areas. India has now emerged to be a giant user of ICTs, occupied second position among the Asian nations in Internet penetration with 121 million (10 per cent) Indians now having access to Internet, 926 million people having access to mobile telephone, 8.7 per cent having access to newspapers and 99 per cent having access to radio and television. The penetration of ICTs and mass media is getting intensified in an unprecedented speed. While these digital technologies posited to reduce and mitigate the technological, digital and knowledge gaps between rural and urban areas and among various segments of population, enhanced physical connectivity with fast expansion of highways, railway and airline are in the making to reduce spatial diversities and cultural and communication gaps among people. All these initiatives have now been accompanied by increasing investment in infrastructural development, establishing new educational, business, IT hubs, shopping mall, high-class hotels and restaurants, amusement parks, highways, railways, airports and many such related areas. The emerging economic scenario has made the state propose several new bills in the parliament pertaining to Foreign Direct Investment in Indian Telecom Industry, retail sector, to bring structural change and innovation in the areas of ICTs. Significantly, the expansion in ICTs has been spearheaded by the private sector that has got greater control over the Internet, mobile, television, radio and newspaper than the public sector. This expansion, however, has not simply been for a technological connectivity but for an economic investment and financial connectivity of global capital that is made endured by inculcating a new sociocultural milieu therein.

Shifting Economic Foundation

Along with economic liberalisation, expansion of education and ICTs across the space India has been experiencing an improved educational status of its work force, emergence of new avenues of employment and increasing occupational diversification, proliferation of knowledge-based economic activities and global interdependence. These are widely accompanied by a fast growth rate of economy with sharp decline in work participation in agriculture and its contribution to the GDP, while very fast increase in work participation in the service sector and its contribution to GDP of the country. Though agriculture and industry have also experienced significant growth in the post 1990s, the growth in the service sector has surpassed those of others and more and more workers shifted from agriculture to non-agricultural sectors and despite global economic slowdown growth in the service sector it has remained the highest among all sectors of economy in recent years. Prominently enough, the service sector has emerged to be the overwhelming contributor to GDP with 61 per cent and the second highest provider of employment with 27 per cent in the country.

Along with these changes, the knowledge economy and the knowledge workers have been posited to enter the centre stage of India with an increasing ratio of their presence in economic activities. As the penetration of knowledge economy has been accompanied by the expansion of its own infrastructure, it has created space for the emergence of support service providers and manual workers of various sorts. The process of expansion of ICTs, economic globalisation and education has created a new economic momentum in India that is widely characterised by increasing rates of work participation, mobility and migration of work force, expansion of the scope of knowledge jobs for the educated and skilled workforce and varieties of nonknowledge jobs for the illiterates and semiliterates. They altogether have paved the way for the expansion of knowledge economy.

III. The Emergence of Knowledge Society in India: Social Divides and Hierarchy

The emergence of this new order is not autonomous of India's traditional heritage, pre-existing spatial and social divides and of multiple social realities that are formed through intense interactivity between tradition and modernity, agrarianism, industrialism and post industrialism and continuity and change. Within these multiple social realities, the emerging economic momentum has set in motion varieties of alternative choices, new forms of mobility and logic of marginality and formation of new collective identities. Knowledge society in India as is in the making within the pre-existing structural arrangements has produced unequal space for mobility and integration of its population with the emerging economic momentum and varieties of contradiction therein.

Knowledge Society's Encounter with Caste, Ethnic, Gender and Spatial Divide in India

Despite the newly induced economic and social stimuli, the traditional correlations between higher social status and higher degree of integration with new economic forces have remained still valid in contemporary India. The higher caste, ethnic and gender status in Indian society that have remained positively linked to higher educational status, access to ICTs and upward occupational mobility, have shown a higher degree of integration with knowledge society. Again as the urban areas have a higher degree of penetration of education and ICTs and mass communication networks, in general these have been penetrated faster by the forces and milieu of knowledge society than the rural areas across the country. The extent of penetration and receptivity towards it has been higher among the general categories and a section of the other backward classes than among the scheduled castes, scheduled tribes and women across the space. However, women from the higher castes have higher degree of participation in knowledge jobs than those of the women from the lower castes. As a higher degree of educational achievement is positively linked to a higher degree of integration with knowledge society, large segments of marginalised people having least or low level of access to education and skill have low level of integration with knowledge society.

Unequal Space for Mobility and Occupational Hierarchy

Similarly, as higher access to education and ICTs is positively linked to higher quantum of upward social and occupational mobility, the people from traditional higher social background having higher access to education and ICTs achieve higher degree of upward social and occupational mobility. However, ICTs have emerged to be a potential leveller through their increasing penetration. The majority of the marginalised people despite having low level of access to computer and Internet, have got a high degree of access to mobile telephone; and it has become a great enabler for them not only to put them in a wider world, but also to facilitate them to form alternative networks for gaining access to new avenues of employment, social and spatial mobility, to become part of wider and alternative employer–employee relations and to come out of primordial and oppressive social arrangements and at places to reconstruct subjugated identity through resurgence of subjugated networks.

However, though this has helped a section of them to get an access to alternative livelihood options and to rearticulate social connectivity, these have not been able to break the key barriers of deprivation, inequality and social segregation, and determinants of downward and horizontal mobility of large sections of them who continue to occupy subordinate social and political position, and remain to be the outsiders from within. Their traditional social status remaining linked to inadequate access to knowledge/education, ICTs and economic and cultural resources still contributes to their sustained downward or horizontal social mobility. Herein through its functioning the emerging knowledge society, while has produced several new varieties of inequality, has also reinforced many of the pre-existing inequality, injustice, domination and exclusion, and has become an extension of pre-existing denial and deprivation. The course of knowledge society has been neither uniform nor unilaterally progressive, but rather paradoxical. In fact, the emergence of knowledge society in India is reflective of the observation that its emergence is not a discrete, rather an evolutionary, phenomenon (Black, 2003), and is not unprecedented (Castells, 2001; Preston, 2001). It has liberated many segments of society while reinforcing many of the pre-existing inequalities. Thus, in many ways, old deprivations and inequalities have taken new forms in the present context by acquiring several new dimensions by way of reinforcing the hierarchy of occupation. It carries many features of the industrial revolution (Deane, 1980; Rowe and Thompson, 1996); and appearing to be the latest stage of the 'modern project' (Giddens, 1991) of capitalism, industrialism, modernity and surveillance (Black, 2003) that have given birth to 'informational capitalism' (Castells, 1996), and made knowledge a subject of the market through a process of its instrumentalisation and commoditisation (Black, 2003; cf. Sellen and Harper, 2002) whereby the society has emerged to be more segregated than consolidated.

New Occupational Momentum: Knowledge Jobs and the Periphery

The new occupational momentum has produced an occupational hierarchy by forming a core with a limited number of workers by maximising their significance, while relegated the vast others to the periphery of different degrees through wide-scale informalisation of work force, expansion of its support services and retention of its association with the social and spatial hierarchy in many parts of the country. While the work condition of knowledge workers and their support service providers have been predominantly characterised by higher social status, vertical upward mobility and security; the nonknowledge workers' working conditions are linked to low social status, downward and horizontal mobility, job insecurity, casualisation and informalisation of work participation.

By evolving knowledge as the key resource, knowledge society has placed knowledge workers at its core, which is supplemented by a huge chunk of workers who are immediately linked to the core and provide support services for expansion and sustenance of knowledge jobs. A small section of the service providers are the middle men and the entrepreneurs who function as human resource providers, labour contractors, suppliers dealing with computer hardware, ICTs and other electronic media devices, transport providers, while the others are the skilled and semiskilled workers.

At the bottom of the occupational hierarchy is the vast mass of manual/unskilled workers to provide varieties of physical labour both in the society and in the organisational structure. In the rural areas, they are drawn from among the existing labour force in agriculture and form the illiterate and semiliterate marginal labour force. In the urban areas, they are predominantly drawn from the migrant labourers and from poor socioeconomic background. The fast expansion of these categories of workers and their working conditions widely contribute to the informalisation of work participation in contemporary India. Devoid of the capacity for integration, they have been horizontally mobilised to opt for alternative source of livelihood security through engagement with all varieties of manual activities. However, for them response to new occupational momentum, movement from one sort of brawl activity to another, migration from rural to rural or rural to urban areas and urban to urban areas for employment and earning a livelihood have resulted in horizontal occupational mobility, and these have been without a substantial change in the quality and condition of their life. The fast expansion of slum and informal economy, retention of huge segment of people in utter poverty and livelihood insecurity both in rural and in urban areas are reflective of quantitative expansion of rural poverty and under development.

In India, occupational and social hierarchy has got sharpened with the increasing gap between the core knowledge workers as the knowledge rich and the informed, on the one hand, and the non-knowledge workers as knowledge poor and the uninformed, on the other. It has brought affluence for a few, while retained impoverishment for the many. It came closer to the observation that knowledge society has 'sharpened class divides based on a major cleavage between technocrats: the dominant classes who dispose of knowledge and control information' (the knowledge haves) and those whose livelihood and lifestyles are governed by the technocrats (knowledge have-nots) (A Touraine 1974 cf. Lyan, 1986). It has made ICTs a tool in the hand of powerful to oppress the uninformed leading to the exclusion of the devalued by the conquerors of technology of information society (Castells, 1996). In this society, information has been endowed with life-enhancing qualities and to be without information is to be deemed disempowered and disengaged; the 'information-rich' are considered advantaged while the 'information-poor' are deemed to be disadvantaged on a number of levels (Castells, 1996). Though it has been widely idealised to be a balanced, progressive, rational, participatory, less hierarchical and democratic, meritocratic and a new society (Evans, 2004), it has emerged to be divided both socially and digitally, and producing new underclass out of those excluded from the information revolution.

The emerging economic momentum is more guided by the urge for market stability, increased productivity and organisational profit, controlled work force for time-bound delivery than by the ideal of a stable work force with liberty, security and choice. The emerging occupational hierarchy helps maintain these arrangements by promoting an environment of job insecurity and loss of liberty among a large section of knowledge workers, service providers and manual workers through culture of contract labour and outsourcing of several key activities of the organisation. The emerging strategy of the government and nongovernment agencies to go for contract employment, outsourcing or piecemeal work through private agencies for engaging manpower in all varieties of office work related to secretarial, housekeeping, cleaning, etc., activities has widely contributed to the formation of an informal sector within the formal sector wherein a large segment of these workers are made subject to beck and call work relation and a work situation conditioned by stress, long working hours, lack of freedom and near absence of alternative choice. The state and of the corporate world that keep these section of workers off the roll of regular employees to burden off themselves from their labour welfare responsibility.

In India again, while the conventional knowledge workers enjoy an amount of job and professional security, the new knowledge workers encounter variety of challenges to ensure such security. Their job prospect, remuneration, choices and security are conditioned widely by economic boom and recession in the developed world. Such job insecurity pushes a large section of knowledge workers to switch over from one area of specialisation to another and one job to another, and from one company to another. Many of them either lose jobs or tend to accept low salary with the recession in the western world. Apparently, market stability is maintained largely through segregation, hierarchy and insecurity of labour force.

The progression of knowledge society in India has again been accompanied by a host of contradictions. It is akin to the global scenario that, on the one hand, emphasises on the multi skilled, knowledge-based work culture with 'flexible' methods of working (Lash and Urry, 1994), on the other produces instability, insecurity and unemployment especially among the low-grade workers who remain as the reserve army of labour to respond to the economic boom and recession, on the other (Warhurst and Thompson, 1998). While it promises to empower each segment of society by enhancing their intellect, in essence it helps in maximising profits for the multinational corporations and worsens the conditions of workers intensifying low wage, poverty, class, gender and race divides and disability in society in everyday life (Muddiman, 2003), put the workers in unequal power relations in the employment market (Castells, 1996, 1997; Evans, 2004), contributes to persistence of inequalities and the growth of global economic forces (Hornbay and Clarke, 2003) by promoting the ideology of informational capitalism.

Knowledge society has promoted imperfect globalisation for India through the coexistence of the network society, as a global structure, with industrial, rural, communal or survival societies as the reality with different geometries and geographies of inclusion and exclusion (Castells, 2004). The newly formed economic momentum till pushes a vast segment of Indian people to survive at the margin of society – socially, economically, culturally and politically – without getting adequate access to the opportunities for capacity development, literacy, skill, training and formal education and ICTs. It has brought a new momentum of segregation in the labour market to which the large section of labour force remains marginalised and responds to it only by offering its physical potential while the minority responds as the knowledge workers through its intellectual capability.

IV. Knowledge Society, Marginality and its New Forms

The emerging occupational momentum besides reproducing the pre-existing hierarchy, employment insecurity has also contributed to the construction of new varieties marginalised out of its own functioning. Within this emerging world, marginality is being shaped and extended among those segments of population who are not only deprived of the opportunities for education and skill development, access to ICTs, but have also posited themselves in an unequal, insecure and peripheral working conditions. In many ways, marginality has taken new form and cultivated several new groups along with the continuation of vast segments of the pre-existing ones, even though the emerging knowledge society has elevated the economic status of a section of marginalised. In general, knowledge society in India experiences the presence of the following types:

I   *Structurally marginalised:* They are located within the structural arrangement of knowledge society, and contribute to the expansion of this society without getting substantive scope of upward social mobility. The quantum of this marginalisation is absolute.

   (a) Migrant workers working in the informal sector out of livelihood compulsion and experiencing only horizontal mobility.

   (b) Workers getting organically linked with the knowledge society by providing cheap labour and remaining socially neglected, economically underpaid and politically disempowered.

   (c) Workers becoming victims of market segregation out of the penetration of knowledge economy.

   (d) Workers becoming victims of displacement, environmental degradation and pollution.

   (e) Traditionally, marginalised within the structural arrangement: they are part of historical continuity and are cumulatively marginalised in the present context. They include the:

   • Historically identified social categories that have not been able to acquire the required education and skill and not having adequate access to education and ICTs for several reasons.

   • Workers continue to acquire insignificant social status and get insignificant economic rewards despite making significant contribution to the economy (e.g. agricultural and construction labourers, small cultivators, tenants, etc., manual workers of all sorts engaged in traditional nexus.

2   *Functionally marginalised:* They have acquired a marginalised status within the emerging functional arrangements of knowledge society even though they are posited with the possibility of upward mobility. A vast part of their marginalisation is relational.

(a) New knowledge workers working in insecure and stressful working conditions without choice and voice and pushed to respond to the global recession and boom.

(b) Old knowledge workers working as ad hoc, non-permanent workers in the organisation. The quanta of those categories of workers are in the increase in tremendous speed because of the emerging outsourcing and hiring and firing culture.

(c) Educated and trained workers compelled to be employed in a low position with mismatch between their acquired educational qualification and their placement in the organisational structure.

(d) Educated and trained youth accepting jobs in different areas of their specialisation, out of job shortage in own areas of specialisation and suffering from low esteem and job dissatisfaction.

(e) Knowledge workers victimised by the terror tactics of management in the form of denial of due promotion, social security and welfare, etc., benefits against all prevailing norms, remain unorganised and non-unionised under the whims of the management.

(f) Non-knowledge workers remaining under constant threat of losing of jobs in the wake of global recession and boom.

3   *Neo-marginalised:* They are not marginalised historically but have acquired this status because of reshuffling of economic and the opportunity structure. They include:

(a) A sizeable section of people from the general categories that have not been able to acquire the required education and skill and do not have adequate access to ICTs for several reasons.

(b) People of all categories who are unable to get integrated with the emerging consumer culture and the ICT–driven sociocultural milieu.

Though many of these categories are mutually inclusive many dimensions of the structurally marginalised are historically cumulative and socially relational; and of the functionally marginalised and neo-marginalised socially relational and situationally cumulative. The emerging facets of marginalisation in knowledge society are being legitimised by the emerging culture of silence, passivity and collective withdrawal of dissent from real public space. While the traditional facets of marginalisation has remained ingrained with the pre-given sociocultural values, the emerging facets of it are legitimised by strict adherence to the rule of law that discourages trade unionism in work place, encourages culture of hire and fire and effectively demonstrates the global threat of recession. Significantly, within the emerging consumer culture and growing affluence of knowledge workers voice against their marginalisation seldom gets a space for collective resistance and self-expression.

The knowledge workers are economically affluent and are consumerists. The growing economic affluence and submersion to consumerism of a leading segment of knowledge workers only reinforce passivity through contradictory perceptions of threat and possibility. On the one hand, they are inspired to work to indulge in consumerism through affluence, on the other, generate a culture of passivity and tolerance to domination with a perceptive threat that their resistance may cause damage to their affluence and thereby to the habit of comfort and consumerism. Growing culture of consumerism among the core segment of knowledge workers, who invariably represent the dominant section of Indian middle class, contributes increasingly to competition, flux, fluidity among themselves and passivity in collective voice against social repression. Economic neo-liberalisation has not only produced conspicuous consumers, out of knowledge workers and youth in particulars and of people in general but has also brought into being new sociocultural milieu to make its influence hegemonic and to culturally subject each segment of society to the waves of market forces. These consumers widely function as the preservers of market dynamics and social stability under economic neo-liberalism, even though they look for alternative politics.

V. New Socio-Cultural Momentum for Market Stability

Along with the emerging frame economic neoliberalism, expansion of education, penetration of ICTs, emergence of new occupational hierarchy, economic prosperity and affluence of a section on people, on the one hand, and marginalisation of vast section of people, on the other, a new sociocultural milieu is in the making across the space in India. Though this sociocultural milieu is metro/urban centric, youth focused, fashion and consumption oriented, and global in texture it is being spread among all sections of population either to be active agents or passive consumers of it. This socio-cultural milieu is predominant with western cultural values and practices and MNC-driven consumerism on which traditional cultural norms, values and practices have little control.

Most of these practices are ICTs driven and of recent origin that have revolutionised all areas of social activities including those of business, shopping, education, socialisation, collective mobilisation, healthcare, advocacy, career counselling, beautification, matrimonial, friendship and match selection, banking, tours and travel, sports, music, arts, spiritualism and religion and all other areas as one needs in his/ her day-to-day existence. These activities have commoditised in each moment of social existence, converted the whole world into a site of production and consumption of information, made the public addicted to it all through their active time starting from morning tea to office journey, railway station to airport, drawing room to boardroom, office hours to personal time, social gathering to professional meeting and formal to intimate actions. Inculcating the culture and habit of being on the network either through phone, email, Facebook, Skype, blog, Twitter, webcasting or any new media, the neo-liberal market has produced consumer out of every user of ICTs as no interaction is free. More the intensity of social interaction more is the commodification of social relation and more the expansion of market forces. Such interactions, invariably, are accompanied by new commercial images, information and temptation those are difficult to resist for being and becoming a global citizen. By injecting a culture of competitive consumerism and inculcating a culture of multiple consumers' choices, knowledge society not only reproduces consumerism but also socialises the new generation child in a global culture embedded in consumerism.

In fact, all free people find themselves enslaved in constructing their needs in terms of the dictum of the media and the market and not by the ontology of their social being and becoming. These choices are constructed as real and are made many a time unconsciously as inevitable needs. These needs are shaped by global market forces and the multinational corporations bringing in a host of contradictions with the ideal image of a knowledge society. Though the knowledge society is supposed to make the world interconnected and interdependent with a common human destiny, in essence it has moved forward as a globalised economy and culture with a common agenda to promote new cultural imperialism wherein western culture and imperatives predominate over a loss of the rest of the world (Evans, 2004). The stateless giant multinational corporations have emerged to be the dominant players in the global market and potential threats to the national interests of many of the poor countries who find themselves unable to catch up with the richer ones and are posited in a relationship that is 'overwhelmingly not just one of interdependence, but of dependence' (Lyon, 1988).

Within the thick of such sociocultural momentum, societies in India experience the arrival of a new generation of youth who are products of economic liberalisation, globalisation and ICTs who are not willing to be conditioned by traditionality but to get sunk in the current of global cultural practices. They socialise in the ICTs boom, computers, videogames, laptops, mobile phones, Bluetooth, email, Facebook and Skype as against their parents or grandparents who were socialised mostly in agrarian and industrial technologies and cultures. These youth exercise their own choice in interaction with the wider world, even though their parents make failed attempts to condition their future, life and choices within the given frame of parental sacrifice and role stereotypes. They are the 'E-Gen', the 'e-credo' and the 'desi zeppies' with deep-down orientation to ICT driven consumerist lifestyle and culture who have no guilt feeling of conspicuous consumption in having the latest brand of ICTs gazettes, clothes, body wire and motor vehicles. They live in the present at against the lifestyle of their parents and grandparents who prefer to live in future even at the cost of the present. Though they are predominantly visible in the mega cities and in the urban areas and among the upper social and economic strata of society, their emergence has been quite explicit even in the rural areas and among the lower socioeconomic strata with a low intensity though. They have made their presence felt not only in the virtual, but also in the real world which is being an appropriate representative of the information age. They look for alternative choices in most domains of society-economy, culture and politics. They, however, inject more fluidity than solidarity to the pre-existing social order, their lifestyle itself represents a criticality to the traditional social order; develop contestation to many of the pre-existing realities and largely contribute to the fragmentation of everyday reality. The emerging sociocultural milieu in the guise of globalisation brings in western consumerist flow and values widely at the cost of localised ethos. Though it has brought a wide variety of choices, it has been shaping the predominant western orientation of consumerism. The demographic dividend of India now stands for encashment by the neo-liberal market forces.

The emerging cultural milieu, however, is unable to integrate a large segment of society especially the structurally marginalised within its own ambit in effective terms even though they have emerged to be a loose nod of this cultural milieu by compulsion. In the process of interaction and mobility, many of them lose not only the required space to preserve, practice and promote own cultural choice, but also become dependent on the market-driven available alternatives on which they seldom have control. Within the emerging economic and social milieu, this section of people has emerged to be the outsiders from within, and survive as global 'marginal man' who resides in urban areas as immigrants, and in rural areas as native but are integrated to none culturally and politically. These marginal men are without adequate skill, knowledge and education, are integrated with this emerging social order only through their capacity to provide manual labour and to bear the burden of insecure, futureless and imbalanced growth. They are exposed to their alternative networks and volatile mass media that exhibit and construct alternative and global market-driven lifestyles. They are posited to be consumers, viewers and listeners of this entertainment industry and culture mostly at the cost of loss of their own cultural identity. Traditionally, the cultural mosaic of Indian society that has remained layered with prevalence of great traditional among the literati and the little tradition among the nonliterati, the villagers and the common mass has been layered and fragmented further with emergence of new socio-cultural milieu. Notwithstanding, the increased layering and limited inclusion in the global consumerist milieu, an imposition of western/global cultural practices over the localised ones has been emerging to be a reality.

Breaking the Barriers

In the emerging knowledge society with the scope of private investment getting phenomenally expanded, relationship between market and the state becoming explicitly stronger, politicians becoming visibly corrupt, administrators becoming indifferent to the public cause, justice has become costly and time consuming, majority of the civil society getting co-opted by the state, public becoming self-centred, intellectuals becoming self-righteous, common people feel the brunt of marginalisation in each and every moment of their existence in India. While a section of common people has developed the art of pretention of being powerful forming a cyber community, the educated enterprising ones try their lots by rubbing their shoulder with the politically influential personalities, affluent social categories use their money and muscle power to hold the social and political command, majority are grinded under the wheel of marginality in many dimensions of their lives. However, marginality being a dynamic process gets contested through diverse means.

In the changing socioeconomic landscape, marginality has acquired uneven characters in India and has got shifted from one domain to another very frequently. While a section of marginalised people has been able to break the pre-existing barriers of marginality either through the state or individual initiatives, for the majority who are at the periphery of knowledge society as providers of support services it has been slow. However, by bringing about multiple economic options, engineering the process of migration, enhancing the scope of horizontal mobility, introducing multiple employer-employee relations, facilitating alternative livelihood options and enabling and empowering people through ICTs the knowledge society has widely paved the way to challenge the barriers of traditional marginality for vast section people. In the wake of increasing mobility, interconnectivity and increasing realisation of their potential hitherto subjugated networks is being resurged. The knowledge and realisation of own potential, though immediately physical in nature, help them to go for alternative choice enabling them to break the barriers of un/underemployment and primordial domination in the place of origin and new forms of coercion in the place of arrival. An enabling environment to develop contestation against the localised hegemonic domination is in the making to cope with the tyranny of powerlessness, neglect, uncertainty and subjugation of various forms.

These contestations are not necessarily always in the form of articulation of organised protest, but in the form of availing alternative options for mobility and livelihood security, not acceding to coercive bondage and terms of work participation, and at places articulation of alternative political choice. However, these contestations seldom get the scope of consolidation as knowledge society has produced space for the formation of multiple identities through varied work relations that are simultaneously located in diverse social processes. It produced more fluidity than solidarity in contemporary social order of the marginalised that are yet to be connected and consolidated through a common concern across the space. Significantly, the possibly of such consolidation gets frequently diluted under the flow of new sociocultural momentum.

VI. Multiple Economic and Social Realities: Fluidity vs Solidarity

The developmental dynamics of India have been accompanied by a host of contradictions. While on the one hand, it has achieved a high rate of economic growth on the other hand, it has retained a vast section of population to live in abject poverty, despite the increase in food production millions live in hunger; regardless of having emerged as a knowledge superpower, a vast segment of population has remained either literate or semiliterate, and in spite of being a land of spiritualism the domination of mafia and criminals prevails over the common man in many parts of the country. In the wake of power getting concentrated in the hands of a limited few, rule of law is altered to safeguard those few and cry for justice of ordinary people becomes an object of mockery and the practice of democracy only becomes a cruel joke to many. These contradictions add widely towards the shaping of social dynamics of emerging India at the grassroots.

In a globalising world with the deep-down interpenetration of market liberalisation, and emergence and reproduction of multiple social collectivities societies in India have been posited within a spatial and historical continuum whereby many of the pre-existing economic, social and political institutional arrangements, values and customs, norms and ideals continue to coexist along with the new ones de/reshaping each other profusely. Within these processes, the social and economic foundation of contemporary India is framed by the coexistence of multiple nodes of economic organisation that is characterised as part agrarian, part industrial and part knowledge based, part formal, part informal, part modern and part primitive, part local and part global, part inclusive and part exclusive. Thus, India stands today within the momentum of multiple social interactivities, structures and processes that interact simultaneously to usher in fast economic and social transformation. With this momentum and fluidity, India is posited to experience the formation of multiple identities and fluidity in these identities similar to what is observed by Toffler (1970) in the Western context in late 1960s, an age of shock with the dizzying disorientation in the social institutions, new turning points of political conflicts and an alternative consciousness (Toffler, 1970, 1980). This transformation has also seen the arrival of new social movements at the grass roots that aim to transform 'human relationship at their most fundamental level' (Castells, 1997).

Knowledge society has helped promote the resurgence of subjugated networks, knowledge and identity at the grassroots. The historical neglect and circumstantial injustice that are inflicted on the marginalised are now articulated on a regular basis across the space to relook their marginal identity and to form languages of protest in everyday discourse. Being situationally integrated with global market forces as providers of cheap labour and consumers of products produced by these forces, on the one hand, and developing networks for alternative choices, on the other, they develop a critique of the present world and articulate a resistant identity against the forces of domination. However, as they try to get integrated with variety of economic and political forces their identities remain far from being unified; they rather contribute paradoxically to fluidity, at one end, and to solidarity, on the other. Notwithstanding such paradoxes have emerged to be interconnected as a harbinger of change in society to challenge and critique the structure of domination. In one way or the other, they produce a protest identity out of their everyday experience.

The knowledge society, however, has reproduced a community of status quoist by facilitating the emergence of entrepreneurs and affluent segments workers from among the traditionally oriented social groups in India. These groups have taken advantage both of their pre-existing economic background, social networks, political connections, educational backgrounds and access to ICTs and the emerging new avenues of financial investment both in the knowledge and non-knowledge sectors to maximise their economic interest and further their social and political influence. Though, they extensively use ICTs and are exposed to the outside world they reinforce traditionality in everyday life. They go by traditional horoscope, caste-based marriage, practice of dowry and adherence to religious dogmas in political discourse. They are status quoist, and develop nexus with the political leaders and religious entrepreneurs to further their economic ventures, largely help expansion of the informal sector to further their interest along with the expansion of knowledge economy. They help inculcating a traditionally oriented legitimising identity as their ways of life.

ICTs function as a double-edged weapon; while it liberates a section of people, it also helps consolidate areas of conservatism and absolute. A section views the expansion of ICT-mediated interaction as a threat to their traditional structure of authority, get united against its use by the youth, students and especially women, some also use it to propagate their absolute thought for a political or other social purpose to gain a long-term benefit. A section of religious leaders and followers propagating extremist view are the case to this point. They use ICTs and mass media to propagate and generate a community of followers with hate against others. Thus, it contributes to the formation of a project identity by carving out a space for themselves creating a community of excluders by excluding the others. Besides the religious extremist groups, efforts of a few caste groups curb the use of ICTs by the female members of these groups only to reflect the resurgence of traditionality in a modern context.

The emerging of knowledge society has kept a section of society to be socially, economically and politically undetermined and in a state of constant flux cutting across their boundaries of social, economic and spatial positioning. This is widely caused by overburdening of information in public space whereby the real appears not only to be deceptive but also fragmented with increasing flow of migration, occupational mobility, emergence of multiple social and cultural interactivity. As the power of ICTs and new mass media now is in wide use to bring out new facts and figures, to construct new image and to reconstruct the scenario on a daily basis, for them there is neither a uniform image nor a common identity. This has produced multiple identities for an important section of people who get swayed by the overburdening of information and availability of multiple choices in employment, network, social and cultural practices and political affiliation. They are never fixed, unavailable to take political or collective position; appears to be more fluid than consolidated in all collective engagements. They predominantly represent themselves through multiple identities, which are contradictory, in one context, and complementary, in another.

While multiple identities are explicit and reflexive of identities in one form or another, there have again been identities of silence and passively whereby large chunks of population prefer to remain silent spectators or passive in attitude to take a position, assert their identity and entitlement even as citizens. For a section, this is deliberate to be legitimising through silence, for another it is simply lack of awareness, while for a vast section it is a fear of loss of livelihood security and their public assertion only repeats the phrase that 'nothing can be changed'! However, these are not fixed, rather transitional in nature and look for appropriate moments to be a part of a visible assertive process.

In fact, the coexistence of multiple identities – the protest, legitimising, project, multiple and passive identities – are reflective of imperfect globalisation, part formation of knowledge society, emergence of social and economic imbalances and deconsolidation of pre-existing social order in India. As the knowledge society is yet to be fully formed, the process finds itself in a whirlpool of multiple sociocultural realities that have unsettled many of the pre-existing social forces. Herein, the contemporary social realities appear to be more fluid than consolidated as ever.

Socially, knowledge society is envisioned to usher the foundation of a new society that is widely characterised by mobility and dispersal of population, objects, images, information and wastes and their virtual travel and movements as social reality (Urry, 2000), emergence of virtual organisation (Deane, 1980) and immensely interactive world as a site of production and consumption of goods and services at a global scale, and of social, cultural, economic and political engagement. Knowledge society in India has emerged to be a part of a world, as various scholars point out in the Western context, that experiences unpredictable mobility of people as fluids that have no clear point of departure, or arrival (Castells, 2004), no designated physical location (Melucci, 1996), 'ordered across time and space', and is free from the hold of specific locales, recombining them across wide time, space and distances ... which create new forms of fragmentation and dispersal (Giddens, 1991). It is in a process of integration with wider world that is getting fragmented socioculturally through the construction of multiple identities.

Construction of new identity is central to the network society wherein identity locates itself within the interplay of local and global interconnectivity as self-reflexivity. In knowledge society, collective identity as reflection of collective solidarity has emerged to be problematic as social collectivities that are usually understood as well-knit 'community' get loosely organised, are loosely formed without being founded in a specific locale, many a times independent of geographical boundary, based on temporarily perceived ideals and interests cross-cutting many a time contradictory interests and goals. This fluid and fuzzy membership makes the social order and the preestablished communities very weak in network society. Within these emerging complexities, social systems increasingly manifest fluid-like characteristics and become increasingly subject to shockwaves of fluidarity rather than solidarity, public experience of self rather than collective identity (Urry, 2000; cf. McDonald, 2002).

In India along with the first expansion with the forces of globalisation, ICTs, education, sociocultural disembeddedness and multiple identities are in the making at the grassroots. Social collectivities are formed based on economic class or professional, ethnic, regional, caste, gender, environment, human rights and related interests and identities with same sets of people getting collectively engaged on diverse issues, interests and identities. Thus, the processes of solidification and fluidity of collective identity go on hand in hand and the dynamics of 'identity' and 'interest', 'morality' and 'rationality', 'primordiality' and 'modernity', 'autonomy' and 'dependence' function as a combination of these composite social processes by becoming both situationally dichotomous and complementary. Through increasing interconnectivity with the wider world they have emerged to be highly flexible as social collectivities that are regularly mobilised on the principle of fragmentation at one end and unification on the other, and are in a process of continuous renewal and rejuvenation and are in the process of crystallisation of a composite culture reflexivity, resonance and resilience. These flexible identities are shaped as a reaction to sustained marginality, at one end, and receptivity to new worldviews, on the other, that have emerged out of the expansion of education, literacy and enhanced virtual and physical connectivity. With the sustained interconnectivity with political actors, civil society activists and with the market players as well these collectivities have now emerged to be highly mobilised and flexible and have taken the form of social movement society: an interconnected collectivity regularly mobilised on the principle of fragmentation at one end and unification on the other, and in a process of continuous renewal and rejuvenation (SinghaRoy, 2010). In the world of cultural interactivity and co-construction, public spaces are available for generating new thoughts, activating new actors and generating new ideas. The social movement actors by 'producing new knowledge, by reflecting on their own cognitive identity, by saying what they stand for and by challenging the dominant assumptions of the social order develop new ideas that are fundamental to the process of human creativity. It develops worldviews that restructure cognition and recognise reality itself that are important source of new social images and transformation of societal identities' (Eyerman and Jamison, 1991). In fact the emergence of knowledge society has paved the way for the formation of alternative sensitivity and politics.

The society in India is posited to unfurl a great transformation from its predominantly agrarian to a knowledge-based society. This transformation has been accompanied by a host of shifts in the organisation of production, political ideology of the state and the relationships between the state, market and people, on the one hand, and in the process of construction of collective identity, on the other. These shifts are shown in the figures mentioned in the following section.

VII. Shifting Political, Economic, Social and Cultural Panorama from Passing Agrarian to Emerging Knowledge Society in India

India's shift towards an industrial society has not been as conspicuous as it has been towards the knowledge society. Rather India has missed the industrial revolution. The slow and limited pace of industrialisation, the state-sponsored initiatives for change and transformation have not been able to wither away the agrarian legacy from Indian society. Significantly, in recent years, resurged India has encountered a phenomenal shift from its conventional agrarian setting to a knowledge based one being educationally, digitally and globally enabled, with a diverse intensity though. However, the pre-existing political, economic, social and cultural dynamics continue to exist in modified form with receding intensity to influence the emergence of a new social arrangement. Here we describe the receding influence of the pre-existing society as the 'passing agrarian society' that is in the process of being transformed into a new one. The knowledge society however is yet to be fully formed. However it is emerging at a fast pace with cumulative shifts in all domains of the society from those of the previous arrangements and practices. We describe it as 'emerging knowledge society' to delineate the ascendance of a new social order which is the process of consolidating and accommodating the shifting panoramas in its fold. These shifts in the political, economic, social and cultural panoramas are shown in Figure 10.1, 10.2, 10.3 and 10.4, respectively. These shifts involve wide spectrums of change from those of state philosophy and initiatives to individual ideals and actions in major domains of lives.

The Political Panorama

A. Post-independent India was predominantly an agrarian society till the early 1990s. The political foundation of the Indian state that was founded on the philosophy of a welfare state has been shifted to political philosophy of economic neo-liberalism in the wake of globalisation and emergence of knowledge society therein after the 1990s. In fact, there has been a conspicuous shift from a protectionist state towards that of a liberal one.

B. In the passing agrarian-based society socialism was the cherished idea of the state and the society, but in the emerging society capitalism is privileged over socialism by the state and the market.

C. Mixed economy, that was the dominant operational principle of market dynamics in the passing agrarian society, is being largely replaced by the capitalist principle of free market dynamics in the emerging society. Significantly, the principle of capitalism is now privileged over socialism through various mechanisms like privatisation, public–private partnerships etc.

D. While centralised planning, state-controlled industrialisation were the dominant strategies for change in the passing agrarian society, market drive initiative for industrialisation, public–private partnership

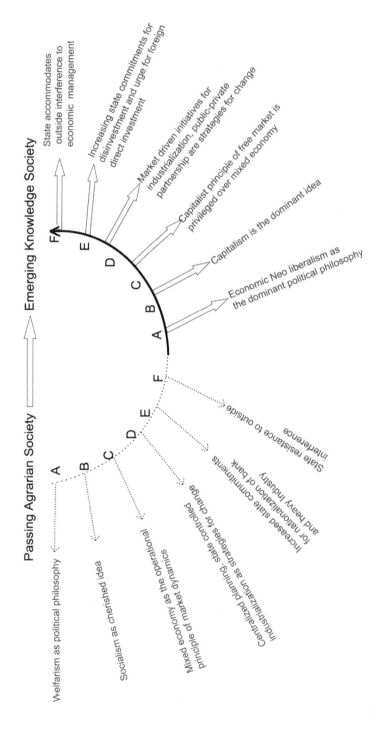

Figure 10.1 Shifting Political Panorama from Passing Agrarian to Emerging Knowledge Society in India

have emerged to be prime strategies for change in the emerging knowledge society.

E. In the transitional agrarian post-independent India state commitments for nationalisation of banks and heavy industrialisation were made very explicit to augment the socialist path of development and modernisation. In the emerging society state commitments have been shifted in favour of increasing disinvestment of nationalised industries and concerns paving the way for increasing foreign direct investment by liberalising trade policies to usher fast economic growth and social development.

F. In the passing agrarian society the state resisted outside interference in the economic policies of the nation. In the emerging society the neo-liberal state accommodates outside interference to economic management, accepts the Structural Adjustment Programme of the International Monetary Fund, and liberalises the trams trades to accommodate the conditions of Multinational Corporations etc.

Economic

A. In the transitional agrarian society in India land and physical labour were major resources while in the emerging knowledge society human being, their skill and intellectual potential are recognised as key resources.

B. While agriculture was the major source of employment in the passing agrarian society, service and manufacturing have together emerged as potential sources of employment in the emerging society. These are most likely to overweigh agriculture in future.

C. Agriculture was the major source of GDP in the passing agrarian society in India, while the service sector has emerged to be the major source of GDP in the emerging knowledge society.

D. In the passing agrarian society agriculturalists were the key and dominant section of workers, in the emerging society service workers are emerging as the key and dominant section of workers.

E. While the landlords were the economically dominant category in the passing agrarian society, the knowledgeable are in the process of emerging to be the economically dominant category in the emerging knowledge society.

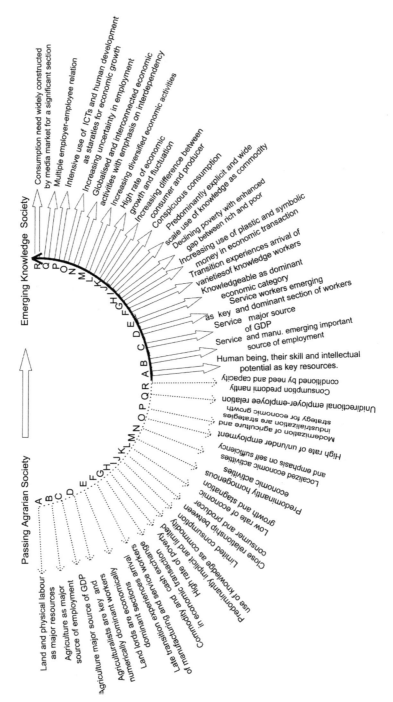

Figure 10.2 Shifting Economic Panorama from Passing Agrarian to Emerging Knowledge Society in India

F. The passing agrarian society has experienced the arrival of manufacturing and the service workers at the later phase of its transition, the transition of present society experiences the arrival of varieties of globally interconnected knowledge workers at a large scale.

G. While commodity and cash exchange were predominantly in use in economic transaction in the passing agrarian society, the emerging knowledge society experiences the increasing use of plastic and symbolic money in economic transaction.

H. High rate of poverty was widely linked with the passing agrarian society, while declining poverty ratio with enhanced gap between the rich and poor has emerged to be an important feature of emerging knowledge society in India.

I. The passing agrarian society was characterised by predominantly implicit and limited use of knowledge as a commodity, while the emerging knowledge society has emerged to be characterised predominantly by the explicit and wide scale use of knowledge as a commodity.

J. The passing agrarian society was founded on the ideals of limited consumption but the emerging knowledge society is taking shape based on conspicuous consumption.

K. Close and interpersonal relationship between consumer and producer was an integral part of the passing agrarian society, while increasing difference between consumer and producer, and increasing impersonality have become integral parts of the emerging knowledge society.

L. The passing agrarian society has perennially experienced low rate of economic growth and sustained economic stagnation (except in the areas of Green Revolution), while the emerging knowledge society experiences a high rate of economic growth, however with globally interconnected fluctuation.

M. In the passing agrarian society economic activities were predominantly homogenous, while in the emerging knowledge society economic activities have emerged to be increasingly diversified.

N. In the passing agrarian society emphasis was on localised economic activities and economic self-sufficiency; however, in the emerging knowledge society emphasis has been on the globally interdependent and interconnected economic activities.

O. The passing agrarian society experienced high rate of un/under employment. In the emerging knowledge society while rate of unemployment has declined, it has generated increasing uncertainty in the employment scenario of the country.

P. In the passing agrarian society modernisation of agriculture and industrialisation were the predominant strategies for economic growth, while in the emerging knowledge society intensive use of ICTs and development of human capability have been viewed as the key strategies for economic growth.

Q. Unidirectional employer–employee relations were a key feature of the passing agrarian society, while multiple and unstable employer–employee relations are important dimensions of the emerging knowledge society.

R. In the passing agrarian society consumption was predominantly conditioned by need and capacity, while in the emerging knowledge society consumption need is predominantly conditioned by media and market.

Social

A. Modernisation was the major social process in the passing agrarian society, while globalisation has emerged to the key social process in the emerging knowledge society.

B. In the passing agrarian society agrarian reforms and Green Revolution were the key strategies for structural transformation, while educational reforms and knowledge revolution have become key strategies for social transformation in the emerging knowledge society.

C. High rate of illiteracy and low level of skill development was associated for long with the passing agrarian society, while high rate of literacy and high level of skill development has been a characteristic feature of emerging knowledge society.

D. The passing agrarian society has witnessed a high rate of population

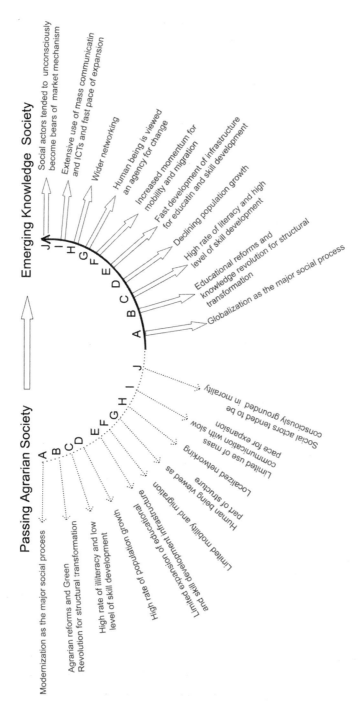

Figure 10.3 Shifting Social Panorama from Passing Agrarian to Emerging Knowledge Society in India

growth, while the emerging knowledge society experiences a declining rate of population growth.

E. The passing agrarian society has seen a limited expansion of infrastructure for educational and skill development, while the emerging knowledge society is founded on fast development of infrastructure for education and skill development.

F. While limited mobility and migration were linked to the passing agrarian society, increased momentum for mobility and migration have emerged to be important dimensions of the emerging knowledge society.

G. In the passing agrarian society human being were viewed as a part of structure, while in the emerging knowledge society human being is viewed an agency for change.

H. The passing agrarian society was founded on localised networking, while the emerging knowledge society is founded on wider and intensive networking.

I. Limited use of mass communication and slow pace of its expansion were the important dimensions of the passing agrarian society. Extensive use of mass communication and ICTs and fast pace of its expansion are the key features of the emerging knowledge society.

J. In the passing agrarian society social actors consciously tended to be grounded in morality, while in the emerging knowledge society social actors unconsciously tended to be the bearers of market mechanism.

Cultural

A. The passing agrarian society was predominantly founded on primordial cultural practices, while the emerging knowledge society, though emerging to be secular, reinforces primordiality in a new context.

B. Predominantly exclusive and localised identities were constructed in the passing agrarian society. While multiple, highly flexible and interactive identities with increased fluidity are widely constructed within the emerging social processes of knowledge society.

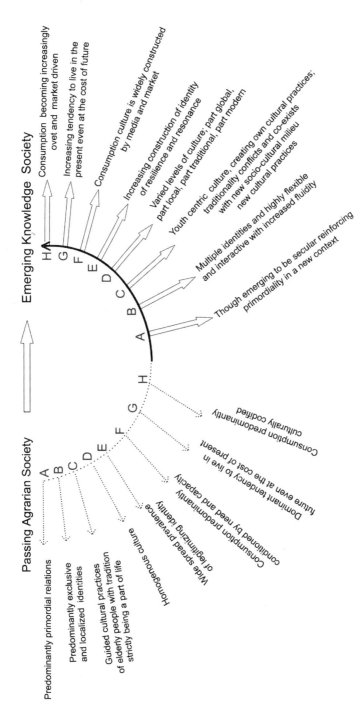

Figure 10.4 Shifting Cultural Panorama from Passing Agrarian to Emerging Knowledge Society in India

C. In the passing agrarian society cultural practices of elderly people was strictly adhered to with tradition strictly being a part of life. The emerging knowledge society experiences the arrival of a youth centric culture with alternative cultural practices. Here traditionality conflicts and co-exists with new socio-cultural milieu.

D. Homogenous culture was linked to the passing agrarian society, while the emerging knowledge society experiences the arrival of varied levels of culture that are part global and part local, part traditional and part modern, even though globality prevails over the rest.

E. The passing agrarian society has experienced the widespread prevalence of legitimising identity both at the end of the dominant and the subordinate. The emerging knowledge society experiences the increasing construction of identity of resilience and resonance.

F. In the passing agrarian society, consumption was predominantly conditioned by need and capacity, while in the emerging knowledge society consumption need is widely constructed by media and market.

G. In the passing agrarian society the dominant tendency has been to live in future even at the cost of present, while in the emerging knowledge society increasing tendency has been, especially among the youth, to live in the present even at the cost of present.

H. Consumption is predominantly codified by cultural practices in the passing agrarian society but in the emerging knowledge society consumption is increasingly becoming market and media driven.

It is important that none of the domains is autonomous; rather these are interlinked and relational and have cumulative impacts on social transformation. Herein the agrarian society is in a transitional form; and the knowledge society is yet to take a full and final shape and yet to get a discrete identity. In the process of such being and becoming the emerging knowledge society accommodates a host of the features of the passing agrarian society within its ambit producing lots of fluidity and fuzziness, anomalies and inconsistencies at the one end and concretisation of the foundation of a new social order on the other. Significantly the process of concretisation of the foundation of a knowledge-based new social order prevails over the rest. This transition is shown in Figure 10.5:

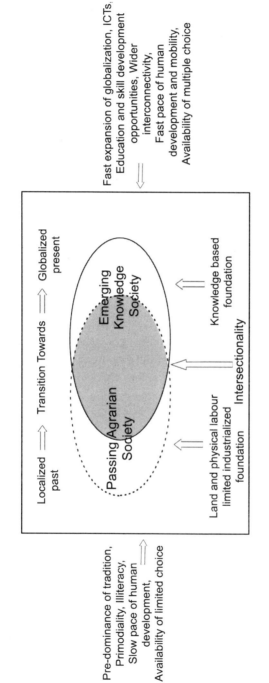

Figure 10.5 Transition from Localized Past to Globalized Present

The transition towards a knowledge society has been conspicuously delineated by the shift in societal foundation from those of its localised past that was based on land and physical labour, limited industrialisation, and was widely conditioned internally by the predominance of tradition, primordality, illiteracy, slow pace of human development and availability of limited choice. Significantly, this transition has been towards a globalized present founded in knowledge widely conditioned by exogenous forces, fast expansion of globalisation, ICTs, education and skill development opportunities, wider interconnectivity, fast pace of human development and mobility and availability multiple choice to stimulate and generate unlimited knowledge potential of people. As these societies are yet to be discreet, they cover vast areas of inter-sectionality causing transitional fluidity and inconsistencies. However, notwithstanding such inter-sectionality the ascendency of knowledge society prevails over the passing agrarian society.

VIII. The Despair and Hope

The emerging India is indeed experiencing a new form of dispersal and fragmentation and also a dark side of development with the advancement of knowledge society. Knowledge society through the interpenetration of ICTs/mass media and education, developing wider connectivity and mobility of people has unfolded the dark side of development in the contemporary world. Economic prosperity and knowledgability have been accompanied by increasing lust for money and power, corruption and trust-deficit, crime and violence, break in the traditional institutions and practices, lack of morality and ethics in public life and increasing difference between public discourse and personal action. Along with market liberalisation, India has been experiencing not only proliferation of new avenues of investments, but also increasing alliances between the businessmen, politicians and the criminals at all levels of interactivity and political actions – the national, regional, district and the village. It is not only the scams related to large ICTs, educational, infrastructure developments, defence deals, coal mining, etc., that have engulfed the country, but also at the local level initiatives like that of the construction of village roads, school buildings, supply of midday meals, MGNREGS, public distribution system etc practice of corruption has emerged to be rampant. It is not surprising that India has acquired the dubious distinction of becoming one of the most corrupt nations in the world acquiring 95th position at the bottom of transparency.

Media and ICTs penetration at different levels in society while rejuvenating connectivity and social bondage, have brought destruction to many of the old systems of social control. Easy exposure to bare body and skin shown in the new and mass media, easy availability of pornographic materials not only push and provoke a section of vulnerable youth also the perverted adult alike, to crime and delinquency of various sort. Frustration, repression and alienation in daily life diverts many towards obscene attractions that are easily available on the Internet and in the local market as 'blue-chips', and promote the tendency to be involved in violence, crime and sexual offences against women and children. While the traditional social control system is breaking down, and these cultural forms do not match the mindset of new age children, they take recourse to easy source of entertainment as available in the television, and in new and mass media. Societies in India experience sudden and phenomenal increase in the incidence of rape and eve-teasing, varieties of violence against women and children, sexual harassment in workplace, organised crime and gang rape. Importantly a part of these crimes are executed either with the influence or use of ICTs.

As the enhanced mobility has set in motion the dislocation in joint living, the elderly parents and young children are left to themselves in many places to decide their destiny. Within this youth-centric, global cultural milieu many members of elderly generation get an overwhelming marginal position, emerged to be unwanted immigrants, neglected and insecure. Seventy-year-old Gangadhar from Delhi migrated here as a young office assistant. All through his life, he and his wife spent every amount of their money, time and energy for the education of their child who was successful in becoming an engineer and is currently serving in the United States as a software engineer. However, Gangadhar and his wife are not welcome in the United States and they are left to themselves. Gangadhar says they can neither go back to village to resettle, nor can stay here comfortably, as they feel insecure as everybody is busy in their own affairs. They will prefer an old-age home if available around. In fact, such is the story of many of the elderly parents both in rural and in urban areas.

Knowledge society by injecting an element of competition in minds of children and their parents alike not only shaped a 'competitive society' out of 'cooperative' one, but also injected a culture of trust deficit and falsehood in everyday discourse for an important segment of socially. In this competetive society children are guided not only to be knowledgeable, but also to be competitive, socialised to be 'practical'. The elders are adviced by their friends and colleagues to be pragmatic and diplomatic and juniors to be submissive and uncritical to authority. They collectively accept the slogan that 'everybody is corrupt' and 'nothing can be changed' and so 'change yourselves'. Consequently, dissents are discarded as irrelevant, and people's voice, whatsoever little available, is mocked as disgruntled nuisance of participatory democracy under the crusher of neo-liberal market drives. Accordingly, collective assertions tend to take a back seat and passivity of academia, middle class and of the civil society prevails to provide legitimacy to hegemony of the power elite and the corporate world.

Higher the level of education lesser is the response to public exigencies and higher withdrawal from public/social service. As the dominant collective value has been self-centric, the corrupt politicians use the available social space in connivance with criminals to keep the common citizens away from the corridors of power. In the wake of passivity and withdrawal of the secular knowledgeable and not allowing their entry in the political domain through several strategic means, politics of primordially and lineage get strengthened at all levels of Indian democracy. An analysis of Dinesh Trivedi (2013), a Member of Parliament, reveals a linear relationship between age and hereditary occupation of parliamentary seats. To him, when India's biggest advantage today is its youth and the lower House of Parliament (Lok Sabha) is constituted by a large number of young and educated MPs quite a large number of members have entered Parliament because of their family connections. 'As much as 70 per cent of all women members in the Upper and Lower House have politically influential family background… The younger the MPs the higher the likelihood they have entered the hallowed portals through family routes. All MPs under the age of 30 have assumed the mantle of a parent or a relative'. About their quality of performance in the parliament and lifestyle, he aptly laments 'Unlike their forerunners, the new kids on the block refuse to venture out of their comfort zones, happy with their latest SUVs, designer outfits and branded watches. Most of the MPs in the 1990s did not hesitate to use the regular minibus provided by Parliament; sprawling, luxurious cars in Parliament's parking lot were a rare sight. But today, BMWs, Mercedes, Audis and the odd Rolls Royce crowd the Parliament...Time was when Parliament not only functioned, but were relevant; but today, it has lost its relevance. It seems that we have lost touch with the country's ethos and the values for which our freedom fighters martyred themselves.... The polity today is marked by a huge disconnect between the talented youth outside Parliament who have done India proud in every field – sport, the arts, music and education – and the young MPs within whose contribution to nation-building has so far been negligible' (Trivedi, 2013).

While knowledge society brings in an amount of withdrawal from real public/collective action, it promotes the culture of snooping and surveillance on public/citizen by the authority. Concern for privacy is ignored in the name of institutional need. Besides on many occasions even private discourses get recorded for manipulation, exploitation and extortion. Both the hidden and mobile camera and voice recording devices have become tools for oppression of powerless and insecured. Even though the otherwise is possible the traditionally dominant sections are seldom posited to take advantage of it, while the poweful are. In fact, it has emerged to be a society of suspicion wherein unknowingly the difference between the public and private is blurred.

By cultivating human mind through education and ICT, knowledge society is in the process to convert the entire humanity to be the community of intellectuals. However, human history is replete with the fact that all intellectual acts are not necessarily moral ones. These are more guided by the mind to gain wealth, power and recognition than by heart that looks for love, affection, integrity and peace. It is yet to prove how far the impact on the people will be able to combine the act of heart and mind together, as the knowledge society is posited to create more of a man of intelligence than a man of morality.

New Signs and Hopes

In all, knowledge society has appeared to be a continuum in the great transformative trajectory in India. It is in the process of having a shape of its own in the midst of pre-existing agrarian and industrial, rural and urban, traditional and modern arrangement by resurging unprecedented momentum in the social, economic, political, and cultural lives in India. The overwhelming flow of economic neo–liberalism is yet to smash the underpinning of a society that is founded on the philosophy of a socialist and mixed economy. India's tryst with economic liberalism is not a new one in the journey of its political economy. However, the recent invasion of economic neo-liberalism is a unique one. It has unleshed huge creative brainpower to integrate domestic forces with the global processes at a mass scale bringing phenomenal shift in all domains of life. However, the explicit shift, that these forces have brought into the state perspectives on economic development, educational and ICTs expansion, has unfolded a host of paradoxes in the social existence without bringing discontinuity with the past that has retained the affluence of few and marginality of many. It has again produced new forms identity, at one end, and fluidity in those identities, on the other. Despite these paradoxes, these economic, technological, social and cultural shifts have ushered a great transformation in society with more people getting across to knowledge and skill, ICTs, getting spatially and occupationally mobilised, getting adopted to global cultural consumerism, opting for non-agricultural jobs, and simultaneously getting marginalised and living under poverty, experiencing crime, violence, suicide, corruption and becoming powerless. All great transformation brings big upheaval affecting the life, work, culture and politics of largest segment of people; and is posited experience such transformations.

Though the emerging knowledge society has brought a host of contradictions, anomalies, disorientation and dichotomies, these have also unfolded new sign of life with added opportunities and challenges for all sections of population. The social scientists cannot avoid these challenges, but accept it. The challenge lies with the fact that the present moment of the society is 'marked by the appearance new problems which is required to be understood no longer by invoking another order of the phenomena – the laws of the capitalist development or the consequences of modernisation'. The post-industrial world is characterised by new modes of development with new varieties of opportunities and challenges (Touraine, 1981).

India today stands in the threshold of another great transformation that aims to liberate its citizen with their own strength from the realities of ignorance, poverty, domination and isolation. Knowledge society has laid its foundation on education and knowledge by igniting human mind to be the source of its key capital. Education as a liberating force has produced space for social critically of its own despite the market-driven efforts to control it. As it promotes human mind and recognises it as the centre of power, the knowledge society provides the platform for liberation of human being from the clutches of domination and exclusion. In that sense, knowledge society has engaged to be the hope of future and ultimate choice for India in general and for the marginalised section of population in particular. The process of liberalisation is in the making and critiquing the existence that has just begun.

With the arrival of knowledge society in India a self-empowered society is in the making by shaking the foundation of all pre-existing social, economic and political formation that would be new society in its own term to redefine the newness. This newness would be based on self–reflexivity, resonance and resilience of its people's creative and critical engagement. The process has began that provides people multiple livelihood options and new choices, make them mobile, self–reflexive, resonant and resilient, helps construct multiple identities as critique both against pre-existing hegemony from within and the emerging hegemony from outside. The resurgence of new identities has been shaping out of penetration of education and increasing interconnectivity would bring a new history for the millions whose voices have remained subjugated in the past. As Toffler (1990) points out, today knowledge is becoming the 'ultimate substitute' and replacing the traditional form of power. In the knowledge age, entirely new relationships between leaders and the led are required, relationships which nurture and build upon the subordinate's knowledge, rather than demand particular behaviour or 'blind obedience' (Toffler, 1990). In contemporary India, critical reflections are in the making at the grassroots level that not only question the culture of blind obedience but also provide alternative choices. These critical reflections now produce a collective identity of resilience and resonance of diverse form to lay the foundation of a new India.

Bibliography

Abrar, P. 2013. *The Economic Times*. Bangalore, January 22:1.

Ambani, M. and K. Birla. 2000. *Report on a Policy Framework for Reforms in Education, Special Subject Group on Policy Framework for Private Investment in Education, Health and Rural Development, Prime Minister's Council on Trade and Industry*. New Delhi: Government of India.

Amin, A. (ed.) 1994. *Post-Fordism: A Reader*. Oxford: Blackwell.

Anderson, B. 1989. *Imagined Communities*. London: Verso.

Ansari, M.M. 2012. 'Miles to go,' *The Indian Express*, July 31.

Appadurai, A. (ed.). 1986. *The Social Life of Things*. Cambridge: Cambridge University Press.

———— 1996. *Modernity at Large: Cultural Dimensions of Globalization*. Minneapolis: University of Minnesota Press.

Appiah, K. A. 2008. 'Education for Global Citizenship,' *National Society for the Study of Education* 107(1): 83–99.

Balakrishanan, N. 2001. 'Information and Communication Technologies and the Digital Divide in the Third World Countries' *Current Science* 81(8): 966–72.

Banerjee, S. 2008. 'A Political cul-de-sac: CPI(M)'s Tragic Denouement,' *Economic and Political Weekly* XLIII(42): 12–15.

Barbar, B. 1992. 'Jihad versus McWorld,' *The Atlantic Monthly* 269(3): 53–65.

Barker, C. and D. Galasinski. 2001. *Cultural Studies and Discourse Analysis: A Dialogue on Language and Identity*. London: Sage.

Bartelson, J. 2000. 'Three Concepts of Globalisation,' *International Sociology* 15(2): 180–96.

Bauman, Z. 1987. *Legislators and Interpreters*. Cambridge: Polity.

———— 1994. 'Deciding 21st Century,' *New Statesman and Society,* 1st April: 24–5.

Bell, D. 1961.*The End of Ideology*. Cambridge, MA: Harvard University Press.

———— 1974. *The Coming of Post Industrial Society: A Venture in Serial Forecasting*. London: Heinemann.

———— 1976. *Coming of Post-Industrial Society: A Venture in Social Forecasting.* Harmondsworth: Penguin.

———— 1980. 'The Social Framework of the Information Society,' in *The Microelectronics Revolution*, edited by T. Forester. Oxford: Blackwell.

Beteille, A. 2000. *Antinomies of Society: Essays on Ideologies and Institutions.* New Delhi: Oxford University Press.

Bhatia, B. 2010. 'Innovation and Research to Steer India's Knowledge Economy,' *The Times of India*, February 15.

Black, A. 1998. 'Information and Modernity: The History of Information and the Eclipse of Library History.' *Library History* 14(1): 39–45.

———— 2003. 'The Information Society: A Secular View,' in *Challenge and Change in the Information Society*, edited by S. Hornby and Z. Clarke, 18–41. London: Facet.

Blaney, D. L. and M. K. Pasha. 1993. 'Civil Society and Democracy in the Third World: Ambiguities and Historical Possibilities.' *Studies in Comparative International Development* 28(1): 3–24.

Blumer, H. 1951. 'Social Movements,' in *New Outline of Principles of Society*, edited by A. M. Lee. New York: Barnes & Noble.

———— 1996. *Symbolic Interactionism: Perspective and Method.* Englewood Cliffs, New Jersey: Prentice Hall.

Boshier, R. and C. N. Onn. 2000. 'Distance Constructions of Web Learning and Education,' *Journal of Distance Education* 15(2): 1–16.

Bourdieu, P. And L. Wacquant. 1999. 'On the Cunning of Imperialist Reason,' *Theory Culture and Society* 16(1): 41–58.

Brennan, J. 2008. 'The Future of Higher Education and the Future of Higher Education Research,' *Higher Education* 56(3): 381–93.

Bryson, J., P. Daniels, N. Henry and J. Pollard (eds.). 2000. *Knowledge, Space, Economy.* London: Routledge.

Buechler, S. M. 2000. *Social Movements in Advanced Capitalism.* Oxford: Oxford University Press.

Business Standard, September 9, 2008.

Byres, T. J. 1981. 'New Technology, Class Formation and Class Action in the Indian Countryside.' *The Journal of Peasant Studies* 8(4): 405–54.

Cassidy, J. 2002. *Dot. Con. The Greatest Story Ever Sold.* London: Allen Lane.

Castells, M.1983. *The City and the Grass Roots: A Cross-Cultural Theory on Urban Social Movements*. Berkeley, CA: University of California Press.

———— 1989. *The Informational City*. Oxford: Blackwell.

———— 1996. *The Rise of Network Society: The Information Age Economy, Society and Culture* Vol. I. Oxford: Blackwell Publishers.

———— 1997. *The Power of Ideality: The Information Age, Economy, Society and Culture*, Vol II. London: Blackwell Publishers.

———— 2001. *The Internet Galaxy Reflections on the Internet, Business, and Society*. Oxford: Oxford University Press.

———— 2004. *Informationalism, Networks and the Network Society: a Theoratical Blueprint* in The Network Society: A Cross Cultural Perspective edited by M.Castells. Northampton, MA: Edward Elgar Publishing, Inc.

Census of India. 1961. Government of India, Ministry of Information and Broadcasting, New Delhi.

———— 1971. Government of India, Ministry of Information and Broadcasting, New Delhi.

———— 1981. Government of India, Ministry of Information and Broadcasting, New Delhi.

———— 1991. Government of India, Ministry of Information and Broadcasting, New Delhi.

———— 2001. Government of India, Ministry of Information and Broadcasting, New Delhi.

———— 2011. Government of India, Ministry of Information and Broadcasting, New Delhi.

Cerutti, F. 2001. 'Political Identity and Conflict: A Comparison of Definition,' in *Identities and Conflicts: The Mediterranean*, edited by F. Ceruttiu and R. Ragiorieri. New York: Palgrave.

Chanda, R. 2002. *GATS and Its Implications for Developing Countries: Key Issues and Concerns*. Washington DC: World Bank, Department of Economics and Social Affairs.

Chandhoke, N. 1995. *State and Civil Society: Exploration in Political Theory*. New Delhi: Sage Publications.

Colley, C. H. 1902. *Human Nature and Social Order*. New York: Scribner.

CNBC. 2012. 'India's Secret Weapon: Its Young Population,' by Ansuya Harjani, November 2, 2012, http://finance.yahoo.com/news/indias-secret-weapon-young-population-134507535.html.

Cohen, J. L.1985. 'Strategy or Identity: New Theoretical Paradigms and Contemporary Social Movements.' *Social Research* 52(4): 663–716.

———— 2003. *Communal Heavens: Identity and Meaning in the Network Society.* Hong Xiuquan.

———— and A. Arato. 1994. *Civil Society and Political Theory.* London: MIT Press.

Cohn, S. F., S. E. Barkan, and W. A. Halteman. 2003. 'Dimensions of Participation in a Professional Social Movement Organization,' *Sociological Inquiry* 73(3): 311–37.

Coser, L. 1956. *The Functions of Social Conflict.* Glenceo, IL: Free Press.

Dahrendorf, R. 1959. *Class and Class Conflict in Industrial Society.* Stanford, CA: Stanford University Press.

David, P. 1975. *Technical Choice, Innovation and Economic Growth: Essays on American and British Experience in the Nineteenth Century.* London: Cambridge University Press.

Deane, P. 1980. *The First Industrial Revolution.* Cambridge: Cambridge University Press.

Dickie-Clark, H. F. 1996. 'The Theory of the Marginal Man and its Critics,' in *The Marginal Situation*, edited by H. F. Dickie-Clark. London: Routledge and Kegan Paul.

Digital Empowerment Foundation. 2007. *e-Content for Development.* New Delhi: DMF.

Dijk, J. V. 1999.*The Network Society: Social Aspects of New Media.* London: Sage Publications.

Drucker, P. F. 1968.*The Age of Discontinuity: Guidelines to Our Changing Society.* London: Heinemann.

———— 1994. 'The Age of Social Transformation,' *The Atlantic Monthly*, November: 53–80, http://www.owl.ru/eng/womplus/1997/drucker.htm.

Dutton, H. 1996. *Information and Communication Technologies: Visions and Realities.* Oxford: Oxford University Press.

Edsalt, S. 2000. *GATS to Impact Public Education: Education on Live: August 2000.* Education and Skill Development Services Sector, *NSW Teachers Federation* http://www.nsdcindia.org/pdf/education-skill-development.pdf.

Edwards, M. 2000. *NGO Rights and Responsibilities.* London: The Foreign Policy Centre.

Etzkowitz, H. and M. N. Richter. 1991. 'Technology and Society,' *Encyclopaedia of Sociology, Vol. V.* New York: Macmillan Publishing Company.

Evans, F. 2004. *Maintaining Community in the Information Age: The Importance of Trust, Place and Situated Knowledge*. New York: Palgrave Macmillan.

Evans, T. and B. King (eds.). 1991. *Beyond The Text: Contemporary Writing on Distance Education*. Geelong: Dakin University Press.

Eyerman, R. and A. Jamison. 1991. *Social Movements: A Cognitive Approach*. Cambridge: Polity Press.

Ferguson, M. 1992. 'The Mythology about Globalisation,' *European Journal of Communication* 7:69–93.

Foucault, M. 1979. *Discipline and Punish: The Birth of Prison*. New York: Vintage/Random.

———— 1980. *Power and Knowledge: Selected Interviews and Other Writings 1972-77*, edited by Colin Gordon. Pantheon: New York.

———— 2006. 'Govern Mentality,' in *The Anthropology of the State: A Reader*, edited by A. Sharma and A. Gupta. Pondicherry: Blackwell Publishing 131–43.

Fox, M. 1989. 'Unreliable Allies: Subjective and Objective Time,' in *Taking Our Time: Feminist Perspectives on Temporality*, edited by J. Forman and C. Sowton. Oxford: Pergamon Press.

Frase, P. and B. O'Sullivan. 2004. *The Future of Education under the WTO*. www.Campusdemoeracy.org/wtoed.html.

Friedman, T. L. 2005. *The World is Flat: A Brief History of the Twenty-First Century*. New York: Farrar, Straus and Giroux.

Fukuyama, F. 1989. 'The End of History?' *The National Interest, Summer*, http://www.kropfpolisci.com/exceptionalism.fukuyama.pdf.

———— 1992. *The End of History and the Last Man*. New York: Free Press.

Germani, G. 1980. *Marginality*. New Jersey: Transaction Books.

Giddens, A. 1982. 'Power, the Dialectics of Control and Class Structuration,' in *Social Class and Division of Labour*, edited by A. Giddens. Cambridge: Cambridge University Press.

———— 1984. *The Constitution of Society: Outline of a Theory of Structuration*. Cambridge: Polity Press.

———— 1990. *Modernity and Self-Identity*. Cambridge: Polity Press.

———— 1991a. *The Consequences of Modernity*. Cambridge: Polity Press.

———— 1991b. *Modernity and Self-Identity*. Cambridge: Polity Press.

——— 1999. *Runaway World: How Globalisation is Re-shaping our Lives*. Cambridge: Profile Books.

Gill, S. S. 2003. 'Globalization: Higher Education Will Suffer,' *The Tribune*, July 20, 2003.

Gist, N. P. and R. D. Wright. 1973. *Marginality and Identity: Anglo Indians as a Racially Mixed Minority in India*. Leiden: EJ Brill.

Gordon, M. M. 1964. *Assimilation in American Life: The Role of Race, Religion, and National Origins*. New York: Oxford University Press.

Gorz, A. 1982. *Farewell to Working Class*. London: Pluto Press.

Government of India. 1947. *Radhakrishnan Commission Report 1947*. New Delhi: Ministry of Education.

——— 1966. *Report of the Education Commission 1964–1966*. New Delhi: Ministry of Education.

——— 1986. *National Policy on Education*. New Delhi: Ministry of Human Resource Development.

——— 1990. *Report of the National Commission on Rural Labour*. New Delhi: National Commission on Rural Labour.

——— 1998. *Higher Education in India: Vision and Action: Country Paper of UNESCO World Conference on Higher Education in 21st Century*, Paris, October 5–9, 1998.

——— 2001. *National Human Development Report 2001*. New Delhi: Planning Commission.

——— 2007a. *Sachar Committee Report*. New Delhi: Ministry of Minority Affairs.

——— 2007b. *Selected Educational Statistics 2006–2007*. New Delhi, Ministry of Human Resources Development.

——— 2008a. *Annual Report 2008*. New Delhi: Ministry of Human Resource Development.

——— 2009. *Annual Report 2008*. New Delhi: Ministry of Human Resource Development.

——— 2010a. *Annual Report 2009–2010*. New Delhi: Ministry of Communications and Information Technology, Department of Electronics and Information Technology.

——— 2010b. *Annual Report*. New Delhi: Ministry of Information and Communication.

————— 2010c. *Monthly Economic Report*. New Delhi: Economic Division, Ministry of Finance.

————— 2011a. *Annual Report 2010*. New Delhi: Ministry of Human Resource Development.

————— 2011b. *Selected Educational Statistics 2010–2011*. New Delhi: Ministry of Human Resources Development.

————— 2013b. *Mid-Year Economic Analysis 2012–2013*, Department of Economic Affairs, Economic Division. New Delhi:Government of India.

————— 2010. *Annual Report 2009*. New Delhi: Ministry of Human Resource Development.

————— 2012a. *All India Survey on Higher Education 2011–2012(Provisional)*. New Delhi: Ministry of Human Resource Development.

—————2012b. *Educational Statistics at a Glance*. New Delhi: Ministry of Human Resource Development.

————— 2012c. *Report to the People on Education 2011–2012*. New Delhi: Ministry of Human Resource Development.

—————2012a. *Annual Report 2011–2012*. New Delhi: Ministry of Communications & Information Technology, Department of Electronics and Information Technology.

————— 2012b. *Annual Report 2011 Ministry of Human Resource Development*. New Delhi.

————— 2012c. *Annual Report 2012*. New Delhi: Directorate General of Employment and Training, Ministry of Labour.

————— 2012d. *Educational Statistics at a Glance*, New Delhi: MHRD.

————— 2013. *Analysis of Budgeted Expenditure on Education 2009–10; 2011–12*. New Delhi: Ministry of Human Resource Development.

Government of West Bengal. 2004. *West Bengal Human Development Report 2004*. Kolkata: Developmemt and Planning Department.

Gramsci, A. 1998. *Selections from the Prison Notebooks* (reprint). Chennai: Orient Longman.

Grmani, G. 1972. 'AspectosTeoricos de la Marginalidad,' *Revista Paraguaya de Sociologia* 9(30). (op. Cited. Parleman, J. E.1976. *The Myth of Marginality: Urban Poverty and Politics in Rio de Janeiro*. London: University of California Press.)

Guha, R. 1998. *Dominance without Hegemony: History and Power in Colonial India*. New Delhi: Oxford University Press.

Gultung, J. 1979. *Development and Technology: Towards a Technology of Self-Reliance*. New York: United Nations.

Gupta, D. 2005. 'Wither the Indian Village: Culture and Agriculture in Rural India,' *Economic and Political Weekly* XL(8):751–58.

Hammer, T. 2003. *Youth Unemployment and Social Exclusion in Europe: A Comparative Study*. Bristol: The Policy Press.

Haq, M. U. 1997. *Human Development in South Asia*. New Delhi: Oxford University Press.

Hara, N. and R. Kling. 2001. 'Student's Frustration with a Web-based Distance Education Course,' *First Monday*, 4(12), http//firstmonday.org/issues/issue4_12/hara/index.html.

Harris, D. 1987. *Openness and Closure in Distance Education*. London: Flamer.

Harris, R. and R. Rajora. 2006. *Empowering the Poor: Information and Communication Technology for Governance and Poverty Reduction*. New Delhi: UNDP-APDIP.

Harvey, D. 1989. *The Condition of Post-Modernity*. Oxford: Blackwell.

Hassan, R. 2002. *Media, Politics and the Network Society*. Oxford: Open University Press.

Hayes, R. M. 2003. 'Economics of Information,' in *International Encyclopedia of Information and Library Science*, edited by J. Feather and P. Sturges. London: Routledge.

Hoggart, K. 2005. 'Inequalities at the Core: A Discussion of Regionality in the EU and UK,' in *Contested Worlds: Introduction to Human Geography*, edited by M. Phillips. Aldershot: Ashgate Publication Ltd.

Hornby, S. and Z. Clarke (eds.). 2003. *Challenge and Change in the Information Society*. London: Facet Publishing.

Jacobs, G. and N. Asokan. 2003.*Toward a Knowledge Society*. Pondicherry: The Mother's Service Society.

Jarvis, P. 1993. *Paradoxes of Learning: On Becoming an Individual in Society*. San Franciso: Jossy-Baisc.

Jenkins, C. 1983. 'Resource Mobilisation Theory and the Study of Social Movements,' *Annual Review of Sociology* 9: 527–53.

Jessop, B. 1994. 'The Transition to Post-fordism and the Schumpeterian Workfare State,' in *Towards a Post-Fordist Welfare State?* edited by R. Burrowsand B. Loader. London. Routledge.

———— 2000. 'The State and the Contradictions of the Knowledge Driven Economy,' in *Knowledge, Space, Economy*, edited by J. R. Bryson, P. W. Daniels, N. D. Henry and J. Pollard. London: Routledge.

———— 2002. *The Future of the Capitalist State*. Oxford: Polity.

———— 2003. 'The Future of State in an Era of Globalisation,' *International Politics and Society* 3: 30–46.

Johannessen, A. 1997. 'Marginalitet som Socialpolitisk utfordring,' Paper Presented at the 9th Nordic Society Research Seminar, cf. Moller, I. H. 2002. *Understanding Integration and Differentiation: Inclusion, Marginalisation and Exclusion*. www.Eurozine.comurozine.

Jordan, T. 1999. *Cyber Power: The Culture of Politics of Cyberspace and the Internet.* London: Routledge.

Juris, J. 2004. *Transnational Activism and the Cultural Logic of Networking.* Unpublished PhD Thesis in Anthropology, Berkeley, CA: University of California.

Keniston, K. 2000. *Bridging the Digital Divide: Lessons from India.* http//www.int.edu.people.

Klein, N. 2001. *No Logo*. London: Flamingo.

Kolaja, J. and S. J. Kaplan. 1960. 'Case Study in Multiple Marginality,' *Phylon* 21: 338.

Kumar, K. 1993. 'Civil Society: An Inquiry into the Usefulness of an Historical Term,' *British Journal of Sociology* GG(3): 375–95.

Labour Bureau. 2012. *Employment and Unemployment Survey 2012*. Government of India: New Delhi.

Larana, E., H. Johnston, and R. Guesfield. 1984. 'Identities, Grievances and New Social Movements,' in *New Social Movements: From Ideology to Identity*, edited by E. Larana, H. Johnston, and R. Guesfield. Philadelphia: Temple University Press.

Lash, S. and Urry, J. 1994. *Economies of Signs and Space*. London: Sage.

Latchem, C. and D. E. Hanna. 2002. 'Leadership for Open and Learning,' *Open Learning* 17(3): 203–15.

Le Roux, J. 2001. 'Re-examining Global Education's Relevance Beyond 2000,' *Research in Education* May, 65:70–80.

Levy, S. 2001. *Hackers: Heroes of the Computer Revolution*, 2nd edn. New York: Penguin.

Lewis, O. 1996. 'The Cultural of Poverty,' *Scientific American* 215(4): 19–25.

Lind, J. and I. H. Moller.1999. 'The Labour Market in the Process of Change? Some Critical Comments.' *CID Studies* 22.

Longman, L. 2010. 'Global Justice as Identity: Mobilization for a Better World,' in *Dissenting Voices and Transformative Actions, Social Movements in Globalising World*, edited by D. K. SinghaRoy. New Delhi: Manohar Publication.

Luhmann, N.1982. *Differentiation of Society*. New York: University of Columbia Press.

Lyon, D. 1988. *The Information Society Issues and Illusions*. Cambridge: Polity Press.

Lyotard, J. F. 1986. *The Postmodern Condition: A Report on Knowledge*. Manchester: Manchester University Press.

Macaulay's Minute of February 2, 1835, http://www.columbia.edu/itc/mealac/pritchett/00generallinks/macaulay/txt_minute_education_1835.html.

Machlup, F. 1962. *The Production and Distribution of Knowledge in the United States*. Princeton: Princeton University Press.

Mann, H. 1985. *The Sources of Social Power: A History of Power Form the Begining to AD 1760, Vol.1*. Cambridge: Cambridge University Press.

Mann, M. 1993. *The Sources of Social Power: The Risk of Classes and Nation States 1860–1914, Vol.2*. Cambridge: Cambridge University Press.

Marris, A. and C. McClurg Mueller. 1992. 'Master Frames and Cycles of Protests,' in *Frontiers of Social Movement Theory*, edited by A. Marris and C. McClurg Mueller. New Haven and London: Yale University Press.

Masuda, Y. 1981. *The Information Society as Post-Industrial Society Masuda*. Bethesda, MD: World Future Society.

———— 1990. *Managing in the Information Society: Releasing Synergy Japanese-Style*. Oxford: Basil Blackwell.

McDonald, K. 2002, 'From Solidarity to Fluidity: Social Movements Beyond 'Collative Identity' — The Case of Globalization of Conflicts,' *Social Movement Studies* 1(2): 109-128

Mead, G. H. 1934. *Mind, Self, and Society*. Edited by Charles W. Morris. Chicago: University of Chicago Press. (op. cited Stryker 1990).

Meadows, A. J. (ed.). 1987. *The Origins of Information Science*. London: Taylor Graham.

Meadows, D. H. (ed.). 1972. *The Limits to Growth*. New York: Pan University.

Melucci, A. 1996a. *Challenging Codes: Collective Action in the Information Age*. Cambridge. Cambridge University Press.

Melucci, A. 1996b. 'The Symbolic Challenge of Contemporary Movements,' in *Social Movements: Perspectives and Issues*, edited by S.M. Buechler and F.K. Cylke Jr. California: Mayfield Publishing Company.

Menon, M. 2012. *Report of the Committee to Suggest Measures to Regulate the Standards of Education Being Imparted Through Distance Mode*. New Delhi: Ministry of Human Resource Development, Government of India.

Merriam, S. B. 2010. 'Globalization and the Role of Adult Continuing Education: Challenges and Opportunities,' in *Handbook of Adult and Continuing Education*, edited by C. Kasworm, A. Rose, and J. Ross-Gordon, 401–9. Los Angeles, CA: Sage.

Merrill, R. S. 1972. 'The Study of Technology,' in *International Encyclopedia of Social Sciences. Vol. 15*. New York: Macmillan Company and Free Press.

Miles, I. 1996. 'The Information Society: Competing Perspectives on the Social and Economic Implications of Information and Communication Technologies,' in *Information and Communication Technologies-Visions and Realities*, edited by W. H. Dutton. Oxford: Oxford University Press.

Ministry of Communications & Information Technology. 2012. *Annual Report 2011–2012*, Department of Electronics and Information Technology. New Delhi: Government of India.

Ministry of Finance. 2010. *Economic Survey*, Department of Economic Affairs. New Delhi: Government of India.

————— 2011. *Economic Survey*, Department of Economic Affairs, New Delhi: Government of India.

————— 2012. *Economic Survey*, Department of Economic Affairs, New Delhi: Government of India.

————— 2013a. *Economic Survey*, Department of Economic Affairs, New Delhi: Government of India.

Moore, L. and Steele, J. 1991. *Information Intensive Britain*. London: Policy Studies Institute.

Mosca, G. 1939. *The Ruling Class*. New York: McGraw Hill.

Muddiman, D. 2003. 'World Gone Wrong? Alternative Conceptions of the Information Society,' in *Challenge and Change in the Information Society*, edited by S. Hornby and Z. Clarke, London: Facet Publishing. 42–59.

Mullaly, B. 2007. 'Oppression: The Focus of Structural Social Work,' in *The New Structural Social Work*, edited by B. Mullay. Don Mills: Oxford University Press, pp. 252–86.

Mumford, L. 1961. *The City in History: Its Origins, Its Transformations, and Its Prospects*. London: Secker and Warburg.

Myrdal, G. 1944. *An American Dilemma*. New York: Harper and Brothers.

Naisbitt, J. 1986. *Reinventing the Corporation: Transforming your Job and Your Company for the New Information Society*. London: Nicholas.

National Crime Record Bureau (NCRB). 2012. *Report of the National Crime Record Bureau*, NCRB, Ministry of Home Affairs. New Delhi: Government of India.

National Knowledge Commission. 2006. *Report to the Nation 2007*. New Delhi: Government of India.

————— 2006. *NKC Impact: Knowledge Initiative in the Eleventh Five Year Plan*. New Delhi: Government of India.

————— 2007. *Report to the Nation 2007*. New Delhi: Government of India.

————— 2009. *Report to the Nation 2006–2009*. New Delhi: Government of India.

————— 2008. *Towards a Knowledge Society*. New Delhi: Government of India.

National Sample Survey Organization. 1983. 'Household Consumer Expenditure,' NSS 38th Round. Ministry of Statistics and Programme Implementations. New Delhi: Government of India.

————— 1992. *Operational Holdings in India 1991–1992, NSS 48th Round, Ministry of Statistics and Programme Implementations*. New Delhi: Government of India.

————— 1993. 'Household Consumer Expenditure,' NSS 50th Round. Ministry of Statistics and Programme Implementations. New Delhi: Government of India.

————— 1997. *Employment and Unemployment Situation in India 1993–1994. NSS 50th Round*, Department of Statistics. New Delhi: Government of India.

————— 1998. *Migration in India 1983 NSS 49th Round*, Department of Statistics. New Delhi: Government of India.

————— 2000. *Employment and Unemployment Situation in India 1999–2000, Part I&II, NSS 55th Round, Ministry of Statistics and Programme Implementations*. New Delhi: Government of India.

————— 2001. *Literacy and Levels of Education in India 1999–2000 NSS 55th Round, Ministry of Statistics and Programme Implementations*. New Delhi: Government of India.

————— 2004. *Employment and Unemployment Situation in India 2005, NSS 60th Round, Ministry of Statistics and Programme Implementations*. New Delhi: Government of India.

National Sample Survey Organization. 2005. 'Levels and Patterns of Household Consumer Expenditure,' NSS 51st Round. Ministry of Statistics and Programme Implementations. New Delhi: Government of India.

———— 2006a. *Employment and Unemployment Situation in India Part I & II. 2004–2005, NSS 61st Round, Ministry of Statistics and Programme Implementations.* New Delhi: Government of India.

———— 2006b. *Some Aspects of Operational Holdings in India 2002–2003 NSS 59th Round, Ministry of Statistics and Programme Implementations.* New Delhi: Government of India.

———— 2008. *Employment and Unemployment Situation in India 2005–2006, NSS 62 Round, Ministry of Statistics and Programme Implementations.* New Delhi: Government of India.

———— 2010. Employment Unemployment Situation in India 2007-08, 64th Round. Government of India : New Delhi

———— 2010a. *Employment and Unemployment Situation in India 2007–2008 NSS 64th Round, Ministry of Statistics and Programme Implementations.* New Delhi: Government of India.

———— 2010b. *Migration in India 2007–2008 NSS 64th Round, Ministry of Statistics and Programme Implementations.* New Delhi: Government of India.

———— 2010c. *Some Characteristics of Urban Slums 2008–2009 NSS 65th Round, Ministry of Statistics and Programme Implementations.* New Delhi: Government of India.

———— 2011. *Key Indicators of Employment and Unemployment in India 2009–2010, NSS 66th Round, Ministry of Statistics and Programme Implementations.* New Delhi: Government of India.

———— 2012. *Employment and Unemployment Situations among Social Groups in India 2009–2010, NSS 66th Round, Ministry of Statistics and Programme Implementations.* New Delhi: Government of India.

———— 2013. *Key Indicators of Employment and Unemployment in India 2011–2012, NSS 68th Round, Ministry of Statistics and Programme Implementations.* New Delhi: Government of India.

National Skill Development Corporation. 2006. Human Resource and Skill Requirements in the National Social Watch Coalition. *Citizen's Report on Governance and Development.* New Delhi.

NCEUS.2008. *The Report of the National Commission for Enterprises in the Unorganised Sector.* New Delhi: Government of India.

Night, J. 2002. *Trade in Higher Education Services: The Implications of GATS.* London: The Observatory on Borderless Higher Education.

Noble, F. D. 2001. *Digital Diploma Mills: The Automation of Higher Education.* New York: Monthly Review Press.

Norris, P. 2000. 'Global Governance and Cosmopolitan Citizens,' in *Governance in a Globalizing World*, edited by J. Nye and J. Donahue. Washington, DC: Brookings Institution Press, 155–77.

Oommen, T. K. 1985. *From Mobilization to Institutionalisation: The Dynamics of Agrarian Movement in 20th Century Kerala.* Bombay: Popular Prakashan.

Outlook India 2004. *The Zippies Are Here.* January 12; 1.

Palfreyman, D., T. Tapper, and S. Thomas. 2012. 'Series Editors' Introduction,' in *Universities in the Knowledge Economy*, edited by P. Temple. London: Routledge.

Park, R. E. 1928, 'Human Migration and the Marginal Man,' *American Journal of Sociology* 33: 881–93.

Paschal, 2001. *Reshaping Communications*, London: Sage

Perkin, H. 1989. *The Rise of Professional Society: England since 1880.* London: Routledge.

Perlman, J. E.1976. *The Myth of Marginality: Urban Poverty and Politics in Rio de Janeiro.* London: University of California Press.

Peters, O. 2002. *Distance Education in Transition: New Trends and Challenges.* Odenburg: Biblio and Kg. and Informations System Der University Odemburg.

Pitroda, S. 2008. 'Foreword' *to Towards a Knowledge Society, National Knowledge Commission.* New Delhi: Government of India.

Planning Commission. 1985. *Seventh Five Year Plan 1985–1990.* Vol. I & II. New Delhi: Government of India.

————— 1992. *Eighth Five Year Plan 1992–1997*, Vol. I & II. New Delhi: Government of India.

————— 1998. *Ninth Five Year Plan 1997–2002*, Vol. I & II. New Delhi: Government of India.

————— 2001a. *India: Knowledge Super Power, Strategy for Transformation, Task Force Report.* New Delhi: Government of India.

————— 2001b. *National Human Development Report, Planning Commission.* New Delhi: Government of India.

————— 2003. *Tenth Five Year 2002–2007*, Vol. I, II & III. New Delhi: Government of India.

————— 2008. *Eleventh Five Year Plan 2007–2012*. Vol. I, II & III Inclusive Growth. New Delhi: Government of India.

————— 2011. *Faster, Sustainable and More Inclusive Growth: An Approach to the Twelfth Five Year Plan (2012–2017)*. New Delhi: Government of India.

————— 2012. *Annual Status of Higher Education in States and UTs, 2012*. New Delhi: Government of India.

Planning Commission. 2013. *Twelfth Five Year Plan 2012–2017*. Vol. I & II. New Delhi: Government of India.

Polanyi, K. 2001. *The Great Transformation*. Boston: Beacon Press.

Porat, M. U. 1977. *The Information Economy: Definition and Measurement*. Washington, DC: US Department of Commerce.

Poster, M. 1990. *The Mode of Information: Poststructuralism and Social Context*. Cambridge: Polity Press.

————— 1995. *Postmodern virtualities, in Cyberspace, Cyberbodies, Cyberpunk*, edited by M. Featherstone and R. Burrows. London: Sage.

Prensky, M. 2001. 'Digital Natives, Digital Immigrants,' *On the Horizon* 9(5): 1–6.

Preston, P. 2001. *Reshaping Communications: Technology, Information and Social Change*. California: Sage.

Redfield, R. 1959. *The Folk Culture of Yucatan*. Chicago: University of Chicago Press.

Robertson, R. (ed.). 1992. *Globalisation, Social Theory and Global Culture*. London: Sage.

Robins, K. 1995. 'Cyberspace and the World We Live In,' in *Cyberspace, Cyberbodies, Cyberpunk*, edited by M. Featherstone, and R. Burrows. London: Sage.

Rowe, C. and Thompson, J. 1996. *People and Chips, The Human Implication of Information Technology*. Third edition. London: McGraw-Hill.

Rucht, D. and F. Neidhardt. 2002. 'Towards a Social Movement Society? On the Possibilities of Institutionalizing Social Movements,' *Social Movement Studies* 1(1): 1–30.

Scally, C.A. 2013. 'Trends in Global Education: Globalization, Education, and New Social Movements. Athabasca University,' *GLST* 611 (Unpublished Paper).

Schiller, D. 1999. *Digital Capitalism: Networking the Global Market System*. Cambridge, MA: MIT Press.

Schumacher, E. F, 1973. *Small is Beautiful: Study of Economics: As if People Mattered*. London: Blond Briggs.

Scott, M. 2001. 'Danger-Landmines! NGO-Government Collaboration in the Ottawa Process,' in *Global Citizen Action*, edited by M. Edwards and J. Gaventa. Boulder, CO: Lynne Rienner Publishers, 121–34.

Sellen, A. J. and Harper, R. 2002. *The Myth of Paperless Office*. Cambridge: MIT Press.

Sen, A. 1999. *Development as Freedom*. New Delhi: Oxford University Press.

Sen, A. 2000. *Social Exclusion: A Critical Assessment of the Concept and its Relevance*. Asian Development Bank.

SinghaRoy, D. K. 2001. 'Critical Issues in Grassroots Mobilizations and Collective Action,' in *Social Development and Empowerment of the Marginalized Groups: Perspectives and Strategies*, edited by D. K. SinghaRoy. New Delhi: Sage.

———— 2004. *Peasant Movements in Post-Colonial India: Dynamics of Identity and Mobilisation*. New Delhi: Sage Publication.

———— 2005. 'Peasant Movements in Contemporary India,' *Economic and Political Weekly*, 24 December 2005.

———— 2010a. 'Changing Trajectory of Social Movements in India: Search for an Alternative Analytical Perspective,' in *Dissenting Voices and Transformative Actions: Social Movements in Globalising World*, edited by D. K. SinghaRoy. New Delhi: Manohar Publication.

———— 2010b. 'Marginalisation and the Marginalized: Some Reflections on the Relational- Cumulative Dynamics,' in *Surviving against Odds: Marginalization and Marginalised in a Globalising World*, edited by D. K. SinghaRoy. New Delhi: Manohar Publication.

Smith, P. J. and E. Symthe. 1999. 'Globalisation, Citizenship and Technology: The MAI Meets the Internet,' *Canadian Foreign Policy* 7(2): 83–105.

Smythe, E. and P. J. Smith. 2003. 'NGOs, Technology and the Changing Face of Trade Politics,' in *Delicate Dances: Public Policy and the Non Profit Sector*, edited by K. L. Brock. London: McGill-Queen's University Press.

Sinha, S. K. 2004. *Age of the Zippi*. Outlook India.com. January 12.

Soja, E. 1989. *Postmodern Geographies: The Reassertion of Space in Critical Social Theory*. London: Verso.

Sorenson, G. 2004. *The Transformation of the State: Beyond the Myth of Retreat*. Basingstoke and New York: Palgrave Macmillan.

Sorokin, P. 1959. *Social and Cultural Mobility*. New York: The Free Press.

Splichal, S. 1994. *Media Beyond Socialism*. Boulder. CO: West View.

Srinivas, M. N. 1978. *The Changing Position of Indian Women*. New Delhi: Oxford University Press.

Stryker, S. 1990. 'Identity Theory,' in *Encyclopeadia of Sociology*. Edited by E. E. Borgatha and M. L. Borgatha. Vol. 2. New York: Macmillan Publishing.

Stewart, A. 2001. *Theories of Power and Domination*. London: Sage.

Sullivan, B. 2001. 'Millions don't want to be Wired,' *Technology and Society*.

Tait, A. 1994. 'The End of Innocence: Critical Approaches to Open and Distance Learning,' *Open Learning* 9(3): 27–36.

Taylor, C. 1990. 'Modes of Civil Society,' *Public Culture* 3(1): 95–118.

Telecom Regulatory Authority of India. 2006. *Indian Telecom Services Performance Indicator*, April-TERI 2006, Ministry of Telecommunication. New Delhi: Government of India.

————— 2011a. *Indian Telecom Services Performance Indicator*, December 2012, Ministry of Telecommunication. New Delhi: Government of India.

————— 2011b. Recommendations on Telecom Equipment Manufacturing Policy, Ministry of Telecommunication. New Delhi: Government of India.

————— 2012. *Indian Telecom Services Performance Indicator*, June 2012, Ministry of Telecommunication. New Delhi: Government of India.

Terras, M. 2007. 'Challenge and Change in the Information Society,' edited by S. Hornby and Z. Clarke, *Literary and Linguistic Computing*, 22 (3): 372–74.

Therborn, G. 2000. 'Globalizations: Dimensions, Historical Waves, Regional Effects, Normative Governance.' *International Sociology* 15(2):151–79.

Thompson, P., C. Warhurst and G. Callaghan. 2000. 'Human Capital or Capitalising on Humanity: Knowledge, Skills and Competencies in Interactive Service Work,' in *Managing Knowledge: Critical Investigations of Work and Learning*, edited by C. Prichard, R. Hull, M. Chumer and H. Wilmott. London: Macmillan.

Thorat, S. 2008. 'Emerging Issues in Higher Education – Approach and Strategy 11th Plan,' in *Higher Education in India - Issues Related to Expansion, Inclusiveness, Quality and Finance*, edited by S. Thorat. New Delhi: University Grants Commission.

Times of India. August 3, 2012:15.

———— 2013. '43% of Teaching Slots in IITs Lying Unfulfilled,' March 13.

———— July 1, 2013.

Toffler, A.1970. *Future Shock*. New York: Random House Publishing Group.

———— 1980. *The Third Wave*. London: Pan Books.

———— 1990. *Power Shift: Knowledge, Wealth, and Violence at the Edge of the 21st Century*. New York: Bantam Books.

———— and H. Toffler. 1995. *Creating a New Civilization: The Politics of the Third Wave*. Atlanta: Turner Publishing.

Tonnies, F. 1957. *Community and Society*. East Lansing: Michigan State University Press.

Touraine, A. 1974. *The Post-industrial Society*. Wildwood House: London.

———— 1981. *The Voice and the Eye: An Analysis of Social Movements*. Cambridge: Cambridge University Press.

Trivedi, D. 2013. 'Politics, the New Zamindari,' *Times of India*, July 26:20.

Tuomi, I. 1999. 'Data is More than Knowledge, Implications of the Reversed Knowledge Hierarchy for Knowledge Management and Organizational Memory,' *Journal of Management Information Systems* 16(3): 107–21.

Turek, J. 2003. *Review of Maurell Castell's Publication, The Information Age*. www.cap-imu.de/fgz/reviews/30.php.

UNDP. 1992. *Human Development Report*. New Delhi: UNDP.

———— 1993. *UNDP and Civil Society*. New York: UNDP.

———— 1995a. *Declaration of the Social Development Summit, Copenhagen*. New York: United Nations.

———— 1995b. *World Bank 1997 World Development Report 2007*. New Delhi: Oxford University Press.

———— 1996. *Human Development Report*. New Delhi: UNDP.

———— 2000. *Human Development Report*. New Delhi: UNDP.

———— 2001. *Human Development Report 2001*. New Delhi: Oxford University Press.

———— 2007. *Human Development Report 2007*. New Delhi: Oxford University Press.

———— 2008. *Human Development Report 2008*. New Delhi: Oxford University Press.

———— 2010. *Human Development Report*. New Delhi: UNDP.

————— 2011. *Human Development Report.* New Delhi: UNDP.

————— 2012. *Human Development Report.* New Delhi: UNDP.

UNICEF. 2009. *The State of the World's Children-2009.*UNICEF.

————— 2005. *Understanding Knowledge Societies,* New York: Department of Economic and Social Affairs, Division for Public Administration and Development Management.

University Grant Commission. 2011. *Inclusive and Qualitative Expansion of Higher Education12 Five-Year Plan, 2012–17,* New Delhi.

————— 2012a. *Higher Education in India at a Glance,* New Delhi.

————— 2013. Higher Education in India at a Glance, New Delhi.

Urry, John. 2000. 'The Importance of Social Movements,' *Social Movement Studies* 1(1): 185–203.

————— 2000. Sociology beyond Societies: Mobilities for the Twenty-First Century, Routledge: London and New York.

————— 2000. 'Mobile Sociology,' *British Journal of Sociology* 51(1): 185–203

Veer Der Van, R. 2009. 'The Transformation of the Welfare State: what is Left of Public Responsibility,' in *Globalization and the State: Sociological Perspectives on the State of the State,* edited by W. Schinkel. London: Palgrave Macmillan, 36–61.

Warhurst, C. and P. Thompson. 1998. 'Hearts, Hands and Minds: Changing Worked and Workers at the End of the Century,' in *Workplaces of the Future,* edited by P. Thompson and C. Warhurst. London: Macmillan.

Webster, F. 1994. 'What Information Society?' *The Information Society* 10:1–23.

————— 1995. *Theories of Information Society.* London: Routledge.

————— 2000. 'Information, Capitalism and Uncertainty,' *Information, Communication and Society* 3(1): 69–90.

White, L. A. 1949. *The Science of Culture.* New York: Farrar, Straus and Cudahy.

Wieviorka, M. 2005. 'After New Social Movements,' *Social Movements Studies* 4(1): 1–19.

Williams, R. and D. Edge. 1996. 'The Social Shaping of Technology,' *Research Policy* 25(6): 865–99.

Winston, B. 1998. *Media, Technology and Society: A History from the Telegraph to the Internet.* London: Routledge.

Woolgar, S. 1996. 'Technologies as Culture Artefacts,' in *Information and Communication Technologies: Visions and Realities*, edited by W. Dutton. Oxford: Oxford University Press, 87–102.

World Bank. 1997. *World Development Report 1997*. New Delhi: Oxford University Press.

————— 1999. *World Development Report 1999*. New Delhi: Oxford University Press.

————— 2000. *World Development Report 2000*. New Delhi: Oxford University Press.

————— 2006. *World Development Report 2006*. New Delhi: Oxford University Press.

————— 2008. *World Development Report 2008*. New Delhi: Oxford University Press.

————— 2010. *World Development Report 2010*. New Delhi: Oxford University Press.

————— 2012. *World Development Report 2012*. New Delhi: Oxford University Press.

WTO 2001. WTO.www.wto.org

Young, J. 1999.*The Exclusive Society*. London: Sage.

Websites accessed

http://eindia.eletsonline.com/2012 (e-India).

http://esaconf.un.org Missing Girl Child in India.

http://fdiindia.in/.

http://indiabudget.nic.in.

http://mospi.nic.in/Mospi_New/upload/NAD_Press_Note_31may12.pdf.

http://www.angelfire.com/nd/ram.

http://www.ibef.org/industry/education-sector-india.aspx.

http://www.iie.org/en/Services/Project-Atlas/India/Indias-Students-Overseas.

http://www.indianexpress.com/news/panchayat-bans-love-marriage-bars-women-below-40-from-shopping/973963.

http://www.internetworldstats.com/top20.htm.

http://www.investindia.gov.in/?q=education-sector.

http://www.ncwof.org.au/edu.

http://www.oifc.in/sectors/education.

http://www.reuters.com/article/2012/12/05/us-india-phones-elopement-idUSBRE8B407E20121205.

timesofindia.indiatimes.com/2013-01-08/india/36215366_1_khap-panchayat-ban-alcohol-hisar-village.

www.cid.harvard.edu, Washington Consensus.

www.ibef.org, Foreign Direct Investment.

www.india.stat.com.

www.internetworldstats.com, 2009, 2011.

www.internetworldstats.com/stats3.htm, 2009, 2012.

Index